The Supersonic BONE

The Supersonic BONE

A Development and Operational History of the B-1 Bomber

Kenneth P. Katz

Pen & Sword
AVIATION

First published in Great Britain in 2022 and reprinted in 2022 by
Pen & Sword Aviation
An imprint of
Pen & Sword Books Ltd
Yorkshire – Philadelphia

ISBN 978 1 39901 471 7

Typeset by SJmagic DESIGN SERVICES, India.
Printed and bound in India by Replika Press Pvt. Ltd.

Pen & Sword Books Limited incorporates the imprints of Atlas, Archaeology,
Aviation, Discovery, Family History, Fiction, History, Maritime, Military,
Military Classics, Politics, Select, Transport, True Crime, Air World, Frontline
Publishing, Leo Cooper, Remember When, Seaforth Publishing, The Praetorian
Press, Wharncliffe Local History, Wharncliffe Transport, Wharncliffe True
Crime and White Owl.

For a complete list of Pen & Sword titles please contact

PEN & SWORD BOOKS LIMITED
47 Church Street, Barnsley, South Yorkshire, S70 2AS, England
E-mail: enquiries@pen-and-sword.co.uk
Website: www.pen-and-sword.co.uk

Or
PEN AND SWORD BOOKS
1950 Lawrence Rd, Havertown, PA 19083, USA
E-mail: Uspen-and-sword@casematepublishers.com
Website: www.penandswordbooks.com

highly effective in conflicts completely different from the global thermonuclear war for which it was designed to deter, if possible, and fight if all else failed.

The story of the B-1 is one of interconnections between military requirements, doctrine and strategy, technology, and politics. It's also a story of people: aeronautical researchers, engineers, program managers, production workers, Presidents of the United States and their appointees, commanders, aircrew, maintainers, and many others.

Most American military aircraft have an official name as well as a designation: the F-4 Phantom II, the C-130 Hercules, the CH-47 Chinook, and the P-51 Mustang, for example. Often, those who fly and maintain a type of aircraft will give it an informal name that is more commonly used than the official name. The B-52 Stratofortress became the BUFF, the UH-1 Iroquois was always called the Huey, F-16 Fighting Falcon was referred to as the Viper, and the S-3 Viking got the nickname Hoover. The B-1A never got an official name and the B-1B was officially named the Lancer only in 1990. The official name was promptly ignored and the B-1 came to be known as the BONE (B-One). To this day that's what the B-1 community calls its aircraft.

Acknowledgements

This book was made possible by the assistance of many people and I am grateful for each of their contributions.

US Air Force public affairs personnel provided access to official US Air Force support and facilitated my visit to Dyess AFB. Thank you to Major Anastasia D. Schmidt, Technical Sergeant Andrew A. Davis, Senior Airman Emily L. Copeland, Airman 1st Class River Bruce, Airman 1st Class Kylee A. Thomas, and Carla A. Pampe. At Dyess AFB, Major John F. Hough was my instructor pilot during an unforgettable session in the B-1B simulator. Numerous personnel at Dyess AFB shared their knowledge and facilitated my photography.

Jeannine Geiger of the Air Force Test Center History Office supplied me with historical photographs of B-1A and B-1B flight testing.

The Strategic Air Command & Aerospace Museum in Ashland, Nebraska graciously allowed me to photograph the B-1A bomber in their collection. Thank you to Deb Hermann for arranging permission.

Michael Simons of the National Electronics Museum provided me with previously unpublished photographs of radars.

Several talented photographers and illustrators contributed their work to this book: Roelof-Jan Gort, Ken Middleton, Erik Simonsen and Ian Tate.

A large number of individuals shared with me a treasure trove of photographs, manuals, and documentation which immeasurably added to the depth and comprehensiveness of this book. Many people who have developed, manufactured, tested, maintained, supported or flown the B-1 spoke to me about their experiences with this historic weapon system. Their subsequent reviews of the manuscript greatly improved its detail and accuracy. Craig Baumann, Master Sergeant Archie E. Browning, USAF (retired), Staff Sergeant Anthony B. 'Blaine' Cason, USAF (honorably discharged), Lieutenant Colonel Ricky W. Carver, USAF (retired), Technical Sergeant Darrell W. Chesnut, USAF (retired), Lieutenant Colonel 'Chunks', USAF (retired), Senior Master Sergeant Wesley T. 'Skip' Clark, USAF (retired), Colonel Jonathan M. 'Claw' Creer, USAF, Colonel Charles R. 'Russ' Davis, USAF (retired), Captain Scott M. Dayton, USAF (honorably discharged), Kenneth Decker, Chief Master Sergeant Jerry Densmore, USAF (retired), Technical Sergeant Michael D. DeWitt, USAF (retired), Major Norman K. 'Keith' Dodderer, USAF (retired), Technical Sergeant Kyle C. Fagin, USAF (retired), Lieutenant Colonel Gary H. 'Smokey' Flynt, USAF (retired), Technical Sergeant David J. Fransen, USAF (retired), Chief Master Sergeant George A. Gilbert, USAF (retired), Colonel Gordon P. 'Guv' Greaney, USAF (retired), Lieutenant Colonel Timothy 'Nogs' Griffith, USAF, Lieutenant Colonel Lawrence H. 'Larry' Haskell, USAF (retired), Colonel Stephen A. Henry, USAF (retired), Colonel David L. 'Lowell' Hickey, USAF (retired), Lt Col Daemon E. 'PBAR' Hobbs, USAF (retired), Lieutenant Colonel Kevin R. 'Hooter' Houdek, USAF (retired), Lieutenant Colonel John R. 'Ray' Houle, USAF (retired), Technical

ARS	Air Refueling Squadron
ASOS	Air Support Operations Squadron
ATB	Advanced Technology Bomber
ATS	Air Turbine Starter
AWACS	Airborne Warning and Control System
BAF	Benefield Anechoic Facility
BLOS	Beyond Line of Sight
BMS	Bombardment Squadron
BMW	Bombardment Wing
BPE	Bomber Penetrativity Evaluation
BS	Bomb Squadron
BTF	Bomber Task Force
BW	Bomb Wing
C^2R^2	Combat Crew Rest and Relaxation
CAMS	Core Automated Maintenance System
CAOC	Combined Air Operations Center
CASS	Consolidated Aircraft Support System
CBI	Computer-Based Instruction
CBP	Continuous Bomber Presence
CBM	Conventional Bomb Module
CBU	Cluster Bomb Unit
CCTS	Combat Crew Training Squadron
CG	Center of Gravity
CITS	Central Integrated Test System
CJTF-OIR	Combined Joint Task Force - Operation Inherent Resolve
CMUP	Conventional Mission Upgrade Program
CNI	Communications, Navigation, and Identification
CPT	Cockpit Procedures Trainer
CRT	Cathode Ray Tube
CTF	Combined Test Force
DAS	Defensive Avionics System
DAY	Dial-A-Yield
DC	Direct Current
DEC	Digital Engine Controller
DEU	Display Electronic Unit
DFE	Derivative Fighter Engine
DFP	Desired Flight Path
DMS	Defensive Management System
DSIF	Defense System Integration Facility
DSO	Defensive Systems Officer
DSUP	Defensive System Upgrade Program
DT&E	Development Test & Evaluation
EAR	Electronically Agile Radar
EBADS	Engine Bleed Air Distribution System
EBS	Expeditionary Bomb Squadron

ECI	External Compression Inlet
ECBM	Enhanced Conventional Bomb Module
ECM	Electronics Countermeasures
EDU	Electronic Display Unit
EMUX	Electrical Multiplex
EMP	Electro-Magnetic Pulse
ENSIP	Engine Structural Integrity Program
EO	Electro-Optical
EOG	Expeditionary Operations Group
ERS	Engineering Research Simulator
ERSA	Extended Range Strike Aircraft
EVS	Electro-optical Viewing System
EWO	Electronic Warfare Officer
EWO	Emergency War Order
FCGMS	Fuel/Center of Gravity Management System
FDC	Flight Director Computer
FIDL	Fully Integrated Data Link
FLR	Forward-Looking Radar
FOT&E	Follow-on Operational Test & Evaluation
FRR	Flight Readiness Review
FSD	Full Scale Development
FUFO	Full-Fuzing Option
GE	General Electric
GPS	Global Positioning System
HF	High Frequency
HML	Hinge Moment Limiting
HP	Hewlett-Packard
HSI	Horizontal Situation Indicator
IBS	Integrated Battle Station
ICBM	Intercontinental Ballistic Missile
IDG	Integrated Drive Generator
IFAST	Integration Facility for Avionics System Test
IFF	Identification Friend or Foe
ILS	Instrument Landing System
INS	Inertial Navigation System
IOC	Initial Operational Capability
IOT&E	Initial Operational Test & Evaluation
IR	Infra-Red
ISIS	Islamic State in Iraq and Syria
JASSM	Joint Air-Surface Stand-off Missile
JDAM	Joint Direct Attack Munition
JPF	Joint Programable Fuze
JSOW	Joint Stand-Off Weapon
JSTPS	Joint Strategic Target Planning Staff
JTAC	Joint Terminal Attack Controller

JTF	Joint Test Force
KIA	Killed In Action
KIAS	Knots Indicated Airspeed
KT	Kiloton(s)
LAMP	Low-Altitude Manned Penetrator
LAR	Launch Acceptability Region
LASL	Los Alamos Scientific Laboratory
LD	Low Drag
LLNL	Lawrence Livermore National Laboratory
LRASM	Long Range Anti-Ship Missile
LRCA	Long-Range Combat Aircraft
MAC	Mean Aerodynamic Chord
MASSG	Manned Aircraft Studies Steering Group
MCI	Mixed Compression Inlet
MEC	Main Engine Control
MFD	Multi-Function Display
MOS	Mission Objective Sheet
MPRL	Multi-Purpose Rotary Launcher
MRT	Miniature Receive Terminal
MSOGS	Molecular Sieve Oxygen Generating System
MT	Megaton(s)
MX	Missile Experimental
NAA	North American Aviation
NACA	National Advisory Committee for Aeronautics
NAR	North American Rockwell
NASA	National Aeronautics and Space Administration
NATO	North Atlantic Treaty Organization
NEPA	Nuclear Energy for the Propulsion of Aircraft
NIAR	National Institute for Aviation Research
OAS	Offensive Avionics System
OC-ALC	Oklahoma City Air Logistics Center
OEF	Operation Enduring Freedom
OIF	Operation Iraqi Freedom
OIR	Operation Inherent Resolve
ORA	Operational Readiness Assessment
ORI	Operational Readiness Inspection
ORS	Offensive Radar System
OSO	Offensive Systems Officer
OT&E	Operational Test & Evaluation
OWF	Overwing Fairing
PAL	Permissive Action Link
PDM	Programmed Depot Maintenance
PF	Panoramic Format
PFRT	Preliminary Flight Rating Test
PGM	Precision-Guided Munition

PIO   Pilot-Induced Oscillation
PIRA   Precision Impact Range Area
PLZT   Polarized Lead lanthanum Zirconate Titanate
PMR   Pacific Missile Range
psi   pounds per square inch
RADC   Rome Air Development Center
RAF   Royal Air Force
RCS   Radar Cross-Section
RFS   Radio Frequency Surveillance
RMIP   Reliability and Maintainability Improvement Program
SAC   Strategic Air Command
SAL   Strategic ALCM Launcher
SALT   Strategic Arms Limitation Treaty
SAMTEC   Space and Missile Test Center
SAR   Synthetic Aperture Radar
SATAF   Site Activation Task Force
SCAD   Subsonic Cruise Armed Decoy
SCAS   Stability and Control Augmentation System
SECBM   1760 Enhanced Conventional Bomb Module
SEF   Stability Enhancement Function
SIOP   Single Integrated Operational Plan
SIS   Stall Inhibitor System
SLAB   Subsonic Low Altitude Bomber
SLBM   Sea-Launched Ballistic Missile
SMCS   Structural Mode Control System
SMS   Stores Management System
SPO   System Program Office
SPORT   Space Positioning, Optics, and Radar Tracking
SRAM   Short Range Attack Missile
SST   Supersonic Transport
SWL   Strategic Weapons Launcher
TA   Terrain Avoidance
TAC   Tactical Air Command
TACAN   Tactical Air Navigation
TDS   Towed Decoy System
TES   Test and Evaluation Squadron
TSF   Threat Situation Format
TST   Time-Sensitive Target
TF   Terrain-Following
TFPE   Thermal Protection Flashblindness Equipment
TFR   Terrain-Following Radar
TFX   Tactical Fighter Experimental
TO   Technical Order
TOV&V   Technical Order Validation and Verification
TSF   Threat Situation Format

TWF	Tail Warning Function
UARRSI	Universal Air Refueling Receptacle Slipway Installation
UHF	Ultra-High Frequency
USAF	United States Air Force
VG	Variable-Geometry
VSD	Vertical Situation Display
VSDU	Vertical Situation Display Upgrade
WCMD	Wind Corrected Munitions Dispenser
WCT	Wing Carry Through
WIA	Wounded In Action
WS	Weapon System
WSMR	White Sands Missile Range
WST	Weapon System Trainer
WTR	Western Test Range

Chapter 1

The Rise of the American Strategic Bomber

'The day has passed when armies on the ground or navies on the sea can be the arbiter of a nation's destiny in war. The main power of defense and the power of initiative against an enemy has passed to the air.'

Brigadier General William L. 'Billy' Mitchell
Chief of Air Service, American Expeditionary Forces, November 1918

As this book was being written, the B–1B Lancer had almost twenty years of nearly continuous combat in the Middle East and South-West Asia, while also projecting power in Europe and the Asia/Pacific regions. By all accounts, the B–1B has been a highly successful weapon system in America's wars of the twenty-first century. But it has been employed in ways that would have been unimaginable when the swing-wing bomber was first conceived.

The concept of strategic bombing was developed in the aftermath of the First World War. Airpower advocates such as Hugh Trenchard in the United Kingdom, Billy Mitchell in the United States, and Giulio Douhet in Italy envisioned that bombers could fly over the stalemated war in the trenches to deliver knockout blows directly against the enemy's homeland. Implementing strategic bombing required airplanes with long range and a heavy payload of bombs, navigation capability, and accurate bombsights.

During the Second World War, the Germans tried and failed to conduct an effective strategic bombing offensive against Great Britain, while the United States and United Kingdom mounted a massive strategic air offensive against Germany. It was extremely costly in both human and material terms. The Allied strategic air campaign failed either to break German civilian morale or to halt industrial production. But it did grind down German airpower to the point that France could be invaded, and effectively opened another front whose defense consumed a significant portion of Germany's human, material, and industrial resources.

Strategic bombing in the Second World War reached its apotheosis in the Pacific theater. Equipped with the advanced Boeing B-29 Superfortress bomber based in the Mariana Islands, the Americans burned numerous Japanese cities to the ground. Two nuclear bombs dropped from B-29s increased the effectiveness of strategic bombing a thousand-fold. Japan surrendered without being invaded. In less than three decades, strategic bombing had developed from an idea to the most revolutionary advance in the history of warfare.

Within a few years of the end of the Second World War, the Soviet Union became engaged in the Cold War with the United States and its allies. The Cold War was fought in many ways: ideology, culture, economics, diplomacy, insurgency, and limited war in places like Korea. But just as strategic airpower was viewed as the alternative to trench warfare in the aftermath of the First World War, the Americans viewed strategic airpower, now armed with nuclear weapons, as the alternative to the deployment of a ruinously expensive conventional deterrent to Soviet aggression. If the Soviets launched a general war, ground forces would act as a tripwire and

B-17G 'Thunderbird' flies in formation with its descendant, the Boeing B-52 Stratofortress. The Boeing B-17 Flying Fortress was America's first operational four-engine heavy bomber. 'Thunderbird' is owned by the Lone Star Flight Museum in Houston, Texas. (*Master Sergeant Michael A. Kaplan/US Air Force*)

victory would be achieved by the bombers that would have turned the Soviet homeland and its satellite countries into blasted, irradiated wastelands.

To implement this strategy, the Army Air Forces (AAF) formed the Strategic Air Command (SAC) in 1946. In turn, AAF separated from the United States Army to become the independent United States Air Force (USAF) in 1947, with SAC as its most important component. At first, the B-29 bomber was the mainstay of SAC. The B-29 was first replaced by the Boeing B-50, an improved version of the B-29, and then by the Boeing B-47 Stratojet, SAC's first jet bomber. Even with aerial refueling, these bombers had to stage from forward bases in Alaska, the United Kingdom, North Africa, Okinawa, and other places to reach targets in the Soviet Union. Another early SAC bomber was the immense Convair B-36 Peacemaker. The B-36 had intercontinental range but being propeller-driven it was really from the previous generation. What SAC wanted was a jet bomber with both intercontinental range and high speed.

The jet-powered long-range bomber appeared in the form of the Boeing B-52 Stratofortress, arguably the most important warplane of the post-Second World War era. It was designed in 1948, first flown in 1952, and initially delivered to SAC in 1955. The B-52 gave SAC the capability to launch from bases in the continental United States and refuel in the air from tanker aircraft to fly to the Soviet Union. A B-52 would then penetrate Soviet air defenses at high altitude and speed to deliver nuclear weapons anywhere in the Soviet Union, including at night and in inclement weather. As thermonuclear weapons supplemented and then largely replaced nuclear weapons, the devastation that the B-52 force could deliver increased by orders of magnitude, to the point where it was likely that an all-out nuclear attack on the Soviet Union, Communist China and other Communist countries would have killed hundreds of millions of people in a single day. Although not understood at the time, it is now thought likely that the

The Boeing B-52 Stratofortress brought together the intercontinental range and large payload of the B-36 with the high-speed performance of the B-47 in one aircraft. The key technology that enabled the B-52 was the Pratt & Whitney J57 twin-spool turbojet engine. The aircraft in this photograph are the B-52D model, which was the first model to be put in large-scale production. (*New England Air Museum collection*)

massive radioactive fallout from this attack might have eventually eliminated most human life in the northern hemisphere. While unimaginably horrific, SAC and the strategy of massive retaliation must be regarded as a total success, since the threat of nuclear annihilation prevented the Cold War from turning into a third World War.

For every weapon, there will be a countermeasure, and as the B-52 entered service, the USAF was already beginning to consider its successor. The Soviet Union was developing jet-powered fighter interceptor aircraft and surface-to-air missiles to shoot down the B-52. What SAC needed was a means to evade these threats and deliver weapons against heavily defended targets. The search for the replacement started the USAF and the American aerospace industry down an extraordinarily convoluted path that half a century later would see the B-1B Lancer dropping precision-guided bombs on terrorists long after the Soviet Union had ceased to exist.

Chapter 2

B-70 Valkyrie

'My feeling is, and it is very strong, that we must maintain manned aircraft in our retaliatory force as well [as intercontinental ballistic missiles].'

Lieutenant General Bernard A. Schriever
Commander, Air Research and Development Command, 1959–1961

WS-110A

SAC was satisfied with the B-52, which gave it extraordinary striking power delivered with jet performance at intercontinental range. But the development time for modern weapon systems is so long that when a new weapon system is introduced into service, it is time to begin developing its replacement. As far back as 1953 (two years before the delivery of the first B-52 to SAC), the industry periodical *Aviation Week* reported:

No decision has been reached, but a proposal is circulating around USAF headquarters to eliminate all but a small part of the Boeing B-52 production program. Feeling in some USAF quarters that the difference between B-47 and B-52 performance is not worth the cost of the latter program. Strategic Air Command also anticipates getting supersonic bombers soon enough to make to make the B-52 strictly a short interim measure.

As the B-52 approached service introduction, the USAF began to explore options for the next generation of strategic bombing system. Each option that was considered was audacious in its own way. The high level of funding that Congress lavished on the military in general during the period and the USAF in particular meant that the USAF did not have to pick one option, but instead proceeded with all of them.

Weapon System (WS)-107A was a truly revolutionary concept, the Intercontinental Ballistic Missile (ICBM). Guided ballistic missiles saw limited service in the Second World War in the form of the German A-4 (called the V-2 in German propaganda), and there had been some development of longer-range ballistic missiles since then, but the ICBM needed greatly increased range compared to the A-4. Implementing an ICBM would require vast improvements in structures, light-weight thermonuclear warheads, powerful and efficient rocket engines, and long-range guidance and navigation. To hedge risk, the USAF developed both the SM-65 Atlas missile under WS-107A-1 with Convair as its prime contractor and the SM-68 Titan under WS-107A-2 with Martin as the prime contractor.

The great attraction of the ICBM was that it flew though outer space on the way to its target, so fast and high that it rendered air defenses obsolete. The ICBM was unstoppable. The risks of the ICBM included its technical feasibility, its reliability, and its ability to accurately place a nuclear warhead on the target. The bomber pilots who ran SAC also experienced initial difficulty accepting a weapon system that put their crews in launch control centers pushing buttons, rather than in cockpits. In the end, WS-107A would not only be the basis of the American ICBM program but also lay the foundation for much of the American civil and military space programs.

The SM-65 Atlas was the product of the WS-107A-1 program to develop America's first intercontinental ballistic missile. This particular missile is on display at the Strategic Air Command & Aerospace Museum in Ashland, Nebraska. (*Author*)

The WS-110A was less revolutionary in concept than a WS-107A in that it was a manned bomber, but what a bomber! In 1955, Mach 1 flight was less than a decade old, Mach 2 flight had been achieved in only a few experimental aircraft, and no human being had ever flown at Mach 3. WS-110A envisioned an aircraft with the range and payload of the B-52 but flying at higher altitudes and perhaps as fast as Mach 3. It's indicative of the technological optimism of the period that such an airplane could have been seriously considered.

The third of the programs, WS-125A, was even more ambitious than WS-110A. At least WS-110A used jet engines, which were an existing technology. WS-125A was based on implementing the Aircraft Nuclear Propulsion (ANP)/Nuclear Energy for the Propulsion of Aircraft (NEPA) work into an operational bomber. In theory, nuclear propulsion would give a bomber unlimited range. The USAF gave contracts to Convair and Lockheed to develop WS-125A.

WS-125A turned out to be an utterly impractical concept, proceeding in fits and starts until finally cancelled in 1961 and never producing an actual aircraft. It might have been possible to protect the crew from the radiation created by a nuclear power plant, but a nuclear-powered bomber would have been impossible to maintain safely. The crash of a nuclear airplane would have caused an environmental catastrophe. Even in an era of infatuation with the promise of nuclear technology and a widespread lack of concern about environmental protection, a nuclear-powered bomber was impractical and unacceptable.

B-58A Hustler

WS-110A was not the first USAF supersonic bomber program. Preceding it was the Convair B-58A Hustler. Part of the famed family of Convair delta-wing aircraft that included the XF-92A, F-102 Delta Dagger, F-106 Delta Dart, and F2Y Sea Dart, the B-58A first flew in 1956 and entered SAC service in 1960. With its elegant and sleek appearance and blazing Mach 2 maximum speed, the B-58A captured public attention and remains a favorite of aviation fans to this day.

The Convair B-58A Hustler was the first American supersonic bomber. It was fast, beautiful and unloved by SAC, which disliked its short range, high operations and maintenance costs, and poor safety record. (*US Air Force*)

As impressive and beautiful as the B-58A undoubtedly was, SAC never liked it. It was never designed for intercontinental range, and the actual airplane that was built had even less range than the specification. Major General John McConnell, the SAC Director of Plans, observed that 'as long as Russia – and not Canada – remained the enemy, range was important.' The complex and technologically immature systems of the B-58A resulted in poor reliability and maintainability. The B-58A was a very demanding aircraft to fly and had a poor safety record, with almost one quarter of the 116 examples built having crashed. Calculations showed that a bombardment wing equipped with the B-58A Hustler cost three times as much to operate and maintain as a wing equipped with the B-52 Stratofortress, and the B-52 wing could deliver more weapons at a greater range. Only two wings of Hustlers were acquired, and after only a decade in operational service the B-58A was grounded with little regret. The last B-58A was retired on 16 January 1970.

Development

In October 1954, SAC published requirements for the next generation of the strategic bomber to be operational in 1965. Essentially, the requirement called for an airplane with the range and payload of the B-52 and at least the speed of the B-58A. Key requirements for the bomber included:

- 50,000lb payload
- 6,000 nautical miles range
- Mach 0.9 cruise speed
- Mach 2+ dash speed to and over the target
- Use existing runways and maintenance facilities

The SAC requirements were the basis of the System Requirement No. 22 (SR-22) for WS-110A that was issued by Air Research and Development Command (ARDC) on 15 April 1955, ARDC being the component of the USAF responsible for the development of new weapon systems. ARDC selected Boeing and North American Aviation (NAA) to compete to build WS-110A through letters of intent issued on 11 November 1955 and development contracts dated 9 December 1955. Curtiss-Wright, Allison, Pratt & Whitney, and General Electric (GE) competed to power WS-110A with their J67, J89, J91, and J93 turbojet engines respectively. Curtiss-Wright soon dropped out of the competition. Both Boeing and NAA chose the GE J93 engine. The USAF put GE under contract on 26 July 1957. The J91 effort was not wasted. It became the basis of the J58, which would propel the Lockheed Blackbird family of Mach 3+ airplanes.

Boeing submitted the Model 804-4 design to the USAF in November 1957. It had a trapezoidal wing with a highly swept leading edge, canards, a single vertical tail, and six J93 engines in individual nacelles, three under each wing. The Model 804-4 had a maximum gross weight of 542,000lbs, was 206ft in length, and had a wingspan of 94.5ft.

The new NAA design had several features that distinguished it from its Boeing competitor. Like the Model 804-4, the NAA airplane had six J93 engines and canards. Unlike the Boeing airplane, the NAA airplane had a delta wing, and the engines were grouped together under the

The Model 804-4 was Boeing's design to meet the requirements of WS-110A. Never built, this artist's depiction shows its sleek lines. (*Erik Simonsen*)

rear of the wing. The NAA design had two vertical tails. The most innovative aspects of the NAA aircraft were compression lift and folding wingtips.

In 1956, National Advisory Committee for Aeronautics (NACA) researchers Alfred J. Eggers and Clarence A. Syverston published a classified technical paper on a phenomenon called compression lift. Using compression lift, a supersonic airplane could fly with greater lift and less drag by surfing on its shockwaves. NAA engineers studied the NACA report and used it to design their bomber. The placement of the engines in the NAA design required a large wedge-shaped inlet to be located ahead of the engines and underneath the delta wing, such that the inlet did double duty by feeding air to the engines and creating the shockwaves at the right place to generate compression lift.

The second innovation in the NAA design was folding wingtips. At supersonic speeds, the wingtips were folded down. Primarily, the folding wingtips increased directional stability, allowing for smaller and lighter vertical stabilizers. In addition, the folding wingtips assisted in capturing the increased pressure under the wing, magnifying the compression lift effect. Furthermore, when the wingtips were folded down, the center of lift moved forward, which reduced trim drag.

Compared to the Boeing aircraft, the NAA design was more complex. The folding wingtips were massive structures and absolutely had to be able to be retracted, because the airplane could not be landed if they remained in the lowered position. The massive variable-geometry inlet also was complex. The aft fuselage under the delta wing needed to contain the ducts

A top view of the XB-70A A/V-1 reveals some of its distinctive structure features, including the long slender forward fuselage, the canards, the large delta wing, and the dual vertical stabilizers. (*National Museum of the US Air Force*)

No part of the B-70 was more critical to its performance than the massive air inlets under the delta wing. The inlets both contributed to compression lift and supplied air to the six massive turbojet engines. The inlets had movable ramps to optimally position the shock waves during supersonic flight. (*NASA*)

leading from the inlet to the engines, leaving no good place for the main landing gear. As a result, the main landing gear had to be designed to fold up in an elaborate manner to fit into the available space, increasing its complexity.

NAA delivered its design to the USAF in October 1957. ARDC, Air Material Command and SAC evaluated the two designs, and NAA design was the clear winner, its innovative technology providing superior performance. The USAF announced the selection of NAA on 23 December 1957. In February 1958, the WS-110A aircraft received the designation of B-70. After a contest, the B-70 gained the name Valkyrie on 3 July 1958.

Cancellation

Despite the enthusiasm of the USAF in general and especially SAC for a supersonic bomber to replace the B-52, the B-70 program faced skepticism from the Eisenhower administration, in particular from its budget director Maurice Stans. The United States was recovering from a mild recession in the late 1950s, defense spending had greatly increased in the preceding years, and this was an era when a balanced budget for the Federal government in peacetime was considered non-negotiable. By 1959, the ICBM program was showing considerable progress and no longer was it unthinkable that long-range missiles could completely replace bombers in the strategic nuclear role.

On 1 December 1959, the B-70 program was cut back to a single XB-70A prototype and development work on the AN/ASQ-28 computer for its weapon system. It was believed that the advanced AN/ASQ-28 would be useful in a variety of applications beside the B-70. The USAF used its influence to expand the program to a second XB-70A and third aircraft, the YB-70A, which would have a full fit of mission systems.

During the 1960 presidential campaign, John F. Kennedy ran on a hawkish platform including support for the B-70. But after the inauguration of Kennedy, defense policy was run by the powerful Secretary of Defense, Robert S. McNamara, who had a background as an academic and business executive. During the Second World War, he had served in the AAF headquarters as the leader of a team of statistical analysts. McNamara believed in the superiority of data-driven cost-effectiveness calculations over the intuitive (and in his perspective, hidebound and parochial) preferences of the uniformed military. In McNamara's opinion, ICBMs '[made] unnecessary and economically unjustifiable the development of the B-70 as a full weapon system.' By July 1961, the program had been scaled back to only the two XB-70A aircraft, to be used as Mach 3 technology demonstrators rather than prototype bombers. The USAF fought back with a concept for a Reconnaissance/Strike aircraft, the RS-70, which was a B-70 that would use advanced sensors to detect targets that had been missed by previous waves of attacks. On 5 March 1964, the program was conclusively limited to two aircraft to be used for flight research, not bomber development.

In hindsight, was the decision to cancel the B-70 production bomber program a good one? Certainly, the effectiveness of the early ICBMs was probably overrated. These missiles used a self-contained inertial navigation system (INS) to determine their position as they guided to the target. As well as extraordinarily accurate sensors and on-board computers (initially analog, later digital), the ICBMs relied on two critical things. The first need was a map of the earth's gravity, which varied by geographic location. The sensors in the INS measured total acceleration; the gravity data was subtracted from the total acceleration to yield the acceleration of the missile. The second requirement was for highly accurate coordinates of the targets. An ICBM did not 'see' its target; it flew to a set of coordinates. If target mapping was inaccurate, the ICBM would miss the target even if it navigated perfectly. Consequently, geodesy, gravimetry, and high-resolution photo-mapping of targets in the Soviet Union were the focus of high-priority work at the time, but not yet fully mature. Unlike an ICBM, a bomber with an on-board crew could still locate and accurately attack targets in the face of mapping uncertainties. It was also true that the early missiles were fairly unreliable.

While ICBM advocates may have oversold their preferred weapon system, it is still questionable whether the B-70 was the right bomber for the time. The shoot-down of a Central Intelligence Agency U-2B high-altitude reconnaissance plane on 1 May 1960 highlighted the capability of surface-to-air missiles. No matter how high an aircraft flew, a missile could be built to intercept it. The Lockheed Blackbird family of aircraft defied this generalization, but those aircraft used an early form of radar low observability (stealth) that the B-70 did not have. Flying very low to use terrain to mask the flight of a bomber was a more promising tactic than flying very high. Paradoxically, the B-52 had low altitude capability but the B-70 did not. Furthermore, accurately dropping an unguided bomb from a very high-altitude Mach 3+ aircraft was difficult. The Mach 3+ speed at weapon separation magnified the effects of even minute variations in weapons aerodynamics and aircraft flowfield. The offensive avionics system could measure the winds at altitude but could only estimate them between the drop altitude and the target. The immense explosive power of strategic nuclear weapons would have compensated for some of these inaccuracies, but the B-70 would probably have been a less effective bomber than anticipated. In summary, the B-70 was magnificent, but an ill-conceived weapon system.

General Thomas S. Power, retired Commander in Chief of the SAC, explained the reason for the cancellation of the B-70 program in 1965:

> What really 'killed' this airplane, in my opinion, was the fact that it was designed for flight at very high altitudes which was very desirable at the time it was conceived. But this became a serious deficiency when the Soviets developed their present extensive system of high-altitude antiaircraft missiles.

Flight Testing the XB-70A

Despite the cancellation of the bomber program, NAA, GE and the USAF had a truly extraordinary aircraft under construction. The first aircraft was designated XB-70A and carried tail number 62-0001. In the program, it was known as Air Vehicle 1 (A/V-1). A/V-1 rolled out of the NAA facility at Air Force Plant 42 in Palmdale, California on 11 May 1964 in a highly publicized fashion. Several months of ground engine runs and then taxi tests followed, while the B-70 team worked out systems problems and readied the aircraft for first flight. The XB-70A undertook its first flight on 21 September 1964, with NAA test pilot Alvin S. White as pilot and Colonel Joseph E. Cotton in the co-pilot seat. Over the course of the flight test program, A/V-1 and its sister ship A/V-2 (tail number 62-0207) explored the B-70 flight envelope to Mach 3+. The XB-70A proved to be a remarkable flying machine. It was also a temperamental one, experiencing a long series of problems with its steel honeycomb structure, inlets, landing gear, and hydraulics. Had the B-70 gone into production, it would have been an enormous and perhaps insurmountable challenge to turn the Valkyrie into a reliable weapon system. On 8 June 1966, A/V-2 had a mid-air collision which resulted in the loss of the aircraft and the death of test pilot Major Carl S. Cross.

A/V-2 could be externally distinguished from A/V-1 by the black radome under the nose, 5-degree wing dihedral angle, and its tail number. The folding wingtips were a distinctive feature of the B-70 design. (*US Air Force*)

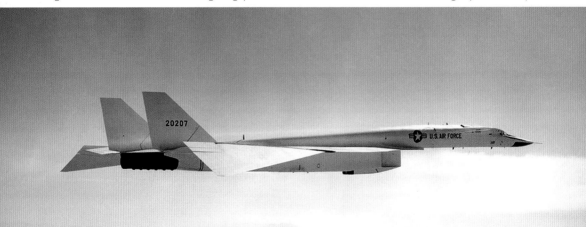

The Legacy of the Valkyrie

Almost six decades after the XB-70A rolled out of its hangar in Palmdale for the first time, it remains the most exotic-looking aircraft of all time and the fastest bomber ever built. It is ironic that the mighty B-70 Valkyrie never advanced beyond the prototype stage, whereas the B-52H, the ultimate model of the B-52 which was acquired as an interim bomber to bridge the gap until the B-70 entered service, is on track to potentially remain in service for a century. The B-70 had no technical influence on the Lockheed Mach 3+ family of aircraft, including the famous SR-71A.

Interestingly, the most lasting effect of the B-70 may have been on the Soviet Union. The MiG-25 (NATO reporting name Foxbat) interceptor was specifically designed to counter the B-70. The high-altitude S-200 (NATO reporting name Gammon, US Department of Defense designation SA-5) surface-to-air missile system was also intended to defend against the B-70. Although the B-70 never went into production or operation, both the MiG-25 and S-200 did, seeing widespread service with the Soviet Union and other states to which it supplied weapons.

But in a broader sense, the B-70 lived on. NAA, its subcontractors, GE, and the USAF had learned how to design, build, and test a large supersonic bomber. The same team would get an opportunity to apply those lessons on a new bomber program, and in subtle ways the influence of the B-70 would be seen in the bomber that followed.

Had the B-70 gone into production and entered service with SAC, this scene created by renowned aerospace illustrator Erik Simonsen would have actually occurred. The B-70B is in pre-contact position behind a KC-135A tanker. The window just forward of the canard is for a systems operator. A Skybolt missile is carried under each wing. (*Erik Simonsen*)

Chapter 3

B-1A

'I would like to emphasize that this program is vitally important to the Air Force. If we are to have a strong and credible strategic force through the 1980s and 1990s, we must have the B-1 as the ultimate replacement for the B-52.'
                    Major General Douglas T. Nelson, B-1 System Program Director

What Should Replace the B-52? (Redux)

The cancellation of B-70 production presented an existential threat to the bomber generals who ran the USAF in general and SAC in particular. Strategic bombers were at the core of their organizational, professional, and personal identities. These were men whose formative experiences had been flying bombers in the Second World War and then building the SAC bomber force into the mightiest military unit in human history. That the ICBM might supplant the manned bomber as a core element of the American strategic deterrent force was unthinkable to them, but entirely thinkable to their elected and appointed civilian superiors, who were not necessarily enamored with flying machines but instead prized cost-effectiveness.

While the great question of what bomber might follow the B-52 was being considered, the state of the art of ICBMs had advanced greatly. The Atlas and Titan I were liquid-fueled, which meant that they needed fueling facilities at the launch site, an elaborate operational sequence to prepare for launch, and a large missile crew. Some of the limitations of the first-generation of ICBMs were overcome by the Minuteman and Titan II missiles that followed them. The former had solid propellant and the latter had storable liquid propellant that did not require the missile to be fueled immediately prior to launch. Both missiles were maintained ready for launch in hardened silos, meaning that they were less likely to be caught on the ground in a surprise attack. The capability to intercept and destroy an ICBM after it was launched was at least a decade in the future. It was conceivable that the B-52 marked the end of the line for the strategic bomber.

The arguments for missiles were further strengthened by the advent of the sea-launched ballistic missile (SLBM). The first generation of SLBM was the Polaris, launched from submerged nuclear submarines. The Polaris was less accurate and had a shorter range than ICBMs but was even more difficult to destroy in a surprise attack, since its launch pad was mobile and underwater. There were also issues of inter-service rivalry; Polaris made the US Navy a full partner with the USAF in the nuclear deterrence mission.

The most important advocate of missiles for strategic deterrence was Secretary of Defense Robert S. McNamara, who served in the administrations of President John F. Kennedy and his successor, Lyndon B. Johnson. McNamara was an extraordinarily strong-willed, powerful and influential holder of his office, and his ideas drove a decade of weapons development

Above: The LGM-30 Minuteman was a more practical and effective weapon than the first-generation ICBMs (Atlas and Titan I). With its solid propellant engines, it could be kept ready for rapid launch without the need to fuel the missile. (*F. J. Hooker/US Air Force*)

Right: Based in hardened underground silos and requiring no fueling facilities, the Minuteman was well protected against a preemptive attack. Most maintenance on the missile was performed in the silo. (*Technical Sergeant Bob Wickley/US Air Force*)

and procurement decisions as well as the conduct of the Vietnam War. His staff of civilian analysts challenged the previously uncontested military control over weapon system acquisition decisions. He frequently clashed with the high-ranking military officers who served under him, none more than the USAF generals who pressed for a new bomber to replace the B-52. In a barely veiled direct criticism of McNamara in 1963, General Thomas D. White, the recently retired USAF Chief of Staff, said:

> In common with many other military men, active and retired, I am profoundly apprehensive of the pipe-smoking, tree-full-of-owls type of so-called professional 'defense intellectuals' who have been brought into this nation's capital. I don't believe a lot of these often over-confident, sometimes arrogant young professors, mathematicians and other theorists have sufficient worldliness or motivation to stand up to the kind of enemy we face.

In fairness to the USAF bomber generals, even the new generation of ICBMs had their problems. The Atlas and Titan I ICBMs missile launch facilities were at a fixed location and either soft or only lightly hardened, so they were vulnerable to surprise pre-emptive attack. The hardened silos of the Minuteman and Titan II were much tougher targets, but improved Soviet ICBM guidance and navigation accuracy could eventually put them at risk. Vulnerability to surprise attack was no small matter to a country that had suffered the raid on Pearl Harbor two decades earlier. Because the missiles could not be recalled after launch, they could only be launched after a Soviet attack had been positively verified, which might be too late. The ability to shoot down ICBMs with anti-ballistic missile systems was in development. Developing an effective anti-ballistic system posed extraordinarily difficult problems, but the 1960s were a time when optimism about technological developments was frequently justified.

Furthermore, the ability of ICBMs to actually destroy targets was extremely uncertain. The INSs of ICBMs were astonishing feats of precision engineering, but like all precision equipment, the missile navigation and guidance systems were not perfect. Furthermore, the missile engines might not stop providing thrust at exactly the correct time, which would mean that the position and velocity vector of the re-entry vehicle at separation would have an error which would propagate into miss distance at the target. After separation, the re-entry vehicle was no more controlled than a thrown ball. Target-mapping inaccuracies, gravitational field, and errors in wind estimates created additional uncertainties and miss distance at the target. All these factors heightened concerns that the ICBMs were less lethal than they appeared. All of these factors were magnified for SLBMs, where the exact location of the launch platform, a moving and submerged submarine, was uncertain.

In contrast, a manned bomber with ground-mapping radar and a skilled crew was either immune to these sources of error or could correct for them in real time at the target. In peacetime, bombers were routinely flown on training missions over instrumented target sites, so trends in bombing accuracy could be measured with abundant data. An American bomber that survived a surprise attack and penetrated Soviet defenses had a good probability of actually destroying even the most hardened Soviet targets with an accurately dropped thermonuclear bomb. The confidence level for target destruction with an ICBM or SLBM was lower.

Fortunately for bomber advocates, a new doctrine arose to justify, (or less generously, rationalize), the continued existence of the SAC strategic bomber fleet. The United States settled on a nuclear force structure called the triad, which consisted of strategic bombers, ICBMs and SLBMs. The diversity of forces within the triad had significant benefits. The unique advantages of each leg of the triad compensated for the disadvantages of the other legs, and in general avoided the risk of 'having all one's eggs in one basket'. In the words of General Powers:

> The advantages of a mixed force of bombers and missiles are enhanced by the addition of the Polaris submarines. The integrated combination of these three entirely different types of strategic weapon systems gives us very high assurance that our deterrent cannot be wiped out, from one day to the other, by some dramatic technological breakthrough on the part of the Soviets. Moreover, this combination lends strength and credibility to a deterrent that must have unmatched flexibility, superior striking power and war-winning capability in order to be and remain effective.

The triad justified the US Air Force keeping its beloved bombers in addition to the ICBM force, and allowed the US Navy to fully participate in the strategic nuclear mission with its SLBM force. Each leg of the triad had its own contractors and bases, which meant that the beside its military value, the triad created many corporations and Congressmen with vested interests. The doctrine served institutional and political interests and gave the United States an assured deterrent, albeit at a considerable cost to taxpayers.

USAF bomber advocates formulated a set of arguments supporting the continued maintenance and modernization of the strategic bomber fleet in the missile age. As he approached retirement, General LeMay (formerly the Commander-in-Chief of SAC and now the Chief of Staff of the USAF) commented on the risk of not developing a new bomber:

> If we don't have a war, it won't matter. If we do, and we don't have a new bomber, we are apt to lose. For a considerable future, we need a manned system. There are certain things a manned system can do better. The next war will be different from the last, and the side with the most flexibility will have the advantage. The side that has the mixed force and can react with missiles and bombers is apt to beat the side that has only missiles. So we must have a manned system for the foreseeable future to exercise judgement and to react to surprises.

In his book *Design for Survival*, retired USAF General Thomas S. Power made the case for the manned strategic bomber in more detail. Power had been LeMay's successor as Commander-in-Chief of SAC. Power was writing as a private citizen, but there's little doubt that his words reflected the thinking of USAF bomber generals. Power acknowledged the advantages of ICBMs and touted his own significant role in introducing them into SAC. But he also emphasized the unique capabilities of manned strategic bombers:

- Bombers could be launched and then recalled and recovered, unlike ICBMs for which the decision to launch was an irrevocable decision. Given the twin concerns of the deterrent force getting destroyed on the ground by a surprise attack and the risk of spurious warnings, this was an important point.
- Bombers could carry a broader range of weapons and deliver them with greater accuracy.

- Bombers could attack from a wide range of directions and altitudes, unlike ballistic missiles with their fixed and predictable trajectories.
- Bombers with an onboard crew can deal with unpredictable situations and their crews can make real-time decisions.
- Bombers are more reliable than missiles. Bomber crews are able to train in a more realistic manner than missile crews. Bombers can be routinely operationally tested.
- Bombers are a valuable hedge against a breakthrough in anti-missile defense.
- Bombers on airborne alert or 'special missions' can present a 'clearly visible expression of national intent and demonstrate this country's determination and capability to protect its interests and those of its allies'.
- Bombers can be used in non-nuclear conflicts, unlike ICBMs. General Power could not have known it at the time, but the B-1B bomber that would eventually be the fruit of the decades-long effort to create a follow-on to the B-52 would excel in exactly this role.

The urgent need for a new strategic bomber grew as the B-52 fleet began to age and shrink. First to go were the B-52B aircraft. The B-52B had been the first operational version of the B-52, which had first been delivered to SAC in 1955. Under Project *Fast Fly*, the B-52B was retired as were all B-47 Stratojets and KC-97 tankers. On 8 December 1965, Secretary of Defense Robert S. McNamara announced that all B-52C, D, E, and F Stratofortresses and B-58A Hustlers would be phased out by June 1971. If the triad was to be maintained, what would be the next strategic bomber for SAC?

Wings That Swing

The planform of a high-performance airplane is a compromise. Ideally it would have a large wing area for take-off and landing, to reduce the airspeed required to maintain sufficient lift to fly and therefore the required length of the runway. For cruise, it would have a high aspect ratio, the ratio of wingspan to chord. High aspect ratio translates into high efficiency. The ideal wing for a jet airplane cruising at medium to high subsonic airspeeds for cruise would be moderately swept, as in modern jet airliners. At high speeds, the ideal wing would have a high sweep angle and a lower aspect ratio. The high sweep angle reduces drag at transonic and supersonic speeds by delaying the onset of compressibility drag associated with shock waves. A shorter and wider wing reduces bending moment on the wing root, permitting a lighter structure. But while swept wings reduce the drag that occurs at high speed, they also introduce new problems at low speeds and at high angles of attack, particularly during take-off and landing. The wing planform has to balance the conflicting demands of the two ends of the performance envelope. Clearly, the shape of the wing that the designer chooses for an airplane is a compromise, based on requirements including maximum speed, maneuverability, required minimum runway length, and range, and the relative importance of those different requirements.

The variable-geometry (VG) wing, alternatively called variable-sweep or swing-wing, was a clever idea to give an airplane the equivalent of not one wing but a set of wings, from which one can be chosen based on the phase of flight. In the spread configuration, a VG wing offers benign low-speed handling qualities, maximum lift and subsonic aerodynamic efficiency. In the fully swept configuration, the VG wing has low transonic and supersonic drag and superior supersonic stability characteristics. As with all things aeronautical, there are trade-offs. A VG wing needs a pivot and a mechanism to control sweep angle which introduces structural and mechanical complexity and increases cost and weight. But the potential aerodynamic improvements of VG wings were so appealing that it was an idea worth pursuing.

Amongst the war trophies acquired by the United States in the aftermath of the surrender of Germany in 1945 was the experimental Messerschmitt P.1101, a VG demonstrator. Like many German late-war aviation projects, it was ahead of its time, never flew, and represented a waste of resources for a country that had desperate and unmet short-term needs. Germany's waste became America's technological windfall, and the uncompleted P.1101 aircraft and its documentation became the object of study. NACA had been researching VG and advocated that the USAF fund a VG technology demonstration. Bell Aircraft Corporation, which had received the P.1101 airframe from the USAF, received a USAF contract to design and build the X-5. Unlike the P.1101 that could only change its wing sweep on the ground, the X-5 could change its wings sweep in flight.

The X-5 pioneered the variable-geometry wing configuration. Note how the wing roots translate to the rear as the wings swing forward and the wing roots translate forward as the sweep angle increases. (NASA)

Bell built two X-5 research aircraft, with USAF tail numbers 50-1838 and 50-1839. The VG wings on the X-5 could be symmetrically swept between 20.25° and 58.7° (often expressed as 20° and 60° respectively in various sources) on hinges just outboard of each side of the fuselage. Electric motors drove jackscrews which changed wing sweep angle, with limit switches at each end of the sweep angle range. There was a manual back-up capability for the pilot to move the wings. The change in wing sweep angle caused unacceptably large changes in the center of lift and center of gravity, so the entire wing assembly had to be articulated along the longitudinal axis of the X-5 to compensate for these changes. An additional set of jackscrews moved the wings forward and aft on a track. The aspect ratio of the wing varied between 2.16 at 58.7° sweep angle and 6.09 at 20.25° sweep angle.

The X-5 flew between 1951 and 1955. The aircraft had bad stall and spin characteristics, which killed USAF test pilot Major Raymond A. Popson when 50-1839 spun out of control. Most X-5 research flights were conducted by NASA, a majority of them being flown by NACA research pilot Joseph A. Walker, who would later perish when his F-104N collided with the XB-70A. The last X-5 sortie (in 50-1838 on 25 October 1955) was a familiarization flight to broaden the experience of a young NACA research pilot named Neil A. Armstrong, who would later go on to greater things. The X-5 had proven that a VG aircraft would work, and that the handling deficiencies of the aircraft were more related to the particular characteristics of the X-5 design than the VG configuration in general. It also demonstrated that the need to translate the wings forward and aft when sweep angle was changed unacceptably increased the complexity and weight of a VG aircraft, making it an impractical feature for an operational aircraft.

As with the B-70 and its compression lift concept, NACA (after 1958, the National Aeronautics and Space Administration, NASA) played an essential role in making VG a practical

The F-111 was the first operational aircraft with variable-geometry wings. The fixed gloves that moved the wing pivot points outboard were a NASA invention that eliminated the need to translate the wings forward and aft when the sweep angle changed. (*Master Sergeant Kevin J. Gruenwald/US Air Force*)

design option. NASA researchers including William J. Alford, Jr., Edward C. Polhamus and Thomas A. Toll, working with British team members including the noted aeronautical engineer Barnes N. Wallis, developed a concept in which only the outer part of the wing was VG, and the pivot points for the VG outer portion were contained in a fixed inner portion of the wing called the glove. The forward portion of the glove was swept and part of the aft portion of the VG outer wing was tucked into the aft portion of the glove when the VG outer wing was fully swept. By moving the pivot points outboard, the movement of the wing aerodynamic center was minimized when the VG outer wing changed its sweep angle, eliminating the need for forward and aft translation of the wing. Furthermore, favorable interaction between the fully swept wing and the horizontal tail further enhanced stability. Wing tunnel tests at NASA Langley Research Center in 1958-59 were used to refine and verify the new VG configuration.

The innovation from Polhamus, Toll, Barnes and associates was timely, because a major new fighter program was starting. In February 1960, the USAF Tactical Air Command (TAC) staff briefed NASA Langley on requirements for a new tactical fighter that combined short take-off and landing capability with long range, high-altitude supersonic performance, and very low altitude high-speed flight. NASA Langley's VG technology was a good fit for TAC's requirements.

Secretary of Defense McNamara and his staff were highly critical of what they perceived as unnecessary and wasteful duplication between the different armed services. They advocated a program which would develop aircraft that could be used for multiple services and missions. In February 1961, McNamara ordered the different service requirements be combined into the multi-service Tactical Fighter Experimental (TFX) program. The TFX was designated the

With its swings fully swept back, the F-111 was capable of high speed even at very low altitudes. (*Ken Hackman/ US Air Force*)

F-111, and there was an F-111A version for the USAF which would be a TAC fighter bomber, and a carrier-based F-111B to meet US Navy requirements for fleet air defense. The F-111 was big, heavy, and fast. VG wings gave the F-111 the combination of take-off and landing distance that the USAF wanted, ability to be catapulted off of aircraft carriers and land on them that the US Navy required, range, endurance, and Mach 2+ speed. General Dynamics (formerly Convair) was the prime contractor for the F-111.

Continuing the theme of commonality, a third variant of the F-111 appeared, the FB-111A. The FB-111A was a strategic bomber for SAC. On 10 December 1965, McNamara announced that 210 FB-111As would replace the early model B-52s and the B-58As. SAC accepted the first operational FB-111A on 8 October 1969. On 19 March 1969, Secretary of Defense Melvin R. Laird reduced the FB-111A buy, and in the end only 76 FB-111As were built.

The FB-111A was of limited value to SAC. Its speed and terrain-following avionics made it a very difficult target for enemy air defenses, but its range was too short to be a useful strategic bomber. It also had a relatively small payload of weapons and lacked the extensive electronic countermeasures system with a dedicated crew member to operate it that SAC preferred. F-111 in its various TAC versions was nominally a fighter but actually it was a light tactical bomber and was excellent in that role when the bugs were worked out and the avionics evolved and matured. The F-111B was a failure as a carrier-based fighter; the US Navy eventually met that requirement with the purpose-built F-14 Tomcat, which also had VG wings.

Whatever the deficiencies of commonality as it was implemented in the F-111 program, the F-111 had proven the viability of VG wings for high-performance military aircraft.

The FB-111A was a strategic bomber version of the F-111 that equipped two SAC bombardment wings. The FB-111A appealed to Secretary of Defense Robert S. McNamara's desire to achieve economic efficiency through commonality, and also put off the need to spend a large amount on developing a new bomber. Its small size for a strategic bomber meant it was deficient in unrefueled range, payload, and electronic countermeasures. (*Master Sergeant Ken Hammond/US Air Force*)

America's Most Studied Aircraft

If the United States intended to keep a strategic bomber force and the B-70 was not the answer, what should be the characteristics for the aircraft that would replace the B-52? The USAF and its contractors conducted studies in the early and mid-sixties to define this new bomber. The Subsonic Low Altitude Bomber (SLAB) of 1961 morphed into the Extended Range Strike Aircraft (ERSA, 1963), then the Low-Altitude Manned Penetrator (LAMP, 1963), Manned Aircraft Studies Steering Group (MASSG, 1963) and Advanced Manned Penetrator (AMP), followed by the Advanced Manned Precision Strike System (AMPSS, 1964). Boeing, General Dynamics, and NAA were the AMPSS contractors. AMPSS evolved into the Advanced Manned Strategic Aircraft (AMSA).

In 1964, Secretary of Defense Robert S. McNamara stated:

> Various options are open for replacing the B-52s in the seventies, if a replacement requirement exists at that time. In case supersonic speed and high altitude are needed for a future strategic bomber, the experience from three different Mach 3 planes, currently in the research and development phase, will be available – the XB-70, the A-11 [the actual classified designation of this aircraft was A-12], and the SR-71. In case low-level penetration capabilities turn out to be the key to future bomber effectiveness, the lessons being learned in the from the F-111, for example, will be applicable … the fiscal year 1965 budget includes funds for a special study on an Advanced Manned Strategic Aircraft, a long-range, low altitude penetrator to serve as an airborne missile platform.

A close reading of McNamara's words ('if a replacement requirement exists at that time') reveals that he remained unconvinced about the need for a new bomber, but funding AMSA gave momentum to the program. The controversy continued into the following year. In early 1965, McNamara's testimony before the House Armed Services Committee reiterated his skepticism about the value of manned strategic bombers:

> I see little merit to the argument that bombers are needed in the assured destruction role because our missiles are not dependable. But I do recognize that presently unforeseeable changes in the situation may occur against which a bomber force might possibly provide a hedge. Therefore, as will be discussed later, I propose to maintain indefinitely bomber units in our strategic offensive forces.

The key AMSA performance requirements were a top speed of Mach 2.5 at high altitude, Mach 1.2 at low altitude over flat terrain, and Mach 0.9 during terrain-following flight. AMSA could take off from a 6,000ft long runway and fly 5,000 miles without refueling, including 2,000 miles at Mach 0.85 at sea level. The bomber would be armed with both nuclear bombs and a new missile called the Short Range Attack Missile (SRAM) and designated AGM-69. Evidence of F-111 influence on AMSA included VG wings, a crew escape capsule instead of individual ejection seats, and a Terrain-Following Radar (TFR).

What eventually would become the B-1 was still a paper airplane, but now it was a defined concept rather than a nebulous desire for a B-52 replacement. The contractors for the AMSA airframe work were the traditional trio of Boeing, General Dynamics and NAA. Curtiss

Wright, GE, and Pratt & Whitney worked on the engines for AMSA, while International Business Machines and Hughes Aircraft investigated avionics. The USAF awarded the AMSA study contracts in 1965. Study contracts with several companies for the electronic warfare system to protect AMSA were also signed.

Perhaps the most difficult and critical deliverable of the study contracts was to optimize the mission, airframe, and engine. Each of these three factors affected the others in an interactive manner. For example, a high-bypass engine was more efficient at subsonic airspeeds but was also heavier and required a bigger airframe, which would also weigh more and have more drag. In contrast, a low-bypass engine was more efficient at supersonic speeds but less efficient at subsonic speeds. It was lighter and had less impact on the airframe. But if the majority of the flight was to be at subsonic speeds, then the extra fuel that was needed would increase the weight of the airframe. The result was a large multi-dimensional matrix of mission, airframe, and engine options. A configuration analysis computer program was used to evaluate the options so that the optimum combination could be chosen. The optimum configuration was biased towards efficient cruise and high-subsonic low-level flight. Augmenters would provide the extra thrust for take-off and supersonic flight. The augmenters would guzzle fuel when they were used, but they would only be used for short periods of time, so the total system-level impact of the augmenters was favorable compared with the alternatives.

The USAF uniformed leadership, General LeMay and then his successor as Chief of Staff, General John P. McConnell, made AMSA their highest priority development program. Secretary McNamara had never warmed to the need for a new bomber. To him, AMSA was most likely a program whose technological spin-offs could be used to upgrade the remaining B-52s and the FB-111A. However, McNamara did want 'to retain the option to maintain indefinitely bomber units in our strategic offensive forces', so he did not conclusively reject a new bomber.

Secretary of the Air Force Harold Brown, who had previously been McNamara's Director of Defense Research and Engineering prior to becoming the civilian leader of the USAF, was another person with influence on AMSA during this period. Brown was a stronger supporter of manned strategic bombers than McNamara but skeptical of the cost-effectiveness of AMSA, which promised to be the most expensive weapon system of the era. He stated that the 'advent of long range ballistic missiles has clearly changed – and reduced – the role of the strategic bomber in thermonuclear war' but also that 'the strategic bomber is needed as part of a balanced missile/bomber force for the foreseeable future.' This was essentially a restatement of the triad doctrine of strategic nuclear force development. However, he was still unconvinced of the need for AMSA, unless 'all other weapon systems have been measured against it in terms of versatility and cost, as well as capability, and found wanting.' The unwillingness of the civilian leadership in the Department of Defense to commit to development of AMSA led to insiders insisting that the acronym actually stood for 'America's Most Studied Aircraft'.

AMSA Becomes the B-1A

The change in American administrations in 1969 greatly altered the course of the American strategic bombers. On 19 March 1969, McNamara's successor, Melvin R. Laird, announced accelerated funding for AMSA at the same time that he reduced procurement of the FB-111A.

AMSA was designated as the B-1 in the following month. [Author's note: In accordance with the American military aircraft designation system in effect in 1969, the first model of the B-1 should have been designated the B-1A. In practice, the first model of the B-1 was almost always called the B-1 instead of the B-1A until the advent of the B-1B program, after which the first model was retroactively called the B-1A. For this book, the first model of the B-1 will always be called the B-1A and the term B-1 will be reserved for those situations where it applies to both the B-1A and B-1B.]

The USAF was thrilled that Laird supported its new bomber, after the opposition of McNamara. In the words of Lieutenant General Marvin McNickle, the USAF Deputy Chief of Staff for Research and Development, in 1969:

> I don't think that you can afford a 100% reliance on missiles or any other simple type of system. Even with an effective missile force, we still need the flexibility that a strategic aircraft gives you. You can send it out and recall it, but you wouldn't launch your missiles until you know that you had been attacked. Once the missiles are out of the hole, you can't recall them.

The structure of the B-1A program would be heavily influenced by Deputy Secretary of Defense David Packard. Packard was a true icon of American engineering and technology management. He was the co-founder of the leading electronic firm Hewlett-Packard (HP) and regarded as the 'father of Silicon Valley'. Laird knew that he would personally be consumed with the Vietnam War, Strategic Arms Limitation Treaty (SALT) negotiations, and working with Congress. He would need Packard and his skills to reform the defense acquisition system and cost-effectively modernize the American military. In some ways, Packard was like McNamara, in that both were accomplished business executives before serving in the Department of Defense. But their approaches were different: McNamara had a more abstract systems analysis mindset, whereas Packard was at heart an engineer. According to a study written by USAF Major Brian M. Frederickson and published in 2020:

> Packard championed a sequential, incremental, 'fly-before-you-buy' approach to defense procurement. He believed that prototyping and hardware demonstration provided the most effective path to mature technologies and lower risk before making a production decision. An ardent opponent of concurrency – which overlapped development and production – Packard wanted companies to prove the capability of their technologies and systems via hardware demonstrations rather than design studies and sales pitches. Packard's approach in the Pentagon mirrored his methods at HP. HP made production decisions based not on analytical studies and designs on paper but instead on inventions and hardware components upon which he could feel and observe their performance and capabilities. In short, the 'fly-before-you-buy' approach required competing teams to demonstrate the superiority of their product, rather than the superiority of their salesmanship.

A major impact of Packard's reforms was the separation of B-1A Full Scale Development (FSD) and production. The decision to proceed with FSD did not necessarily imply a decision to proceed with production. Instead, a production decision would be informed by test results and made only when sufficient data was available. Another impact was that Packard, an electronics expert, understood that electronics technology was advancing much faster than the more mature fields of airframe and engines. Therefore, Packard chose a system and contractual approach that broke the B-1A into four prime contracts (airframe, engine, offensive avionics system, and defensive avionics system) rather than have a single prime contractor with the engine and avionics systems suppliers being subcontractors to that prime contractor.

On 3 November 1969, the Air Force Systems Command, the research, development and acquisition command of the USAF, issued the request for proposals for B-1A FSD. The draft request for proposals was 'one of the largest paper monsters ever produced', as each office in the USAF bureaucracy added its own requirements for documentation. Deputy Secretary Packard, the ever-practical engineer, questioned each proposal deliverable and cut the request to a more manageable size before it was released to industry. Boeing, General Dynamics, and North American Rockwell (NAR, formerly NAA) would compete for the airframe, and GE and Pratt & Whitney for the engine. It was an important opportunity for each of the companies. For Boeing, B-52 and KC-135 production had ended, its commercial airliner business was about to enter a downturn, and NASA contracts for the Saturn rocket were soon to wind down. General Dynamics had nothing to follow the F-111. NAR had a fantastic run with military aircraft, but work had been sparse in the 1960s. That decade at NAA/NAR had been dominated by NASA work on the Apollo spacecraft and Saturn rocket, which was ending. Each of the three contractors perceived that the future of their military aircraft business was at stake. They submitted their proposals for the B-1A in early 1970.

During November 1969, the USAF appointed Brigadier General Guy M. Townsend as the program manager for the B-1A. Townsend was a highly experienced bomber test pilot who was the first USAF pilot to fly the B-47, the co-pilot on the first flight of the B-52, and the director of the XB-70 test force at AFFTC during the planning phase prior to first flight. He had also been the program manager for the C-5 Galaxy. Townsend was joined by Brigadier General Douglas T. Nelson as his deputy. Nelson replaced Townsend as the B-1 system program director in September 1970, was promoted to major general, and served in that role through January 1974.

The engine competition pitted GE's GE9 engine against the Pratt & Whitney JTF20 powerplant. The range and speed of the B-1 required the use of an augmented turbofan engine, with the augmenter providing the high thrust for supersonic flight and the turbofan providing the efficiency for a long cruise range. Each company had been funded for some development work by AMSA and also generic engine research sponsored by the USAF. In addition, both companies had an extensive heritage on which to draw. Also, both companies had been developing afterburning turbofan engines with the military designation of F100 for the USAF F-15 Eagle fighter and the closely related F400 for the advanced F-14B version of the US Navy's F-14 Tomcat.

Pratt & Whitney had supplied the first afterburning turbofan, the TF30, for all F-111 variants as well as the Grumman F-14A Tomcat, which replaced the unsatisfactory F-111B as the new fighter for the US Navy. The JTF20 used a scaled gas generator core from the STF-200C engine, which had been Pratt & Whitney's company-funded technology demonstrator for the engine that it would propose for what would eventually become the C-5A Galaxy transport. The STF-200C had been running on a test stand since April 1964. The JTF20 added a fan optimized for the B-1 mission and an augmenter to the scaled STF-200C core.

The NAR design for the B-1A underwent over 22,000 hours of wind tunnel testing. The variable-geometry feature meant that from an aerodynamic testing perspective, the B-1A was not one airplane but rather a family of airplanes. Wind tunnel runs covered the range of wing sweep angles. (*NASA*)

GE had been the contractor for the USAF's last new bomber engine, the J93. The GE9 was based on the GE1, which was intended to create a family of engines based on a common gas generator core design for bombers, fighters and transports. The GE1 started its test stand runs in November 1963.

Even before the USAF selected the airframe contractor, it chose IBM and the Autonetics Division of NAR to develop components of the offensive avionics. On 5 June 1970 Secretary of the Air Force Robert C. Seamans, Jr. announced the winners of the airframe and engine competitions: NAR and GE, respectively. NAR would supply five flight test aircraft and two for ground testing (one for structural load testing and the other for fatigue testing). GE would build forty F101-GE-100 engines, the F101 being the military designation given to the GE9. In accordance with Packard's philosophy, he issued a memorandum to Seamans that stated, 'The [B-1] authorization is for development programs only. A decision has not been made whether the B-1 will be authorized for production, when production might be authorized, or what level of production will be authorized.'

The year 1970 was not an auspicious time to begin FSD on a major new weapon system. Congress was displeased with cost overruns such as those on the F-111 and the C-5A Galaxy transport aircraft. The Vietnam War was enormously divisive in the United States, and military spending in general was out of favor. Congress reduced funding for B-1A FSD.

On 18 January 1971, Seamans approved a scaled-down program that consisted of only three flight test aircraft and twenty-seven engines. Ground structural testing would be conducted on pieces of the airplane rather than a full structural test article. First flight was now scheduled for April 1974, production go-ahead in April 1975, and initial operational capability (IOC) in December 1979 with 65 B-1As, with a total planned production run of 244 bombers. The USAF awarded an Offensive Avionics System (OAS) integration contract to Boeing on 13 April 1972. The last major contract issued by the USAF was to AIL, a division of Cutler-Hammer, for the critical Defensive Avionics System (DAS).

From Paper to Metal

B-1A FSD began in earnest after contract signing. Richard F. Walker was the B-1 program manager at NAR, with Robert E. Greer serving as his deputy. When NAR reorganized to create its B-1 Division in August 1972, Greer was promoted to lead that business unit and the B-1 program. He was a retired USAF general officer with a strong background in engineering and program management who had been hired by NAR to lead its effort on the

A free flight model was used to test stability and control in a wind tunnel. Data collected in the wind tunnel reduced the risk of flight testing. (*NASA*)

second stage of the Saturn V rocket, which NAR had been under contract with NASA to design and build.

The B-1A aerodynamic configuration, including weapons separation, was refined in over 22,000 hours of wind tunnel testing. Engineers and draftsmen needed to create tens of thousands of drawings, detailing every single part and assembly. In an era where computer-aided design did not exist, these drawings were produced by hand on sheets of vellum. Every part then needed to be analyzed to verify that it was strong enough to endure the stresses and fatigue that it would experience in service. The critical loads varied by part of the airplane. For example, the landing gear might face its greatest load at a high-speed, high sink rate, heavy-weight landing. The maximum load on the radome on the nose might be imposed by the aerodynamic pressure of high-speed flight at low altitude. The windshield might be most severely tested by a bird strike.

The application of a new analytical technique called fracture mechanics was pioneered during B-1A FSD. Fracture mechanics is the discipline of metallurgy concerned with the study of the propagation of cracks in materials and the resistance of materials to that propagation. Using fracture mechanics, critical structural parts of the B-1A were designed to limit the growth of cracks in the metal, which made for a more durable aircraft able to

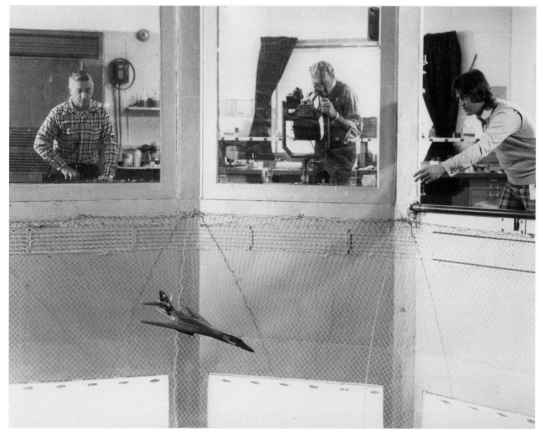

The NASA Langley Research Center 20ft spin tunnel was a wind tunnel with an upward flow of air. The free-flying B-1A model was hand-launched to evaluate spinning and spin recovery characteristics. The actual aircraft was prohibited from being deliberately stalled or spun and would most likely be unrecoverable if it did get in such a condition. (NASA)

A 6 per cent scale model of the B-1A was tested in the AEDC 16ft transonic wind tunnel to gather drag, stability, and control data. (*Chuck Klein collection*)

endure the rough ride of high-speed low-level flight. Other structures and material technology pioneered during FSD were a new specification for titanium and diffusion bonding to weld together the titanium. The B-1A primary structure was mostly manufactured of aluminum, steel, and titanium.

In January 1971, NAR began construction of a full-scale mockup. The mock-up was a useful tool for NAR engineers to visualize the location of structure and equipment. Another interesting mock-up was a full-scale model of the B-1 wing pivot joint, with Plexiglas windows at strategic locations to observe the operation of the VG mechanism. A USAF team of 208 personnel conducted a formal examination of the mock-up on 18–31 October 1971, resulting in 297 requests for changes to the design. The requests were in the areas of maintainability, safety, operations, logistics/support, and survivability/vulnerability. For example, one request was to improve leg room in the cockpit. Another was to improve lighting in the bomb bay.

The crew escape capsule was a good example of the complex challenges that were accomplished during FSD. As part of the AMSA studies, it was determined that the best way to provide an emergency escape capability for the crew was to use an escape capsule like the one on the F-111, although larger because the F-111 had a crew of only two. B-1 crews might have to escape at high altitude or low altitude, at very high speeds, and over water or rough terrain. But engineering the escape capsule was an enormously complicated task. Essentially it was an aircraft in itself that needed to contain the crew stations and be carried by another aircraft.

It needed two rocket engines to separate from the B-1 in a controlled manner, sensors for the flight controls, a strong and watertight structure, flotation bladders and self-righting bags for water landings, impact attenuators for land, and parachutes. The escape capsule needed to fit on the B-1A in a streamlined manner yet be aerodynamically stable after it separated over a wide range of airspeeds. In order to provide aerodynamic stability, two stabilizing fins and three spoilers were inflated or deployed by gas generators after separation. The module design was tested in a wind tunnel. The parachute system was tested by dropping an object with the mass and drag of the crew module from a B-52; the parachutes deployed after the drop. Using the test results, the parachute system was redesigned until it provided the required reliability and performance. The rocket-propelled ejection sequence of the capsule was tested on the high-speed track at Holloman AFB, with the first all-up sled test being conducted on 15 February 1973. Drop tests of capsules on water and land tested those flotation and impact attenuation.

NAR constructed nine full-scale structural sections of the aircraft for ground testing, such as the wing carry-through (WCT) structure which was the structural core of the entire airplane. That structure connected the fuselage to the wings and included the pivots for the VG wings. The structural test articles were loaded to verify their strength, and the data from the tests was compared to stress calculations to verify the analysis. Loading was first increased to the design limit, and then the structural sections were loaded to failure to verify that their ultimate load was at least 150 per cent of the design load limit.

An engine is the most important part of an aircraft, because it affects the performance, reliability, and operating costs more than anything else. The parts of an engine work under enormous stresses and high temperatures. The F101 would need to endure the fatigue induced by the frequent throttle movements that B-1A pilots would make during terrain-following flight. It would also need to handle ingesting ice that might be shed by the inlets or birds that got sucked into them – both hazards of low-level flight. Even if the ice or birds damaged the engine, the engine needed to contain the damage within it and not catastrophically disintegrate.

The USAF had previously decided that the durability of its aircraft engines needed to be improved. The result of this demand was the Engine Structural Integrity Program (ENSIP), and the F101 was the first engine designed to conform with the requirements of ENSIP. The impact of ENSIP was profound and pervasive; it influenced the design and testing of every part of the F101, including operating environment, design life, external and maneuvering loads, margins of safety, and material properties. ENSIP required a fundamental reconsideration of the way that engineers designed and analyzed engine components. Before ENSIP, designers assumed that components could be designed not to fail. ENSIP was based on the realization that all components can fail, and therefore the key to engine durability is to reduce the probability and impact of failure. ENSIP encompassed both the design of the engine, and inspection and maintenance procedures in the field and depot. The F101 utilized new high-temperature alloys, new fabrication technology, and advanced engine cooling techniques; some of the latter could be traced back to the pioneering work on the J93.

The USAF contract for the F101 called for GE to deliver 23 XF101-GE-100 ground test engines and 23 YF101-GE-100 flight test engines. Of the ground test engines, two went to Rockwell International (as NAR was renamed in 1973) for ground testing of a complete B-1A nacelle. Three flight test aircraft required twelve engines; the remaining eleven were spares. The GE program manager for the F101 was James E. Worsham.

The first F101 Preliminary Flight Rating Test (PFRT) engine ran in a test cell in February 1972. A problem with the F101 that was discovered and fixed in ground testing was a low-amplitude, high-frequency 'screech' in the augmenter; this was fixed by adjusting

Four General Electric F101 augmented turbofan engines powered the B-1. The XF101-GE-100 was used for ground testing. The YF101-GE-100 was installed in the B-1A flight test aircraft. (*Chuck Klein collection*)

the fuel flow pattern and redesigning the flame holder. The F101 compressor occasionally rubbed against its casing, which was resolved by opening up tolerances. After over 2,000 hours of engine run time, PFRT was completed in March 1974. The final tests for PFRT were run at the USAF's Arnold Engineering Development Center (AEDC). Test runs at AEDC included subsonic and supersonic operations, full- and partial-power operations with six different inlet distortion patterns, and simulated test flights at fourteen points in the flight envelope. A critical capability for PFRT was provided by the J-2 cell at AEDC, which could simulate flight at altitude. The PRFT was a critical requirement for the first flight of the B-1A (which would also be the first flight of the F101), verifying that the F101 was safe for flight.

The F101 could be safe for flight testing, yet not fully compliant with requirements. Engine development and testing continued after the completion of PFRT. For example, the XF101-GE-100 demonstrated a 5 per cent deficiency in specific fuel consumption during PFRT. That deficiency needed to be rectified prior to production, or the B-1A would have inadequate range to accomplish its mission. Specific fuel consumption was decreased (i.e. improved) by small incremental improvements to seals, clearances and pressure drops in F101 components. The formal and comprehensive qualification of production (as opposed to test) F101 engines proceeded in parallel with the flight test program, with the key demonstrations being low cycle fatigue, engine life cycle tests, altitude operation, and endurance.

The engine is only one part of the aircraft propulsion capability, which includes the fuel system and the air inlets. The purpose of the engine inlet is to present outside air to the face of the jet engine. This deceptively simple description belies the complexity of implementing that purpose: the air must be in the correct quantity and arrive at the correct speed, with as little energy in the air as possible converted to heat as it is compressed, and with uniform distribution over the face of the engine. Furthermore, these things must be done over the entire flight envelope of the aircraft (very large in the case of the B-1A), over the full range of angles of attack and sideslip angles that the aircraft can attain and be as light-weight as possible. For the team at Rockwell designing the B-1A, designing the inlets for the four engines was amongst the most challenging aspects of FSD, comparable in difficulty with the VG wing mechanisms and pivot structure.

The B-1A had two nacelles under the fixed parts of the wings and attached to the wing carry-through structure. Each nacelle contained two separately compartmented engines, an auxiliary power unit (APU), and shaft-driven accessories such as electrical generators and hydraulic pumps. Each engine was fed by its own air duct, which led from the inlet to the engine face. The inlets were two-dimensional, with compression ramps mounted in a vertical plane. Because aerodynamic heating is proportional to the square of the Mach number, the maximum temperature of the inlet of the Mach 2+ B-1A was only half of that of the Mach 3+ B-70, which allowed the B-1A to avoid the use of the exotic materials that the B-70 had required. The nacelles of the B-1A were 'toed in' half a degree to align with the local flow outwash angle at cruise conditions.

The original inlet design of the B-1A was for a mixed-compression inlet (MCI). At Mach 1.7 or faster in the MCI, the air entering the inlet was first slowed down by oblique shocks external to the inlet, and the final deceleration to subsonic airflow was performed inside the inlet. The MCI had the benefits of thermodynamic efficiency (as the flow decelerated, more of its energy was captured as pressure increase and less dissipated as heat) and less drag. However further studies showed that the MCI was excessively complex, heavy and expensive. On 29 August 1972, the MCI was replaced by an external compression inlet (ECI) design, in which all the compression of the air was done outside the lip of the inlet. The change from MCI to ECI decreased the weight of the aircraft by the not inconsiderable amount of 1,350lbs and also decreased mechanical complexity, at some cost in aerothermodynamic efficiency. A change of this significance, twenty-seven months into FSD, was of huge consequence and only with the most strenuous effort did it not delay the entire FSD program. The scope of the effort included the use of four different wind tunnel models, including a full scale inlet with an actual F101 engine that was tested in the 16ft transonic and supersonic wind tunnels at AEDC.

While Rockwell produced most of the aircraft structure during FSD and was responsible for integrating the aircraft, most of the systems came from a network of subcontractors. The subcontractors provided specialized technologies and products without which the B-1A would have been a hollow, earth-bound shell.

The Supersonic Super-Bomber

The B-1A reflected a new set of priorities in aircraft design. The B-70 had been driven by the desire to fly faster and higher. The new generation of aircraft had more sophisticated requirements, in which avionics, systems integration, human factors, cost-effectiveness, reliability, maintainability, and survivability were more important than raw performance. In retrospect, the new formula must be judged a great success. The most extravagant and even outlandish aircraft of the late fifties such as the B-70 had little impact; the best aircraft of the seventies like the B-1, F-15 and F-16 have had long service lives. When Rockwell International rolled out the first B-1A on 26 October 1974, at long last the USAF had the new bomber which it had spent nearly two decades pursuing.

The sleek and streamlined curves of the B-1A were beautiful, and if an inanimate object can be described this way, almost sexy. The most distinctive airframe feature was the VG wings, which could vary in sweep from 15° to 67.5°. The B-1A was 151.2ft long and had a wingspan 136.7 ft (15° sweep) to 78.2ft (67.5° sweep). The B-1A maximum gross take-off weight was 395,000lbs; most of this weight would be fuel and weapons. The airframe was primarily constructed of aluminum, with titanium only used in specific areas where the strength and temperature resistance of that expensive material were required. Canted vanes mounted on each side of the forward fuselage were part of the Structural Mode Control System (SMCS) to reduce structural bending oscillations. The B-1A was capable of aerial refueling.

The crew sat in a capsule that in an emergency would separate from the aircraft with rocket engines and descend to land under parachutes. The first two B-1A aircraft would have a crew of three (pilot, co-pilot and flight test engineer). Subsequent aircraft would have an Offensive System Operator (OSO) and a Defensive System Operator (DSO) in addition to the two pilots. Both the OSO and DSO would be rated USAF navigators, with the OSO concentrating on navigation and weapons delivery while the DSO operated the defensive electronic systems.

The ultimate purpose of the B-1A was to deliver weapons. The aircraft had three bomb bays, each with a rotary launcher which could carry eight SRAM missiles or eight nuclear bombs.

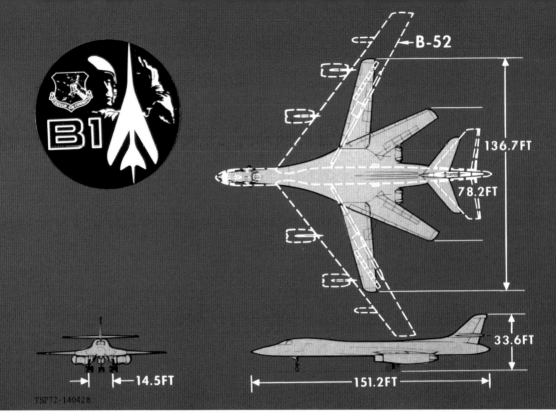

The B-1A was smaller and lighter than the B-52. VG wings were the most distinctive design element of the B-1A. (*Stephen Henry collection*)

The B-1A had a combat crew of four sitting in an escape capsule. The pilot sat in the front left seat, the co-pilot sat in the front right seat, the DSO sat in the rear left seat, and the OSO sat in the rear right seat. There were instructor seats between the pilots and between the DSO and OSO. (*Stephen Henry collection*)

THE CREW

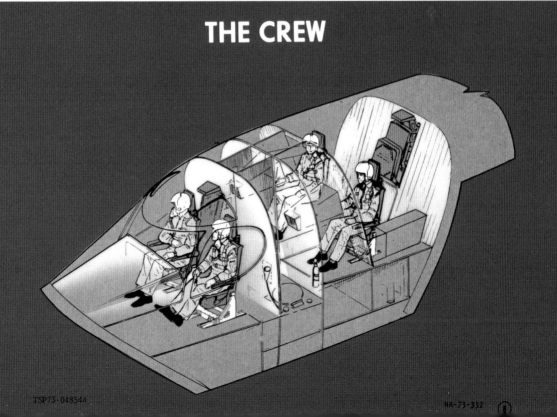

The B-1A had four YF101-GE-100 augmented turbofan engines, each with a maximum thrust of 30,000lbs when augmented and 15,000lbs of thrust without augmenter. The engines were mounted in pairs in nacelles under the aft fuselage. Each nacelle also had a secondary power system with an Auxiliary Power Unit (APU). The inlet at the forward part of each nacelle had multiple moving parts which efficiently supplied air to the engines over the operating envelope of the aircraft.

The OAS handled the navigation and weapons delivery tasks. It used digital computers for computation and data management. The B-1A had a ground mapping radar and a TFR; the OAS was optimized for high-speed flight while hugging the terrain.

The DAS, also called the AN/ALQ-161 Electronic Countermeasures (ECM)/Radio Frequency Surveillance (RFS) system, monitored, jammed, and deceived enemy radars, protecting the B-1A from being detected and engaged by radar-guided weapons.

Its design and features made the B-1A a fearsome strategic bomber. From an alert posture, it could race at high speed from its base to avoid being destroyed by a surprise attack, refuel in the air from a tanker, and reach the Soviet Union. Penetrating Soviet air defenses, it could outrun fighters-interceptors, use terrain and electronic countermeasures to hide from enemy defenses, blast enemy radar and surface-to-air missile sites with SRAM missiles, and then accurately drop thermonuclear weapons on targets day or night in any weather condition.

Flight Testing the B-1A

Testing a modern military aircraft is an expensive and elaborate process. Long before the aircraft flies, its aerodynamics are measured in wind tunnels. System testing starts at the component level, proceeds to tests of systems in the laboratory, then moves to the aircraft on the ground. Only after the aircraft is thoroughly checked out on the ground is it ready to fly for the first time. To mitigate risk, flight testing is incremental, starting at the most benign test condition and building up to more demanding ones in small steps. Development flight testing is broadly divided into two categories: flight sciences and mission systems. 'Flight sciences' includes performance, air data system, stability, control, structural loads and dynamics, propulsion, and stores separation – how the aircraft functions as a vehicle. Another term for flight sciences is performance and flying qualities. 'Mission systems' pertains to offensive and defensive systems including sensors, navigation, weapons delivery, and electronic countermeasures – how the aircraft functions as a weapon system. Reliability and maintainability, human factors evaluation, technical order (maintenance manual) verification and validation, training development, and climatic testing are also part of the flight test program.

Prior to the B-1A, flight testing of new USAF aircraft had been sequential. First the contractor conducted flight testing to develop the aircraft and demonstrate that it met the contract specifications. Then the Air Force Flight Test Center (AFFTC) at Edwards AFB conducted Developmental Testing & Evaluation (DT&E) to assess the aircraft and its systems. DT&E was followed by Operational Testing & Evaluation (OT&E), in which the using command (SAC in the case of the B-1A) evaluated the operational effectiveness and logistics supportability of the weapon system. The problems with the sequential approach to testing were three-fold:

- The sequential approach took too much time.
- It was inefficient, because there was unnecessary duplication of test points between the different categories of testing.
- The inability of the operators and maintainers of the using command to obtain hands-on experience and provide feedback early in the process meant that aircraft were being produced that had major deficiencies when they entered service.

In response to these problems, the B-1A flight test effort was organized as a Joint Test Force (JTF), which combined all flight test work into a single team. The B-1 JTF was assigned to AFFTC and consisted of team members from AFFTC, Rockwell International and the other contractors, and SAC's 4200th Test and Evaluation Squadron (TES). The role of 4200th TES was to perform Initial Operational Test & Evaluation (IOT&E), a subset of the full OT&E. The hope was that the JTF concept would speed up the development and entry into service of the B-1A, eliminate unnecessary duplication of tests, and allow SAC to have an early look at the weapon system. Another participant in the JTF was the Air Force Test and Evaluation Center (AFTEC). AFTEC provided an additional analysis and reporting channel independent of the developing and using commands.

The B-1A flight testing was planned in three phases.

- Phase 1 testing was to provide the data needed to support a production decision, that decision having been delayed until May 1976 by the time that detailed flight test planning was underway in 1973. The purpose of Phase 1 testing was risk reduction rather than comprehensively covering all requirements. Was there a 'show–stopper' that would make it unwise to proceed to production? It was not only Phase 1 flight testing that needed to be completed before the production decision, but also F101 qualification testing and ground testing of airframe fatigue.
- Phase 2 testing would start after the production decision and use the three FSD test aircraft to complete the technical development and demonstration of the weapon system.
- Phase 3 testing would use the first four production aircraft to verify that the B-1A was operationally effective and suitable.

The B-1 JTF had three aircraft at its disposal as a result of the 18 January 1971 descoping program, which was really too few for the enormous job of flight testing a new airframe, a new engine, a new OAS, a new DAS, and the integration of all of these elements. The program office formally referred to these aircraft as A/V-1, A/V-2, and A/V-3. However, common usage in the JTF was to call them Ships 1, 2, and 3, respectively.

B-1A Ship 1 had USAF tail number 74-0158, the '74' indicating that the contract for its production was issued in fiscal year 1974. Ship 1 was the primary platform for flight sciences work. It would be used for the first flight and envelope expansion. As the flight sciences aircraft, Ship 1 was not fitted with OAS or DAS. It had a crew of three, with two pilots and a flight test engineer (FTE). Ship 1 was heavily instrumented to collect flight test data. Some of the data

B-1A 74-0158 (Ship 1) is under assembly at the Rockwell International facility in Palmdale, California. The escape capsule has not yet been installed. (*Stephen Henry collection*)

could be telemetered to a ground station and used in the mission control room for real-time monitoring, which improved the safety and productivity of the test flights. All of the data was recorded on board the aircraft for post-flight analysis.

B-1A Ship 2 (tail number 74-0159) was similarly configured to Ship 1. The 1971 descoping had also cost the program its dedicated structural test article for ground testing, so Ship 2 would undergo static proof loading after assembly before starting its flights. Ship 2 was instrumented to measure structural loads. In the flight test program, it would be used to collect load data in flight as well as to supplement Ship 1's flight sciences work.

B-1A Ship 3 (tail number 74-0160) completed the trio of FSD flight test aircraft. It was the platform for mission systems testing. Ship 3 had a full crew of four members, but since it was fitted only with OAS, the fourth crew member was a flight test engineer and not a DSO. Note that the absence of the DAS in any of the FSD aircraft meant that the DAS would have no flight testing prior to the production decision. Ground testing of DAS was necessary to solve as many problems as possible, but it was not a substitute for flight testing which exposed the DAS to the dynamic flight environment and radio waves being propagated in the open. Ship 3 was the aircraft most relevant to IOT&E being conducted by 4200th TES.

AFFTC stood up the JTF as early as 1971. Two early JTF members were Colonel Emil Sturmthal and Kenneth L. Martin. Sturmthal had flown the last flight of the XB-70A two years earlier and became the JTF director. Martin was a civilian employee of AFFTC, a flight sciences expert who was the first USAF flight test engineer assigned to the JTF. It might seem premature to staff the JTF three years before first flight, but early involvement allowed flight testers to obtain a deep understanding of the aircraft systems as well as have adequate time to plan the tests and define instrumentation and data requirements. Sturmthal and Martin got the opportunity to join the flight test team of the Anglo-French Concorde SST for three sorties, adding to their experience with large supersonic airplanes.

Sturmthal, Martin and other AFFTC personnel soon were joined in the JTF by Colonel William R. Payne of 4200th TES, who would command that squadron and lead the SAC IOT&E contingent for the B-1A. Payne had previously set a number of records in the B-58A Hustler. 4200th TES was completing FB-111A OT&E as the B-1 JTF was being stood up, so it brought recent and relevant experience to the team. Its pilots, navigators, engineers, and maintainers had dual roles. As well as fully participating in the activities of the JTF, they reported directly to SAC on the operational effectiveness and suitability of the B-1A so that SAC could make a recommendation on the production decision.

By 1974, the B-1 program leadership had turned over. Major General Abner B. Martin was now the USAF system program director. He was a rated pilot and had spent much of his career in program management assignments for ballistic missiles.

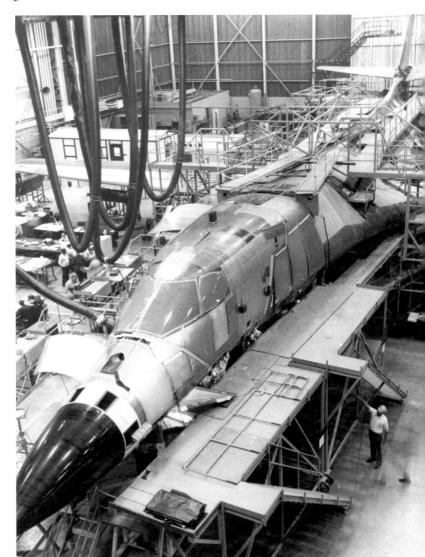

At this stage of assembly, the escape module has been installed. (*US Air Force*)

The formal rollout of Ship 1 on 26 October 1974 was a festive and highly publicized event attended by thousands. (*Stephen Henry collection*)

Rockwell rolled out Ship 1 from its final assembly facility at Air Force Plant 42 in Palmdale, California on 26 October 1974. Like the XB-70A A/V-1 rollout ten years earlier, it was a festive and highly publicized event attended by a large number of dignitaries. Rollout also signified the hand-off of Ship 1 from Rockwell's manufacturing department to its flight test department, which now had to accomplish a large number of steps to prepare Ship 1 for its first flight.

In 1974, the JTF named the members of the first flight test crews for the B-1A. Richard Abrams was the Rockwell flight test engineer. The Rockwell test pilots were Charles C. Bock, Jr. and Tommie D. 'Doug' Benefield. They were joined by Martin, Sturmthal, and test pilot Lieutenant Colonel Edward D. McDowell, Jr. from AFFTC. John Hill was the Rockwell director of flight test.

Starting and running the engines and APUs was the most significant part of pre-flight testing. The engines had been started and operated as part of the PFRT, and the APUs had also been tested on a stand-alone basis, but now they were part of a complete integrated airplane, including being controlled from the cockpit, being supplied with fuel by the airplane, and powering the electrical, hydraulic, and environmental control systems. In turn, the electrical, hydraulic, and environmental control systems had all been operated on a stand-alone basis, but

B-1 FLIGHT TEST CREWS

ROCKWELL INTERNATIONAL   UNITED STATES AIR FORCE

CHARLIE BOCK
Chief Pilot

COL TED STURMTHAL
Chief Pilot

DOUG BENEFIELD
Project Pilot

LT COL ED McDOWELL
Project Pilot

DICK ABRAMS
Flight Engineer

KEN MARTIN
Flight Engineer

Abrams, Bock and Sturmthal composed the prime crew for the first flight of the B-1A. Benefield, Martin and McDowell were their back-ups. Abrams and Martin were flight test engineers. The other four were test pilots. (*Chuck Klein collection, Rockwell International*)

now their generators, pumps, and bleed air sources were being driven by the engines or APUs. Ground engine runs started with a single engine, and worked up to all four engines running, up to full augmented thrust.

The Automated Flight Test Data System (AFTDS) at AFFTC needed to be integrated with the telemetry system on the B-1A and the flow of data from the B-1A to AFTDS verified. Real-time monitoring of telemetry data made flight testing safer and more productive. An engineering team in the control room could monitor the instrumentation for exceedances and call for a test abort if needed. Using real-time data, the test team could decide to expand the envelope or repeat a test during a flight without need to land the airplane, retrieve data tapes, process the tapes and analyze the data after the flight. Testing with a control room team monitoring telemetry was not a new technique. Both the X-15 and XB-70A flight test programs had used it, and NASA raised it to a high art during its space missions. AFTDS introduced a new generation of the technology to AFFTC.

The final step before first flight was taxi testing. Taxi tests verified the proper operation of the wheels, brakes, and landing gear. Low speed taxi tests came first, followed by high-speed taxi tests on the runway up to 135 knots indicated airspeed (KIAS). With completion of the taxi tests, Ship 1 was ready to take to the air.

The crew for Flight 1-1 (23 December 1974) was Bock (pilot), Sturmthal (co-pilot) and Abrams (flight test engineer). The original test card for Flight 1-1 was ambitious, with a 2.6 hour flight that included landing gear retraction and extension, slats and flaps retraction and extension, and wing sweep angle being changed from the take-off position of fully spread (15°) to a 20° angle. Presumably the USAF and Rockwell scaled back the plan to the bare minimum to achieve the first flight milestone before the end of 1974 in the simplest possible way. A decade earlier, NAR had been under pressure to fly the XB-70A at supersonic speeds on its maiden flight, and

Ship 1 is taxiing. The flat terrain in the background makes it likely that the photograph was taken at Palmdale, before the first flight. (*US Air Force*)

that flight had experienced serious problems. The lesson had been learned. Ship 1 would be regarded as having a successful first flight if it put air under the tires with no excessive drama. Popular culture perpetuates the image of fearless test pilots pushing the envelope; by 1974 the reality was that to mitigate risks, flight testing was done in small increments, with each step preceded by simulation and analysis.

On Flight 1-1, Ship 1 had a gross take-off weight of 280,000lbs, considerably less than the B-1A planned maximum gross weight. It departed Runway 07 at Palmdale in full augmentation, with an F-111 flying chase. Bock initiated rotation at 145 KIAS, and Ship 1 lifted off at 160 KIAS after having used 4,400ft of runway. The aircraft reached 190 KIAS after take-off, before Bock leveled it off and trimmed it at 10,000ft altitude and 180 KIAS for handling checks in the 15° wing sweep angle, slats and flaps extended, landing gear extended configuration in the restricted airspace of the Edwards AFB range. The crew also conducted throttle transients of the two left engines to evaluate their response to control inputs. Bock conducted a simulated approach to landing and go-around at altitude to evaluate aircraft and engine handling during those maneuvers, and then flew an airspeed calibration test point in formation with an A-37B that had a calibrated airspeed system. The landing on Edwards AFB Runway 04 was uneventful, bringing Ship 1 to its new home. Ship 1 had a landing weight of 248,000lbs, and the flight duration was 1.3 hours. The only two anomalies noted during the flight was that Ship 1 flew slightly left wing heavy, which was probably caused by a small fuel imbalance and easily corrected with lateral trim, and one of two redundant take-off/go-around computers in the flight control system was inoperative, which had no impact. The B-1A was no longer just a concept, a controversy or a massive program. It was a flying machine.

The next flight (Flight 1-2, 23 January 1975) continued envelope expansion. Bock, Sturmthal, and Abrams took off from Edwards AFB, this time with a gross weight of

After taking off from Palmdale on its first flight on 23 December 1974, Ship 1 has just landed at Edwards AFB. The flaps are lowered to the landing position and the spoilers on the wings are deployed. (*Air Force Test Center History Office*)

300,000lbs. They cycled the landing gear and then retracted it again and then retracted the slats and flaps before evaluating handling qualities in this configuration. The wings were swept back to 20° and 25°. The center of gravity was shifted by transferring fuel between tanks. Airbrakes were deployed for the first time. The maximum altitude reached during the flight was 16,000ft and the maximum speed was Mach 0.7. A T-38A with a calibrated air data system provided a reference to measure the accuracy of the air data system on the B-1A as the two aircraft flew in formation at a higher speed than was done with the A-37B on Flight 1-1. The crew started both APUs in flight. Flight time was 3.4 hours. Two deficiencies were noted on the flight: limit load factor could be reached with very little stick displacement, and a low-amplitude low-frequency pitching oscillation caused by the Stability and Control Augmentation System (SCAS) was observed. Both would need to be corrected with adjustments to the flight control system.

Flight 1-3 (11 February 1975) reached 20,000ft altitude but was terminated prematurely when the crew was notified of an overtemperature condition in the avionics bays, later determined to be caused by a small leak in the cooling system. Ship 1 dumped fuel to get down to the allowable landing weight, thus testing that function. In a demonstration of the complexities of designing an SCAS for an aircraft as complex as the B-1A with its wide performance envelope, center of gravity range, weight range, and wing sweep angles, the enhancement to the SCAS implemented as a result of Flight 1-2 results caused a new problem, a slight tendency to pilot-induced oscillation (PIO) on landing final approach. By the time of B-1A FSD, analytical methods and simulator technology had advanced to the point where the flying qualities of new aircraft were generally very good from the first flight, but invariably there were some problems

Ship 1 was the primary B-1A test aircraft for envelope expansion, flutter, flying qualities, and propulsion testing. Ships 1 and 2 could be easily recognized by their long, striped nose booms. (*Stephen Henry collection*)

that were only discovered in flight tests. Finding these stability and control issues was one of the primary objectives of the flight sciences work. Ken Martin, the back-up flight test engineer for the B-1A, had by this time been promoted to manage the AFFTC branch that did this work in collaboration with contractor engineers such as those at Rockwell; as a result, he never got to fly in the B-1A.

The cooling leak was quickly fixed, and Flight 1-4 was conducted on 19 February 1975. On this flight, Bock and Sturmthal switched seats so that an AFFTC pilot was the aircraft commander in the left seat for the first time. The left two engines were stopped and then started with the APU. In preparation for aerial refueling, one of the F-111 chase airplanes acted as the tanker so that the Ship 1 crew could evaluate the formation-flying characteristics of the B-1A for that operation. Envelope expansion continued. Flight 1-4 reached Mach 0.75, 23,000ft altitude, and lasted 4.6 hours. In comparison to the XB-70A at a similar point in its flight test program, the B-1A had shown itself to be a reliable machine.

The formation flying in Flight 1-4 paved the way for the first dry hook-ups (no fuel transfer) with a KC-135A tanker on Flight 1-5 (18 March 1975). Aerial refueling was not only an essential operational capability, but it was needed to increase flight test productivity. The Phase 1 flight test objectives were heavily weighted towards the high-speed, low-altitude regime where fuel consumption was higher, so aerial refueling enabled longer test missions. Sturmthal and Bock could achieve contact with the KC-135A aerial refueling boom, but there was a slight

Every B-1A flight test mission involved one or more chase aircraft. The chase aircraft crew could observe leaks or other problems, watch out for terrain and traffic while the B-1A crew focused on the test point, and take photographs. The F-111 was the chase aircraft of choice for the B-1A because of its similar airspeed and altitude capabilities. (*US Air Force*)

tendency to PIO, another issue for the engineers to address. Flight 1–5 was eventful in other ways. The flight had a delayed take-off because an engine bleed air valve was stuck open. The Central Integrated Test System (CITS) aided in identifying the problem, validating the value of that digital system. After the flight began, the VG wings were fully swept in flight for the first time, and the SMCS also was operated in flight for the first time. SMCS counteracted the tendency of the long fuselage of to the B-1A to 'twang' when it was buffeted by turbulence or flight control movements, particularly at low altitude.

Flight 1-6 (10 April 1975) marked a major achievement, the first supersonic flight of the B-1A. Top speed and altitude on this flight were Mach 1.05 and 29,500ft, respectively. For the first time, the B-1A took fuel from a KC-135A, allowing Flight 1-6 to be 6.4 hours in duration. Other achievements included the first airborne operation of the flutter excitation system, the first in-flight opening and closing of the weapons bay doors, and the first operation over the Space and Missile Test Center (SAMTEC)/Western Test Range (WTR) and Pacific Missile Range (PMR). Testing in the WTR and PMR would be important for future flights because Edwards AFB is at a field elevation of 2,311ft above sea level, which meant that the B-1A had to be tested elsewhere to evaluate its high-speed performance in the denser air near sea level. The range checks on Flight 1-6 verified that voice communications and data could be relayed from WTR and PMR to the mission control center at AFFTC. Throughout the program, test runs would be conducted in this airspace, typically starting off the California coast near the Oregon border and going as far south as Los Angeles or in the opposite direction.

The wings of Ship 1 are swept full aft to 67.5° degrees for high-speed flight. (*Stephen Henry collection*)

The first six flights had taken almost four months to accomplish and logged a total of 19.6 hours of flight time. Starting with Flight 1-7, the pace of flights increased with a focus on clearing the low-altitude, high-speed portion of the flight envelope that was the focus on the Phase 1 objectives required for the production go-ahead decision.

Perhaps the most important aspect of these flights was an intensive effort to verify that the B-1A was free of flutter within the specified flight envelope, using the flutter excitation system. Flutter is a dynamic instability of the aircraft structure as it moves through the air. Aircraft structures are not rigid. If there is positive feedback between the airframe's deformation and the force exerted by the airflow, the aircraft structure can catastrophically disintegrate. Flutter testing was complicated on the B-1A by the SCAS and SMCS, which created further perturbations to the airframe in addition to the purely aeroelastic feedback. All of these interactions needed to be measured in flight. Flutter testing is one of the most hazardous types of flight testing.

The flutter excitation system on Ships 1 and 2 featured hydraulic-driven inertial exciter beams (commonly called 'flutter wands') on the wing tips, horizontal stabilizer, and vertical stabilizer. The flutter wands were driven in angular oscillations and applied loads to the airframe. The frequency of the excitation were swept through a range or could be set at a specific value. The flutter excitation system was controlled by the co-pilot with a panel on his side console. During flutter testing, the B-1A telemetered critical data to the mission control center so that engineers could monitor the parameters that would indicate the onset of flutter and radio up to the aircraft to terminate the test point before the aircraft entered a hazardous condition.

Between Flights 1-7 (21 April 1975) and 1-25 (19 December 1975), Ship 1 completed the first year of B-1A flight test operations. In addition to flutter testing, major achievements during these flights included:

- Four more crew members (Rockwell test pilot Benefield, AFFTC test pilot McDowell, 4200th TES test pilot Major George W. Larson, and AFFTC flight test engineer Pat Sharp) flew in the B-1A.
- The test pilots conducted flying qualities evaluations of SCAS improvements on multiple flights.
- The B-1A performed a supersonic run of more than 30 minutes and conducted its first aerial refueling from a KC-135A tanker operated by an operational SAC unit (Flight 1-7, 21 April 1975).
- The B-1A performed a maximum gross weight take-off (Flight 1-8, 30 April 1975).
- Multiple electrical failures caused the SCAS and trim system to disconnect. Ship 1 then experienced roll and pitch excursions. Engine control also reverted to a back-up capability. The electrical failures prevented the flaps from being extended, which provided an unplanned opportunity to do a flaps-up landing in Ship 1 on the immense dried mud flat of Rogers Dry Lake rather than on the paved runway at Edwards AFB (Flight 1-10, 13 June 1975; for the superstitiously inclined, this flight was on a Friday).
- On Flight 1-13 (8 August 1975), an access door to the #2 engine failed and separated from the aircraft. The #2 engine was shut down, and Ship 1 was landed with three engines running. Before the next flight, additional instrumentation was added to measures loads on the nacelles. Flights 1-14 (26 August 1975) and 1-15 (4 September 1975) were devoted to understanding this problem.

- Flight 1-16 (12 September 1975) was the first flight with an all-USAF crew.
- The B-1A demonstrated a simulated emergency landing gear extension (Flight 1-21, 7 November 1975). On the flight, Ship 1 also achieved Mach 0.83 runs at 200ft above ground level (AGL) over the Edwards AFB range and tower fly-bys for airspeed calibration.
- The flight envelope expanded to a maximum speed of Mach 1.6 and maximum altitude of 50,000ft (Flight 1-24, 26 November 1975). Other accomplishments were aerial refueling to the maximum in-flight gross weight (higher than the maximum gross take-off weight) and simulated terrain following at Mach 0.85 at 500ft AGL.
- The longest flight of the year was 8.2 hours in duration (Flight 1-25, 19 December 1975)

The first year of B-1A flight test operations had been successful, with the B-1A demonstrating critical capabilities, an increasing flight rate, and no major deficiencies. The B-1 JTF had established a solid foundation for future testing.

Bastian 'Buzz' Hello replaced Robert Greer as the president of Rockwell's B-1 division and the B-1 program manager. He was an experienced aerospace engineer and manager. During his military service during the Second World War, he was a project engineer on the P-80, the first operational American jet fighter. After the war, he worked at Martin on aircraft and missiles. The investigation into the tragic Apollo AS-204 fire during ground test that killed three astronauts led to the discovery of mismanagement and negligence at NAR, the prime contractor for the Apollo spacecraft. There was a significant management turnover at NAR, which hired Hello to turn around its Apollo spacecraft operations at the NASA Kennedy Space Center. Hello led NAR's Space Shuttle work before being assigned to the B-1 position.

After Flight 1-25, Ship 1 entered an extended lay-up. The Automatic Flight Control System (AFCS) and Automatic Inlet Control System (AICS) were activated. Modified and strengthened engine bay doors addressed the failure seen on Flight 1-13 and investigated on the two following flights. There were also changes to the electrical system. Additional test instrumentation was installed to investigate unexpected engine vibration. Flight 1-26 (unknown day in March 1976) was a post-functional check flight. During the lay-up, Rockwell and GE engineers had been working on the engine vibration problem, the solution being an exhaust nozzle area ratio schedule modification. Flight 1-27 (23 March 1976) verified that the engine modification solved the problem and also tested AICS at Mach 1.6 and 40,000ft altitude. With AICS now functional, the B-1 JTF could expand the envelope of the B-1A beyond Mach 1.6.

While Ship 1 was flying and then in lay-up, and Ship 2 was undergoing structural ground tests, Rockwell was preparing Ship 3 for flight. Ship 1 had proven that the B-1A could fly; Ship 3 was needed to test the B-1A mission systems. Ship 3 rolled out of the Rockwell final assembly facility in Palmdale on 16 January 1976. It took to the air on Flight 3-1 (1 April 1976) and flew to Edwards AFB. As well as a general functional check of the aircraft, the crew exercised various parts of OAS. Flight 3-1 was the first time that a B-1A flew with a crew of four. Pilot Bock, co-pilot McDowell and flight test engineer Abrams were joined by Lieutenant Colonel K. Warren Brotnov, the first USAF navigator to fly as a B-1A crew member, who was the OSO. Brotnov was well-qualified for the OSO seat. Before his military service, he had worked at Boeing as a flight test engineer on the KC-135 Stratotanker. He held the USAF aeronautical rating of Master Navigator and also had USAF experience as an engineer in planning, teaching, and flight testing assignments.

B-1A 74-0159 (Ship 2) nears the completion of its assembly and checkout in Palmdale. (*Stephen Henry collection*)

Ship 2 was actually the third B-1A to fly, because it was used for ground structural testing before its first flight. For those tests, it was covered with approximately 300 mounting points for the loading devices to distribute the load over the airframe. Note that the tail cone is not installed. (*Stephen Henry collection*)

B-1A 74-0160 (Ship 3) was the third FSD aircraft but the second to fly. Like all B-1 aircraft, it was assembled in Palmdale from parts built in multiple locations. (*Stephen Henry collection*)

Flight 3-2 (20 April 1976) was a short one because of an engine problem, but Flight 3-3 (28 April 1976) was a success, with test points for navigation, manual terrain following, and simulated weapons releases. Flight 3-3 also was the first time that a B-1A flew with five crew members. Joining pilot Bock, co-pilot McDowell, and flight test engineer Abrams were OSO Brotnov from AFFTC and Boeing flight test engineer George C. Dostal. The B-1A linked its AFCS and TFR for automatic terrain following on Flight 3-5 (22 May 1976).

Meanwhile, Ship 1 was both expanding the envelope and selling the program. Flight 1-28 (9 April 1976) achieved Mach 1.9 at 43,000ft. Flight 1-29 (15 April 1976) was a familiarization flight for Senator Barry M. Goldwater. Goldwater was a supporter of the B-1 as well as a retired major general in the USAF Reserve and a rated command pilot. Secretary of Defense Donald H. Rumsfeld followed Goldwater on Flight 1-30 (19 April 1976). Rumsfeld was an officer in the US Navy Reserve and a naval aviator. Envelope expansion resumed on Flight 1-31 (30 April 1976) as Ship 1 hit Mach 2.12 and 50,000ft altitude. During this flight, it performed aerial refueling five times and took on 200,000lbs of fuel.

The JTF fleet grew on 14 June 1976, when Ship 2 started Flight 2-1 in Palmdale and then joined its siblings at Edwards AFB. With three aircraft now actively flying, the pace of progress increased significantly. Flight 2-2 continued the functional checkout of Ship 2 (9 July 1976) but was terminated prematurely because of a hydraulic problem. Flight 2-3 (23 July 1976) was the first flight used to measure loads using Ship 2's structural instrumentation. It was also a familiarization flight for Major General Thomas P. Stafford, who was now the AFFTC commander but had previously won renown as a Gemini and Apollo astronaut. Before his selection as a NASA astronaut, he had been a highly regarded test pilot at AFFTC. Ship 2 was used to explore the most extreme airloads and maneuver loads that the B-1A was designed to handle, working within the flutter envelope that had previously been cleared by Ship 1. Loads testing was done at a variety of Mach numbers, altitudes, weights, centers of gravity, and speed brake configurations (retracted or extended). The results of Ship 2 flight tests were compared against calculations, component ground tests, and Ship 2 ground loads tests to validate the structural design and analysis of the B-1A.

Meanwhile, Ships 1 and 3 continued to be used for flights. Flight 1-33 (16 June 1976) featured the first stores separation, when an inert SRAM was ejected from the rotary launcher in the intermediate weapons bay at Mach 0.6 and 10,000ft altitude. Flight 1-34 (25 June 1976) was the final test point for aerial refueling envelope expansion. Flight 1-35 (16 July 1976) focused on bomb bay door opening and closing, which was more challenging than it

Ship 3 takes off from Edwards AFB. It was the platform for OAS testing including navigation, weapons delivery, and terrain following. (*US Air Force*)

might sound, considering that the doors needed to operate in the high dynamic pressure of high-speed, low-altitude flight. On Flight 3-7 (29 June 1976), auto-terrain following was done at 750 feet AGL. USAF Chief of Staff General David C. Jones had a familiarization flight on Flight 3-8 (15 July 1976) and he was followed by system program director Martin on Flight 3-9 (16 July 1976). Flight 3-9 was not just a familiarization flight, because auto-terrain following was done at 400ft AGL. 15 July 1976 had a notable first that reflected the increased pace of progress, since Ships 1 and 3 were in the air at the same time, on Flight 1-35 and 3-8 respectively. Flight 3-11 (12 August 1976) was the first terrain following flight on an operationally realistic low-level route off the AFFTC range. All previous terrain-following flights had been conducted over the AFFTC range against a single terrain feature, which was not operationally representative but did allow for data from different test points to be easily compared against each other.

   Flight 1-37 (27 August 1976) featured the first supersonic bomb bay door operation. During Flight 1-38 (13 September 1976), the B-1A dropped Mk 82 non-nuclear bombs for the first time. The ability to drop non-nuclear bombs was a significant argument in favor of the B-1. Unlike ICBMs, bombers were useful not only for nuclear deterrence but also in conventional war.

Airmen access the equipment bays on B-1A Ship 3. During flight tests, Rockwell was primarily responsible for aircraft maintenance, but Air Force maintainers also worked on the aircraft to evaluate maintainability, verify technical orders (maintenance manuals), and train a cadre for future operational units. (*Stephen Henry collection*)

Flight 3-14 (24 August 1976) was the first dedicated IOT&E flight. SAC Commander-in-Chief Russell E. Dougherty joined a 4200th TES crew for that mission. Flight 3-15 (31 August 1976) featured the crew doing an alert start and flying a high-speed escape profile, as if the base were under attack. Flight 3-16 (2 September 1976) repeated the alert start and escape and added simulated weapons delivery. In building block fashion, the IOT&E flights used the full range of airframe and OAS capabilities first demonstrated in DT&E to execute operationally representative combat missions. After the three IOT&E flights, automatic terrain following was flown at 200ft AGL on Flight 3-17 (14 September 1976).

November 1976 was the 24th month of B-1 flight testing. The flight logs for the aircraft at that time were:

Ship 1	44 flights	223 hours
Ship 2	10 flights	40 hours
Ship 3	24 flights	155 hours

One notable member of the JTF who joined it in August 1976 was Captain Jerry L. Ross. Ross was an AFFTC flight test engineer and one of the first engineers to graduate from the USAF Test Pilot School, attendance at which had previously been limited to pilots. He was the lead AFFTC engineer for B-1A stability, control, and flying qualities and flew on twenty-three test missions. When not flying in the B-1A, he served as a test director in the control center or flew in the F-111 chase aircraft. Ross would go on to be selected as a NASA astronaut in 1980 and is the co-holder of the record of most spaceflights by an individual, having logged seven on the Space Shuttle.

B-1A flight testing continued into 1977 with Phase 2.

The B-1A flight test program provided convincing evidence that the combined contractor, DT&E, and IOT&E testing approach was superior to the previous sequential testing. While adjusting to the new approach required some change in attitudes and put a premium on collaboration and compromise, it was the fastest and most efficient way to get to the completion of Phase 1 testing. Flights were the most visible part of the test program, but the evaluation of maintenance, logistics, and training was equally important. The USAF had previously fielded aircraft which were not supportable in the field and was determined to not repeat that experience with the B-1A. The combined testing approach pioneered at the B-1 JTF became the standard at AFFTC and it remains in use in the twenty-first century.

The Society of Experimental Test Pilots awarded Rockwell chief test pilot Bock its Iven C. Kincheloe Award in 1976 for outstanding professional accomplishment in the conduct of flight testing. The Society of Flight Test Engineers recognized flight test engineer Abrams for outstanding achievement in his field with the Kelly Johnson Award in 1977.

The Robert J. Collier Trophy is the most prestigious American aerospace award. It recognizes those who have made 'the greatest achievement in aeronautics or astronautics in America, with respect to improving the performance, efficiency, and safety of air or space vehicles, the value of which has been thoroughly demonstrated by actual use during the preceding year.' In 1977, the Collier Trophy for 1976 was awarded to the USAF and Rockwell for the design, development, management, and flight test of the B-1 weapon system. The Collier Trophy turned out to be the high point of what would be a very bad year for the B-1 program.

Ship 3 could be distinguished from Ships 1 and 2 by its short nose boom without stripes. It had a tracking target on its nacelle. Ship 3 was the first B-1A to have OAS installed. (*Brad Purvis collection*)

'A Technologically Marvelous Anachronism'

To those people involved in the B-1 program, it was self-evidently a winner. As in all complex development projects, there were problems, but none that threatened the ability of the B-1A to become a highly capable weapon system. However, the B-1 program faced other serious problems which had little to do with the successful flight test program being conducted over the high desert of Edwards AFB.

The B-1 was perhaps the most politically controversial weapon system program in American history, rivaled only by the Strategic Defense Initiative (often nicknamed 'Star Wars') a decade later. It was expensive and its timing could not have been worse. FSD coincided with a number of trends that were adverse to the B-1. The Vietnam War had soured many Americans on national defense. Increased awareness of environmental degradation and poverty created a strong sentiment to reallocate priorities from defense to domestic social needs. Inflation and recession put great stresses on the American economy. To critics, the B-1 appeared to be an egregious example of 'overkill'; the immoral product of a runaway nuclear arms race and a military-industrial complex that was out of control.

The USAF and Rockwell strongly supported the B-1. Rockwell's lobbying campaign was intense and even heavy-handed; it may have actually alienated some potential Congressional supporters of the B-1. The leadership of both the AFL-CIO and the United Autoworkers Aerospace Council also supported full funding of the B-1A. Neither organization was a disinterested party; many of the workers who would build the B-1A were members of those unions.

The Campaign to Stop the B-1 was the focus of efforts to halt the B-1 program. At its core was the American Friends Service Committee, joined by thirty-five other organizations. The American Friends Service Committee and some of the other groups were pacifist in ideology; justifying pacifism in the face of the Soviet threat pushed them into ideological territory that was effectively anti-American and pro-Soviet. Other members of the coalition held more mainstream positions. The Campaign operated on a small budget but had significant grassroots support and the general tenor of the times was favorable to it.

Members of Congress, including Senators, were also divided on the issue of the B-1. Defense hawks tended to support it, while those of a doveish orientation generally opposed. The B-1 program promised to create hundreds of thousands of jobs across the country, which meant that the legislators were also influenced by the economic impact of it on their constituencies. That the largest number of jobs would be created in California (home of the Rockwell International B-1 program) and Ohio (home of the GE aircraft engine plant), and that both California and Ohio were populous states in which both Democrats and Republican were competitive, did not escape the attention of politicians looking forward to upcoming elections.

While the B-1A flight test program moved ahead, the Department of Defense still felt the need to justify the B-1 program to Congress. It chartered the Joint Strategic Bomber Study to re-evaluate the merits of the B-1A compared to alternatives. The alternatives that were studied were a stretched FB-111A which was called the FB-111G, a re-engined B-52, and a derivative of the Boeing 747 airliner armed with cruise missiles. The study concluded that the B-1A was the preferred choice. Secretary of the Air Force John L. McLucas presented the results of the study to the Senate Armed Services Committee on 17 April 1975. The B-1's critics were not mollified by McLucas' testimony.

The 1976 presidential campaign pitted Democratic challenger James E. Carter against Republican incumbent President Gerald R. Ford. Ford supported the B-1 and Carter opposed it. In September 1976, Congress restricted funding of B-1A to $87 million per month through February 1977, which effectively moved the decision point until after the winner of the 1976 election was inaugurated in office. Carter won the election, but outgoing Ford administration Secretary of Defense Donald Rumsfeld authorized proceeding with B-1A production on 2 December 1976. The authorization included purchasing and fabricating production tooling, the first lot of three production B-1A aircraft, and long-lead procurement for the second lot of eight production aircraft.

Meanwhile, SAC planned for the deployment of the B-1A and its introduction into operational service. The training squadron would receive its first B-1A in 1980, the first bombardment wing equipped with the B-1A was planned to reach Initial Operational Capability (IOC) in

1982, and the completion of the deliveries for the full fleet of 244 aircraft was scheduled for 1986. Since the B-1A would be based at airfields that previously held the B-52 and it was sized to be compatible with B-52 facilities, a major airbase infrastructure upgrade was not required as part of the B-1A introduction.

President Carter entered office in January 1977 and faced a decision on the B-1. He had campaigned against the B-1 but once in office undertook a major re-evaluation of the program. That re-evaluation was heavily affected by a new development, the air-launched cruise missile.

SAC already had the GAM-77 Hound Dog (later re-designated the AGM-28) air-launched cruise missile in service. The B-52 carried the Hound Dog. SAC regarded Hound Dog as a marginally effective weapon. The combination of the heavy W28 nuclear warhead and the relatively inefficient J52 turbojet engine resulted in a missile that was so large that a B-52 could carry only two, one under each wing. The aerodynamic drag of the big Hound Dog missiles noticeably reduced the range of the B-52 that carried them. Furthermore, the Hound Dog was developed before the advent of integrated circuits. Its electronics were heavy, power-hungry, and unreliable, and its navigation accuracy was poor.

But technological developments were dramatically changing the potential of air-launched cruise missiles. In July 1970, USAF began development of the Subsonic Cruise Armed Decoy (SCAD) to be carried by bombers. SCAD could either carry a small nuclear warhead (the 'Armed' part of its name) which would make it impossible for Soviet air defenses to ignore it, or a 200lb electronic warfare package.

SCAD posed a significant challenge to the B-1 program. It was small enough that a B-52 could carry a large load of them; it had a long enough range that a B-52 delivering SCAD would not need to penetrate the concentrations of Soviet air defenses that were located around the most important targets. The entire justification of the B-1 was that its extensive and advanced capabilities were needed to penetrate sophisticated air defenses. A single cruise missile was probably an easier target than a B-1A, but a swarm of cruise missiles might overwhelm an air defense system and some would get through. In June 1971, Senator William Proxmire, a critic of the B-1, charged that the USAF was obstructing development of SCAD to protect the B-1 program. A USAF study in early 1973 concluded that SCAD was essential to ensuring the future ability of the B-52, but not the B-1, to penetrate Soviet air defense. Since the B-1 was planned to replace the B-52, from a USAF perspective SCAD was not a priority. A Senate report stated:

> The Air Force has proceeded with this program solely as a decoy, notwithstanding the direction of Congress. It is generally recognized that the Air Force has resisted pursuing SCAD with an armed warhead because of its possible use as a standoff launch missile. This application could jeopardize the B-1 program because it would not be necessary to have bomber penetration if a standoff missile were available as a cheaper and more viable alternative.

With SCAD floundering and costs escalating, SCAD was cancelled on 30 June 1973. However, on 19 December 1973, Deputy Secretary of Defense William P. Clements, Jr. established the Air-Launched Cruise Missile (ALCM) program and directed it to use the products of the SCAD program to the maximum extent possible. What emerged from the program was the Boeing AGM-86A ALCM, with a Williams Research Corporation F107-WR-100 turbofan engine.

The AGM-86A ALCM was carried on the same rotary launcher as the SRAM. The ALCM had a successful first powered flight on 5 March 1976. On its fourth flight it demonstrated full guidance and navigation capability, including updating its navigation calculations with terrain elevation information. Both supporters and opponents of the B-1 program understood that ALCM had become a competitor to the B-1A.

As he considered the B-1, President Carter had a multitude of objectives that competed to be satisfied:

- Maintain a viable nuclear deterrent force
- Promote peace and security through arms control agreements with the Soviet Union
- Choose the lowest-cost solution that is adequate
- Meet campaign promises made to supporters
- Appear to be strong on national defense

Carter was passionate about arms control. To negotiate an arms control treaty with the Soviet Union that had a chance of being ratified, and then to have the political credibility to persuade enough senators to ratify it, required President Carter to project strength on the question of national security.

There were a large number of potential alternatives explored by President Carter, his staff and his Department of Defense appointees. They included:

- Retire the B-52 with no replacement and rely on ICBMs and SLBMs for deterrence.
- Acquire 244 B-1A bombers (the full planned production run).
- Acquire a smaller production run of B-1A bombers.
- Modernize the B-52 to carry ALCM instead of acquiring the B-1A.
- Develop another bomber instead of acquiring the B-1A. There were various concepts for these aircraft, including a transport-like aircraft such as 747 carrying a large number of ALCMs and a stretched version of the FB-111 (a smaller bomber that was used to supplement the B-52).

Only three of these alternatives received serious consideration by policy makers: the full planned production run of the B-1A, a limited production run of the B-1A, and modernize the B-52 to carry air-launched cruise missiles (ALCM) instead of acquiring the B-1A. Eliminating in its entirety the bomber leg of the triad would have saved considerable funds, and the ICBM and SLBM forces were capable of inflicting devastation on the Soviet Union without assistance from bombers. But maintaining the bomber leg of the triad decreased risk, a matter of no small consequence in matters of nuclear deterrence. Also, such a drastic and unilateral act of disarmament would have projected weakness and reduced American influence in the arms control negotiations that were so important to President Carter. Furthermore, unilateral disarmament and the elimination of all US Air Force bomber bases would have aroused fierce opposition in Congress and the Senate. A new aircraft would require at least a decade and many billions of dollars to bring to production. This effort would be both expensive and cause a gap in the capability of the bomber force.

A variety of arguments on the operational effectiveness of B-1A vs. B-52/ALCM were made in the open literature. Perhaps the most influential report on the issue was written by Alton

H. Quanbeck and Archie L. Wood with the assistance of Louisa Thoron and published by the Brookings Institution. It concluded:

> There are marked economic advantages for a bomber force that carries standoff missiles [i.e. ALCM], which would be an alternative to the B-1 in modernizing the bomber force.
> There appear to be no significant military advantages to be gained by deploying a new penetrating bomber in preference to this alternative.

A healthy degree of skepticism would be warranted for even the most rigorous, well-informed and objective analyses. Any analysis would have to make assumptions about the capability of Soviet air defenses a decade in the future, the reliability of autonomous terrain-based cruise missile navigation systems over enemy territory that had only be mapped by satellite, the circumstances of nuclear war, and the ability of men and machines to function as intended in the unprecedented situation of a war involving thousands of nuclear weapons. These uncertainties could result in a wide range of outcomes. The bottom line was that both options had significant potential to place targets in the Soviet Union at risk. The Soviet leadership ran a tyrannical regime but fortunately it did not consist of people who were psychotic, delusional, suicidal or martyrdom-seekers. It is reasonable to conclude that either the B-1A or B-52/ALCM options in concert with the ICBM and SLBM forces was sufficient to provide a robust deterrent, but the B-52 modified to carry ALCM was considerably less expensive.

In his memoir, Secretary of Defense Harold Brown recalled his recommendation:

> Early in 1977 I advised President Carter that it would be a good idea to produce a few B-1 aircraft at a very low rate of production. That way we could keep the B-1 option open without committing to any specific number of aircraft while we saw how our new generation of ballistic and cruise missiles came along, including the MX. I was concerned about the difficulty of getting our aircraft through enemy defenses so I recommended upgrading existing B-52s and equipping them with air-launched cruise missiles. My thinking was that instead of building many expensive, high-speed B-1 bombers to make deep strikes into enemy territory, we could focus on developing highly effective cruise missiles that could be carried aboard less expensive subsonic aircraft like the B-52.

Under Secretary of Defense for Research and Engineering William Perry was a strong Administration voice against the B-1A and in favor of the B-52/ALCM:

> I also undertook a fundamental rebuilding of the air leg of the Triad, the aging B-52 force. As the Soviet Union increased its already extensive air defense deployments, the concern grew that many B-52s would be shot down before reaching their targets. The previous administration had moved to replace the B-52s with the B-1, which was nearly ready for production. My first action was to cancel the production plans for the B-1, a technologically marvelous anachronism, because it did not significantly improve our ability to penetrate the massive Soviet air defense network. (I wanted to cancel the program entirely, but to keep the support of some strong B-1 proponents in Congress, I agreed to maintain a small

Advances in propulsion, avionics, and miniaturized thermonuclear weapons had a revolutionary impact on cruise missiles. A B-52 could carry twelve Boeing AGM-86B ALCMs instead of two Hound Dogs. The ALCMs had longer range and were more reliable and accurate. (*Stephen Henry collection*)

B-1 research and development program.) My second action was to authorize and closely oversee the development of the Air-Launched Cruise Missile (ALCM) program. The B-52s would carry the cruise missiles and launch them several hundred miles from the Soviet Union, where the bombers could not be reached by the Soviet surface-to-air missiles deployed densely around targets in the USSR. Further, we developed rotary launchers for the ALCMs, each of which could carry eight ALCMs; each B-52 could carry one rotary launcher. The capacity of the B-52 could be expanded to a total of twenty nuclear bombs by adding two external pylons, each of which could carry another six missiles.

Carter received delegations of both pro-B-1 and anti-B-1 senators to argue their cases. In his 7 June 1977 diary entry, he expressed dissatisfaction with the pro-B-1 argument ('I had a meeting today with the proponents of the B-1 bomber, who pointed out all the advantages of it, conveniently forgetting that there is such a thing as a cruise missile …'). Carter was more impressed by the 10 June meeting with the anti-B-1 group. He had multiple discussions with Secretary of Defense Brown, who straddled the fence and supported both the B-52/ALCM and a limited production run of the B-1A to mitigate the risk of the new ALCM technology. Carter retired to the presidential retreat at Camp David with a thick binder of memoranda, reports, analyses, articles and editorials. On 30 June 1977, President Carter announced his decision to cancel production of the B-1A bomber. In a national television address, he stated:

This has been one of the most difficult decisions that I have made since I have been in office. Within the last few months, I've done my best to assess all the factors involved in the production of the B-1 bomber. My decision is that we should not continue with the deployment of the B-1, and I am directing that we discontinue plans for production of this weapons system. The secretary of defense agrees that this is a preferable decision. The existing testing and development that is now underway on the B-1 should continue to provide us with the needed technical base in the unlikely event that more cost-effective alternative systems should run into difficulty. In the meantime, we should begin development of cruise missiles using air-launched platforms such as B-52s, modernized as necessary.

Secretary Brown elaborated on Carter's decision the day after the announcement:

My recommendation to the president, and his decision not to proceed with production of the B-1, were based on the conclusion that aircraft carrying modern cruise missiles will better assure the effectiveness of the bomber component of U. S. strategic power in the 1980s. Both the B-1 and the cruise missile offer high assurance of survivability and penetration. But the president and I are convinced that the cruise missile will provide more certainty for our defense.

For the second time, the USAF had been thwarted in its desire to obtain a long-range supersonic bomber to replace the B-52, and for the second time Rockwell International (formerly NAR) had designed, built, and flown that supersonic bomber, only to have it cancelled. Twenty-three years had passed since SAC had published the requirements to replace the B-52, and now it appeared that SAC would continue to operate the B-52 for the indefinite future, albeit in a modernized and re-armed configuration.

The ALCM changed the concept of the bomber from a vehicle that penetrated the target to a delivery platform for stand-off weapons. Cruise missile advocates and critics of the B-1 argued that modifying the existing B-52 fleet to carry the ALCM was less expensive than acquiring the B-1 and at least as effective. (*Author*)

Chapter 4

From A to B

'I have directed the Secretary of Defense to revitalize our bomber forces by constructing and deploying some 100 B-1 bombers as soon as possible, while continuing to deploy cruise missiles on existing bombers.'

President Ronald W. Reagan, 2 October 1981

Down But Not Out

President Carter's cancellation of B-1A production provoked vociferous opposition from the airplane's supporters. The B-1 retained considerable support in Congress and elsewhere. A barely noticed part of President Carter's announcement ('The existing testing and development program now underway on the B-1 should continue to provide us with the needed technical base in the unlikely event that more cost-effective alternative systems should run into difficulty. Continued efforts at the research and development stage will give us better answers about the cost and effectiveness of the bomber and support systems, including electronic countermeasures techniques') endorsed the continuation of B-1 flight test at a lower level of activity, which was duly funded by Congress. To President Carter, the continuation of B-1A flight testing was a necessary compromise. To B-1 supporters, it was a way to keep the program alive.

In response to the cancellation, Rockwell stopped work on the first lot of production aircraft except for Ship 4, which was 45 per cent complete and was intended to join the flight test effort. Some 10,000 Rockwell employees were laid off, leaving approximately 6,000 to support flight test and Ship 4 construction. The associate contractors and subcontractors also would experience lay-offs, reassignments to other work, or reduction in planned hiring because of the cancellation. USAF personnel working on the B-1 program did not face job loss, but they were disappointed and frustrated by the decision.

While the effects on design engineering and production were dramatic, the B-1 JTF continued to carry out its work on Phase 2 of the flight test program. Flight 3-39 (8 July 1977) was the first test mission after the 30 June 1977 announcement by President Carter. It was a busy flight that was representative of the range of avionics and weapons tests: B61 nuclear bomb separation at 0.6 Mach and 10,000ft altitude, an SRAM launch rehearsal, and measurement of weapon bay acoustics and weapon bay spoiler characteristics at several points in the envelope. The test program did not actually drop real nuclear weapons; instead, Ship 3 had dropped an inert BDU-38/B which had the same size, shape, weight, center of gravity and moments of inertia as a real B61.

Ship 1 made its first flight after the cancellation on 14 July 1977. Flight 1-54 featured airspeed calibration, flutter tests, and tests of the fuel system and engines. Flight 2-29 (16 August 1977) was the first flight of Ship 2 after the cancellation. It continued the Ship 2 loads program, with

B-1A 76-0174 (Ship 4) was intended to be the first of a second lot of B-1A aircraft that would have ejection seats instead of the escape capsule and be fitted with DAS. The openings through which the ejection seats would pass are visible in the top of the forward fuselage. Ship 4 was the only aircraft of this lot that was actually completed and flew. (*Anthony Spencer collection*)

measurement of structural loads during maneuvers. Between them, Flights 1-54, 2-29, and 3-39 illustrated that an extensive variety of flight tests were needed on a new type of complex, high-performance combat aircraft.

The last test mission for Ship 1 was Flight 1-79 (18 July 1978). In a total of 405.3 flight hours, Ship 1 had first demonstrated the airworthiness of the B-1A and then accomplished the majority of the flight sciences test points. As the focus of the flight test program shifted from flight sciences to mission systems, Ship 1 was no longer needed. It became a source of parts, cannibalized to keep the other B-1A prototypes flying.

The grounding of Ship 1 left Ship 2 to carry out the remainder of the flight sciences tests. Thoroughly instrumented to collect structural loads data, Ship 2 was the aircraft of choice to probe the limits of the performance envelope. Flight 2-51 (24 August 1978) saw Ship 2 fly at Mach 2.0. On Flight 2-52 (5 October 1978), it reached Mach 2.22, the highest speed of any B-1.

The most serious B-1A inflight emergency since Flight 1-10 was experienced on Flight 2-53 (17 October 1978). Generator #2 malfunctioned, and the resulting electrical power transient caused the flight control system to make the aircraft perform an uncommanded pitch maneuver. At altitude, an uncommanded maneuver only required the immediate and full attention of the crew. But had it happened during terrain following, during aerial refueling, or while taking off or landing, the result could have been catastrophic. After the pitch excursion, the crew returned Ship 2 to Edwards AFB. The electrical power and flight control systems required modification to prevent a recurrence. The flight sciences-oriented Ship 2 competed its test flights on Flight 2-60 (27 February 1979) and joined the grounded Ship 1, with 282.5 flight hours logged.

Important flight sciences findings included:

- At the aft center-of-gravity limit, the horizontal tail needed to be trimmed differently than predicted. Therefore, the failure of even one hydraulic system in the low–altitude, high-speed part of the flight envelope would cause an uncontrolled pitch-up. Pending redesign, the aft center-of-gravity limit was moved forward for flight in the low–altitude, high-speed envelope.
- At certain speeds in the transonic range, the air loads on the wing caused it to bend. The wing bending moved the location of the shock wave on wing, which altered the pressure distribution on the wing. The interaction between the elasticity of the wing structure and the shock wave location and subsequent pressure distribution overcame the structural damping of the wing and caused a dangerous divergent oscillation.

After the SRAM launch rehearsal on Flight 3-39, another SRAM launch rehearsal on Flight 3-40 (19 July 1977) verified the interface with the White Sands Missile Range (WSMR) in New Mexico. Ship 3 launched the first live AGM-69A SRAM from a B-1A over WSMR on Flight 3-41 (28 July 1977). The launch parameters were an airspeed of Mach 0.6 and 10,000ft altitude, with the missile ejected from the front weapons bay before it ignited its rocket motor. Ship 3 accurately aligned and initialized the SRAM guidance and navigation system, and the SRAM flew accurately to its target. After the launch, Ship 3 flew to northern California, then descended for a 400ft AGL terrain-following run to Edwards AFB.

For the remainder of 1977, Ship 3 test flights were focused on expanding the weapons separation envelope, with inert shapes representing the B43 and B61 nuclear bombs and the SRAM. These flights demonstrated the benefits of spoilers which had been added to the B-1A to improve the vibration and acoustic environment in the weapons bays. It was also learned that the aircraft needed stiffened weapons bay doors to reduce high vibration levels in the bays. Flights 3-49 (6 October 1977), 3-51 (18 October 1977), and 3-52 (28 October 1977) verified the interface between the B-1A, SRAM, and SAMTEC/WTR. Ship 3 launched a SRAM on SAMTEC/WTR on Flight 3-53 (10 November 1977). The SRAM was launched from the aft weapons bay of Ship 3. At SRAM launch, Ship 3 was at 0.85 Mach (faster than the first SRAM launch on Flight 3-41) and 1,000ft altitude (lower than on Flight 3-41). The combination of higher speed and lower altitude meant that the dynamic pressure on the airplane and missile were much higher than during the first SRAM launch, but the missile separated cleanly from Ship 3 and flew accurately. There were a total of sixty-one weapons releases from the B-1A, of which forty-three were of the B61.

Flight testing of Ship 3 in 1978 and subsequent years covered further navigation, radar, and weapons testing. Eventually, the glossy white paint on the upper surfaces of Ship 3 was replaced by a tan, brown and green desert camouflage scheme. Ship 3 also got a prominent dorsal spine that was a traveling wave tube for the Kuras-Alterman Crosseye system, an experimental electronic countermeasures set. Crosseye jamming affected radar systems that used monopulse tracking, which was a counter-countermeasure to traditional deception jamming techniques. With crosseye jamming, the target intercepted the transmitted monopulse radar signal, manipulated it, and returned it to its source in a way that would mislead the monopulse radar.

B-1A Ship 4 did not fly until 14 February 1979. Bearing the tail number 76-0174, Ship 4 was the first production aircraft from the three that had been authorized on 2 December 1976.

It incorporated improvements that resulted from lessons learned during early flight test, as well as being built on production tooling. What most distinguished Ship 4 from its predecessors was that four ejections seats replaced the crew ejection capsule and also that it was the first B-1A to have the AIL Division of Eaton Corporation (Eaton having purchased Cutler-Hammer in 1978) AN/ALQ-161 DAS installed. Although nominally a production aircraft, Ship 4 was dedicated to DAS testing and was not intended to be delivered to an operational unit. Ship 4 had another distinction. The Rockwell project manager for Ship 4 was Pat Swanson, the first woman to serve in that role at the company. Swanson had started in the company as an engineering library clerk and moved up in the engineering ranks at a time when very few women were working as engineers. Flight 4-1 (14 February 1979) from Palmdale to Edwards AFB was Ship 4's first flight. Later in 1979, Ship 4 would acquire the same Crosseye traveling wave tube and desert camouflage paint scheme as Ship 3.

Since the B-1A was no longer a production program, the last phase of flight testing of Ships 3 and Ship 4 was an AFTEC-managed program called the Bomber Penetrativity Evaluation (BPE). The objective of BPE was to learn the value of various technologies and tactics applicable to penetrating enemy air defenses rather than qualify the B-1A DAS for operational use, since the B-1A was no longer an aircraft headed for production. The results of the BPE would be useful to whatever bomber programs the USAF might have in the future. Left unsaid was that the study was a low-key way to keep the B-1 program alive and moving forward under President Carter.

Ship 4 first flew on 14 January 1979. This photograph depicts that first take-off from Palmdale. Flight 4-1 was a 4.7-hour functional checkout of the new aircraft and it ended with a landing at Edwards AFB. (*Russ Davis collection*)

BPE involved flying the B-1A against various ground-based and airborne systems that were considered to be representative of present and future Soviet air defense capabilities. The USAF F-15A Eagle fighter and the E-3A Sentry airborne warning and control aircraft were used in these tests. While not publicized, presumably the B-1A also flew against actual Soviet radars which had been captured a few years before by the Israelis during the 1973 Yom Kippur War and shared with the United States.

Ship 3 acted as the control in the experiments. It provided baseline data without the AN/ALQ-161 DAS. Ship 4 would then fly the same profile against the same threats using the AN/ALQ-161 DAS. Comparing the results of the Ship 3 and Ship 4 flights provided information on the incremental operational effectiveness of the AN/ALQ-161. Scripted scenarios with the B-1A flying against a single threat preceded more operationally representative tests in which the B-1A flew against multiple threats. The data from these tests was used to update and validate computerized models of bomber penetration, which could be used to develop and optimize future bomber designs. BPE included a human factors component to understand the best way to combine automation and a human operator in DAS operations in complex, high-workload situations with multiple threats.

An important person during BPE was Captain Charles R. 'Russ' Davis, an engineer and DSO assigned to the 4200th TES at Edwards AFB. Davis was an experienced SAC EWO who had flown 179 combat missions in the B-52 during the Vietnam War and also served on a staff in theater. In 1976, he reported to the 4200th TES to provide engineering support to the B-1 JTF. In USAF parlance, this was a 'rated supplement assignment', a non-flying position to broaden the careers of pilots and navigators. After the production cancellation in 1977, SAC returned its

B-1A Ship 4 was the only B-1A with DAS installed and was used for testing that system. (*Major Bill Hayes/US Air Force*)

The B-1 JTF at Edwards AFB has all four B-1A aircraft in their original glossy white paint scheme. Ship 4 is to the left. Its tail radome has been swung to the side to access components of the DAS. Ship 3 is in the left rear corner of the hangar and undergoing maintenance. Ship 1 is in the right rear corner of the hangar and Ship 2 is in the right foreground. Ships 1 and 2 appear to be roped off and inactive. (*Stephen Henry collection*)

Ship 3 was painted in the desert camouflage scheme by the time this photo was taken on 1 February 1980. When in desert camouflage, Ship 3 can be distinguished from Ship 4 because it has deflated stabilizing fins for the escape capsule folded on the side of the forward fuselage, while Ship 4 with its ejection seats does not. Unlike Ship 4, Ship 3 did not have black radomes on the forward wing gloves, which were just painted in the same desert camouflage colors as the rest of the airplane. (*Master Sergeant Paul J. Herrington/US Air Force*)

Right: Aerial refueling was not only an operational requirement for the B-1A, but also a necessity for efficient test missions, since the B-1A often flew at high thrust settings and low altitude, which consumed fuel rapidly. In this photograph, a KC-135A Stratotanker refuels Ship 3. Note the cheek antennas for the Kuras-Alterman Crosseye system above the SMCS vanes. (*Brad Purvis collection*)

Below: Hoses supply B-1A Ship 3 with cooling air for its avionics. The slats are extended, revealing the white paint on the fixed leading edge of the wing into which the slats retract. (*Erik Simonsen collection*)

B-1A pilots, OSOs and DSOs assigned to the 4200th TES to operational and staff assignments, with the exception of test pilot Major Larson, who remained at the B-1 JTF. When the need arose for a B-1A DSO to fly on Ship 4, Davis was the logical choice, and he operated the AN/ALQ-161 DAS during many of the tests.

Ship 3 retired from flying on 15 April 1981, having flown on 138 sorties for 829.4 hours. Flight 4-70 (30 April 1981) concluded the B-1A flight test program with 378.0 hours flown by Ship 4. Combined totals for the four B-1A aircraft across Phase 1 and Phase 2 were 347 flights for 1895.2 hours.

Left: B-1A Ship 4 Flight 4-39 was promoted as the 'first all-SAC flight'. From left to right, Major Charles R. 'Russ' Davis (DSO), Charles C. Bock, Jr. (pilot), Lieutenant Colonel John R. 'Ray' Houle (OSO), and Captain L. Daley Autry (co-pilot). Davis, Houle, and Autry were assigned to the 4200th TES. Bock, a retired USAF officer, was a SAC veteran. (*Rockwell International/Russ Davis collection*)

Below: Banked to the left, Ship 4 displays the dorsal Crosseye wave that was installed on Ships 3 and 4. The desert camouflage paint scheme was FS30140 (flat brown), FS30400 (flat tan), and FS34201 (flat green) on the top and sides. (*US Air Force*)

Ship 4 displays the glossy white paint on the bottom of the desert camouflaged B-1A aircraft. (*Staff Sergeant Bill Thompson/ US Air Force*)

With its wings swept forward, Ship 4 flies formation in the precontact position with a KC-135A tanker. Aerial refueling in the B-52 was notoriously difficult but B-1 pilots had it much easier behind the tanker. (*Stephen Henry collection*)

Connected to the tanker, Ship 4 replenishes its fuel supply. It was much more efficient to refuel in the air than return to Edwards AFB for refueling on the ground and then make another sortie. (*Stephen Henry collection*)

Maintainers have used a stand to position a 'hat' in front of the left side fairing radome, which covered the fuselage side fairing compartment. This compartment had DAS transmitters and receivers that protected the left forward quadrant of B-1A Ship 4. The 'hat' absorbed radio frequency radiation from the DAS emitters and dissipated it in the form of heat. Black hoses fed cooling air to the avionics when neither the engines nor APU were running. The cart provided liquid cooling for DAS equipment on the ground. (*Staff Sergeant Bill Thompson/US Air Force*)

Stretch, SWL, and Stealth

In the aftermath of the cancellation of B-1A production by President Carter, the focus of strategic bomber force modernization shifted to the ALCM and the modernization of the later models of the B-52, the B-52G and B-52H, to carry and launch ALCM. The existing AN/ASQ-38 bombing and navigation system in the B-52G and B-52H was a relic of 1950s analog electronics technology. The AN/ASQ-38 needed to be replaced not only because of its general obsolescence, but because a modern digital system was needed to initialize and align the ALCM navigation system and download mission data to the missiles. The new B-52G/H OAS that replaced the AN/ASQ-38, designated the AN/ASQ-176, was based on the B-1A OAS. Like the B-1A OAS, the AN/ASQ-176 was integrated by Boeing and used inertial navigation, digital computers, and video displays. To cool the avionics inside the ALCMs, the B-52G and B-52H needed a revamped environmental control system, which was supplied by Hamilton Standard, who had been the subcontractor for the comparable system on the B-1A. Between the post-cancellation flight test work, various elements of the ALCM program, and also the preservation of B-1A production tooling, the industrial base for the B-1 was being maintained.

The desire of some people to have a penetrating strategic bomber, as opposed to a stand-off bomber that launched missiles from afar, continued in some quarters. One idea promoted by General Dynamics and supported by General Richard H. Ellis, the Commander-in-Chief of SAC between 1977 and 1981, was a more ambitious FB-111 upgrade than the FB-111G concept studied in 1975. First called the FB-111H and then the FB-111B/C (both unofficial designations), the concepts for this airplane were focused on stretching the airframe of the FB-111A (presumably this would have been the FB-111B) and perhaps also the F-111D tactical fighter (presumably designated the FB-111C) to carry more weapons and also for the aircraft to be re-engined with two F101 engines from the B-1.

General Dynamics touted the FB-111H as an alternative to the B-1. Nominally an upgrade to existing aircraft in the inventory, it was essentially a new aircraft with F101 engines, new avionics, new landing gear, and a stretched airframe that would have just used some pieces from existing aircraft. The FB-111H was later referred to as the FB-111B/C, the -111B being a rebuilt FB-111A and the FB-111C being a rebuilt F-111D. (*General Dynamics*)

In theory, the improved FB-111 was a way to rapidly field a new penetrating bomber. In practice, it was an ill-conceived idea. A stretched airframe with new engines, an APU, new landing gear, and new avionics was not a simple upgrade; it was tantamount to a newly designed airplane that happened to re-use some pieces of its predecessor. In 1980, General Dynamics and Ellis claimed that the first FB-111B/C could be delivered in January 1983, before the B-1 could be delivered. This date was preposterous. By 1980, the B-1A had been flying for over five years. In contrast, the FB-111B/C was a paper airplane that had not even started FSD. The improved FB-111B/C still had the fundamental deficiency of the FB-111A and also the FB-111G concept, in that it lacked intercontinental range except through the copious use of aerial refueling.

Also in circulation at this time were various ideas for cruise missile carriers other than the B-52, to be based on existing wide-body transports. The Boeing 747, Lockheed C-5, Lockheed L-1011, and McDonnell Douglas DC-10 were all considered. A major problem with this idea was that the adaptation of a transport to a cruise missile carrier was much more complicated in practice that it appeared. The aircraft would need to be redesigned to be hardened against electromagnetic pulse effects of nuclear weapons and they would need essentially a new fuselage design. After all these changes, the wide-body cruise missile carrier would offer no cost advantage relative to a purpose-built military aircraft.

On the theory of 'if you can't beat them, then join them', Rockwell touted the B-1 as an ALCM carrier. In testimony before the House Armed Services Committee in September 1977,

One potential solution to the search for a new strategic bomber was a wide-body transport modified to carry ALCMs. An illustration shows what an ALCM carrier derived from a Boeing 747 airliner might have looked like. (*Erik Simonsen*)

Bastian Hello had advocated completing not only B-1A Ship 4 but also Ships 5 and 6. He observed that the B-1 could be modified to carry sixteen ALCMs internally and another ten to twelve externally.

Rockwell developed the concept of the Strategic Weapons Launcher (SWL). SWL was obviously derived from the B-1, but unlike the B-1 it had a fixed sweep wing and was an ALCM carrier without the high-speed performance of the B-1. Since the wing pivot was the most expensive and challenging structure element of the B-1, SWL would have been less expensive than the B-1A. Rockwell estimated that a SWL would cost $35–45 million per aircraft compared with $56.1 million for a swing-wing B-1A. The empty weight of SWL would also be considerably lighter than the B-1A. Compared to the B-1A with its three weapons bays (eight SRAM or bombs in each bay, for a total of twenty-four), SWL would have two long weapons bays (eight ALCMs in each bay) plus eight ALCMs carried under the fixed sweep wings and twelve more under the fuselage, for a total of thirty-six ALCMs. A SWL with a pure stand-off role and no penetrating mission would also have simplified, less capable, and less expensive OAS and DAS. Left unproven was whether SWL would have been significantly better than a modified B-52 for the ALCM mission. A further development of SWL was called the Strategic ALCM Launcher (SAL). At the peak of interest in the SAL concept in 1979, there was a proposal to modify B-1A Ship 3 to become the SAL prototype, which never reached fruition.

Showing a very strong resemblance to the B-1A on which it was based, the SWL had fixed-sweep wings and carried 16 ALCMs internally and 20 externally. The logic of the SWL concept was dubious, since the airframe and engines of this aircraft were based on a high-speed, low-altitude penetrating bomber but the SWL was incapable of acting in that role. (*Erik Simonsen*)

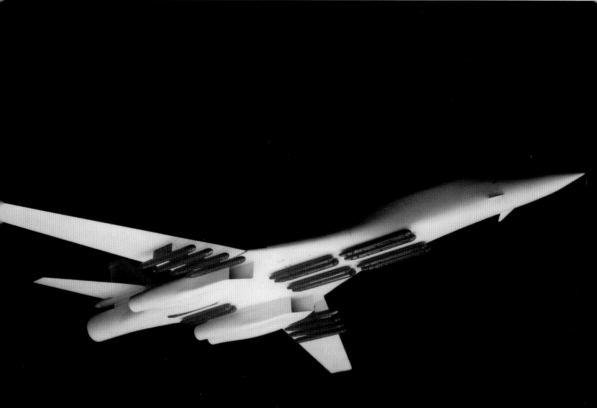

A more promising alternative for a strategic bomber was emerging from the 'black world' of classified programs. The losses inflicted on combat aircraft over North Vietnam and then the Middle East by radar-guided air defense systems of Soviet origin were deeply troubling to the USAF. There were several approaches to countering this threat: suppressing and destroying air defenses, jamming their radars, and making airplanes invisible to radar. In fact, the B–1A had elements of all three in its design. While not invisible to radar, the B–1A was said to have a radar signature that was one tenth that of the B–52. But the B–1A was a conventional aircraft with some radar signature reduction features. Classified research and development was advancing radical changes in aircraft design in which the primary consideration was low observables rather than aerodynamic performance, leading to revolutionary new configurations that looked like nothing else that had ever flown.

The first major flight demonstration of this low observables technology (commonly called 'stealth') was the *Have Blue* aircraft designed and built by Lockheed. *Have Blue* was not truly invisible to radar, but its radar signature was so small that radars could not distinguish the radar return from the *Have Blue* from radio frequency noise in the environment and the radar receiver itself. There is a story that a radar was being used to measure the radar reflectivity of a *Have Blue* model mounted on a pole. The radar was unable to detect the model, but then in the middle of the test, a signal was suddenly detected. Had the test revealed a flaw in stealth technology? Actually, it had not. What had actually happened was that a bird had landed on the model and its radar signature was larger than *Have Blue*. Stealth advocates regarded the technology as the greatest advance in military aviation since the jet engine.

The ATB was a revolutionary bomber that would use low-observables technology to evade enemy defenses. Opponents of the B-1 argued that the ATB was more advanced than the B-1 and made it obsolete and unnecessary. Eventually, the ATB would become the Northrop B-2A Spirit, a flying wing. (*Technical Sergeant Matthew Plew/US Air Force*)

The first production application of low observables was the Lockheed *Senior Trend*, later designated the F-117A. The F-117A was nominally a fighter; actually it was a small single-seat tactical bomber. But the next step was to scale up low observables to create a true strategic bomber built around the technology. This program was called the Advanced Technology Bomber (ATB). Without any details, Secretary Brown revealed the existence of the ATB program on 22 August 1980, shortly before the 1980 election. In the words of Brown, and referring to *Have Blue*, although not by name:

> Stealth technology enables the United States to build manned and unmanned aircraft that cannot be successfully intercepted with existing air defense systems . . . We have demonstrated to our satisfaction that the technology works.

To opponents of the B-1, the ATB revelation was a checkmate move from a political perspective. They could now argue that the B-1 was not only wasteful and unnecessary, it had also been rendered obsolete by the ATB.

The Revival of the B-1

The cancellation of B-1A production occurred in a political environment that was unfavorable to the program. The Cold War had spawned the divisive and eventually unpopular Vietnam War. Arms control treaties and détente with the USSR seemed to many Americans to be a better means of preventing nuclear war than increasingly expensive weapon systems like the B-1.

But a few years later, as the 1980 election approached, the American political situation had changed greatly. Advances by the Soviets and their proxies in places like Afghanistan led many Americans to believe that détente with the Soviet Union invited aggression. The Soviet Union greatly increased the power and capabilities of its military forces, discrediting arms control in the eyes of many. When the pro-American regime in Iran fell and was replaced by a radically anti-American theocracy, the subsequent hostage crisis made President Carter appear weak.

The 1977 B-1A production decision by President Carter had not conclusively resolved the issue of the B-1. Rockwell continued to promote the B-1. To a considerable extent, the B-1 became a proxy for broader concerns about the direction of American national security during the Carter administration. The platforms of the two major American political parties reflected the continuing importance placed on the B-1 issue.

The Democratic Party, running President Carter at the top of its ticket for re-election, reaffirmed its opposition to the B-1 in its 1980 platform:

> The Democratic Administration has determined to cut waste in defense spending. The B-1 bomber was cancelled because it was technologically obsolete.

In contrast, the Republican Party nominated Ronald W. Reagan to challenge President Carter for the presidency. Reagan was a noted conservative with a hard line on the Soviet Union; he decried what he claimed was the degraded state of the American military under President Carter. The failed raid to rescue the American hostages in Iran buttressed his argument.

The Republican Party became the political home of those Americans who wanted greater military expenditure and a more confrontational policy towards the Soviet Union. The Republicans harshly criticized President Carter's B-1 decision and explicitly supported the B-1 in their 1980 platform:

> Mr Carter cut back, cancelled, or delayed every strategic initiative proposed by President Ford. He cancelled production of the Minuteman missile and the B-1 bomber. He delayed all cruise missiles, the MX missile, the Trident submarine and the Trident II missile. He did this while the Soviet Union deployed the Backfire bomber and designed two additional bombers equal in capability to the B-1, and while it deployed four new large ICBMs and developed four others . . . Nuclear weapons are the ultimate military guarantor of American security and that of our allies. Yet since 1977, the United States has moved from essential equivalence to inferiority in strategic nuclear forces with the Soviet Union. This decline has resulted from Mr. Carter's cancellation or delay of strategic initiatives like the B-1 bomber, the MX missile, and the Trident II submarine missile programs and from his decisions to close the Minuteman production line and forego production of enhanced radiation weapons . . . In addition, we will proceed with . . . accelerated development and deployment of a new manned strategic penetrating bomber that will exploit the $5.5 billion already invested in the B-1, while employing the most advanced technology available.

Reagan decisively defeated President Carter's re-election bid in 1980 and was elected president. His inauguration in January 1981 signaled a new beginning for the B-1.

B-1: Second Take

To the incoming administration, the B-1 had several attractions. Building the B-1 would be a highly visible way to repudiate the policies of the Carter administration. The new direction on the B-1 sent a powerful message to the Soviet Union, American allies, and the American public. Since developing major new weapon systems took a decade or more, the B-1 was one of the only feasible ways to rapidly reinforce the American strategic nuclear deterrent force.

The attractiveness of the B-1 as a near-term solution was not to be underestimated. All flight test programs reveal problems, but at the time of the Carter decision there was no doubt that the B-1A was a good airplane (which is not the same thing as a cost-effective weapon system). The continuation of B-1A flight test activity after the 1977 production cancellation meant that technology risk reduction work continued, and enough of the industrial base and USAF flight test team remained in place to use them as the basis for reconstituting the full program without delay.

In contrast to the B-1, the ATB in 1981 was no more than a preliminary design. Eventually, the ATB would take to the air in 1989 in the form of the Northrop Grumman B-2A Spirit. But the B-2A was an exotic design at the ragged edge of what was possible, in the spirit of the B-70. It would be well into the 1990s before the B-2A would be mature enough to give SAC an operational capability, and Reagan had a mandate to increase American military strength on an urgent basis. The FB-11B/C remained under consideration, but it was not a serious contender.

The B-1 that was being promoted by the USAF and Rockwell in 1981 was based on the B-1A, but it was not exactly the same aircraft as the one that had been cancelled four years earlier. Called the Long Range Combat Aircraft (LRCA), it could carry ALCMs and had a lower radar cross section than the B-1A. But LRCA would not have a Mach 2+ maximum speed.

On 2 October 1981, President Reagan announced his plan to implement the strategic build-up that was such an important of the platform on which he was elected.

As President, it's my solemn duty to ensure America's national security while vigorously pursuing every path to peace. Toward this end, I have repeatedly pledged to halt the decline in America's military strength and restore that margin of safety needed for the protection of the American people and the maintenance of peace.

During the last several years, a weakening in our security posture has been particularly noticeable in our strategic nuclear forces – the very foundation of our strategy for deterring foreign attacks. A window of vulnerability is opening, one that would jeopardize not just our hopes for serious productive arms negotiations, but our hopes for peace and freedom.

Shortly after taking office, I directed the Secretary of Defense to review our strategy for deterrence and to evaluate the adequacy of the forces now available for carrying out that strategy. He and his colleagues, in consultation with many leaders outside the executive branch, have done that job well. And after one of the most complex, thorough, and carefully conducted processes in memory, I am announcing today a plan to revitalize our strategic forces and maintain America's ability to keep the peace well into the next century.

Our plan is a comprehensive one. It will strengthen and modernize the strategic triad of land-based missiles, sea-based missiles, and bombers. It will end longstanding delays in some of these programs and introduce new elements into others. And just as important, it will improve communications and control systems that are vital to these strategic forces.

This program will achieve three objectives:

- It will act as a deterrent against any Soviet actions directed against the American people or our allies;
- It will provide us with the capability to respond at reasonable cost and within adequate time to any further growth in Soviet forces;
- It will signal our resolve to maintain the strategic balance, and this is the keystone to any genuine arms reduction agreement with the Soviets.

First, I have directed the Secretary of Defense to revitalize our bomber forces by constructing and deploying some 100 B-1 bombers as soon as possible, while continuing to deploy cruise missiles on existing bombers. We will also develop an advanced bomber with 'stealth' characteristics for the 1990s.

In subsequent parts of his remarks, he listed the other elements of his plan. It's indicative of the scale of the American military build-up of this era that the Reagan plan took an 'all of the above' approach. It was no longer a question of arming the B-52 with ALCM or B-1 or ATB. Now all three programs would be pursued simultaneously. Elsewhere in his speech, Reagan advocated strengthening the ICBM and SLBM legs of the triad, as well as nuclear command and control systems and air defenses. In addition to the nuclear force modernization, Reagan advocated extensive increases in conventional military force structure and capabilities. Understood in totality, Reagan's announcement about the B-1 was one part of an extraordinary realignment of national priorities in confronting the Soviet threat.

In the American system of government, the ultimate power to authorize and appropriate funds for programs is held by Congress. The Democratic Party still had a majority in Congress, but Reagan adroitly assembled a bipartisan coalition of almost all Republican and enough Democratic members of Congress to support his rearmament program. The new bomber was based on the LRCA concept and designated B-1B. With authorization and funding secured, the USAF awarded a $20.5 billion contract to Rockwell on 20 January 1982 for the B-1B. Major General William E. Thurman was the B-1B system program director for the USAF and Sam F. Iacobellis was his counterpart at Rockwell.

SAC Commander-in-Chief General Bennie L. Davis was delighted, stating: 'President Reagan's announcement on 2 October 1981 to proceed with the production of 100 B-1B aircraft is a hallmark decision essential to the strengthening of the strategic force.' The USAF had begun work to get a new bomber to replace the B-52 in 1954. That bomber, the B-1B, was finally on its way.

Chapter 5

The Supersonic Cadillac

'The B-1 is not a big fighter. It is a supersonic Cadillac.'
Lieutenant Colonel Thomas S. 'Squeeze' Curran, Jr.,
34th Bomb Squadron commander, 2004–2006

Note

In this chapter, 'B-1' refers to both the B-1A and B-1B. 'B-1A' refers to all four B-1A aircraft unless particular aircraft are specified. 'B-1B' refers to the aircraft in the configuration in which it was delivered from the factory unless otherwise specified.

Design Analysis and Aerodynamic Configuration

The BONE is fast, powerful, and complicated. While ambitious, its design stayed within the envelope of proven technologies from its era, resulting in a relatively smooth B-1A flight test program. Flight testing did not reveal any major problems that threatened the viability of the B-1A, although it did reveal several deficiencies which would need to be fixed in the B-1B.

The most distinctive feature of the B-1 is its VG wings, with a sweep angle that range from 15° fully forward to 67.5° fully swept. The B-1 is not the only VG aircraft. The F-111 was the first mass-produced VG aircraft and it was followed by the Grumman F-14 Tomcat, a carrier-based fighter that replaced the ill-conceived and overweight F-111B naval version of the F-111. In Europe, the British, Germans, and Italians built the Tornado, a low-level strike and reconnaissance aircraft broadly comparable to the F-111. The French designed and flight-tested the Mirage G, which never entered production. The Soviets enthusiastically adopted VG wings, with the MiG-23/-27 (NATO reporting name Flogger), Su-17/-20/-22 (Fitter), Su-24 (Fencer), Tu-22M (Backfire), and Tu-160 (Blackjack) all using them. Each of these designs was initially conceived in the 1960s.

Like bell-bottom jeans and tie-dyed t-shirts from the same era, VG wings turned out to be a fad. The military aircraft with VG wings that reached production had long and useful service lives. But VG wings impose significant penalties on aircraft in terms of cost, weight, and complexity – three attributes that aircraft designers try to minimize. Scaling back requirements for maximum speed and improved aerodynamics, materials, and powerplants allowed the next generation of combat aircraft to have fixed-sweep wings. Besides, VG wings turned out to be incompatible with low observables. The VG wings of the B-1 mark it as a period piece.

With its sinuous curves and sleek shape, the B-1 was a stunning piece of aerodynamic sculpture. There is a widespread belief in the world of aviation that 'If it looks good, it flies

The B-1B sweeps its wings forward for take-off and landing. On the ground, the wings must be swept forward for balance because the aircraft would tip back on its tail if the wings were swept back. (*Author*)

B-1A Ship 4 has its wings fully swept back to 67.5 degrees. This sweep angle is used for terrain following and supersonic flight. (*Staff Sergeant Bill Thompson/US Air Force*)

good.' This principle might seem ridiculous and divorced from hard engineering realities, if not for the fact that it has a high correlation with reality. Perhaps human perceptions of the attractiveness of an aircraft's shape reflect an intuitive grasp of aerodynamics. Beautiful as it is, the B-1 was most certainly shaped by principles of aerodynamics rather than artistry.

Everything in aircraft design is a trade-off. The B-1A was designed for low drag at high speeds, which enabled Mach 2+ speed at high altitude and transonic speeds down to sea level. The wing pivots of the B-1 needed to be moved outboard of the centerline of the aircraft, in accordance with the results of NASA research by Polhamus, Toll, Barnes and associates. It was well known that the fuselage of an aircraft interfered with the optimal flow of air around a wing. One way to minimize interference drag between the fuselage and wing was with a blended transition between the two rather than merely butting the wing up against the fuselage. From an aerodynamic perspective, the center fuselage section of the B-1 is also the inboard portion of the wing; there is no distinct break between wing and fuselage. Not only does the blending of the wing and fuselage reduce drag, but the fuselage of the B-1 creates considerable lift. In the case of the B-1, the compound curves of the airframe were more expensive to fabricate than the simple curves and constant-diameter fuselage barrel sections that might be found on a typical jet airliner.

When viewed from the side, there was a noticeable dip in the middle of the aircraft between the forward fuselage and the aft fuselage. That the center fuselage was wide has already been explained as necessary for the VG configuration. That it had to be lower in the vertical direction than the parts of the airframe forward and aft of it was a result of the area rule concept, which was developed by Richard T. Whitcomb, the renowned aerodynamicist who worked for NACA and NASA. The full body of Whitcomb's work and its impact could justify a book-length exposition; his innovations can be found on almost every modern airplane. The area rule concept is based on the observation that at transonic and supersonic speeds,

The pronounced dip in the center of the B-1 reduces supersonic wave drag through the application of the area rule principle. (*Author*)

the drag of a three-dimensional body caused by shock waves is related to the change (either increase or decrease) in the cross-sectional area of the vehicle over its length. To reduce the intensity of these shock waves, the cross-sectional area should change as smoothly as possible. As the fuselage widened aft of the cockpit to form the fixed glove for the VG wing, the vertical dimension of the fuselage decreased to prevent the fuselage cross-sectional area from increasing. Every inch of the B-1 shape was designed to reduce transonic and supersonic drag. This airplane was built to fly fast.

Despite considerable differences between the B-1A and the B-1B, there was a strong family resemblance. It takes a trained eye to distinguish between the two models. The B-1B airframe had approximately 85 per cent commonality with the B-1A. The B-1B had a maximum gross take-off weight of 477,000lbs compared with the B-1A at 395,000lbs. President Reagan wanted a new bomber in service as soon as possible, and the similarity of the B-1B to the well-tested B-1A was a decisive factor in its favor.

Structure

Aluminum is a beautiful thing.

Aluminum is light and if used properly in structures, quite strong. It's inexpensive. It's easy to drill, mill, and turn. In sheet form, it's easy to form and rivet. Aluminum is electrically conductive, which means that avionics in an aluminum compartment will be shielded from interference, and lightning will flow along, rather than penetrate, its surface.

For all these reasons, most of the B-1 structure is made of aluminum. But aluminum is not a perfect material. It is relatively soft, so structures subject to high localized loads deform

The B-1 structure is primarily constructed of aluminum, which makes the B-1 much more affordable and manufacturable than the B-70. (*Stephen Henry collection*)

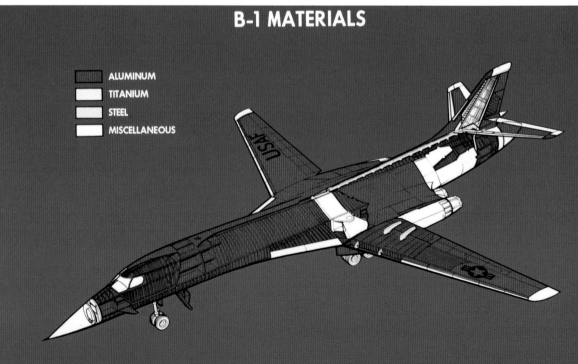

B-1 MATERIALS

ALUMINUM
TITANIUM
STEEL
MISCELLANEOUS

excessively if made of it. With its high electrical conductivity – useful for some purposes – it can't be used where electromagnetic waves need to propagate through it, so windows and radomes need to be made of other materials. Most critically for aerospace applications, aluminum loses its strength at elevated temperatures. The Mach 3+ speed of the B-70 therefore required the use of exotic materials. Keeping the maximum speed of the B-1 lower than Mach 3+ allowed the structure of the B-1 to be constructed predominantly of aluminum, with all its virtues.

The B-1 airframe consists of sections. The modularized structure enabled sections to be manufactured at various locations, and these were small enough to be transported to the final assembly facility. In general, the B-1 airframe uses a semi-monocoque design, in which both stressed skins and internal frames share the loads. The primary structure was designed to be fail-safe with redundant load paths, so the B-1 can maintain structural integrity and fly even if it sustains major structural damage. The B-1B airframe is 8,000lbs heavier than the B-1A structure due to additional reinforcement – its maximum gross take-off weight is 82,000lbs higher than the B-1A's.

The WCT is the backbone of the B-1. It was constructed of diffusion-bonded titanium. Diffusion bonding is a form of welding. The pieces of titanium to be joined are clamped

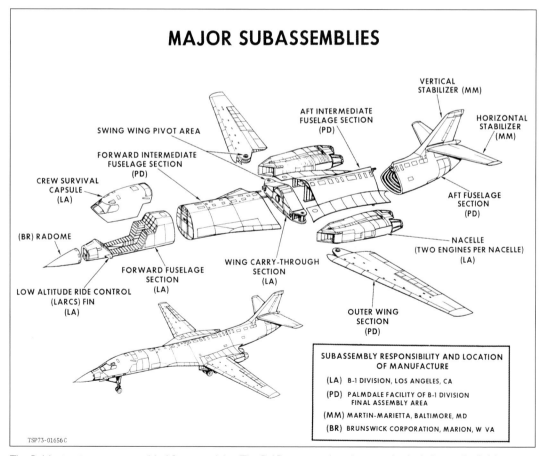

MAJOR SUBASSEMBLIES

VERTICAL STABILIZER (MM)

AFT INTERMEDIATE FUSELAGE SECTION (PD)

HORIZONTAL STABILIZER (MM)

SWING WING PIVOT AREA

FORWARD INTERMEDIATE FUSELAGE SECTION (PD)

CREW SURVIVAL CAPSULE (LA)

AFT FUSELAGE SECTION (PD)

(BR) RADOME

NACELLE (TWO ENGINES PER NACELLE) (LA)

FORWARD FUSELAGE SECTION (LA)

WING CARRY-THROUGH SECTION (LA)

LOW ALTITUDE RIDE CONTROL (LARCS) FIN (LA)

OUTER WING SECTION (PD)

SUBASSEMBLY RESPONSIBILITY AND LOCATION OF MANUFACTURE

(LA) B-1 DIVISION, LOS ANGELES, CA

(PD) PALMDALE FACILITY OF B-1 DIVISION FINAL ASSEMBLY AREA

(MM) MARTIN-MARIETTA, BALTIMORE, MD

(BR) BRUNSWICK CORPORATION, MARION, W VA

TSP73-01656C

The B-1A structure was assembled from modules. The B-1B structure has the same basic design as the B-1A, except that the crew survival capsule is deleted and instead the crew compartment is built into the forward fuselage. Some of the subcontractors for the modules changed from the B-1A to the B-1B. (*Chuck Klein collection*)

together, then pressure and heat are applied to the joint over an extended period so the different pieces become one. The WCT has wing pivots, reacts the loads from the wings, engines, and main landing gear, and contains fuel tanks. Attached to it are the portions of the aircraft forward and aft of the WCT, which joined the aircraft components. The high loads on the WCT made titanium the material of choice.

The movable portions of VG wings are mounted on large titanium pins inserted in the WCT wing pivot points. The pins had to be supercooled prior to installation and expanded upon warming to keep them in place. Each movable wing section contains flight control surfaces and one fuel tank. While wing hardpoints for weapons were envisioned for SWL and SAL, neither the B-1A nor the B-1B have them. The movable wing sections are primarily aluminum with titanium pivot lugs, while the wingtips and some outer wing spin panels are fiberglass. The wings can sweep between 15° and 67.5°.

The over wing fairings (OWFs) streamline the area where the VG wings connect to the fuselage and overlap the nacelles. They also cover and protect the many mechanical, electrical, and fluid connections between the VG wings and the fuselage. The shape and configuration of the OWFs for the B-1A and B-1B differ considerably. Compared to the B-1A OWF, the B-1B OWF is simpler and has less drag. The B-1B OWFs are constructed of movable fiberglass shapes, with inflatable air bladders and a folding panel that fill the gaps in the wing gloves on the aft intermediate fuselage when the wings are forward. On the ground, the OWFs rise to

The WCT is the structural backbone of the B-1. Constructed of titanium, it has the wing pivots. The nacelles with their engines are suspended from the bottom of the WCT. The WCT reacts the loads of the main landing gear. It also contains the main fuel tanks. (*Stephen Henry collection*)

The OWF maintains a streamlined shape when the VG wing moves in and out of the fuselage aft of the wing pivot. The design of the OWF on the B-1A in this photograph varied considerably from the OWF on the B-1B. (*Staff Sergeant Bill Thompson/US Air Force*)

The wing of the B-1 smoothly blends into the fuselage. Called the glove, the inner fixed part of the wing is structurally part of the fuselage. The glove generates a significant fraction of the lift. It moves the pivot points for the VG outer wings outboard, which reduce the trim change when the wings are moved. From B-1A to B-1B, the OWF was redesigned. The B-1B OWF configuration is visible in this photograph. (*Airman 1st Class Christopher Quail/US Air Force*)

allow air to flow into the APUs. After fuel flow increases above 100,000lbs per hour during take-off, the OWFs close and seal the area between the aft wing root and the fuselage.

The left and right nacelles are suspended under the WCT. Each nacelle contains two engines, inlets, one APU, and accessories powered by the engines or APU. Because of the high temperatures in the nacelles, parts of them are constructed of titanium, as are the parts of the fuselage aft of the engine exhausts exposed to high temperatures. The location of the nacelles on the bottom of the aircraft and a variety of access doors on the nacelle improve the maintainability of the B–1. A high proportion of the systems (including the engines) on the B–1 that require frequent inspection, servicing, removal, and replacement are located in the nacelles. Maintainers can access those systems without ladders, stands, or lifts.

The nacelles have inlets to supply the engines with air. The B–1A had inlets of the ECI type. Movable lips driven by electric jackscrews on the inlets' outer edges increased the inlets' capture area for take-off and landing and were automatically scheduled based on airspeed. Each inlet had two variable-position ramp panels, a variable-position throat panel, an air bypass door, and two-position boundary layer bleed-air exit louvers. These components were controlled by the AICS, with manual backup. The purpose of this complex and highly sophisticated inlet was to supply the engines with a smooth source of air and minimum dissipation of energy over the entire range of airspeeds up to Mach 2+. After the test program demonstrated the high-speed performance of the B–1A, the inlets of the B–1A aircraft, other than their movable lips, were fixed in position.

The engine inlets are the most conspicuous external difference between the B-1A and the B-1B. The B-1A inlets enabled the B-1A to fly at a maximum speed of Mach 2.22 but had a large radar cross section. (*Stephen Henry collection*)

At supersonic speeds, the B-1B inlets do not supply air to the engines as efficiently as the B-1A inlets did, but they lower the radar cross section of the B-1B relative to the B-1A. The B-1B is not a true low-observables aircraft, but it presents a smaller return to enemy radars. (*First Lieutenant Katie Spencer/US Air Force*)

Perhaps the most significant change in the B-1B airframe relative to the B-1A was replacing the ECI inlets with fixed-position inlets. The B-1A inlets had been designed for Mach 2+ speeds. The USAF decided that Mach 2+ speed was not a requirement for the B-1B. Aside from their cost, complexity, and weight, the problem with the B-1A inlets is that they greatly contributed to the aircraft's radar cross-section (RCS). Not only did the inlets tend to strongly reflect radar waves, but radar waves could enter the inlets to reflect off the rotating fan blades on the face of the engine, with its distinct and powerful radar signature. Aside from the movable lips that remain from the B-1A, the inlets of the B-1B have a fixed geometry. The interior of the B-1B inlets contain RCS reduction guide vanes (which aircrew call 'potato chips') that block radar waves from directly reaching the engine face. The radar waves that enter the inlet are deflected and dissipated, lowering the RCS of the B-1B by 90 per cent relative to the B-1A. The trade-off of the new inlets was that they lack the capability to efficiently slow and compress incoming air at Mach 2+ to subsonic speeds, so the B-1B is limited to Mach 1.2 (less at some altitudes) and is inefficient at supersonic speeds.

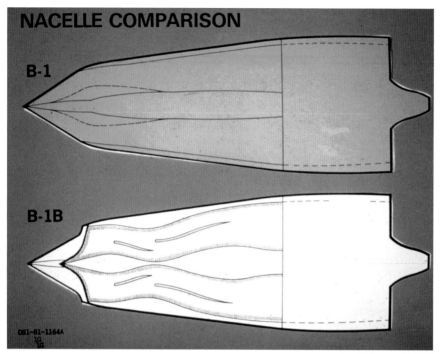

NACELLE COMPARISON

B-1

B-1B

DS1-81-1164A

A simplified top-view cross-section of the inlets shows the differences between the B-1A ('B-1') and B-1B inlets. Note the 'potato chips' in the B-1B inlet. (*Stephen Henry collection*)

Viewed up close, the B-1A inlets had a wedge shape. The movable outer lips of the inlet used for take-off and landing are opened in this image. This photograph is of B-1A Ship 4 which is displayed outside. The plexiglass panels keep birds and other critters from nesting in the aircraft and were obviously not part of the aircraft when it was in service. (*Author*)

Another limitation imposed by the RCS vanes is their tendency to accumulate ice when flying through cold, moist air. Various methods were used in the early years of the B-1B to limit ice accumulation, including electrical heating and Teflon coatings. None of these proved effective, forcing the crews to limit operations in anything more than light icing. However, this limitation was not as restrictive as it might seem. When flying at altitude, crews can avoid icing areas or change altitude if the ice detector warning is triggered. While flying at low altitude, aerodynamic heating is often sufficient to avoid icing.

The forward intermediate fuselage is attached to the forward end of the WCT. Its primary purpose is to contain two 15ft long weapons bays (forward and intermediate) and fuel tanks. A major difference between the B-1A and the B-1B was that the bulkhead between the two weapons bays in the B-1A was fixed. In the B-1B, that bulkhead is movable, so the intermediate bay can be extended to 22ft to accommodate the ALCM. Another difference is that in the B-1A, the weapons bay doors were made of aluminum, whereas in the B-1B they are constructed of lighter and stiffer graphite/epoxy composite materials. The change in materials resulted from weapons bay door-vibration measurements made during the B-1A flight test program. The composite doors reduce RCS when the stores bay doors are open. The B-1B also has weapons bay spoilers that were added during B-1A flight testing. Both the weapons bay doors and spoilers are hydraulically actuated.

The forward fuselage contains the avionics, nose landing gear bay, and the crew compartment. On B-1A Ships 1-3, the crew compartment was an escape module that separated from the

Looking down the inlets on the left nacelle of a B-1B, the RCS reduction vanes ('potato chips') are visible. Note how little of the front face of the engines is visible. Rotating engine parts greatly contributed to RCS, so blocking line of sight to them is important. (*Author*)

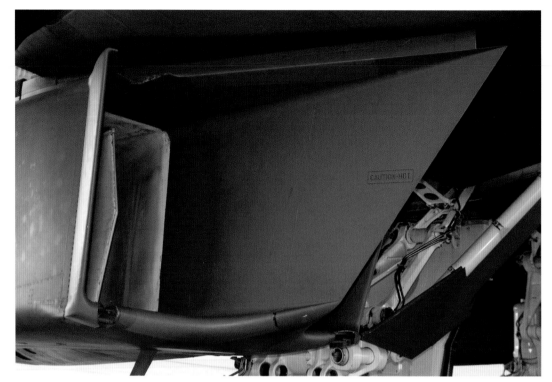

Viewed from the side, the B-1B inlets have a distinctive raked profile. The CAUTION-HOT marking pertains to inlet deicing. The RCS reduction vanes are problematic in icing conditions. They tend to accumulate ice which can be shed into the engine and damage it. (*Author*)

forward fuselage and descended on a parachute. On B-1A Ship 4 and the B-1B, the escape module was replaced by ejection seats. The SMCS vanes are mounted on the forward fuselage, which contains their actuators.

The nose cone is a radome. On the B-1A, the radome was a double-cone shape, whereas the B-1B has a shorter ogival shape. B-1A Ships 1 and 2 could be visually distinguished by the long, striped air data booms on their noses, used to collect precise airspeed data for flight testing. The B-1 radomes are built of polyimide quartz fiberglass, which is nearly transparent to radio-frequency electromagnetic radiation and strong enough to handle air and maneuvering loads.

The aft intermediate fuselage has a 15ft long aft weapons bay, the main landing gear bays, and a fuel tank. Aft of it is the aft fuselage, which contains yet another fuel tank. The aft end of the aft fuselage on B-1A Ships 1–3 had a pointed fairing. On B-1A Ship 4 and the B-1B, the aft end is a rounded radome for the aft-facing antennas of the DAS.

The aft fuselage supports the vertical stabilizer, which has a multipart rudder. The horizontal stabilators extend from the vertical stabilizer in a cruciform configuration. They are mounted on steel spindles extending from the vertical stabilizer and they rotate around those spindles.

A dorsal spine of steel, titanium, and boron composite stretches along the top of the fuselage, stiffening the long flexible fuselage. When the B-1A was designed, advanced composite materials were in their infancy and not yet ready to be used for primary load-bearing structures, except in very limited areas such as the dorsal spine. In contrast to the B-1A, the

B-1A Ships 1-3 had streamlined tailcones. B-1A Ship 4 had a rounded rear radome that covered the DAS equipment that protected the rear aspect of the aircraft, as does the B-1B. *(Author)*

B-1B uses graphite/epoxy composite materials for parts of the wing flap, slat areas, weapons bay doors, landing gear doors and certain other secondary structures. The utilization of graphite/epoxy composite materials in certain secondary structures in the B-1B is indicative of the advances in that material technology in the decade between when the B-1A and the B-1B were designed.

B-1A Crew Stations

The B-1 carries a combat crew of four: pilot, co-pilot, Offensive Systems Operator (OSO), and Defensive System Operator (DSO). The OSO and DSO are aeronautically rated navigators, more recently titled combat systems officers. Unlike the B-52 with its crew of six, the B-1 combines the roles of the navigator and radar navigator into one OSO, with no defensive guns and therefore no gunner. The B-1 could carry two additional crew members, an instructor pilot who sat between the pilot and co-pilot and an avionics instructor who sat between the OSO and DSO.

The B-1A aircraft had different crew compositions. Ships 1 and 2 had neither an OAS nor a DAS, so they only had a crew of three; the third crew member was a flight test engineer. Ship 3 had an OAS but not a DAS, so it had an OSO and a flight test engineer. Various observers, including other flight test engineers, might fill the instructor seats. During the flight, the flight test engineer operated instrumentation systems, monitored the weight and center-of-gravity location, verified aircraft configuration, and backed up the test pilots by reading the test cards and taking notes.

In B-1A Ships 1–3, the crew stations were located in an escape capsule. Determining the requirements for crew escape had been one of the primary tasks of the AMSA studies. Options included traditional ejection seats, individual ejection capsules like those used on the B-70, and a crew escape capsule like the F-111's. Compared to the other options, the escape capsule was superior at high altitude and high speed, had the best post-landing survival performance, and provided equal escape probability for all crew members. The latter point addressed a deficiency in the B-52, in which the primary crew members in the cockpit had ejection seats but any additional crew members such as instructors or crew chiefs would need to bail out manually.

The escape capsule was essentially another aircraft carried by the B-1A. It acted as a piece of the primary load-bearing structure of the B-1A when attached to the airplane, but also needed the strength to endure the violent forces of escape, parachute deployment, and landing on either land or water. Furthermore, it needed to be watertight to avoid drowning the crew during a water landing.

The B-1A escape capsule contained 1,240 components to provide and complete an escape sequence. The sequence could be initiated by the pilot, co-pilot, or combined action of both crew members in the back. In an extremely rapid progression after initiation, the pyrotechnics would shut the valves in the ducts between the environmental control system and the capsule, sever all structural and systems connections between the capsule and the aircraft, ignite the two escape rocket motors, activate a thermal battery powering the rocket control system, and release stored pressurized helium gas to inflate the chin spoilers and stabilizing fins. Two solid-propellant

The crew escape capsule concept had been previously used on the F-111 before it was adopted for the B-1A. It had advantages at high speeds and altitudes and when extra crew members were carried. But it was heavy, complex, and expensive, and less effective than conventional ejection seats at low altitude. Had it been built, the production B-1A would not have had the escape capsule. This escape capsule was a developmental model used for testing. (*Stephen Henry collection*)

rocket motors propelled the escape capsule away from the rest of the B-1A. One motor was gimballed in roll and the other in pitch. The rocket control system signaled actuators to rotate the engines around their gimbals to control the attitude and angular rates of the escape capsule.

Depending on the sensed speed and altitude, a redundant network of detonating cords would fire mortars under specified timing and conditions to deploy two drogue parachutes (medium- and high-speed only) and three 50ft diameter main parachutes. The escape capsule would descend under the three main parachutes, and impact attenuation bladders would fill with gas to soften the blow upon landing. After landing, the crew would manually initiate inflation of the flotation and uprighting bladders (if landing in water), jettison the parachutes, and sever the emergency hatch and side windows to exit the escape capsule (not if landing in the water).

In hindsight, the escape capsule was a bad idea. It had a vast number of features that needed to be inspected and maintained. The complete ejection sequence was exceptionally complex, and there were a large number of single-point failures, any one of which could kill or injure escape capsule occupants. The fatal consequences of the escape capsule concept would become apparent during the flight test program. Even before President Carter canceled B-1A production, conventional ejection seats replaced the escape capsule in plans for future B-1As and were installed on Ship 4. Just as on the B-52, additional crew members on Ship 4 were not seated in ejection seats and would need to bail out of the crew entry door manually.

In Ships 1 and 2, the pilot and co-pilot instrument panels bore a strong family resemblance to the instrument panels on the XB-70A aircraft. An attitude director indicator (ADI) was

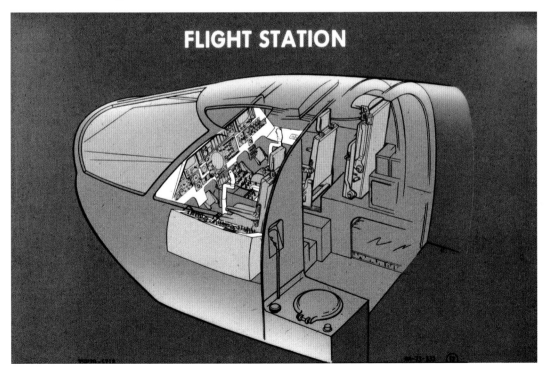

FLIGHT STATION

The pilot is the aircraft commander and sits in the left front seat. The copilot sits to the pilot's right. An instructor pilot seat is located between the pilot's and co-pilot's seats. In the B-1A, the entire crew compartment was an escape capsule, so there were no ejection seats. The chemical toilet was aft of the flight station. (*Stephen Henry collection*)

in front of each of the pilots, with a horizontal situation indicator (HSI) beneath each ADI. Vertical tape-type instruments flanked the ADIs and HSIs. Secondary instruments such as the standby attitude indicator and the fuel management control panel were installed in similar locations on the XB-70A and B-1A instrument panels. The most obvious difference between the instrument panels of two aircraft is that the XB-70A had round-dial instrumentation for six engines, whereas the B-1A had vertical tape-type instruments for four engines. In all cases, the instrumentation on both aircraft was electromechanical. The B-1A had a TFR indicator in the center instrument panel.

Whereas the instrument panels of the XB-70A and B-1A were similar, the pilot controls were different. The B-1A used center-mounted control sticks instead of the yokes on the XB-70A.

In B-1A Ships 1 and 2, the pilots had electromechanical instrumentation, with a circular radar indicator between their instrument panels. The ADIs were flanked by vertical-tape instruments: Airspeed-Mach Indicators to the left and Altitude-Vertical Velocity Indicators to the right. The pilots used control sticks. The co-pilot's throttle levers were on the center console; the pilot's throttle levers were to the pilot's left and are not visible in this photograph. (*Greg Spahr collection*)

The XB-70A had six throttle levers on a center console that both pilots shared. In the B-1A, the pilot and co-pilot had separate sets of four throttle levers for use by their left hands.

In Ships 3 and 4, the pilot and co-pilot instrument panels changed appreciably from the configuration in Ships 1 and 2. Vertical Situation Displays (VSDs) replaced the ADIs. The VSD in the B-1A was one of the first applications of cathode ray tube (CRT)-based video flight displays replacing electromechanical instrumentation in aircraft applications. Electromechanical instruments were limited in what they could be mechanized to display. In contrast, video flight displays could combine information from multiple sources to be displayed in a way that worked best for the user. The VSD reduced the cognitive workload of the pilots, particularly in terrain following (TF) flight. It displayed aircraft attitude, flight path angle, and steering commands, as well as infrared video from the Electro-optical Viewing System (EVS). It was similar to a television screen, but the symbology was sharper and brighter, and the hardware was able to operate in extremes of temperature, shock, vibration, and EMP.

B-1A Ships 3 and 4 had OAS. In these aircraft, the pilots had VSDs to replace the electro-mechanical ADIs. This photograph is of a cockpit development mock-up, not an actual aircraft. (*Greg Spahr collection*)

A pair of analog Flight Director Computers (FDC) calculated pitch and roll steering commands based on inputs from the flight control system, which in turn received data from a variety of sensors including the TFR. The FDCs transmitted the steering commands to the Display Electronic Units (DEU), which generated the symbology to be displayed on the VSDs. Each VSD had its own DEU, but if a DEU failed, the pilot or co-pilot could switch his VSD to receive a video feed from the other DEU. The capability enabled by the VSDs was transformative. Instead of mentally integrating information from multiple sources while skimming over the ground at high speed, perhaps at night or in poor visibility, the pilots could look at a single display of all the information that they needed to control the aircraft, follow their desired flight path, and avoid colliding with the terrain.

The OSO sat in the right rear seat behind the co-pilot in Ships 3 and 4. That this crew member was called an OSO rather than a navigator or bombardier reflected the capability of the OAS. It was the OAS that performed the calculations for navigation and weapon delivery using digital computers. The OSO controlled and monitored the OAS with a radar scope, a Multi-Function Display for OAS data and EVS video, several smaller CRT displays, a track handle, a keyboard, and several control panels.

The flight test engineer sat in the left rear seat on Ships 1–3. He had a dedicated control panel to operate some of the aircraft systems in test-specific modes.

The DSO occupied the left rear seat behind the pilot in Ship 4 only. Like the OSO, the DSO controlled and monitored a system that used digital computers, in this case the DAS. The

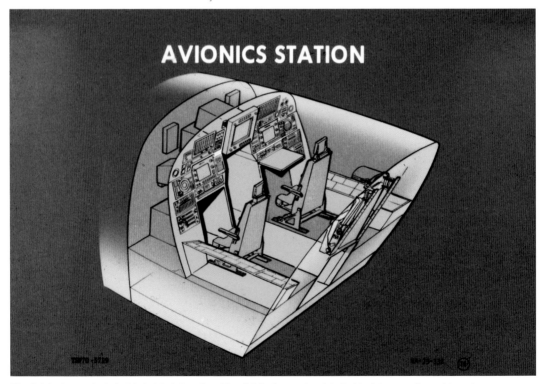

The DSO sits on the left side behind the pilot. The OSO sits on the right behind the co-pilot, with an instructor seat between them. These artists' concepts were made during the design of the B-1A. In some details they are different from the actual B-1A aircraft. (*Stephen Henry collection*)

In B-1A Ships 3 and 4 there was an OSO crew station. The round radar indicator was the centerpiece of the OSO panel, with an MFD for EVS video above it. With his right hand, the OSO used a track handle. At the lower part of the panel, the OSO had a keyboard and alphanumeric display. Two alphanumeric displays for the stores management, a stores management panel below the two displays, and a navigation panel below the stores management panel dominated the center panel between the DSO and OSO. (*Greg Spahr collection*)

Only B-1A Ship 4 had DAS installed or a DSO to operate it. In the other B-1A aircraft, there was a flight test engineer panel in this crew position. The DSO panel was dominated by two large EDUs. The EDU control panels were underneath the EDUs. A keyboard and alphanumeric display were beneath the EDU control panels. (*Stephen Henry collection*)

DSO had a control panel, a cursor control, and two large Electronic Display Units (EDU), which were also CRT displays. The DSO could control the format on each EDU. The two formats were the Threat Situation Format (TSF) and the Panoramic format (PF). The TSF was a heading-up map display that showed the bearing and range of radar emitters relative to the aircraft and its planned flight path. The PF displayed the frequency and signal strength of the emitters.

The B-1A crew entered the aircraft through a hatch using an attached retractable entry ladder aft of the nose landing gear well. On Ship 4, a chemical toilet was located behind the pilot's seat. Each pilot had a windshield strong enough to resist bird strikes, a side window and an upper window. The crew members in the rear seats of the B-1A did not have any windows.

B-1B Crew Stations

The B-1B has a crew compartment that is generally similar to the one on B-1A Ship 4. The pilot and co-pilot instrument panels are built around the VSDs. The small TFR scope on the

The B-1B is one of the last American military aircraft to have instrument panels filled with dedicated controls and displays. The next generation of military aircraft had mostly multifunction electronic controls and displays. (*Brad Purvis collection*)

instrument panel of the B-1A was omitted because the TF information was now displayed on the VSDs. Because of the change in engine inlet design from the B-1A to the B-1B, the AICS controls and indicators are omitted from the B-1B.

The pilots have Thermal Protection Flashblindness Equipment (TPFE), which protects the pilots from being blinded by the brilliant light pulse of a nuclear explosion. TPFE consists of aluminum panels to cover the cockpit windows. The pilots can fly the B-1B with the panels blocking the view out the windows because six of the shields have cutouts for EDU-4/A polarized lead lanthanum zirconate titanate (PLZT) portholes. PLZT is a material with the unusual property that when it is exposed to a bright flash of light, it reduces the intensity of the light to 0.003 per cent of the initial intensity with a reaction time of 150 microseconds, much faster than the blink of an eye. The colloquial term that the crews use for this equipment is 'plizit'.

The B-1B pilot and co-pilot instrument panels are optimized for terrain following. The critical information for that phase of flight are on the VSD or in the instruments and indicators that surround it. (*Brad Purvis collection*)

Because of the changes in the OAS between the B-1A and the B-1B, the OSO and DSO stations are substantially redesigned in the B-1B. In the B-1B, the OSO has two MFDs. A Radar Display Unit replaces the smaller circular radar scope on the B-1A. The DSO retains his two EDUs and gains an MFD of his own.

The ejection seat system on the B-1B is less complex than the B-1A escape capsule, but by no means simple. The Advanced Concept Ejection Seat (ACES) II ejection seat envelope is 0 to 50,000 feet and 0 to 500 knots. The seats operate in two modes: Auto or Manual. Auto mode is used for take-off, landing, low-level flight, or any other critical phase of flight. In Auto Mode, the pilot or co-pilot can initiate ejection of the entire crew. The OSO and DSO can only eject themselves. When the pilot or co-pilot initiate an automatic ejection sequence for the entire crew, the individual seats are fired in the order OSO-DSO-co-pilot-pilot over two seconds to deconflict ejection seats

The co-pilot's wing sweep angle control lever is on the right side of the cockpit. In this photograph, the ball-shaped knob at the end of the lever is visible near the orange 'Remove Before Flight' flag. The pilot has a similar lever to his left. (*Brad Purvis collection*)

from each other or from falling on the parachute canopies of earlier ejections. Each seat is set for a different trajectory to increase its distance from the other seats during a rapid manual ejection.

The sequence for a single seat consists of firing a retraction thruster to position the seat, decompressing the cabin, severing and removing the hatch above the seat, firing another thruster for the OSO and DSO stations to flip work tables out of the way, and then firing the rocket catapult to accelerate the ejection seat upward. The ejection seat has an integral parachute pack, oxygen bottle, locater beacon, drogue parachute, main parachute, and divergence rocket motor to separate the crew members from each other after ejection. It also has arm and leg restraints to prevent the ejecting crew member from sustaining flailing injuries. After parachute deployment, the ejection seat is separated from the crew member.

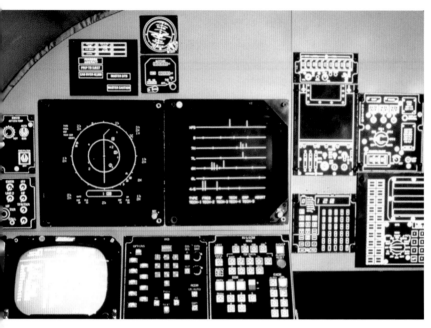

Left: This is a mock-up of the B-1B DSO panel. The left EDU has the TSF and the right EDU has the PF. The MFD to the lower left of the panel is part of the DMS. (*Stephen Henry collection*)

Below: The B-1B OSO panel has a radar display unit with MFDs to the right and below the radar display unit. (*Brad Purvis collection*)

The B-1A had no windows for the OSO on the right and the DSO on the left. (*Author*)

The B-1B has windows for the DSO on the left and the OSO on the right. (*Author*)

If onboard, the fifth (instructor pilot) and sixth (avionics instructor) occupants of the B-1B did not have ejection seats, but instead sat on small fold-out seats. Their bailout procedure was supposed to precede the ejection of the crew members in ejection seats. Successful execution of the bailout procedure required that the aircraft be under control and that the crew could perform the bailout procedure in an orderly manner. After a mishap in which the additional crew members died attempting to bail out, the fold-out seats were removed. Only four crew members would fly in the B-1B from then on.

Unlike the B-1A, the OSO and DSO have small windows on the side of their crew stations in the B-1B. The windows are small and inconveniently located for seated crew members to see out of, so they are humorously called 'day-night indicators'. Together with the engine inlets, these windows provide the most obvious visual means of distinguishing a B-1A from a B-1B.

B-1 System Design Philosophy

The B-1 was designed to accomplish its combat mission with a high degree of reliability, despite sustaining system malfunctions or battle damage. The B-1 can complete its mission with full capabilities even after any one failure in a system and can continue to fly with any two failures in a system. The high degree of mission reliability in the B-1 results from redundant systems and a well-trained crew that can detect and respond to failures and battle damage.

B-1 electrical and electronic systems are hardened against the effects of an electro-magnetic pulse (EMP). Nuclear weapons, particularly those detonated at high altitude, can produce a powerful blast of electromagnetic radiation. An EMP can couple with unprotected circuits and burn them out with voltage and current surges. Equipment on the B-1 was designed and tested to withstand EMPs.

F101 Engine

The B-1 has four GE F101 turbofan engines. The engines were designed to provide the optimum combination of thrust, weight, specific fuel consumption, and durability to match the characteristics of the B-1 airframe and the mission profile. The engines are mounted in pairs, side-by-side, in nacelles attached to the WCT.

The YF101-GE-100 propelled the B-1A. It was a dual-spool, mixed-flow, augmented (afterburning) turbofan. The high-pressure section, also known as the gas generator or core, consisted of a nine-stage compressor, an annular combustor, and single-stage high-pressure turbine. The first three stages of the compressor were variable, as had been GE's practice since the J79. The high-pressure turbine, turbine nozzle, and shroud were air-cooled, a technology pioneered in the J93. The low-pressure section comprised a shaft that rotated concentrically to and inside the high-pressure section shaft on bearings, a two-stage fan, and an uncooled two-stage low-pressure turbine. The augmenter section (afterburner) and variable area convergent-divergent nozzle were aft of the turbine section. The augmenter doubled the engine thrust at the cost of a dramatic increase in fuel consumption rate.

The inlet supplied the engine with air. At maximum thrust, each engine consumed 350lbs of air per second. The air that passed through the fan was divided into two streams.

The stream of air that entered the compressor was compressed. It then mixed with fuel in the combustor, was ignited, and then flowed through the turbine section. As the air flowed through the high-pressure turbine, energy was extracted from it to drive the compressor. Then the air passed through the low-pressure turbine, where more power was extracted to turn the fan.

The other stream of air was contained by the bypass duct shroud that surrounded the core. This air bypassed the core and mixed with the air from the core aft of the turbine section. The YF101-GE-100 had a bypass ratio of 2, which meant that twice as much air flowed in the bypass duct as flowed through the core. The combined streams of air then entered the augmenter and then the nozzle before exiting aft. The nozzle was of the convergent-divergent type. Hydraulic actuators moved an actuator ring that positioned the segmented flaps and seals provided exhaust area variation.

The YF101-GE-100 compressor had a maximum compression ratio of 26.5. Its turbine inlet temperature was 2,500°F to maximize thermodynamic efficiency. Engine components were constructed of exotic alloys to withstand the extreme conditions.

Bleed air was taken from the third stage of the compressor to cool the engine. It was also taken from the fifth and ninth stages of the compressor to supply the pneumatic system. The Main Engine Control (MEC) system, an electro-hydro-mechanical computer, received the engine throttle lever position and start switch position from the pilot. It controlled the fuel flow into the combustor and the variable compressor stages. An innovative feature of the MEC was an infrared pyrometer to measure high-pressure turbine blade temperature. Based on data from the infrared pyrometer, the MEC reduced fuel flow to the engine if the high-pressure turbine blades were at their temperature limit, preventing engine damage.

While the MEC controlled the core, the Augmenter-Fan-Temperature (AFT) control regulated the fan, augmenter, and nozzle. Ignition, starting, lubrication, anti-icing, instrumentation, fire-detection, and fire-extinguishing systems comprised the engines' ancillary systems.

The F101-GE-102 engine in the B-1B has a similar design to the YF101-GE-100 in the B-1A, with numerous detailed changes. Advances in manufacturing technology reduced cost and weight. One improvement was the use of near-net shape forgings, requiring less machining after the forging process and fewer expensive materials. Another new manufacturing process was the use of laser drilling to create the tiny cooling holes in the high-pressure turbine blades. Later in its service life, the Digital Engine Control (DEC) replaced the MEC and AFT.

The F110-GE-102 is an improved version of the F101 that incorporated lessons from B-1A and YF101-GE-100 testing. Although the -100 and -102 were generally similar, the -102 took advantage of advances in materials and manufacturing technology. (*Author*)

The B-1A flight test program revealed that the low-altitude flight environment was more severe than expected, and the -102 engine evolved in response. Engine components were redesigned to endure the increase in thermal cycles caused by throttle transients during terrain-following flight. The -102 fan was modified to be compatible with the B-1B engine inlet. The augmenter and nozzle also were redesigned based on flight test results.

Although GE designed the F101 for the B-1, the engine's impact on aviation extended far beyond that aircraft. In 1974, GE and the French aircraft engine company SNECMA created a joint venture, CFM International, to develop, market, and manufacture the CFM56 turbofan engine. For the CFM56, GE contributed the core from the F101 and SNECMA designed the low-pressure spool with a high-bypass fan. GE and SNECMA intended the CFM56 to be more powerful, more efficient and quieter than the Pratt & Whitney turbofan engines that were then the market leaders in propelling airliners.

Despite its advanced technology and superior performance, the CFM56 had difficulty finding a launch customer, and its corporate parents came close to terminating the project. But in 1979, the CFM International sold the CFM56 to re-engine some DC-8 airliners. Then there was a substantial order of CFM56 engines to re-engine US Air Force KC-135 tankers, with CFM56 engine being designated F108 in military service.

The selection of the CFM56 as the exclusive engine on the Boeing 737-300 airliner in 1981 and the launch of the Airbus A320 airliner in 1984 with the CFM56 as one of two engine options for that airplane made it the legend that it has become. Since then, the CFM56 has become the most-produced commercial jet engine in the history of aviation.

The face of the F101-GE-102 consists of a two-stage fan with movable flap inlet guide vanes. Bleed air from the engine is ducted to the inlet guide vanes and into the engine nose fairing for anti-icing. (*Author*)

The F101-GE-102 has a variable area, converging-diverging, flap-type exhaust nozzle. Each engine has eight sets of three-flap seal groups which define the nozzle. The exhaust nozzle controls the expansion ratio of the engine exhaust gas. In this photo, the #1 engine nozzle is at the military power position. The #2 and #4 nozzles are fully open, which is the position for both idle power and full augmentation. The #3 engine has been removed. (*Airman 1st Class Susan Roberts/US Air Force*)

Meanwhile, GE self-funded the F101 Derivative Fighter Engine (DFE) starting in 1979. The F101 DFE was a modified F101 core with a new fan sized for fighter aircraft combined with a fighter-type afterburner based on the one in the GE F404 engine for the F/A-18 Hornet. The F101 DFE was designed to meet the American military's need for better fighter engines. At the time, the Grumman F-14A used by the US Navy was powered by the Pratt & Whitney TF30 engine. The TF30 was an older engine that was used previously on the F-111 but it made the F-14A underpowered. The General Dynamics (later Lockheed Martin) F-16 Fighting Falcon used the Pratt & Whitney F100 engine. The F100 had spectacular performance but also experienced a host of problems that displeased the USAF.

The American military took an interest in the F101 DFE, which gained the military designation F110. Eventually, the advanced F-14B and F-14D versions of the Tomcat would be powered by the F110-GE-400. The USAF had GE and Pratt & Whitney compete annually to power that year's F-16C and F-16D fighters. Not only would the F110-GE-100 power many F-16C and F-16D aircraft, but competition spurred Pratt & Whitney to improve the F100, to the benefit of both the military and taxpayers. The F110 would later equip some export models of the McDonnell Douglas (later Boeing) F-15 Eagle.

The F118 engine formed another branch of the F101 family tree. Combining aspects of the F101 and F110 but without the augmenter, the F118 would power the Northrop B-2A Spirit bomber. It would also be installed in the Lockheed U-2R reconnaissance aircraft, with the re-engined aircraft being designated the U-2S. Between the original F101, the CFM56, the F110, and the F118, the F101 and its offspring were an enormously successful and influential family of engines.

Secondary Power System

Each of the two nacelles in the B-1 has an APU and two F101 engines. The APU can start the engines and power the electrical, hydraulic and pneumatic systems when the engines are not running. In addition to being started using a control panel above the co-pilot, the APUs can be started from an alert start panel attached to the nose landing gear strut door.

The B-1 was designed to rapidly escape its base to avoid being destroyed on the ground during a surprise attack. The APUs were a critical element of that capability. The B-52 did not have an APU, and so it required a traveling circus of aerospace ground equipment to power its systems on the ground. Because it had the APUs, the B-1 could be dispersed to many airfields without furnishing those airfields with aerospace ground equipment (AGE). While on alert, the first crew member to reach the B-1 would hit the button on the alert start panel, starting the APUs and lowering the crew entry ladder. By the time the crew had climbed the ladder and were seated, the APUs were developing power, and engine start could be initiated. Hastening the B-1 start-up procedure helped get the bombers off the ground and away from their bases before Soviet missiles could reach the bases.

Fuel System

It is only a slight exaggeration to regard the B-1 as a collection of fuel tanks flying in close formation. The weight of the aircraft at take-off depends on its load of fuel and weapons. Often, the gross take-off weight is nearly half fuel. The B-1 fuel system can load, store, and dump fuel, control the aircraft center of gravity (CG), and provide cooling.

The B-1 was designed to use JP-4 fuel, with JP-5 as an alternative. The USAF later replaced JP-4 with JP-8. JP-8 is a less flammable and less hazardous fuel for greater safety and combat survivability. The B-1 has eight internal fuel tanks.

Tank	Location
1	Forward fuselage
2	Forward intermediate fuselage
3	Aft intermediate fuselage
4	Aft fuselage
5 Left Main and Right Main	WCT
6 Left Wing and Right Wing	Outer wings

Fuel tanks No. 1 and No. 4, the most forward and aft of the fuel tanks (also called the ballast tanks), play a critical role in controlling aircraft CG. No. 2 and No. 3 tanks consist of fuel cells on both sides of the weapons bays in those fuselage sections. No. 4 tank is the largest tank in the B-1. Because it is the largest fuel tank and its location is at the far aft end of the B-1, Tank No. 4 makes the B-1 tail-heavy unless its fuel is balanced by fuel in No. 1 and No. 2 tanks. Tail-heaviness due to fuel loading has been responsible for one fatal B-1 accident and several

The No. 4 fuel tank is the largest fuel tank in the B-1 and located in the aft fuselage. Woe to the crew chief who does not carefully monitor the fuel tanks during refueling and allows the No. 4 tank to be filled before the other tanks further forward. After the unbalanced B-1B sits on its tail, he or she undoubtedly will come to the attention of the colonels and chief master sergeants. (*Brad Purvis collection*)

incidents in which, while the aircraft was being loaded with the fuel on the ground, it ended up sitting on its aft end with its nose high in the air.

No. 5 Left and Right tanks (also called the Main tanks) are the header tanks that feed the engines and APUs in the left and right nacelles, respectively. No. 6 Left and Right tanks in the outer wings have fuel lines to the fuselage that can accommodate the variable sweep angles of the outer portion of the wings. The fuel tanks are integral, meaning that the fuel is contained by the structure of the aircraft and not bladders within the structure. Integral tanks are lighter and have higher capacity, but with no bladders the structure itself must be leak-proof.

Each weapon bay can also be fitted with a fuel tank instead of weapons and a launcher. When only one weapons bay tank is carried, the usual practice is to install it in the forward weapons bay. The B-1B had provisions for six 1,000-gallon external drop tanks carried under the fuselage, but they were never tested or acquired.

The B-1 has two ground refueling pressure-type receptacles on the bottom of the right nacelle. A universal air refueling receptacle slipway installation (UARRSI) on the dorsal side of the forward fuselage, forward of the pilots' windshields, is used for aerial refueling with the USAF's standard flying boom aerial refueling system.

An elaborate complex of pumps, valves, fuel lines, and manifolds transfers the fuel from the ground refueling receptacles and UARRSI to the fuel tanks, between fuel tanks, and from the

Additional fuel tanks can be carried in the B-1B weapons bays in place of a launcher and weapons. This tank is being loaded in the forward weapons bay. (*Master Sergeant Val Gempis/US Air Force*)

Before flight, the B-1 needs to be fueled. The R-12 refueling truck connects to a fuel hydrant, which is supplied by underground fuel pipelines. The R-12 pumps the fuel to the airplane. In its right nacelle, the B-1B has two Single Point Receptacles (SPR) from which all of its fuel tanks can be filled. The SPRs are located between the two engines and close to the APU exhaust. The FCGMS measures fuel levels in the tanks and controls the valves so that each tank gets the proper amount of fuel. A crew chief monitors the FCGMS from the cockpit or a fuel control panel. (*Staff Sergeant David Owsianka/US Air Force*)

The B-1B can dump fuel from all of its fuel tanks except the No. 5 Left and Right (Main) tanks through dump valves and outlets near each wingtip trailing edge. *(Technical Sergeant Michael J. Haggerty/US Air Force)*

fuel tanks to the engines and APUs. The fuel transfer equipment can also dump some or all of the fuel in the B-1, except for the fuel in No. 5 Left and Right tanks. No. 1 and No. 3 tanks contain heat exchangers because the fuel in those tanks is used as a heat sink for cooling other aircraft equipment.

The Fuel/Center of Gravity Management System (FCGMS, pronounced 'figimz' or 'fugumz') controls the fuel system. It uses capacitive sensors in the fuel tanks to measure the fuel levels, dual digital electronic processors to process the sensor measurements and control fuel transfer, and control panels for the ground crew and in the cockpit. FCGMS calculates the location of the CG of the aircraft. It automatically commands pumps and valves to transfer the fuel to the correct tanks to attain the desired CG.

Utility Systems

The B-1 needs high-capacity utility systems to operate its complex systems and accomplish its mission.

Each F101 engine is connected to an Accessory Drive Gearbox (ADG) by its power take-off shaft. ADG 2 and ADG 4 also are connected to the left and right APUs, respectively. The ADGs are connected to hydraulic pumps, Integrated Drive Generators (IDGs) and Air Turbine Starters (ATSs). Unlike the other ADGs, ADG 3 does not have an IDG.

Three maintainers from 28th Aircraft Maintenance Unit, 7th Aircraft Maintenance Squadron inspect Accessory Drive Gearbox (ADG) #4 in the right nacelle. Every engine has an ADG. Each of the four ADGs connect to an engine, generator (except #3), air turbine starter, and two hydraulic pumps. ADG #2 and #4 also connect to the left and right APUs, respectively. This design gives the B-1B a high degree of redundancy, enabling it to accomplish its mission even with multiple system failures. *(Staff Sergeant David Owsianka/US Air Force)*

ADG	Nacelle	Engine	APU	Hydraulic Pump	IDG	ATS
1	Left	1		1 Master 2 Slave	1	1
2	Left	2	Left	2 Master 1 Slave	2	2
3	Right	3		3 Master 4 Slave		3
4	Right	4	Right	4 Master 3 Slave	4	4

The ADGs works in four modes:

- The F101 engines power the ADGs, which drive the IDGs and hydraulic pumps. This mode is the normal mode after engine start.
- The APUs power ADGs 2 and 4. This mode drives the IDGs and hydraulic pumps when the engines are not running.
- The left and right APUs drive engines 2 and 4. This mode is used to motor and start those two engines.

- An ATS motors an engine, with the ATS being powered by the pneumatic system. The normal engine start sequence uses the APUs to start engines 2 and 4, and then uses engines 2 and 4 to generate pressurized bleed air to drive ATS 1 and 3 to start their respective engines.

The B-1A did not have the four ATSs inside the aircraft. For the B-1A, the ground crew connected a portable ATS powered with a ground pneumatic cart to each nacelle and disconnected the portable ATS after starting the engines.

The B-1 has four hydraulic systems. Each hydraulic system has a master pump driven by one engine through the ADG and a slave pump driven through the ADG of the adjacent engine in the same nacelle. The slave pumps provide redundancy and add additional capacity when needed. The hydraulic systems are pressurized to 4,000 psi and power numerous systems on the B-1, including the landing gear, flight controls including wing sweep, AICS (B-1A only), weapons bay doors and spoilers, weapon rotary launch drives, blowers, and UARSSI slipway doors. The hydraulic fluid in each system is cooled by passing it through heat exchangers in the No. 3 fuel tank. The hydraulic systems can also be powered by AGE through connections in the nacelles.

The three IDGs powered by ADGs 1, 2 and 4 provide 230-volt 400Hz alternating current (AC) electrical power to four primary AC electrical power buses and the Essential Bus. The buses can be cross-tied in the event of generator failure. Hydraulic system 4 powers an additional emergency generator. An external power receptacle on the left nacelle allows AGE to be connected to the aircraft for electric power while on the ground.

Primary AC Bus 2 and the Essential Bus supply AC electrical power to the forward transformer-rectifier unit which converts the AC power to 28-volt direct current (DC) power for the Forward Main DC Bus. Primary AC Buses 1 and 3 do the same thing to the aft transformer-rectifier unit for the Aft Main DC Bus. Each DC bus also has a battery.

The B-1 can be started completely independently of AGE. The APUs are started with electrical power from the aft battery and hydraulic power from an accumulator. Once started, the APUs drive the electrical, hydraulic, and pneumatic systems and start the engines.

Compressed bleed air from the fifth and ninth stages of engine compressors feed the Engine Bleed Air Distribution System (EBADS). The APUs also supply compressed air to EBADS, as can AGE through pneumatic connections in the nacelles. The hot compressed air in EBADS passes through precoolers in the engine inlet ducts to lower its temperature.

EBADS supplies compressed air to four air cycle refrigeration units, two for avionics and one for the stores (weapons bay) and one for the crew compartment. The air cycle refrigeration units have a compressor and a turbine expander, a heat exchanger, a mixing valve to control the temperature of the discharged air, and a water separator.

The discharge air from the crew compartment air cycle refrigeration unit provides a comfortable (temperature-controlled, ventilated, and pressurized) environment for the crew. The air can be filtered to prevent radioactive particles from entering the crew compartment. AGE can also supply conditioned air to the aircraft for cooling.

The two avionics bay air cycle refrigeration units provided a combination of air and liquid cooling for the extensive avionics systems of the B-1. The stores air cycle refrigeration unit provided cooling for the weapons bays and other equipment in the center and aft sections of the B-1.

Besides the four air cycle refrigeration units, EBADS supplies pneumatic power used by several systems, including the crew entry door seals, the window wash reservoirs, and the inflatable OWF seals.

B-1A Ships 1 and 2 had more austere pneumatic and environmental systems. In those aircraft, the APUs did not supply compressed air to EBADS. B-1A Ships 1 and 2 only had two air cycle refrigeration units – those aircraft did not have OAS, DAS, or actual weapons in their weapons bays, all of which dissipated large amounts of heat.

When below 8,000ft of altitude, the B-1 crew compartment is pressurized to the approximate outside ambient pressure. When above 8,000ft, it is pressurized to the equivalent pressure at 8,000ft. Therefore, the crew does not need to use supplemental oxygen for normal operations. However, supplemental breathing oxygen is available to the crew when needed – in the case of smoke and fumes in the cockpit, a leak, or a failure of the crew compartment's air cycle refrigeration unit. In B-1A Ships 1-3, the standard oxygen system consisted of two insulated containers of liquid oxygen and the equipment to gasify, warm, and regulate the oxygen pressure. This liquid oxygen system was backed up by the escape capsule's emergency oxygen supply in a 1,800 psi bottle.

B-1A Ship 4 and the B-1B have an onboard Molecular Sieve Oxygen Generating System (MSOGS) that generates oxygen-rich breathing air from compressed air supplied by EBADS, so those aircraft do not need to be serviced with liquid oxygen from a specialized ground facility. Those aircraft have a 1,800 psi emergency bottle and also small bottles of high-pressure oxygen in their ejection seats.

Landing Gear System

The B-1 has a tricycle landing gear for taxi, take-off, and landing. The landing gear is retractable, electrically controlled, and hydraulically powered.

The nose landing gear has twin wheels and is steerable by the pilots through their rudder pedals. It retracts forward into the nose landing gear well in the forward fuselage underneath the crew compartment. The left and right main landing gears each have twin tandem wheels (four in total on each side). They are attached to the WCT and retract inward, aft, and up into the main landing gear wells in the aft intermediate fuselage. The emergency landing gear extension function uses different electrical and hydraulics systems than the primary extension/retraction function to provide a redundant means of extending the landing gear.

The tires, wheels, and brakes need to handle the forces and heat generated by a heavy bomber during a high-speed rejected take-off or a hard landing. Each main gear wheel has thermal relief plugs that blow to relieve excessive pressure and protect against explosive tire or wheel failure due to severely overheated brakes. Each main landing gear has two independent braking systems and an emergency braking function. The main landing gear brakes use carbon disks for high performance and light weight. Wheel speed sensors on the main landing gear brakes feed into an electronically-controlled antiskid system, so that the pilots can apply maximum braking force without causing brake lock-up and tire-skidding.

Compared with the B-70, the B-1 landing gear system is uncomplicated and reliable. The B-1's landing gear is track 15.0ft wide, while the B-52's track (including the wing tip outriggers)

The B-1 has retractable tricycle landing gear. Notice how the main landing gear, the nacelles, and the VG wing pivots all converge on the WCT, which is the structural backbone of the B-1. (*Ken Middleton*)

is 148.4ft wide. The B-1 can use many more airfields than the B-52 can. During the Cold War, the alert force's ability to use more airfields – and thus its ability to disperse widely during a crisis – enhanced its survivability. When the B-1 switched to a conventional expeditionary mission, the increased basing flexibility enabled by the B-1's landing gear was an advantage.

Electrical Multiplex System

The Electrical Multiplex (EMUX) system controls the electrical power on the B-1. Instead of having thousands of dedicated point-to-point hard-wired connections, EMUX collects and transmits signals between the aircraft systems on time-multiplexed data buses. The reduced wiring and improved transfer of information between B-1 aircraft systems enabled by EMUX increase reliability, reduce crew workload through increased systems automation, and decrease weight. For redundancy, the EMUX is split into two duplicate buses, MUX 1 and MUX 2. One bus is primary and the other is a backup in case of primary bus failure.

Central Integrated Test System

The Central Integrated Test System (CITS) continually tests all B-1 systems. During flight, it informs the aircrew of aircraft malfunctions for the immediate evaluation of remaining mission capabilities. CITS provides data to the maintenance personnel to detect, isolate, and identify aircraft malfunctions. It also records data for trend monitoring and ground maintenance data processing. In the B-1A, CITS monitors 10,000 parameters using the avionics system, EMUX, and its own data acquisition units. CITS in the B-1B CITS monitors 19,600 parameters

The CITS control and display panel is located between the DSO and OSO crew stations. The CITS maintenance recorder writes system status data to magnetic tape cartridges – removed post-flight for downloading and analysis. A typical CITS scenario might involve the landing gear, where the CITS monitors various landing gear parameters. If the co-pilot moves the landing gear control handle to the retracted position, but at least one landing gear remains extended, CITS identifies the anomaly and records the electrical and hydraulic system parameters at the time of the anomaly. This data is available to the B-1 crew for in-flight troubleshooting through the CITS control and display panel and recorded for post-flight maintenance.

Flight Control System

The B-1 pilots use the flight control system to direct the aircraft on a desired path through the air. The flight control system translates inceptor movement (pilot controls) into effector movement (on the B-1, the horizontal stabilators, spoilers, and rudders). The B-1 flight control system has parallel electronic and mechanical paths.

The B-1 pilots' control sticks and rudder pedals are the primary flight control inceptors. The pilot and co-pilot controls are mechanically linked but can be disengaged if one pilot's controls jam or experience multiple hydraulic systems failures. The pilot's control stick moves the mechanical flight controls, augmented by hydraulics to move the massive flight control surfaces. The co-pilot's control stick is connected to the electronic flight control system and moves the control surfaces using fly-by-wire technology. Because the sticks are mechanically connected, the commands to the control surfaces are consistent. Bungees transmit force feedback to the pilots when the control sticks are moved.

The primary mechanical flight control path runs through hydraulic actuators to the horizontal stabilators (pitch control), two inboard spoilers on each wing (roll control), and upper rudder (B-1A yaw control) or upper/intermediate rudders (B-1B yaw control). Each primary flight control surface is powered by a minimum of three hydraulic systems to provide redundancy in case of system failure or battle damage.

The primary electronic flight control system – called the Stability & Control Augmentation System (SCAS) – provides the pilots with optimized flying qualities over the entire flight envelope of the B-1. SCAS uses transducers to measure inceptor position. The SCAS controllers are analog computers that combine inceptor position information from the transducers with data from sensors: the central air data computer (airspeed, altitude, angle of attack (AOA), Mach number), wing sweep angle, weight and CG (from FCGMS), effector positions, rate gyroscopes, and accelerometers. With this information, the SCAS controllers compute the actuator commands, which are electrically transmitted to the actuators.

SCAS controls the horizontal stabilators (pitch control when the stabilators were deflected symmetrically and roll control when they are controlled asymmetrically), two outboard spoilers on each wing (roll control), and the lower rudder (yaw control). The roll control scheme illustrates the capabilities of the B-1 flight control system. Based on the wing sweep angle and Mach number, SCAS commands the optimal application of three effectors – the inboard spoilers, outboard spoilers, and differential stabilator – to provide roll control. SCAS also provides pitch, roll, and yaw trim so the pilots can zero out inceptor forces at the desired control position.

The B-1's secondary flight control system comprises the wing sweep, flaps and slats, and speed brakes. The VG wings are the key to the large flight envelope of the B-1. The pilots use wing sweep levers at the pilot and co-pilot stations to control the wing sweep angle. Two hydro-mechanical assemblies on each wing drive a ball screw actuator that moves the wing. The hydro-mechanical assemblies are mechanically linked to actively maintain identical sweep angles on both wings.

An interlock between the flaps and wing sweep prevents wing sweep angles greater than 20° when the flaps are lowered. An interlock with the landing gear prevents wing sweep angles greater than 35° when the landing gear is extended. The OWF seals the gap aft of the wings when the VG wings are swept forward and maintains a faired airflow at the wing root at all wing sweep angles.

At take-off, the wing-sweep angle is 15 or 20 degrees. The leading-edge slats and trailing-edge flaps extend to provide more lift at take-off speed. In the photograph, the horizontal stabilators are trailing edge up to pitch the aircraft nose up. The three sections of the rudder are clearly visible. (*Roelof-Jan Gort*)

The pilots extend the slats on the leading edge of the movable portion of the wing and the flaps on the trailing edge of the movable portion of the wing to provide high lift for take-off and landing. For other phases of flight, the pilots retract the slats and flaps, which are mechanically synchronized to prevent asymmetrical surface positions. The pilots use thumb slide switches on the No. 4 engine throttle to command speed brake deployment. The spoilers on the wings have a dual role: as roll control when deployed asymmetrically and as speed brakes when deployed symmetrically.

Based on the B-1A's flight test findings, the B-1B gained a hinge moment control system for the horizontal stabilators. The horizontal stabilators control both pitch and roll. Testing revealed that – under some flight conditions with a degraded hydraulic system – high roll control inputs could cause insufficient control authority in the pitch axis, resulting in uncommanded pitch excursions. High-speed, aggressive, low-altitude maneuvering would induce asymmetric aerodynamic loads on the horizontal stabilizers, reducing the rotation rate of the overloaded stabilizer.

Consequently, the jet could develop an uncommanded pitch-up during hard climbing turns, negatively impacting aircraft control. This problem was remedied by adding Hinge Moment Limiting (HML) to the flight control laws. HML maintains tail loads at levels controllable by the hydraulic actuators by matching the rates between the two stabilizers. This solution reduces the roll rate while preserving the more critical pitch authority.

The increase in maximum gross weight from 395,000lbs (B-1A) to 477,000lbs (B-1B) with no increase in lifting surface area means that, at high weights, the B-1B must fly at a higher

Viewed from this angle, the degree to which the slats and flaps increase the curvature of the wing and increase in chord is apparent. (*Staff Sergeant Joshua Horton/US Air Force*)

There are four hydraulically-actuated spoilers on the top of each movable wing. The inner two spoilers on each wing are controlled by the mechanical flight control system. The two outboard spoilers are under the control of SCAS. When the spoilers are deployed symmetrically, they act as speed brakes. Roll control of the B-1 is a combination of asymmetrical deflection of the horizontal stabilators and asymmetrical deployment of the spoilers. The deployed flaps on the trailing edge of the wing are also visible. (*Author*)

AOA to generate sufficient lift. With the wings swept aft, a significant portion of the lift is generated by the forward fixed section of the wings and fuselage. This lift distribution gives the aircraft the unfortunate characteristic that higher angles of attack drive the aerodynamic center of pressure far forward, reducing longitudinal stability.

If the center of pressure moves forward of the CG, the B-1B becomes dynamically unstable. It then departs controlled flight. The B-1B copes with this problem by flying fast, which reduces the need for higher angles of attack, while aggressively moving fuel forward and aft as needed to maintain the CG in a desirable location. The first two production lots of B-1B even have a stall warning system with control stick shakers, stall warning lights, and an aural stall warning tone.

The B-1B adds a Stall Inhibitor System (SIS)/Stability Enhancement Function (SEF) within the SCAS pitch channel to address high AOA flight at heavy weights. SIS provides AOA feedback to reduce the horizontal stabilizer deflection, increasing the apparent stability of the aircraft. It also transmits stick-force cues to the pilots when the AOA limit is approached and automatically uses the stabilator to reduce AOA if the limit is exceeded. The SEF expands on the SIS's capabilities by artificially augmenting aircraft stability beyond the airframe's natural stability limits. The objective of the SIS/SEF is to maximize the use of the entire flight envelope, permitting the aircraft to be flown at the higher gross weights of the B-1B.

Although the B-1 is a demanding airplane to fly with the mechanical flight control system only, SCAS provides excellent handling throughout the flight envelope. The B-1 enables the pilots to fly critical maneuvers like aerial refueling and low-level flight with a low workload, leaving them to concentrate on accomplishing the mission rather than controlling the airplane.

The Automatic Flight Control System (AFCS) gives autopilot functionality to the B-1 to further reduce pilot workload. The basic AFCS modes are flight-path-angle pitch hold and roll-attitude hold. Numerous other AFCS modes build on the basic modes. The AFCS can follow a flight plan programmed into the OAS while automatically following a terrain profile provided by the TFR and maintaining a pilot-selected airspeed or Mach. With these AFCS modes, the B-1 can hit a weapon release point at a highly accurate time-on-target at low altitude under any conditions without the pilots ever touching the control sticks or rudder pedals.

Structural Mode Control System

Despite its appearance as a rigid structure, the B-1 is flexible. Like any flexible structure, the B-1 resonates at particular frequencies. The B-1 crew in the forward fuselage is essentially at the end of a long flexible beam. If flight control inputs or air turbulence excite the airframe at its resonant frequencies, the B-1 crew will be bounced around – uncomfortably and disconcertingly.

The two SMCS vanes on the forward fuselage use feedback from accelerometers to automatically damp out oscillations of the long flexible fuselage. The vanes can deflect both symmetrically and asymmetrically. (*Master Sergeant Joshua L. DeMotts/US Air Force*)

The Structural Mode Control System (SMCS) detects structural bending oscillations using accelerometers located throughout the airframe. SMCS then calculates the forces required to dampen the oscillations and uses two small vanes to generate those forces. One SMCS vane is located on each side of the forward fuselage. The SMCS vanes are electrically signaled and hydraulically powered. Like the horizontal stabilators, the SMCS vanes can operate symmetrically or asymmetrically. SCAS also dampens structural bending oscillations with the lower rudder.

SCAS, AFCS, and SMCS are examples of how advanced control system technology optimizes the B-1 for high performance. The excellent handling and ride qualities can then be added using active controls rather than compromising the airframe and aerodynamics to achieve those characteristics. The low-level ride in a B-1B is relatively quiet and 'Cadillac-smooth', whereas flying the B-52 on the same route is like 'being locked in a shoe box with a vacuum cleaner getting kicked down a hill'.

Communications, Navigation, and Identification

In peacetime, the B-1 requires communications, navigation, and identification (CNI) capabilities to operate safely in the airspace and at airfields. Over enemy territory, the B-1 navigates using the self-contained capabilities of the OAS. With the communications radios, the B-1 crew would receive the commands to launch, proceed past the positive control point, and proceed to attack targets. In general, each CNI system consists of a control head at a crew station, the radio, and one or more antennas mounted outside the airframe. Except for the B-1-specific interphone communication system, the B-1 uses standard USAF CNI systems.

The additions of the Air Force Satellite Communications (AFSATCOM) system and Miniature Receive Terminal (MRT) to the B-1B were indicative of the modernization of strategic command, control, and communications capabilities that coincided with the modernization of strategic weapon systems. The objective of these new communications channels was to thwart the Soviet Union from launching a pre-emptive kinetic or jamming attack on communications systems that would prevent bombers from receiving messages to proceed with their attacks. The other changes reflected the fielding of the next generation of standard CNI systems.

System	Function	B-1A	B-1B
UHF Radio	Ultra-High Frequency line-of-sight communications	AN/ARC-109 (two)	AN/ARC-171 (two)
HF Radio	High Frequency long-range communications	AN/ARC-123	AN/ARC-190
Intercom	Communications between crew members; audio monitoring for all communications systems; aural tones from aircraft systems	AN/AIC-27 (AN/AIC-27A in Ship 4)	ICS-150
IFF Transponder	Identification friend or foe; air traffic control radar beacon system	AN/APX-64	AN/APX-101A

System	Function	B-1A	B-1B
TACAN	Range and bearing to ground radio–navigation facility	AN/ARN-84	AN/ARN-118
ILS	Instrument landing system	AN/ARN-108	AN/ARN-108
Radar altimeter	Measures height above the ground	AN/APN-194	AN/APN-224
ADF	Automatic direction finder to UHF station	AN/ARA-50	
Crash position indicator	Beacon for search aircraft and data recorder	AN/ASH-31	
Secure voice	Voice encryption and decryption	KY-28 (Ships 3 and 4)	KY-59
Rendezvous beacon	Enhances radar return to rendezvous with tanker	AN/APX-78 (Ships 3 and 4)	AN/APX-105
AFSATCOM	Satellite communications		AN/ASC-19
MRT	Very Low Frequency/Low Frequency radio receiver		AN/ARR-85

Offensive Avionics System

The purpose of the B-1 is to put munitions on targets. Every aircraft system supports that purpose, directly or indirectly. Second World War bombers had navigators who used manual techniques such as dead reckoning and celestial navigation with a sextant. Navigation technology advanced rapidly during the war, with radio-navigation and radar ground mapping entering service. However, all of these techniques required the bomber to fly straight and level for extended periods while the navigator took fixes and plotted aircraft position on a paper chart with a pencil. Bombardiers using the optical bombsights from that era also needed the bomber to fly straight and level.

Manual navigation was not feasible on an airplane skimming the earth at transonic speeds, frequently changing course and altitude to avoid threats and terrain. In this situation, the navigation had to be automatic and self-contained. The AN/ASQ-38 bombing and navigation system that entered service with the B-52E Stratofortress was an initial attempt to solve this problem; it demonstrated the limitations of analog and electromechanical computation. Although the F-111 and Grumman A-6 Intruder pioneered new bombing and navigation technology, the B-1A OAS was revolutionary in applying digital computation to the problem.

The OAS places digital computers at the center of the B-1 bombing and navigation functions. It is not an oversight that the B-1 has no crew member called a bombardier or navigator – the OAS is the bombardier and navigator. The OSO delegates the detailed computations to the OAS. His job is to monitor and exercise supervisory control over the OAS. The OSO directs the OAS to do things, and the OAS does them. The B-1 is a human/cybernetic hybrid that uses the best capabilities of its human and digital electronic elements.

Three Avionics Control Units (ACUs) formed the heart of the B-1A OAS. Each ACU was a ruggedized, EMP-hardened digital computer with interfaces to other OAS components. They had identical hardware but unique application software: one supported the DAS, one performed guidance and navigation, and one performed weapons delivery.

The OSO loaded the OAS with data using a data cartridge. He had a full suite of controls and displays for the OAS. The OAS navigation sensors included the AN/APQ-144 forward-looking radar (FLR) for ground mapping, the AN/APQ-146 TFR, an EVS with a forward-looking infrared camera, dual LN-15S internal navigation systems, the AN/APN-200 doppler radar, and the AN/APN-194 radar altimeter.

The magic happened inside the guidance and navigation ACU with an algorithm called a Kalman filter. One of the greatest achievements of applied mathematics, the Kalman filter was an esoteric development until engineers realized that it could be used to blend noisy and biased measurements from various sensors into an estimate of a vehicle's attitude, position and velocity more accurately than any of its input sensor measurements. The first operational application of the Kalman filter was in the Apollo Guidance Computer – astronauts would not have put their footprints on the moon without it.

Each of the B-1A OAS navigation sensors had advantages and disadvantages. The FLR could take accurate radar position fixes but only when the airplane had line-of-sight to a landmark that the radar could distinguish. The LN-15S inertial navigation systems were completely self-contained and provided high-bandwidth updates, but they could not determine their absolute position. Instead, they calculated the current position by integrating accelerations from a known starting point. The gyroscopes and accelerometers inside the LN-15S had biases and scale-factor errors that caused the inertial estimates of position and velocity to drift over time. The AN/APN-200 Doppler radar provided drift-free measurements of ground speed, but the measurements were low-bandwidth and noisy. The Kalman filter was programmed with the statistical characteristics of each sensor. With these sensor characteristics, the sensor data, and the previous calculations of sensor errors, the Kalman filter blended all sensor data into an optimal estimate of attitude, position, and velocity.

Navigating and guiding the B-1A along its planned flight path was one function of the OAS. The B-1A had to be in the right place at the right time to deliver weapons. The weapons delivery ACU pre-armed the nuclear warheads of the bombs and missiles, controlled the rotary launchers in the weapons bays, calculated the ballistics for dropping bombs, loaded SRAMs with their trajectories and targets, aligned the inertial measurement units on the SRAMs, and released the weapons. The ballistic calculations and SRAM transfer alignments used the attitude, position, and velocity data from the guidance and navigation ACU calculated by the Kalman filter.

The most important part of the B-1A TF system was the AN/APQ-146 TFR. The AN/APQ-146 had previously been used on the F-111F. It scanned the region in front of the B-1A to build a terrain profile and then calculated an optimal trajectory that balanced airplane performance, desired terrain clearance, and ground collision avoidance. Besides the TFR, the TF system used data from the OAS, radar altimeter, and flight instruments. The pilots could select TF clearance levels of 200, 300, 400, 500, 750, and 1,000ft AGL. They had a TFR indicator located between their instrument panels and TF guidance cues (climb/descend commands) displayed on their VSDs. The VSDs could also display forward-looking infrared imagery from the EVS. The TF system could be coupled to the AFCS for hands-off TF flight.

The Stores Management System (SMS) translated from the weapons delivery ACU to the physical weapons delivery systems. SMS features included weapons jettison and the unlock and consent capabilities required for nuclear weapons. It communicated with the FCGMS to pre-position fuel before weapons release to maintain the desired CG location. A critical nuclear surety feature of the SMS was that at least two crew members had to perform certain critical actions related to nuclear weapons.

Although the B-1B OAS (designated AN/ASQ-184) has the same general operational concept as the B-1A OAS, the intervening years between their designs produced numerous architecture, hardware, and software changes.

Compared to the B-1A, the B-1B upgraded every sensor in the OAS. The AN/APQ-164 Offensive Radar System (ORS) combines the functions of the TFR and FLR. The ORS has two complete channels of transmitters, receivers, and processors for redundancy; these ORS components are based extensively on their counterparts in the AN/APG-68 radar. The AN/APG-68 radar is used on the F-16C Fighting Falcon and is highly regarded for its reliability. The two radar channels share a single phased-array antenna. The AN/APQ-164 is designed to minimize the ability of the enemy to detect the B-1B.

Controlled by software, the ORS has multiple modes: real-beam ground mapping, monopulse ground mapping with Doppler beam sharpening, TF, terrain avoidance (TA),

The B-1A had a retractable EVS that provided infrared imagery to the pilots' VSDs and the OSO's MFD. The imagery was an aid to flying at low level at night. The B-1B does not have EVS. (*Greg Spahr collection*)

air-ground ranging, ground moving target indicator, weather detection, and rendezvous to find tankers. It also functions as a high-altitude radar altimeter for calculating height above the ground for high-altitude weapons release and as a backup Doppler radar for feeding drift and ground speed to the navigation system.

Later upgrades include a track-while-scan mode similar to a fighter aircraft's air-to-air mode to simplify tanker rendezvous. The phased array antenna is fundamental to the ORS's multimode capability, allowing it to replace two radars in the B-1A. The radar processor can time-share the one antenna, allowing the operator to interleave the various modes (e.g. TF and ground mapping). The antenna can create different beam shapes for different modes while time-interleaving the modes.

High-resolution ground mapping was a major new feature of the ORS with its Synthetic Aperture Radar (SAR) technology. With the high-accuracy phase and Doppler data from ground targets, augmented by precision velocity data from the OAS (calculated by the Kalman filter), the ORS can achieve much higher angular resolution than that provided solely by the antenna beamwidth.

As a young Air Force officer and flight test engineer, the author flew on a BAC 1-11 airliner being used as an airborne testbed for the ORS in support of the B-1B program. On that flight, the high-resolution ground map created by the ORS was sufficiently detailed to distinguish individual lights on the edge of a runway (for perspective, runway edge lights are about the size of a 2-liter soft drink bottle).

For a radar position update, the OSO uses ORS to take a high-resolution ground map centered on the position of a known landmark. The OSO then adjusts the crosshairs on the

The ORS phased array antenna contains a large number of phase shifters and can continue to operate if some of the phase shifters fail. The phase shifters work together to create the optimum beam shape for each radar mode. (*National Electronics Museum*)

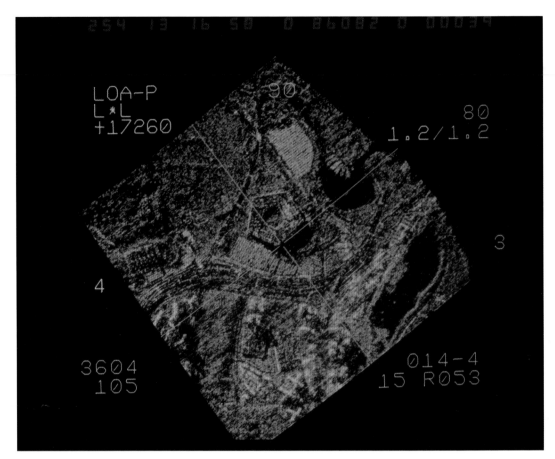

In high-resolution ground mapping mode, the ORS creates a detailed image of objects on the ground. On this ORS high-resolution ground map, the crosshairs have been placed on a corner of the Pentagon. This kind of cultural feature is an excellent radar position fix to input to the Kalman filter running in the Guidance and Navigation ACU and improve the accuracy of the position and velocity estimates. (*National Electronics Museum*)

radar display until they are directly on the landmark and has the OAS take a position fix. The radar position update from ORS tightens up the position estimate in the Kalman filter. The Kalman filter then does an even better job of calibrating the sources of errors in the other sensors, further improving navigation accuracy between radar position fixes.

The ORS has full TFR capability and creates a terrain profile for the 10 miles ahead of the aircraft. The ORS scan rate is adaptive based on the characteristics of the terrain. Instead of continually scanning the terrain, the ORS takes a 'snapshot' and uses that information until the system determines that another 'snapshot' is needed. The objective is to emit radar energy from the ORS as infrequently as possible to minimize the enemy's probability of detecting the emissions, while simultaneously building an accurate terrain profile. Functionally, the TF capabilities of the B-1A and B-1B are similar, though with slightly different Desired Flight Path (DFP) values (i.e. the desired altitude above the terrain). The B-1B is capable of setting a clearance plane above the terrain. Architecturally, the B-1A and B-1B TF systems differed.

The B-1A TF capability used a dedicated TFR, whereas the B-1B TF capability is just an ORS mode.

In the B-1B OAS, the SKN-2440 inertial navigation system, AN/APN-224 radar altimeter, and AN/APN-230 Doppler radar replaced earlier units in the B-1A OAS. The new sensors had the same function as the units they replaced, only with higher accuracy and reliability. The interlude between the cancellation of B-1A production and the decision to proceed with the B-1B had seen significant advances in avionics technology. The opportunity to update the OAS design allowed the B-1B to benefit from those advances. The B-1B OAS does not have EVS, which was omitted as a cost-saving measure.

The ACU complex, controls and displays in the B-1B OAS were thoroughly upgraded compared to the B-1A OAS. Each improved ACU is of the AP-101F type, derived from the AP-101C computers used in the AN/ASQ-176 OAS for the B-52G/H but with two and half times the speed. There are seven ACUs in the B-1B: guidance and navigation, weapons delivery, controls and displays, back-up, TF (two) and a preprocessor used by the DAS.

Defensive Avionics System

The DAS must foil the best efforts of sophisticated air defense forces to shoot down the B-1, although it is only one component of B-1 survivability. Others include the ability of the B-1 on alert to depart its base quickly before the base is destroyed, TF flight to hide the B-1 in ground clutter, and use terrain masking, reduced RCS, and systems redundancies to enable the mission to be accomplished despite battle damage.

The DAS was the most difficult B-1 system to develop. Material properties, atmospheric characteristics, and the laws of physics do not change with malicious intent to thwart the developers of the B-1 airframe, engine, and systems. The DAS must counter evolving threats from an intelligent adversary. The knowledge of those threats, acquired through opaque intelligence sources, is often incomplete and sometimes incorrect. The B-1's threat environment would be different and more lethal after it was fielded than when it was designed. DAS designers needed to 'chase a moving target' in a way that differed from the task of the engineers working on any other part of the B-1.

The black art of ECM came of age during the Second World War. It was imperative to jam or deceive radio-navigation systems, ground-based anti-aircraft radars, radar-equipped fighters, and radio-command-guided anti-ship missiles. When the offending signal was received, an operator used the information provided by the receiver to determine the characteristics of the threat and then select an ECM tactic. The ECM tactic was implemented using a transmitter or an expendable such as chaff.

As electronic threats proliferated in quantity and capability, human operators became overwhelmed and unable to respond swiftly. The B-1 DAS has the same design philosophy as the OAS: a combination of computerized automation with the option to insert a human operator in the loop when adaptability is required. The B-1 DAS differs qualitatively from the electronic receivers and jammers on the B-52. The B-52 is operator-centric, with the Electronic Warfare Officer (EWO) monitoring the electronic threat environment and deciding how to employ the jammers.

In contrast, the B-1 DAS is automation–centric, with a computer analyzing the electronic threat environment and controlling the jammers. The computers engage in 'sensor fusion', integrating the information from multiple receivers into a composite picture. The DAS is reprogrammable on several levels: by the operator and through the rapid deployment of firmware, software, and threat library upgrades.

All signals received by the DAS are automatically categorized by their frequency, pulse width, pulse repetition frequency, bearing, and time of arrival. The frequency, pulse width, and pulse repetition frequency information are compared against a threat library that specifies priority and preferred jamming technique. A fire control radar currently guiding a missile to intercept the B-1 would be a higher priority threat than a target acquisition radar searching for it. The DAS then selects the transmitter and antenna best suited to counter the threat.

The DSO on the B-1 is not merely a passive observer – he can perform monitoring and analysis and then select jamming techniques. Consequently, the B-1 DAS has the best of both worlds: the fast reaction time of an automatic system and the option to put a highly trained human operator in the loop to creatively manage unplanned situations.

The B-1A DAS was designated the AN/ALQ-161. The DAS had three sectors that each covered approximately 120° of the aircraft. The equipment in the left glove covered forward and to the left. Similarly, the ALQ-161 components in the right glove covered forward and to the right. The DAS equipment in the aft radome covered the rear of the aircraft. Presumably the AN/ALQ-161 covered the spectrum of Soviet threat radars at the time of its development and could use ECM techniques including noise jamming and deception jamming. The AN/

The nose radome covers the ORS. Large radomes on the left and right gloves of the B-1B cover the elements of the DAS that protect the front and sides of the aircraft. The radomes are a slightly different shade of gray than the rest of the airframe. (Roelof-Jan Gort)

The rounded radome on the aft end of the B-1B covers the DAS transmitters and receivers that protect the rear aspect of the aircraft. The aft end of the 'stinger' at the intersection of the horizontal stabilators and the vertical stabilizer houses the DAS tail warning function. There is also a small DAS component on the back of the tip of the vertical stabilizer. (Roelof-Jan Gort)

ALQ-161 was computerized for automatic responses to threats and presented digitized information to the two EDUs used by the DSO.

The B-1A had four AN/ALE-48 chaff dispensers and four AN/ALE-49 flare dispensers on the dorsal side of the forward intermediate fuselage that ejected expendables. Chaff consisted of thin strips of aluminized material cut to specific lengths to maximize their RCS to radars of a particular frequency. Flares emitted heat at a similar frequency to the hot exhaust nozzles of jet engines. The purpose of chaff and flares was to create attractive targets that would draw radar and infra-red homing missiles, respectively, away from the B-1A.

The results of the BPE have never been declassified. Nonetheless, the AN/ALQ-161 on B-1A Ship 4 was flown against the most advanced American radars, such as those on the F-15A and E-3A – revealing what concerned the USAF. Presumably these systems were assumed to represent the Soviet air defense systems that a future USAF bomber would face.

When the B-1 was revived in the form of the B-1B, the B-1B was to be equipped with the AN/ALQ-161A as its DAS. The AN/ALQ-161A is an advanced version of the B-1A's AN/ALQ-161, with its design informed by the BPE results, the latest intelligence about the Soviet threat, and advances in avionics technology.

Compared to the AN/ALQ-161, the AN/ALQ-161A has several new features:

- Addition of a Tail Warning Function (TWF), an active radar that covers the aft sector of the B-1B and detects incoming fighters and missiles, even if they are not emitting radar energy.
- Extended warning and jamming coverage at the high end of the frequency range.

- Receivers for early warning/ground-controlled intercept radars at the low end of the frequency range.
- Digital radio-frequency memory to jammed pulse-Doppler radars used on the most Soviet fire control radars at the time of its design.
- ACU of the same sort used by the OAS, functioning as a preprocessor for the DAS.
- DSO controls and displays – the Defensive Management System (DMS) – considered part of the AN/ASQ-184 and integrated with the OAS.

The B-1B also has the chaff and flare dispensers.

Left: The black rectangles on the dorsal side of the fuselage aft of the crew compartment mark the locations of the chaff and flare dispensers. (*Ken Middleton*)

Below: Countermeasure flares are a last-ditch defense against heat-seeking missiles. The theory of operation of the flares is that they are a more attractive target for the missile seekers than the B-1B. (*Master Sergeant Kevin J. Gruenwald/US Air Force*)

Chapter 6

Nuclear Weapons

'The United States acquires and maintains nuclear forces for four principal reasons:

- To deter nuclear attacks on the United States.
- To help deter conventional and nuclear attacks on U.S. allies.
- To strengthen U.S. power and influence in world affairs.
- To engage in nuclear wars should deterrence fail.'

Alton H. Quanbeck and Archie L. Wood with the assistance of Louisa Thoron,
Modernizing the Strategic Bomber Force: Why and How, 1976

Nuclear Bombs

The purpose of the B-1 was to deliver nuclear weapons – or more accurately, if less concisely, to deter war by being able to deliver nuclear weapons. The B-1 always had some conventional capabilities and these would become increasingly important over the life of the BONE, but it was designed for the nuclear mission. The nuclear arsenal of the B-1 included both bombs and missiles.

The Mk 1 Little Boy was the first nuclear weapon used in combat. Delivered by a B-29 Superfortress flying at high altitude, the Little Boy free fell until a radar fuze initiated an airburst. Little Boy detonated with a yield of 15-KT (kilotons, i.e. a blast equivalent to 15,000 tons of high explosives), devastating the Japanese city of Hiroshima. The blast, thermal, and radiation effects of the bomb killed an unknown number of people, but the death toll probably exceeded 100,000.

Between the Mk 1 of 1945 and the B-1A program, nuclear bombs became vastly more powerful through the use of thermonuclear fusion. They also had improved safety and security features. Reflecting the change in strategy and tactics, nuclear bombs were designed for high-speed low-altitude delivery. Hardened targets such as underground command and control facilities and missile silos were the primary targets of the new weapons.

During FSD, the B-1A dropped B43 and B61 shapes (inert practice bombs with the aerodynamic and mass properties of the actual weapons). The B43 from Los Alamos Scientific Laboratory (LASL) had a primary operational mode called 'laydown'. During a laydown delivery, the bomber dropped the bomb, typically at high speed and low altitude. Shortly after release, the bomb deployed a parachute from its tail that slowed it down. Decelerating the bomb reduced the shock when it hit the ground so that it would not break apart on impact. The B43 had a hardened steel spike on its nose. The spike dug into the ground on contact, which kept the bomb in place and prevented it from skidding along the ground further from the aim point. The bomb then lay on the ground (hence 'laydown'), while a timer counted down for a short time until detonation. The delay allowed the bomber to escape the blast zone of the bomb. Because the bomb detonated on the ground rather than as an airburst, its blast radius was smaller because much of the energy of the explosion was absorbed by the ground rather than spread outward. Although less effective against urban/industrial targets covering a large area, a ground burst dug a crater which ideally would vaporize the ground in which a hardened target had been located. The ground burst also transmitted a strong shockwave through the ground which could destroy buried targets even if they were not in the crater. The B43 was produced in five models which had yields that ranged from 70-KT to 1-MT (megatons, equal to 1,000 kilotons).

The B61 from LASL was a second-generation laydown weapon. It was designed for even lower and faster delivery than the B43. The B61 had a dial-a-yield (DAY) feature which meant that a fixed yield was not set at manufacture, as in the B43. Instead, the yield could be selected on the ground before flight, or in later versions of the B61 set by the OSO using OAS and SMS. The B61 also had the Full-Fuzing Option (FUFO), which meant that the bomb mode could be set inflight for free-fall, retarded or laydown by the OSO. In theory, the versatility of the B61 would allow the B-1A crew to perform optimized attacks on targets which bomb damage assessment had shown to have survived the first wave of attack by ballistic missiles. The B61 also had an improved Permissive Action Link (PAL) which prevented the bomb from arming unless a code was entered using the SMS, an important measure to prevent an unauthorized nuclear detonation.

The streamlined shape of the B61 thermonuclear bomb is necessary for high-speed, low-altitude delivery. The nose contains shock-absorbing honeycomb material. The fins stabilize the bomb until the parachute deploys from the tail section. The bomb is suspended from the ejector rack by two hooks with 30-inch spacing. (*Master Sergeant Ken Hammond/US Air Force*)

A series of concentric frangible rings form the shock-absorbing nose of the B83. The actual thermonuclear device is in the forward part of the bomb. The aft third of the bomb contains three pilot parachutes and the 46-foot diameter main parachute. (*Master Sergeant Ken Hammond/US Air Force*)

The first B-1B (tail number 82-0001) performs a laydown of a B83 on the Tonopah Test Range on 11 June 1986 during flight testing. An F-111 chase plane observes the release. The chase crew could notify the B-1B crew and examine the B-1B for damage if the separation was not clean and the B83 hit the B-1B. (*Air Force Test Center History Office*)

Had the B-1A entered service, the B43 would have been replaced by the B77, designed at the Lawrence Livermore National Laboratory (LLNL). The B77 was a state-of-the-art thermonuclear bomb designed for high-speed, low-altitude delivery, with FUFO, DAY, and PAL features. The maximum B77 yield was 1 MT. Designed to be dropped from altitudes as low as 100ft AGL, the B77 had elaborate roll stabilization and dual-parachute retardation systems. The roll stabilization system kept the correct side of the B77 pointing up until the lifting parachute deployed to increase the altitude of the B77 to 300ft AGL. At that altitude, the main parachute deployed to lower the B77 to the ground so it would impact at the desired angle to dig in its nose rather than skip along the ground. The B77 program was cancelled in December 1977, its cancellation being related to the cancellation of the B-1A.

The B-1B was armed with two nuclear bombs, initially the B61 and later the B83. The B83 was a simplified and less expensive derivative of the B77. Like the B77, the B83 was designed at LLNL. With no roll stabilization or dual parachute systems, the B83 had to be delivered from a higher (but still quite low) altitude than the minimum altitude for a B77 drop. The 1-MT ground burst of the B83 put the most heavily hardened and deeply buried targets in the Soviet Union at risk. Even if a B83 had not been able breach certain bunkers built into solid rock, those facilities still needed access to the surface for entry and exit, communications links, and air ducts for breathing and powering generators. An accurately delivered B83 would have made those bunkers into sealed-off tombs for their occupants.

Missiles

The USAF began preliminary work on the AGM-69A SRAM in January 1963. Originally intended for the B-52G/H and the FB-111A, the SRAM became one of the primary armaments of AMSA when that concept emerged. In November 1965, the USAF selected Boeing as SRAM prime contractor over its competitor, Martin.

The SRAM was smaller, lighter, faster, and more reliable than the previous air-launched stand-off missile, the AGM-28 Hound Dog. Prior to launch, its inertial measurement unit was aligned using a position, velocity, and attitude data transfer from OAS. The accuracy of the OAS navigation solution used as the reference for the SRAM transfer alignment was critical to SRAM accuracy; any transfer alignment errors propagated into SRAM miss distance. SRAM had a two-pulse solid rocket motor. The first pulse accelerated the missile away from the carrier aircraft. After the first pulse, the SRAM cruised until the second pulse started to accelerate it towards the target. The SRAM could fly a ballistic trajectory or a TF trajectory using a radar altimeter to measure height above the ground. The maximum range of the SRAM was 35 miles for a low-altitude launch and TF trajectory; longer for a high-altitude launch and/or ballistic trajectory. The primary role of the SRAM was destruction of enemy air defenses. Fired from outside the range of Soviet surface-to-air missiles, the SRAM would approach a radar or missile site at Mach 3 and with a low RCS, making it a very difficult target for radar-guided missiles. The SRAM was not as accurate as a well-aimed bomb, but radars and missile launchers were soft and exposed targets vulnerable to the airburst from the SRAM's 170-KT W69 warhead, a LASL design with DAY and multiple modes. The SRAM also had a secondary role against strategic relocatable targets such as mobile missile launchers.

Three fins controlled the SRAM in flight. Munitions load crews used inert missiles for training purposes. (*Master Sergeant Ken Hammond/US Air Force*)

Members of the 96th Munitions Maintenance Squadron inspect an inert AGM-69A SRAM after removing it from the weapons bay of a B-1B bomber. (*Technical Sergeant Kit Thompson/US Air Force*)

The B-1A conducted two test launches of the AGM-69A SRAM, but the intended version for the production B-1A was the AGM-69B, an improved model. The AGM-69B was cancelled along with the B-1A. It would have had a W80 nuclear warhead, new computer with more memory, higher nuclear hardness, and a solid rocket motor with longer storage life.

The AGM-69A did see operational service on the B-1B, but only for a short time. When the B-1B first went on alert on 1 October 1986, it was armed with B61 and SRAM. Safety concerns over its aging solid-rocket motor and W69 warhead led to its retirement in June 1990. The retirement of the AGM-69A was earlier than desired, but not entirely unanticipated. Its replacement already was under development. In 1985, the USAF issued contracts to Boeing, Martin Marietta, and McDonnell Douglas for the definition of the AGM-131A SRAM II concept. SRAM II was intended to be twice as accurate as the original SRAM with three times the range, in a smaller and lighter missile.

B-1B 82-0001 first fired the SRAM on the Tonapah Test Range on 16 January 1987. The SRAM had previously been fired twice from B-1A Ship 3. Low-altitude launches of the SRAM were a severe test for the missile. Ignition of the solid rocket motor could only be done after the SRAM cleared the launch aircraft but needed to be done as early as possible after clearing the aircraft to avoid having an unpowered missile impacting the ground. The launch conditions on this test were Mach 0.9, 500ft AGL altitude, wings swept at 67.5 degrees, and the SRAM dropped from the intermediate weapons bay. An F-111 is chasing the B-1B. (*Air Force Test Center History Office*)

The USAF awarded the SRAM II contract to Boeing in December 1986. An integrated rocket/ramjet propulsion system had been considered for the missile, but eventually SRAM II got a solid rocket motor like SRAM, although of a new design. Compared to SRAM, SRAM II also had improved electronics, a more accurate inertial system, and extensive use of composite materials that saved 400lbs of weight. There had been considerable pressure from Congress to save money by reusing the W69 warhead on the SRAM II. But it ended up with a new warhead, the W89 from LLNL.

SRAM II had several development delays because of cracks in the new motor and changes in the W89 warhead. B-1B tests of the SRAM II included vibration and acoustics surveys of an instrumented missile shape in the bomb bays, captive carry tests with an inert missile to verify avionics integration between the aircraft and missile, and jettison tests from all three weapons bays. On 27 September 1991, President George H. W. Bush announced sweeping cuts to American nuclear forces as the Cold War was coming to an end. Amongst the reductions was the cancellation of the SRAM II, which was in serious technical trouble with motor cracks and had yet to have its first powered flight.

The AGM-86B ALCM had originally been a competitor to the B-1A, and President Carter's decision to choose to equip the B-52 with the ALCM spelled the demise of the B-1A. But after

The SRAM II never had a powered flight prior to its cancellation because of cracks discovered in the solid-rocket motors. Several JTVs were released from a B-1B. (*Air Force Test Center History Office*)

the cancellation of the B-1A, subsequent B-1 concepts such as SWL, SAL, and LRCA all used the B-1 as an ALCM carrier. The B-1 had considerable merit as an ALCM carrier. Compared to the B-52, it could escape from its base faster in the event of a surprise attack. Also, the 1,500-mile range of the ALCM could keep the B-52 far away from terminal defense such as short-range interceptors and surface-to-air missiles, but the Soviets were developing airborne warning and control aircraft to guide advanced long-range interceptors that might shoot down the B-52 before it launched its load of ALCMs. The B-1 with its superior DAS and lower RCS would make it more survivable against this emerging threat. From the beginning, the B-1B was designed to carry ALCM.

The ALCM load for the B-1B was designed to be twenty-two missiles. Eight ALCMs would be carried internally and fourteen externally on hardpoints underneath the fuselage. The B-1B first launched an ALCM on 24 November 1987. Despite the successful ALCM test launch, the ALCM never achieved operational capability on the B-1B. The reason for the decision to omit the ALCM from the B-1B had nothing to do with engineering. In 1979, President Carter and Soviet leader Leonid Brezhnev signed the Strategic Arms Limitation Treaty 2 (SALT 2) in an attempt to arrest the nuclear arms race. The treaty was highly controversial in the United States, and the Senate never ratified SALT 2. Paradoxically, President Reagan, who opposed SALT 2, directed the American government to essentially comply with the terms of the treaty even through it had not been ratified. The treaty limited bombers to the carriage of no more than twenty cruise missiles. Also, the treaty limited the number of bombers that could be

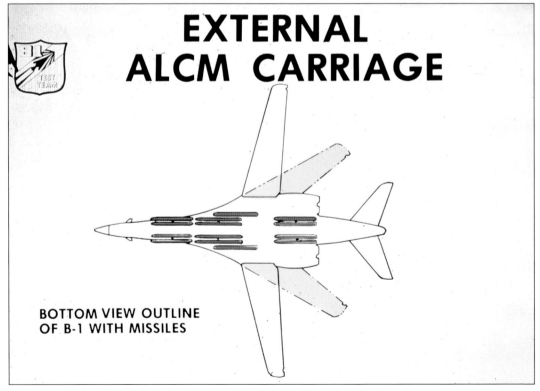

The B-1B was designed to carry 14 AGM-86B ALCMs externally and eight internally. The ALCM capability of the B-1B was never operationally fielded. (*Stephen Henry collection*)

armed with cruise missiles, and equipping the B-1B with them would have exceeded that limit. Consequently, the B-1B never was armed with the ALCM in operational units. The AGM-129A Advanced Cruise Missile (ACM) was the intended replacement for the ALCM. Compared to the ALCM, ACM had longer range, higher accuracy, and most importantly, low observables that gave an extremely small RCS. Some captive-carry testing of ACM was conducted on the B-1B – this entailed in-flight testing of a missile which was powered-up and communicating with OAS but launched. ACM was only actually launched from the B-52H – never the B-1B – and operationally fielded with that aircraft as its carrier.

Launchers

The B-1 had three weapons bays, each equipped with a rotary launcher to carry eight nuclear weapons. The rotary launchers had an electronically controlled, hydromechanical drive to rotate the launcher so that the weapon to be launched was in the bottom position. There were two types of launchers for nuclear weapons, one for bombs and one for SRAMs. The two launchers were similar, but the SRAM rotary launcher had extra equipment needed for the missiles. Attached to the rotary launcher tube, ejector racks with 30-inch hook spacing carried and released the weapons. On the B-1B, the rotary launch tubes were made out of filament-wound graphite/epoxy composites, which saved 400lbs per launcher. A loaded launcher was heavy

Looking forward in the forward weapons bay, the forward pivot point for the rotary launcher is visible. A perforated spoiler at the front end of the weapons bay extends down into the airstream prior to door opening to eliminate cavity resonance and acoustic vibration when the bay doors are open. (*Author*)

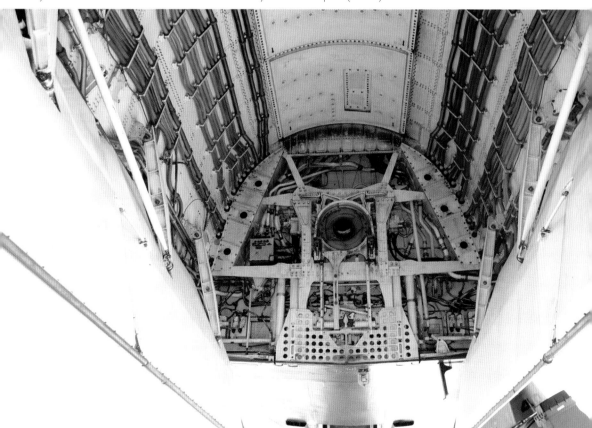

Looking rearward, the store's air conditioning unit provides air to a duct that feeds into the aft pivot point for the rotary launcher. The conditioned air cools the SRAM missile electronics prior to launch. The weapons bay doors have a graphite/epoxy composite skin over an aluminum honeycomb. They are partially open for weapons delivery and fully open for loading and unloading weapons on the ground. (*Author*)

enough that when it rotated, the crew could sense the aircraft rotating around its longitudinal axis in the opposite direction.

Starting with the Lot III aircraft, the B-1B had a movable bulkhead between the forward and intermediate weapons bays to accommodate the longer rotary launcher used for the ALCM. The rotary launcher for ALCM carried eight missiles. When it was installed, no weapons could be carried in the forward bay, only a small fuel tank. The external hardpoints for ALCM or ACM were permanently disabled for reasons of arms control treaty compliance.

This B-1B is carrying six ACM pylons, each of which carries two missiles. The pylons are not actually loaded with missiles in this photograph. The intermediate weapons bay doors are open. (*Erik Simonsen collection*)

Chapter 7

B-1B Development and Testing

'The B-1 offers a way of doing that which is credible and early and which will be noticed by the Soviet Union in a very major way.'

General Lew Allen, Jr., USAF Chief of Staff, 1978–1982

A Better B-1

The B-1B would become America's next bomber, complementing the B-52 and strengthening the airborne leg of the strategic triad while the USAF and Northrop developed the more ambitious B-2A Spirit. Being an interim solution to a need that was perceived to be urgent, the B-1B needed to be affordable and rapidly deployed. Congress established a program cost baseline of $20.5 billion in 1981 dollars. The USAF set a target for Initial Operational Capability (IOC) in 1986.

A key step in executing the B-1B program was to set up a System Program Office (SPO) at the USAF's Aeronautical Systems Division at Wright Patterson AFB, Ohio. The SPO was responsible for managing the research, development, test, production, and acquisition of the B-1B. It contained all the functions necessary to accomplish these tasks, among which were program management, engineering, logistics, manufacturing and quality assurance, and contracting. The SPO managed the contracts with Rockwell and the other contractors. It also funded the test work conducted by AFFTC; the SPO was AFFTC's customer for its test activities and reporting.

When B-1A production was cancelled, the remaining B-1A work was folded into the Strategic Systems SPO, which also had the B-52 OAS, ALCM, and SRAM in its portfolio. With the revival of the B-1, the B-1B SPO was created with Major General Melvin F. Chubb, Jr. as the System Program Director. Chubb had previously been the System Program Director for the Strategic Systems SPO. Chubb's tenure with the B-1B was short-lived. He was soon promoted out of his position and replaced by Major General William E. Thurman.

The normal practice in the development and acquisition of defense systems was that the military worked with a prime contractor. That prime contractor in turn managed subcontractors for engines, avionics, and other systems. Subcontractor management was expensive, and the prime contractor passed those costs onto the military customer. In order to reduce costs, the B-1B SPO took on the role of integrating contractor and the responsibility of coordinating Rockwell, GE, Boeing, and AIL, a function for which it had neither the expertise nor staffing. Consider a situation in which the OAS and DAS were interfering with each other. Under a traditional prime contract, Rockwell would have worked with AIL and Boeing to analyze and solve the problem. With no prime contractor, it fell to the SPO to integrate the work of the different contractors.

The B-1B was a new airplane, but it was not a 'clean sheet of paper' design, being based on the B-1A. To meet the 1986 IOC date, the first B-1B needed to begin flight testing in 1984. This meant production of the first aircraft needed to begin in 1983 and represented a significant challenge for the B-1B team. However, the program risk was deemed acceptable because of the B-1A flight test activity that continued through 1981, parallel technology maturation on the B-52G/H OAS, and industry activity in anticipation of President Reagan's announcement.

Left: Major General William E. Thurman was the B-1B System Program Director from November 1981 through May 1985. He had previously served in the same role on the F-16 program. (*Master Sergeant Mike Dial/US Air Force*)

Below: Data collected during the B-1A flight test program reduced B-1B technical risk and made it feasible to conduct concurrent development, testing, and production of the B-1B. (*Staff Sergeant Bill Thompson/US Air Force*)

Rockwell remained the airframe contractor. On 20 January 1982, the USAF and Rockwell signed two contracts. The FSD contract covered development, test, and associated activities, and cost $1.317 billion. A second contract valued at $886 million covered Lot I production and long-lead items for subsequent lots. GE, Boeing, and AIL (since sold by Cutler-Hammer to Eaton Corporation) had the same roles on the B-1B as they did on the B-1A.

ORS Development

One of the most important changes from the B-1A to the B-1B was the replacement of the FLR and TFR with a single multimode radar, the ORS. Hughes and Westinghouse competed to be the ORS supplier. Boeing, in its role as contractor for OAS, selected Westinghouse to provide ORS in December 1981, shortly after President Reagan announced his B-1B decision.

A radar is a complex piece of equipment. A multimode ORS is more complex, but it can provide significantly higher reliability and performance. Traditionally, airborne radars had used an antenna which was mechanically scanned. The antenna had a fixed radiation pattern, and the mechanical scanning mechanism was prone to failure.

B-52G 59-2568 was the EAR testbed. Sponsored by the Air Force Avionics Laboratory, EAR proved the radar technology that would later be used on the AN/APQ-164 ORS on the B-1B. (*National Electronics Museum*)

Westinghouse, the ORS supplier, modified a BAC 1-11 airliner to be a flying testbed for the AN/APQ-164 ORS. It carried the vanity civil registration N164W (164 for AN/APQ-164, W for Westinghouse). (*National Electronics Museum*)

Boeing's selection of the Westinghouse ORS traced its origins to the Electronically Agile Radar (EAR) program sponsored by the Air Force Avionics Laboratory and developed by Westinghouse. The Westinghouse EAR underwent five years and thousands of hours of testing in labs and BAC 1-11 and B-52G aircraft. The testing demonstrated the reliability and high performance of EAR and its phased-array antenna. Combining the phased-array antenna with a programmable signal processor, EAR could perform multiple functions in a time-interleaved manner. EAR used a phased-array antenna with 1,818 phase-shifter/emitter elements. By having the phase-shifter/emitter elements radiate at slightly different times, the radar beam could take on multiple shapes, with different shapes for different modes. The same phase-shifting mechanism enabled the beam to be moved and scanned without any movement by the antenna. The testing demonstrated the reliability and high performance of EAR and its phased-array antenna.

The original Westinghouse ORS proposal in 1981 used two antennas, one for the FLR modes and one for the TFR mode. But the successful technology development on the EAR program led Westinghouse to propose in February 1982 a single phased-array antenna for ORS to replace the two antennas. Boeing endorsed the change, and SPO director Thurman approved it in March 1982.

Radar technology is developed in a laboratory but needs to be tested in a dynamic environment that cannot be fully replicated in the laboratory. Because of the compressed test schedule, Westinghouse outfitted a BAC 1-11 airliner as an airborne testbed for ORS to reduce

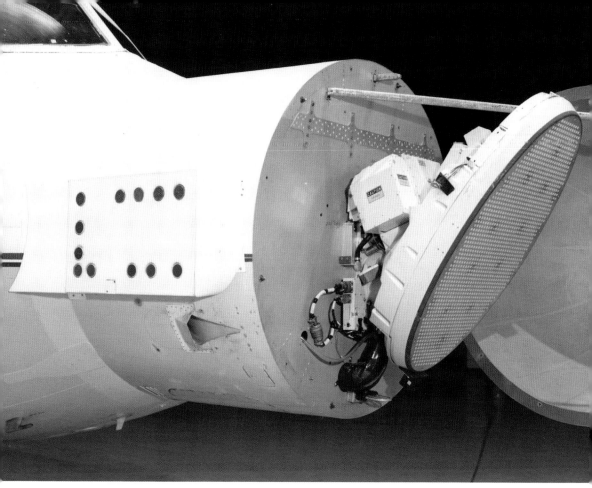

The ORS antenna and electronics were mounted in the highly modified nose of the BAC 1-11. (*National Electronics Museum*)

technical risk. Most of the development testing for ORS would be done on the BAC 1-11. ORS testing on the B-1B itself focused on those functions that required a high degree of integration with other B-1B systems, particularly TF which tied in closely with the airframe and flight control system. The BAC 1-11 was instrumental in resolving early issues on the TF software.

B-1A Ships 2 and 4 Return to the Air

One implication of the compressed B-1B program schedule was that there were less than two years between the first flight of the B-1B in 1984 and the IOC on 1 October 1986. The B-1B was based on the B-1A but it had many new features to test. Ideally, the ramp at Edwards AFB would be filled with multiple B-1B aircraft conducting the full range of flight sciences and mission systems tests. However, achieving the IOC milestone required more than just completing enough of DT&E and IOT&E for SAC to declare the B-1B operational. The first B-1B wing would need its own airplanes to train the initial cadre of aircrew and maintainers and put at least a token force on alert. The one B-1B initially allocated to flight testing would clearly be insufficient by itself, but the B-1A fleet still existed. B-1A Ships 2 and 4 were modified with certain B-1B features to become testbeds for the B-1B. This move tripled the number of flight test aircraft and allowed B-1B flight testing to begin nineteen months before the first B-1B flew.

B-1A Ships 1 and 3 would not return to the air, but maintainers would cannibalize parts from them to keep Ships 2 and 4 flying.

With the resumption of flight testing, AFFTC created the B-1B Combined Test Force (CTF). A CTF was the same thing as a JTF, but since 'Joint' had come to mean multi-service in Department of Defense argot, CTF was the new name. AFFTC assigned test pilot Lieutenant Colonel Leroy B. Schroeder to be the director of the B-1B CTF. Schroeder would be succeeded in August 1984 by Colonel K. Warren Brotnov, who had been the first B-1A OSO. Lieutenant Colonel C. Wayne Staley and then Lieutenant Colonel Harold R. 'Randy' Gaston followed Brotnov. What had previously been called AFTEC was now known as the Air Force Operational Test and Evaluation Center (AFOTEC). Detachment 5 of AFOTEC reported on the B-1B testing directly to the Director of Operational Test and Evaluation, who in turn reported to the Secretary of Defense and Congress. Lieutenant Colonel Robert Vacker led the AFOTEC component of the B-1B CTF.

One of the keys to program success is promoting the program and keeping it politically sold. The test aircraft helped promote the program. B-1A Ship 4 returned to flight with four shakedown and pilot proficiency flights at Edwards AFB (Flight 4-71, 6 August 1982; Flight 4-72A/B, 11 August 1982; Flight 4-73, 17 August 1982; Flight 4-74A/B, 23 August 1982). Then B-1A Ship 4 flew non-stop from Edwards AFB to the Farnborough Air Show in the United Kingdom with the assistance of aerial refueling. Flight 4-75, the longest B-1A flight to date (11.4 hours) occurred on 1–2 September 1982. The crew consisted of Schroeder, Rockwell B-1 chief test pilot Tommie Douglas 'Doug' Benefield, OSO Lieutenant Colonel Tom W. Alexander

Flight 4-70 (30 April 1981), conducted by B-1A Ship 4, was the last flight of the B-1A program. (*Air Force Test Center History Office*)

On 6 August 1982, B-1A Ship 4 underwent a functional checkout, signaling its return to flight status. Pilot Tommie D. Benefield, co-pilot Lieutenant Colonel Leroy B. Schroeder, OSO Lieutenant Colonel Tom W. Alexander, and flight test engineer James A. Leasure were the crew for Flight 4-71. (*Staff Sergeant Bob Simons/US Air Force*)

of the 4200th TES, and Rockwell flight test engineer James A. Leasure. The B-1A was on static display during the airshow; it did not conduct a flight demonstration. William H. Gregory, the editor-in-chief of the influential aerospace industry publication *Aviation Week & Space Technology* gushed: 'The B-1's size and sleek potency awed the public and professionals alike.'

After Farnborough, B-1A Ship 4 returned to the United States, stopping at Andrews AFB, Maryland (Flight 4-76, 13 September 1982) and Offutt AFB, Nebraska (Flight 4-78, 17 September 1982), home of SAC headquarters. Flight 4-77 (17 September 1982) had been intended to go to Offutt AFB, but Ship 4 returned to Andrews AFB when the DSO hatch separated. General Charles A. Gabriel, the USAF Chief of Staff, flew as one of the pilots on Flight 4-77.

Starting in 1982, B-1A Ship 2 underwent a modification period to become the flight sciences testbed for the B-1B. Its SCAS was updated to the B-1B standard. It also added weapons bay spoilers and graphite/epoxy composite weapons bay doors. The latter two features supported weapons tests. Having no OAS, Ship 2 was not intended to test weapons delivery accuracy. The focus of its weapons work would be the vibration and acoustics environment in the weapons bays and the aerodynamic separation characteristics of weapons. A total of 1,700 parameters were recorded on B-1A Ship 2. Fifty-two of the parameters were telemetered to the ground and displayed on strip charts in the mission control room for real-time monitoring.

Above: B-1A Ship 4 crosses the Atlantic Ocean on the way to the Farnborough Air Show on Flight 4-75. At 11.4 hours, Flight 4-75 was the longest B-1A flight to date. (*Technical Sergeant Boyd Belcher/US Air Force*)

Left: (L to R) Lieutenant Colonel Tom W. Alexander, James A. Leasure, Tommie D. Benefield and Lieutenant Colonel Leroy B. Schroeder flew B-1A Ship 4 to and from Farnborough. (*Technical Sergeant Boyd Belcher/US Air Force*)

Below: The B-1B team designed an attractive patch for the Farnborough Air Show. When the patches arrived from the manufacturer, it was discovered that red and blue had been reversed on the flag of the host nation. In the best tradition of engineering resourcefulness, Rockwell flight test engineer James A. Leasure and his wife Sandy painted the correct colors on the patches with model airplane paint and some deft brushwork, averting a minor international incident. (*Technical Sergeant Boyd Belcher/US Air Force*)

B-1A Ship 4 has departed Andrews AFB and is being refueled during Flight 4-78 (19 September 1982) to Offutt AFB, home of SAC headquarters. (*Dennis Plummer/US Air Force*)

B-1A Ship 2 returned to the air to support the B-1B flight test program. At first it retained its glossy white paint but gained a spiffy 'B1B Test Program' logo on its vertical stabilizer. Note the '2' on the nose landing gear bay door. (*US Air Force*)

B–1A Ship 2 completed its modifications and returned to the air on Flight 2-61 on 23 March 1983. The crew consisted of Benefield (pilot), Schroeder (co-pilot) and Leasure (flight test engineer). The crew conducted system and handling qualities checks, opened the forward weapons bay doors, and did 'dry' (no actual fuel transfer) aerial refueling with a KC-135A. Flight 2-61 was prematurely terminated due to an engine vibration warning, landing after 3.3 hours of flight.

Upon returning to flight, B–1A Ship 2 entered a productive period of flight testing. High on the list of testing priorities was the new HML feature in SCAS. Any change in the flight control system required a significant amount of regression testing to verify that the changes didn't adversely affect other characteristics of the system. Vibration and acoustics test results were favorable, with the weapons bay spoilers and composite bay doors having no apparent problems. In addition to the tests, the Ship 2 flight tests allowed a new generation of test pilots and flight test engineers to get checked out in the B–1.

By early June 1983, Ship 2 had completed eleven flights totaling 42.4 hours. During a ground test of the flight control system, the horizontal stabilator controls were damaged when a component came into a contact with a piece of structure. The aircraft was grounded while the incident was investigated. Engineers determined that the root cause of the problem was the way that Ship 2 had been modified to have a B–1B flight control system installed in its B–1A airframe. During the modifications, a bulkhead in the aft fuselage/vertical stabilizer transition area was cut back to make room for the new flight control system and then a doubler was added to the bulkhead to reinforce it. The doubler reduced clearance. At the limit of its movement, a bellcrank contacted the bulkhead, causing the damage. During the grounding, the flight control

Flight 2-61 (23 March 1983) was the first flight of B-1A Ship 2 that was part of the B-1B program. Pilot Tommie D. Benefield, co-pilot Lieutenant Colonel Leroy B. Schroeder and flight test engineer James A. Leasure conducted a functional checkout of systems on the 3.4-hour mission. The crew in an F-111 chase aircraft could spot fluid leaks, loose panels or other problems that the B-1A crew could not see from the cockpit. (*Technical Sergeant William B. Belcher/US Air Force*)

B-1A Ship refuels from NKC-135A 55-3127 on Flight 2-61. On this flight, there was only a dry hook-up and the B-1A did not take fuel. This tanker had decidedly non-standard portholes on the sides through which instruments observed nuclear explosions earlier in its service life. By 1983, it had reverted to being used as a tanker but retained the portholes. (*Technical Sergeant William B. Belcher/US Air Force*)

system and structure of Ship 2 were modified to prevent a recurrence. Ship 2 returned to the air on Flight 72 (8 July 1983).

When B-1A Ship 2 resumed flying in support of B-1B development, it still had its B-1A gloss white paint scheme with prominent B-1B markings on the vertical stabilizer. In 1984 it was repainted in the green and two-tone gray scheme of the B-1B, an event that was remembered, albeit not fondly, by the AFFTC workforce. Ship 2 was painted outside because it was too big to paint inside a hangar. The high winds that are common at Edwards AFB, particularly in the afternoon, blew overspray which ended up in the parking lot outside the B-1B CTF. People were not pleased to find speckles of green and gray on their vehicles.

[Author's note: Some CTF members recall a slightly different story: that the overspray came from painting ground fuel storage tanks and not B-1A Ship 2. It is too good a story to omit from the book just because of some uncertainty.]

Upon returning from its tour to Farnborough, Andrews AFB and Offutt AFB to Edwards AFB (Flight 4-79, 21 September 1982), B-1A Ship 4 entered an extensive modification period to get the new OAS and DAS avionics installed. It next flew on 30 July 1984 and provided a production-representative testbed for avionics testing.

B-1A Ship 4 made its last flight on 16 December 1986, when it flew to Wright-Patterson AFB for display in the United States Air Force Museum. Eventually, it would be replaced in that museum's collection by a B-1B. Ship 4 would be moved in pieces on the ground to the Strategic Air Command & Aerospace Museum in Ashland, Nebraska, where it would be reassembled and placed on outdoor display.

Above: The F-111 chase plane was an essential part of every B-1 test flight. (*Eric Simonsen*)

Left: B-1A Ship 2 has its wings swept fully aft on Flight 2-71 (2 June 1983). During this flight, the left windscreen cracked. After Flight 2-71, the horizontal stabilator controls were damaged during a ground test, necessitating investigation and repair. B-1A Ship 2 would not fly again until 8 July 1983. (*Brad Purvis collection*)

After a test mission, personnel work around B-1A Ship 2 to secure it and download data. The slats and flaps are extended and the spoilers are deployed. (*Air Force Test Center History Office*)

After being retired from flight testing, Ship 4 was originally displayed in the National Museum of the US Air Force. When that museum received a B-1B for its collection, it lent Ship 4 to the Strategic Air Command & Aerospace Museum in Ashland, Nebraska, where it is on display at the entrance. (*Author*)

Flight 2-127

The weather for Flight 2-127 on 29 August 1984 was forecast to be a typical summer day at Edwards AFB: hot and clear. Edwards was a base that got to work early – the air was smoother in the morning before it heated up, which translated into better test data. The flight test team gathered at 0500 local time for a briefing. The airplane would be B-1A Ship 2, with the call sign WIRY 29. The B-1A Ship 2 crew was Major Richard V. Reynolds (AFFTC test pilot), Tommie Douglas 'Doug' Benefield (co-pilot for this flight and the Rockwell B-1 chief test pilot) and Captain Otto J. Waniczek, Jr. (AFFTC flight test engineer). Mervin L. Evenson (Rockwell B-1 test pilot) and Captain Stephen R. Fraley (AFFTC flight test navigator) would fly the F-111 chase aircraft. There was an engineering team in the mission control room led by test director Robert Broughton (Rockwell manager of flight test engineering) and test conductor Major Stephen A. Henry (AFFTC flight test navigator). Flight 2-127 covered a diverse set of flight sciences objectives that took advantage of Ship 2's elaborate instrumentation. The test points included landing gear taxi loads, a 9° pitch attitude take-off, dropping five inert Mk 82 shapes on the Precision Impact Range Area (PIRA), airspeed calibration, minimum controllable airspeed tests, landing gear touchdown loads, and brake effectiveness during landing. In accordance with AFFTC regulations, every test point had undergone a safety review and AFFTC leadership signed off on the test card.

The ground crew and aircrew started up Ship 2, while the engineers in the mission control center verified the telemetry links. The landing gear taxi loads test involved tight turns on the ground at increasing speeds. Data was good, but the ground crew noticed that the test damaged the tires, necessitating a two-hour delay while the aircrew shut down Ship 2 for a tire change by the ground crew. After the tire change, the B-1A departed Edwards AFB with the F-111 in chase.

B-1A Ship 2 eventually got a B-1B-style Strategic paint scheme with green and two tones of gray. In this photograph, it flies over Rogers Dry Lake at its home, Edwards AFB. (*Stephen Henry collection*)

Above: B-1A Ship 2 flies over the desert near Edwards AFB on Flight 2-105 (30 March 1984). Strategic camouflage did a very poor job of concealing the aircraft when it was flying over arid desert terrain. Note the extended spoilers on the wings. (*Paul Reynolds/US Air Force*)

Right: Flight 2-105 (30 March 1984) had a diverse set of flight science test points, with B83 and Mk 82 shape separations, flying qualities evaluation, usable AOA tests, trim change evaluation, and SMCS tests. In this photograph, B-1A is in the landing configuration. (*Paul Reynolds/US Air Force*)

The drop on the PIRA and airspeed calibration runs were uneventful, and the team proceeded to the minimum controllable airspeed test points. The minimum controllable airspeed was the lowest airspeed at which the aircraft had control during an asymmetrical thrust condition such as during an engine failure. The most challenging minimum controllable airspeed conditions were low, slow, and with an aft CG.

The design of the B-1 complicated the test set-up. Because of its long fuselage, the B-1 had a large CG range based on which tanks held the fuel. The sweep angle of the VG wings also affected the CG and the center of lift. The pilots used FCGMS to control the CG location. CG location was set in terms of percentage of Mean Aerodynamic Chord (per cent MAC).

The first minimum controllable airspeed test point was at 55° of wing sweep. At this sweep angle, the allowable CG location was 25–60 per cent MAC, with the smaller number being the forward limit and the larger number being the aft limit. The test point specified a middle location for the CG, which was set at 45 per cent MAC. The pilot set the #1 and #2 engines at maximum thrust and #3 and #4 engines at idle. The Ship 2 aircrew flew the first test point once, then repeated it because the engineers in the control room noticed that the speed brakes were in the deployed condition, which differed from the planned test configuration.

The next test point was to test for minimum controllable airspeed at 6,000ft altitude (approximately 3,500ft AGL in the high desert), 15° wing sweep angle, slats and flaps extended, and landing gear extended, with the CG at the aft location. After setting up for the test point, the pilot would put all engines at full thrust to start a climb and then rapidly move the throttle for the #4 engine to idle. This test point represented an engine failure on take-off.

At this point, a series of errors began which soon would have a tragic ending. The aircrew began to sweep the wings forward from 55° to 15° at 1021:30 local time and configured the slats, flaps, and landing gear for the next test point. By mistake, the CG was left at 45 per cent MAC from the last test point, but the allowable CG range for 15° sweep angle with extended slats and flaps was only 10–21 per cent MAC. Suddenly Ship 2 was tail-heavy. Mission control was monitoring the CG location and wing sweep angle data being telemetered from Ship 2, but the engineers' attention focused on the last test point and the next point, not the current state of the aircraft during the transition between test points. If the B-1A had had a traditional flight control system the pilots would have felt the tail-heavy condition, but SCAS acted as designed and compensated for the CG being too far aft by commanding the stabilators to create a nose-down pitch moment. The master warning and caution lights in front of the pilots lit and sounded an aural tone at 1022:10 local time. FCGMS caused a CG caution light to be illuminated on the caution, warning and advisory panel. Unfortunately, B-1 pilots had become used to momentary illumination of this light during wing sweep angle changes. The CG caution light was hidden from Reynolds by his right knee and it was out of the field of vision of Benefield. Neither Waniczek nor the mission control room had caution, warning, and advisory panels of their own. Waniczek could not see the pilots' panel from his seat in the back. Post-flight analysis revealed that there had been forty-seven times in the past sixty-five flights when the aircraft had gotten into a situation where the CG was too far aft; this notification of a potentially dangerous condition became regarded as a merely transitory nuisance.

What might have become a barely noticed forty-eighth incident turned into a tragedy because of two factors. During a normal flight, FCGMS would have been set to an automatic mode (OPT CRUISE or NORM on the FCGMS control panel) and fuel would have been

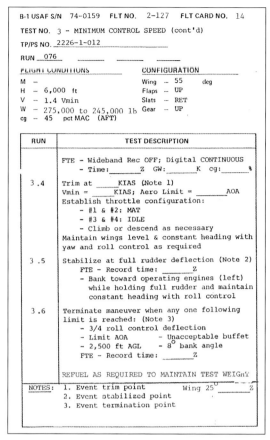

B-1 USAF S/N 74-0159	FLT NO. 2-127	FLT CARD NO. 14

TEST NO. 3 - MINIMUM CONTROL SPEED (cont'd)

TP/PS NO. 2226-1-012

RUN 076

FLIGHT CONDITIONS	CONFIGURATION
M -	Wing - 55 deg
H - 6,000 ft	Flaps - UP
V - 1.4 Vmin	Slats - RET
W - 275,000 to 245,000 lb	Gear - UP
cg - 45 pct MAC (AFT)	

RUN	TEST DESCRIPTION
	FTE - Wideband Rec OFF; Digital CONTINUOUS - Time:_____Z GW:_____K cg:_____%
3.4	Trim at _____KIAS (Note 1) Vmin = _____KIAS; Aero Limit = _____AOA Establish throttle configuration: - #1 & #2: MAT - #3 & #4: IDLE - Climb or descend as necessary Maintain wings level & constant heading with yaw and roll control as required
3.5	Stabilize at full rudder deflection (Note 2) FTE - Record time: _____Z - Bank toward operating engines (left) while holding full rudder and maintain constant heading with roll control
3.6	Terminate maneuver when any one following limit is reached: (Note 3) - 3/4 roll control deflection - Limit AOA - Unacceptable buffet - 2,500 ft AGL - 8° bank angle FTE - Record time: _____Z REFUEL AS REQUIRED TO MAINTAIN TEST WEIGHT
NOTES:	1. Event trim point Wing 25°_____Z 2. Event stabilized point 3. Event termination point

B-1 USAF S/N 74-0159	FLT NO. 2-127	FLT CARD NO. 15

TEST NO. 3 - MINIMUM CONTROL SPEED (DYNAMIC)

TP/PS NO. 2226-1-012

RUN 080

FLIGHT CONDITIONS	CONFIGURATION
M -	Wing - 15 deg
H - 6,000 ft	Flaps - DN
V - Vmca + 9 Knots	Slats - EXD
W - 275,000 to 245,000 lb	Gear - DN
cg - 21 pct MAC (AFT)	CP - L&R APU - START/RUN - Verify L&R Run Lights P - Eng 4 ADG - BRAKE LOCKED

RUN	TEST DESCRIPTION
	FTE - Wideband Rec OFF; Digital Rec CONTINUOUS - Time: _____Z GW: _____K cg:_____
3.7	Trim at Vmca + 9 Knots: _____KIAS (Note 1) Vmin = _____KIAS; Aero Limit = _____AOA With all engines at MAT, establish a climb at Vmca + 9 Knots.
3.8	Throttle #4 - Move rapidly to idle (Note 2) Wait 1 second or until significant roll/yaw deviation has developed.
3.9	P - Take corrective action to arrest roll/yaw excursions (Note 3) - Minimize airspeed loss - Minimize altitude loss - Maintain directional control within ±10° of the heading at throttle chop. TERMINATE TEST WHEN AIRSPEED LOSS OR ALTITUDE LOSS BECOMES EXCESSIVE OR HEADING CANNOT BE MAINTAINED WITHIN 10°. FTE - Record Time: _____Z REFUEL AS REQUIRED TO MAINTAIN TEST WEIGHT
NOTES:	1. Event Trim Point. Wing 25°_____Z 2. Event throttle chop. 3. Event when roll/yaw control is regained.

FORM 2002-8-4 (PAGE 8)

Above left: On Flight 2-127, Flight Card No. 14 immediately preceded the mishap. The CG location was at 45 per cent MAC and the wing was at 55 degrees of sweep. (*Otto Waniczek collection*)

Above right: When the B-1A lost control, the crew was setting up for Flight Card No. 15. Notice all the things that had to change between No. 14 and No. 15. The CG was supposed to go from 45 per cent MAC to 21 per cent MAC. The wings were to sweep forward from 55 degrees to 15 degrees, flaps lowered, slats extended, and landing gear to the down position. Missing the CG change set the aircraft up for loss of control. (*Otto Waniczek collection*)

pumped from the No. 4 tank to the No. 1 tank, moving the CG forward. In flight test, setting the CG was part of the test point and FCGMS was placed in the manual mode (SET on the FCGMS control panel) with the CG setting mistakenly still at 45 per cent MAC from the previous test point, far aft of the 21 per cent MAC aft limit in the current configuration. Furthermore, the pilots were decelerating to 137 KIAS, which decreased the ability of the horizontal stabilators to generate enough lift to create a downwards pitch moment to counteract the aft CG.

At 1023:25 local time, the aircraft performed an uncommanded pitch-up. Reynolds pushed the stick forward. Then the aircraft made some excursions in roll and yaw, departed controlled flight by dramatically pitching up to 70° nose high, and sliced to the right, almost flying tail-first. It's instinctive for pilots to want to regain control of their aircraft, and everybody was certainly aware of the value and importance of bringing a critical asset like Ship 2 back home. By now Ship 2 was in an unrecoverable situation; the crew was just along for the ride.

For the next twenty-nine seconds, Ship 2's pilots tried in vain to restore control. Evenson, in the chase F-111, radioed: 'Hey Doug, have you got it?' Benefield responded, 'No. We are trying to come out of it, maybe.' In the cockpit of Ship 2, the relationship between Reynolds and Benefield may have slowed the response. Reynolds was the aircraft commander but he was also fairly inexperienced in the B-1. Benefield was the co-pilot and subordinate to Reynolds during the flight but he was also vastly more experienced in the B-1. A secondary objective of the flight was for Reynolds to regain his landing currency under Benefield's watchful eye. Who was really in charge of Ship 2? The ambiguity may have consumed precious seconds.

The flight manual for Ships 1 and 2 stated: 'Under uncontrollable conditions, eject at least 15,000ft above terrain, whenever possible', but Ship 2 had started this maneuver at only 3,500ft AGL. When Reynolds initiated ejection, the escape capsule separated from Ship 2 at 1,505ft AGL. It was later calculated that if ejection had been delayed by more than one more second, the parachute canopies would have not had time to inflate and the escape capsule would have smashed into the ground.

The escape capsule rocketed away from Ship 2. The inertial reels on the aircrews' shoulder harnesses should have automatically tightened but did not. The parachutes deployed, but there was a serious problem. The pyrotechnic repositioning bolt on the left rear corner of the escape capsule did not fire properly. The failure caused the capsule harness, to which the parachutes were attached, to prevent the capsule from rotating to a level attitude. Instead of landing in a level attitude on the impact attenuation airbags, the escape capsule slammed into the ground on the right side of its nose. Because of the lack of impact attenuation, the impact was 40+ Gs, far higher than the design load for the escape capsule. Benefield was closest to the point of impact and also the heaviest member of the crew. His seat broke loose and he suffered fatal injuries. Reynolds was severely injured. He tried to aid Benefield but was disabled by his condition. Waniczek was also in bad shape. The escape capsule landed so close to the massive fireball caused by the crashed B-1A and its large fuel load that the escape capsule parachutes melted. The F-111 chase circled over the crash site and radioed for assistance.

It is received wisdom in the aviation community that mishaps are almost never caused by one mistake. In the case of Flight 2-127, a series of small errors – none of which individually

Rockwell test pilot Tommie D. 'Doug' Benefield perished in the Flight 2-127 mishap. Benefield was a retired colonel in the USAF and a former president of the Society of Experimental Test Pilots. (*Paul Reynolds/ US Air Force*)

would have caused a crash – resulted in the loss of a valuable test aircraft and a highly respected member of the flight test community.

A very large anechoic chamber was under construction at Edwards AFB to test electronic warfare systems and other avionics, including the B-1B DAS. In memory of Benefield, it would be named the Benefield Anechoic Facility (BAF). Reynolds would mostly recover from his injuries, return to flight status and go on to serve a full 34-year career in the USAF, which included duty as the B-2A Spirit System Program Director and AFFTC Commander. He ultimately retired as a Lieutenant General and Vice Commander, Air Force Materiel Command. Waniczek left USAF active duty to work for Northrop on B-2A flight test, bringing with him his valuable experience. He transferred to the USAF Reserve, and taught at the USAF Test Pilot School, retiring as a Lieutenant Colonel.

The lessons learned from the demise of B-1A Ship 2 had a profound impact. Although the long fuselage and VG wings of the B-1 made it inherently susceptible to experiencing the CG outside of limits, never again would an aircraft be lost because of this problem.

B-1B Flight Test

The initial focus of the B-1B flight test plan was to get just enough data to evaluate the bomber against specific operational mission criteria to support the 1986 IOC rather than development-oriented objectives. The B-1B CTF implemented a computerized flight test management system. The system supported test planning, scheduling, tracking of progress, and status reporting. The CTF prioritized test points into three categories:

1. The highest priority was demonstration of initial operational capabilities, safety of flight, and nuclear certification.
2. Second priority was to clear an envelope for SAC to conduct training flights.
3. Third priority was to satisfy the remaining DT&E and OT&E objectives and contractual requirements.

The intent was to declare the B-1B to be operational on schedule even if it needed to operate with limitations and then complete any additional tests needed to verify the full operational capability after IOC.

While B-1A Ships 2 and 4 jump-started the flight test program, B-1B #1 (tail number 82-0001) began to take shape. This aircraft was a one-off. At the time of the B-1A production cancellation in 1977, several of the airframe modules for B-1A Ship 5 had been completed and they were stored rather than scrapped. Taking advantage of the high degree of structural commonality between the B-1A and the B-1B facilitated the rapid construction of B-1B #1, using pieces of the never-completed B-1A Ship 5.

In October 1983, only twenty-one months after contract award, GE delivered the first production F101-GE-102 engine for B-1B #1 to the Rockwell final assembly plant in Palmdale. The main landing gear for B-1B #1, from Cleveland Pneumatic Co., arrived in November. That same month, Rockwell production workers in Palmdale placed all the fuselage modules and the vertical stabilizer for the first B-1B in a mating fixture. By January 1984, fuselage structural assembly was complete. With assembly complete, Rockwell moved B-1B #1 to the checkout

Rockwell personnel tow B-1B #1 in preparation for the rollout ceremony. From this angle, the nose radome, engine inlets, and OWF are the most obvious indications that this aircraft is a B-1B and not a B-1A. (*Master Sergeant Mike Dial/US Air Force*)

B-1B #1 had an imposing presence and sleek, flowing lines. (*Master Sergeant Mike Dial/US Air Force*)

The B-1B #1 rollout on 4 September 1984 was a major event which celebrated a program milestone and created favorable publicity. The festive atmosphere was dampened by the crash of B-1A Ship 2 and the death of Doug Benefield a few days earlier. (*Master Sergeant Mike Dial/US Air Force*)

facility on 10 May 1984. For the next four months, the aircraft systems were thoroughly tested. In August, B-1B #1 again moved to the paint hangar. A highly publicized rollout on 4 September 1984 celebrated the USAF's newest bomber, but the festive mood was considerably dampened by the crash of B-1A Ship 2 and the death of Doug Benefield only a few days earlier.

Secretary of the Air Force Verne Orr was the keynote speaker at the B-1B #1 rollout. His remarks started:

Today marks a special occasion for both the United States Air Force and Rockwell International. It has been twenty-two years since the last heavy bomber was built for the Strategic Air Command. With the rollout of the first B-1B, a benchmark in the defense of our nation has been achieved.

As a flight test aircraft, B-1B #1 had been fitted with extensive instrumentation. It had a pitot boom on the radome and flutter wands on the wing tips, horizontal stabilator tips, and upper rudder. An aft-facing camera on the crew entry door and camera pods on the nacelles would take motion pictures of weapons separation. The B-1B also contained the equipment to record the instrumentation data and telemeter it to the ground; this filled the forward weapons bay.

B-1B #1 took to the air for the first time on 18 October 1984, only three years from program initiation. Its crew was Rockwell test pilot Mervin L. Evenson (pilot), co-pilot Lieutenant Colonel Leroy B. Schroeder, OSO Major Stephen A. Henry and flight test engineer Captain

Rockwell personnel prepare B-1B #1 for its first flight. The hoses supplied cooling air when the engines and APU were not running. (*Master Sergeant Mike Dial/US Air Force*)

The flutter wand on the tip of the left stabilator of B-1B #1 is visible. This flight-test specific feature was not found on any other B-1B. (*Master Sergeant Mike Dial/US Air Force*)

David E. Hamilton, Jr. Like Schroeder, Henry and Hamilton were assigned to AFFTC. Waniczek was originally planned to take the first flight but he was recuperating from his injuries, and his back-up, Hamilton, flew in his place. The flight departed Palmdale and landed there. During the 3.2-hour flight, the crew evaluated flying qualities and avionics system operation. Overall, the OAS and DAS worked well, with a few small problems. Post-flight inspection revealed foreign-object damage to engines #2 and #3. The damage to engine #3 was very minor and could be repaired with the engine on the aircraft but #2 engine was replaced with a spare. The crew had been unaware of the engine damage during the flight.

Right: Major Stephen A. Henry was OSO on the first flight of B-1B #1. He had experience as a B-52H radar navigator and a program manager before attending the USAF Test Pilot School. After serving in the B-1B CTF, he worked on the Air Staff as the B-1B Program Element Monitor. Later in his career, he would return to Edwards AFB as the Deputy Commandant of the USAF Test Pilot School and then serve in senior USAF engineering and program management positions. (*Stephen Henry collection*)

Below: B-1B #1 lifts off on its first flight on 18 October 1984. Flight B1-001 featured the functional checkout of aircraft systems. (*Brad Purvis collection*)

The reason that B-1B #1 returned to Palmdale on its first flight rather than Edwards AFB was because a special visitor was coming to Palmdale. The 1984 election was in November, and President Reagan wanted to tout his military build-up and tough stance towards the Soviet Union. That California was the most populous state and the B-1B was creating thousands of jobs in the state was another political benefit for Reagan. The Rockwell plant in Palmdale became the site for a campaign appearance by Reagan, with the just-flown B-1B #1 as the centerpiece. Reagan commended Rockwell and its workers for their efforts on the B-1B:

> Let me congratulate Sam Iacobellis, the men and women of Rockwell, the subcontractors around the country, and the whole aerospace industry. You are doing a magnificent job. And I know there could be no better group of people working together than you – the men and women of our aerospace team here in southern California. The teamwork of the B-1B is something to behold – 5,200 suppliers and subcontractors, 55,000 workers nationwide, with 17,000 workers right here in California – producing quality work ahead of schedule and under cost.

Reagan then explained his defense policy along with criticism of his opponent, former Vice President Walter F. Mondale, who did not support the B-1B:

> No one, absolutely no one, should ever ask the sons and daughters of America to protect this land with less than the best equipment that we can provide. If our sons and daughters can put their lives on the line to keep us free, then I believe it's immoral to give them

Although fully equipped with OAS and DAS, B-1B #1 tended to be used for flight sciences tests since it was an actual B-1B. B-1A Ship 4 also had OAS and DAS but its airframe was in the older B-1A configuration so it became the primary test aircraft for mission systems until it was retired. (*Brad Purvis collection*)

Flight B1-100 on 28 July 1987 had a SIS evaluation and TF checks. It featured the first weapons delivery test in which fourteen Mk 82 shapes were separated from the intermediate and aft weapons bays. At this time, Mk 82 separation dynamics from the aft weapons bay were problematic and the subject of considerable investigation. From the left to right, the Flight B1-100 crew was Addison S. Thompson (Rockwell test pilot and copilot in this flight), Major Harold R. 'Randy' Gaston (AFFTC test pilot), Major Frantz DeWillis (AFFTC OSO), and James A. Leasure (Rockwell flight test engineer). (*Addison Thompson collection*)

anything less than all the tools, all the training and the equipment to do the job right. And it's up to us in this election to choose, and choose wisely, between a strong, safe America – an America at peace – or to slide back to the failed and dangerous policies of the past. There's no clearer issue in this campaign.

B-1B #1 flew from Palmdale to Edwards AFB on 31 October 1984 on a 1.5-hour flight. Besides repositioning the aircraft, objectives for this flight included pitot-static calibration and the preliminary evaluation of the new inlets and their compatibility with the engines. The B-1B CTF now had two aircraft, B-1A Ship 4 and B-1B #1. Both had the full set of mission systems, but since only B-1B #1 had the airframe and engines of a B-1B, it was used for flight sciences work, and B-1A Ship 4 was the primary mission systems test aircraft. With two aircraft now available for testing and less than two years until IOC, the B-1B CTF was working at an intense pace. Production aircraft were being built concurrently with the testing. If any problems were discovered in testing, aircraft that had already been delivered or were in production would need to be retrofitted, which was costly and disruptive. The sooner that problems were found, the smaller their impact. SAC needed an airplane that was safe enough to fly for training as soon as possible and had enough operational capability to justify being put on alert. At AFFTC,

The last flight of B-1B #1 on 22 August 1988 brought it to Ellsworth AFB where it was used as a ground weapons loading trainer. In 1995, a team from the 654th Combat Logistics Support Squadron including Technical Sergeant Kyle C. Fagin dismantled 'The Leader of the Fleet' after it had been cannibalized for useful parts. This sad hulk in a scrapyard in Blossom, Texas is the remains of B-1B #1. (*Brad Purvis*)

the B-1B was the highest priority test program. The other CTFs got used to having their test missions delayed because the B-1B CTF received preferential access to range time, mission control rooms, and data processing services.

The Real Stuff

A B-1B test mission was the antithesis of a casual 'let's kick the tires and light the fires' exercise. From planning through aircraft preparation, test execution, and post-flight data processing and analysis, the work of hundreds of people came together to conduct a mission. Flight testing was exacting work that required a meticulous attention to detail. The failure of even one person to perform a task properly could cause an aborted mission, a poorly executed test point, uncollected or lost data, or even a catastrophe. To many of the people working for the B-1B CTF, both USAF and contractor, it was the highlight of their careers, and for several it was the launch pad to future promotions.

A test plan guided the work of the B-1B CTF. The test plan first came under the scrutiny of the Technical Review Board, an ad hoc group of senior staff who verified that the plan would meet the objectives of the program and was practical to implement. The next step was to meet the Safety Review Board, which was convened by the AFFTC Safety Office. AFFTC procedures required that CTF members review past safety reviews for other programs and lessons learned. Risks were identified and evaluated for the probability that they would occur and the consequences if the risk was realized.

For example, high AOA tests were identified as high-risk tests, with the potential for loss of control of the aircraft. To mitigate the risk of high AOA tests, each maneuver was flown in a high-fidelity engineering simulator before being flown in the B-1B. Beyond neutral stability, AOA was increased in 1° increments; aircraft response needed to be satisfactory before advancing to the next increment. Critical parameters were telemetered to a mission control

It being the first B-1B and having extensive instrumentation, B-1B #1 was the workhorse of the B-1B CTF for several years. (*Stephen Henry collection*)

A close examination of this photograph will reveal the flutter wands on the wingtips and horizontal stabilator tips of B-1B #1. Flutter could cause catastrophic structural damage to the aircraft and clearing the flutter envelope was an essential prerequisite for other types of flight testing. (*Stephen Henry collection*)

room staffed with engineers analyzing the data. After each test point, the engineers compared the actual response of the aircraft and flight control system to the results of the simulation. A difference beyond a certain amount between the simulation and the telemetered data was reason to terminate further testing. The aircrew had rehearsed their response if the test point was terminated and the aircraft needed to be recovered to a safe AOA. The application of this disciplined and systematic approach made flight testing safer and more productive.

The test plan and the computerized flight test management system provided the information for the Mission Objective Sheet (MOS). A Rockwell flight test engineer created an MOS for each test flight. The MOS included the type of tests to be conducted, aircraft configuration, data and instrumentation requirements, time required to conduct the tests, and various performance parameters. Each organization that was part of the B-1B CTF contributed to the MOS.

Flight B1-029 was a typical test flight. Using B-1B #1, Flight B1-029 was intended to accomplish a mix of flight sciences and mission systems tests on 21 February 1986. The original aircrew was led by Lieutenant Colonel Frank T. Birk, the B-1B CTF operations officer. Lieutenant Colonel Steven A. Harmon was the OSO. Due to some late changes, Captain Perry L. Lamy flew as co-pilot and Rockwell flight test engineer James A. Leasure was in the DSO seat. Lamy was a former B-52G pilot who graduated from the USAF Test Pilot School and joined the B-1B CTF. He would later be the B-1B program element manager at SAC headquarters, command the 420th Flight Test Squadron in the B-2A CTF and later the test wing at AFFTC and the Air Force Research Laboratory, being promoted to Major General. Leasure had started his career as an air defense artillery officer in the US Army and had then worked for Boeing on Saturn launch vehicle ground support equipment at NASA Kennedy Space Center. He joined Rockwell in 1975 and went on to become the flight test engineer with the most flights in the B-1.

Lieutenant Colonel Richard V. Reynolds was the test conductor, acting as the single point of communications between the mission control team and the aircrew. Still recovering from the injuries that he suffered on Flight 2-127, he was no longer flying in ejection seat-equipped aircraft but was still involved in test operations.

T-5 days

A Rockwell ground operations engineer defined the configuration of B-1B #1 for the upcoming flight according to the MOS and maintainers prepared the aircraft, its systems, and instrumentation. During this phase of the program, Rockwell had the primary responsibility for the aircraft when it was on the ground. USAF personnel from AFFTC and the 4200th TES assisted the Rockwell personnel to evaluate maintainability and supportability of the B-1B. Any problems written up during the previous flight needed resolution. Rockwell flight test engineering used the MOS to create a test card for Flight B1-029.

T-1 day

The major event of the day was the Flight Readiness Review (FRR). Dozens of people participated in the FRR: management, test director, test conductor, engineers responsible for the technical disciplines and systems that would be tested, B-1B aircrew, chase aircrew, flight test engineers, instrumentation engineers, mission control room personnel, range controllers and photographers. The FRR agenda was standardized from flight to flight. The flight test team reviewed test aircraft configuration and status, support aircraft (chase aircraft and tankers), and range status. It then conducted a page-by-page review of the test card; often there would be some changes penciled in. If the test cards contained test points assessed by the SRB to be medium or high risk, senior leadership at AFFTC needed to be briefed and approve the test cards.

T-12 hours

Fatigue was a known risk factor. The aircrew needed to be in crew rest for the twelve hours prior to show time. Maintainers on night shift closed out problems, fueled the aircraft, serviced hydraulic fluid and oil, loaded film for the stores separation cameras, and performed the preflight inspection. All aircraft documentation needed to be signed off.

T-2 hours

The aircrew, test director, test conductor, ground operations engineer, meteorologist, and range controller met for the preflight briefing at 0900 local time on 21 February 1986. At this time, the test cards might be revised again because of aircraft and instrumentation status or weather. For example, if instrumentation wasn't working on a control surface, it might mean scrubbing all the handling qualities cards/test points for the flight. The aircraft commander would carry out a normal pre-flight crew briefing. At the mission control center, the staff was finishing up the set-up of the mission control room for the flight.

T-1:30 hours

The aircrew went to the life support shop to get their helmets and other personal flight equipment and then rode in a small bus to B-1B #1. Arriving at the aircraft, they reviewed the maintenance forms with the crew chief.

T-1 hour

Left APU start was attempted three times without success. Right APU start was normal. Then the left APU controller circuit breakers were reset and it started without any problems. The aircrew started the engines. All communications and telemetry links were checked. The engineers in the mission control room verified that they were getting good data to their strip chart recorders. Each CTF at Edwards AFB had its own call sign. The B-1B CTF used WIRY. Each pilot had a personal number that was used with WIRY when he was the aircraft commander. On Flight B1-029 with Birk in the front left seat, the call sign was WIRY 21. B-1B CTF operations, maintenance and mission control room used the call signs WIRY OPS, WIRY MAINTENANCE, and WIRY CONTROL respectively. The first F-111 chase aircraft also started engines; those aircraft used the LEAHI call sign. B–1B #1 had more than its share of problems this morning which delayed taxi and take-off by five hours. A flight test was a carefully orchestrated operation with numerous constraints. Delays could lead to mission cancellation if the range was no longer available, the crew was running out of duty time, or it was getting dark. While the team worked the aircraft systems problems, the range controller scrambled to reschedule the range.

T-0

B–1B #1 and LEAHI 24, the first F–111 chase, taxied to the runway. Runway 04–22 at Edwards AFB was 15,000ft long and 300ft wide; it was one of the largest runways in the world. The prevailing winds favored Runway 22. LEAHI 24 took the runway first, lifted off, and flew a left closed pattern. Then B–1B #1 moved into position, and the pilot gave a countdown call to the chase aircraft. On the downwind leg of the closed pattern, the chase pilot used the countdown to be in position to perform the airborne pick-up maneuver. Done properly, the airborne pick-up put the F–111 in formation with the B–1B as it took off. The maneuver required excellent timing and airspeed control to do well. Take-off was at 1220 local time, with rotation at 145 KIAS and lift off at 160 KIAS.

After take-off, the B–1B performed instrumentation checkout maneuvers with left and right sideslips, left and right rolls to 30° bank angle, and a pull-up. The engineers in the mission control room would see the traces of the parameters corresponding to the maneuvers on their strip charts, verifying the end-to-end operation of the instrumentation, telemetry and mission control room.

The first test points were two air data calibration tower fly-bys. The pilots configured the airplane for the test by retracting the landing gear, flaps, and slats, swinging the wings back to 25° of sweep, and flying at a precise airspeed and altitude on a precise ground track past an airspeed calibration tower. The operators in the tower observed the path of the aircraft through a grid. By use of trigonometry, the actual altitude of the aircraft would be calculated. The actual altitude would be compared to the indicated altitude in the cockpit to determine the altimeter error. Air data calibration work was terminated because low-altitude turbulence resulted in poor quality data.

Now under control of the range controller (call sign SPORT, which stood for Space Positioning, Optics, and Radar Tracking), the B–1B set up for B61 drops on the Precision Impact Range Area (PIRA). For this flight, B–1B #1 had instrumentation in the forward weapons bay, eight B61 shapes on a rotary launcher in the intermediate weapons bay, and a single SRAM on a rotary launcher in the aft weapons bay. The weapons had the aerodynamic and mass characteristics of a real B61 but no actual nuclear components. The B–1B dropped two shapes, each drop preceded by a dry run. The first drop was at 0.60 Mach and 25,000ft altitude. The OSO had the critical job of turning on and off the stores separation cameras at the correct times. These high-speed motion picture cameras consumed film at a very high rate. Proper timing captured the shape separation but did not use excessive film which would prevent the subsequent release from being fully documented. The second B61 drop was planned to be done at 0.85 Mach and 200ft AGL. It was not actually conducted because of launcher rotation problems.

!30

12 FEB 86

B-1 USAF   S/N 82-0001   FLT NO: FLT CARD: J-4

TEST NO.·   - B61 MANUAL RELEASE (EAFB)

TP/PS NO. 3136-1-006C

RUN 011 ____ ____ ____ ____

FLIGHT CONDITIONS   and   CONFIGURATION

```
M  -  0.85              Wing   - 67.5   deg
H  -  200 AGL           Flaps  - UP
V  -  540    kt         Slats  - RET
W  -         lb         Gear   - UP
cg -  30 pct MAC        SPEED LOCKUP Sw - LOCKUP
                        q =      960        PSF
```

RUN	TEST DESCRIPTION

19-9	**LIVE RELEASE** *DLVY RESTRICTION ON*
	PRE-IP (IP - ROSAMOND LAKE)
	OSO - Verify CAMERA SYS PWR sw - ON
	    - Verify TM Sel sw - POS. 2
	    - Perform PRE-IP Checklist
	P - Verify NUC PA & REL sw - PA & REL (ON OSO CAI
	    ~~(Nuclear Caution Light - ON)~~
	    - Perform Tone check with SPORT
	    - Call SPORT - DATA ON

20-9
 	
.2
	IP-TO-TARGET (TARGET - PB4)
	SPORT: Countdown to <u>Release</u> on Target
	OSO - NUC LOCK/UNLOCK Sw - UNLOCK
	      (When cleared to arm by SPORT)
	OSO - Verify ~~Nuclear Caution~~ *Caysont Disclosan* Light - OFF
	OSO -(T-30) INT Bay Doors (PART) - OPEN
	    - Chase Verify Spoiler/Doors - Extended
	    - (T- 2) CAMERA WPN MAN RUN sw - ON (HOLD ON)
	    - (T- 0) Release on SPORT CALL
	    - (T+ 10) CAMERA WPN MAN RUN sw - OFF

	POST-TARGET
	P - Maintain level flight for 10 sec
	OSO - INT Bay Doors - CLOSE
	P - ~~Verify Nuclear Caution Light - ON~~
	    - NUC PA & REL sw - NORM (ON OSO CALL)
	    - Notify SPORT - All Switches SAFE/DATA OFF
	OSO - CAMERA SYS PWR - OFF
	    - Perform POST-RELEASE Checklist

Test cards provided the detailed instructions for each test point. Each test card represented the output of months and sometimes years of test planning. Although data from instrumentation was recorded on board the aircraft and telemetered data was also available on the ground, the aircraft crew wrote their own notes on the test cards. Weapons releases tests needed to be done at specific conditions. Note the detailed instructions for the OSO on a Flight B1-029 test card pertaining to the high-speed movie camera that photographed the separation of the B61 shape. (*Perry Lamy collection*)

Later in the flight, B-1B #1 flew test points to collect data on SIS, the engines, ORS, DAS, and subsystems. Because of an off-scale high reading on engine #4, it was shut down and the B-1B returned to land. During landing, application of the wheel brakes using the pedals resulted in severe oscillations. Lieutenant Colonel Birk noted: 'No further braking tests should be conducted until this data has been analyzed an explanation has been given for this condition.' The flight ended at 1555 local time back at Edwards. The flight's activities did not end with engine shutdown. There was a thorough debrief of the test activities and aircraft problems that would need to be addressed by the maintainers. Technicians collected data tapes and motion picture film from the aircraft for post-mission processing.

In the aftermath of Flight B1-029, the engineers analyzed the data. Any unexpected behavior in the areas of B61 separation dynamics or SIS performance might be indicative of a dangerous condition if the envelope was further expanded. Anomalies needed to be understood and the impact on future test flights assessed. Meanwhile, the maintainers performed a post-flight inspection and began to ready the aircraft for Flight B1-030. Mission by mission, the B-1B CTF tested the aircraft so that SAC could get an operationally effective and reliable weapon system.

B-1B #1 was retired from flight testing after Flight B1-137 on 28 April 1988 with 617 flight hours logged. Because it was a one-off constructed in part with B-1A modules it had become a burden to support. Its last flight on 2 August 1988 was to Ellsworth AFB, where it became a static weapons loading trainer. In 1995, the 654th Combat Logistics Support Squadron cut up B-1B #1. Pieces of it were used for live fire test and evaluation. From the perspective of taxpayers, it was wise to use this no-longer useful asset in some productive way. Sadly, a historic airplane was lost forever.

Taming Instability

The B-1B increased its maximum gross weight by 82,000lbs over the B-1A design. The increased weight, long fuselage, and wide range of center of gravity represented a design challenge for flight control engineers. Analysis showed that at heavier gross weights and higher AOAs, B-1B performance was constrained by longitudinal stability issues. However, B-1A testing had shown that there was more lift available close to the stall AOA that could be utilized if the longitudinal instability was counteracted. Rockwell developed a set of flight control system modifications, SIS and SEF, to enable the envelope to be more fully utilized by artificially compensating for the longitudinal instability.

SIS/SEF testing involved an elaborate matrix of test points, with testing at five wing sweep angles (15°, 20°, 25°, 55° and 67.5°) and three CG positions for each wing sweep angle (forward, intermediate, and aft). At each of these conditions, test pilots flew a variety of maneuvers with an emphasis on high AOA. SIS/SEF had to show that not only did it compensate for the natural longitudinal instability of the B-1B at high AOA but that it did not degrade the B-1B flight control system and handling qualities in any other way.

SIS/SEF flight testing was the highest risk flight testing of the B-1B flight test program. If the AOA is high enough, any aircraft can aerodynamically stall, which means that the airflow over the aircraft is disrupted and lift decreases. If the aircraft is in sideslip while it is stalled, it may enter a spin. Because of its shape and mass distribution along the longitudinal axis of the aircraft, aerodynamicists predicted that the B–1B would be unrecoverable if it entered a spin. Things could very quickly go very wrong during a high AOA test of SIS/SEF.

The B–1B CTF used multiple measures to mitigate the risks of this testing. One of the most useful tools was Rockwell's engineering flight simulator at its El Segundo, California facility, which was heavily upgraded in 1985 to support SIS/SEF testing. The Rockwell engineering flight simulator was sophisticated in those areas that were needed for flight dynamics and control development. It had advanced digital computers to model the airframe dynamics and flight control system response in real-time. The digital computer system consisted of a general-purpose computer as host, distributed microprocessors for interfacing, and a parallel process for the real-time modeling of dynamics and control. The SCAS was analog and was simulated accordingly. The simulator had a motion base which was not used during SIS/SEF development. The visual imagery system had forward imagery but no peripheral imagery. The simulator represented the B–1B cockpit, but only those systems relevant to the tests were functional.

The simulator activity in El Segundo and the flight testing at Edwards AFB were closely coupled, with Rockwell flight control system engineer Newell Johnson playing the lead role. The program used the simulator to rehearse test flights before they were flown and to conduct safety evaluations. The strip chart pen-plots created in the simulator during rehearsals were used during flight test as the basis of comparison for the strip chart pen-plots created during the flight tests. B–1B #9 and #28 had built-in position sensors in the SCAS actuators and the horizontal stabilator actuators so they could be recorded on-board and telemetered for real-time monitoring in the control room. Those sensors enabled the control room engineers to ensure that the aircraft didn't use more than 50 per cent of available trailing-edge-down stabilator travel nor more than 60 per cent of the available SCAS servo-actuator stroke from the trim point to ensure that there was always enough pitch authority for a recovery maneuver if it were needed. Instrumentation on the test aircraft captured the actual response of the aircraft. Rockwell engineers used this data to refine the mathematical models of airframe dynamics and flight control responses. The team also used the simulator to investigate flight test anomalies and conduct post-flight evaluations to verify that the simulator and the flight test data matched.

A common method to mitigate risk in high AOA testing is to equip the aircraft with a spin chute attached to its aft end. If the aircraft entered an unrecoverable stall or spin, the pilot would activate the spin chute, which would deploy and create a force to counteract the stall or spin. After recovery, the pilot would jettison the spin chute. The B–1B was much too large to be equipped with a spin chute, which necessitated even more caution during SIS/SEF testing at high AOA. All flight test maneuvers were first rehearsed in the Rockwell engineering flight simulator. The AOA envelope was expanded from benign test points to the edges of the envelope in a cautious and incremental fashion. The engineering team in the mission control room monitored data telemetered from the B–1B, looking for deviations from the responses predicted by the simulation and exceedances or adverse trends of flight dynamics and flight control system parameters. Either the mission control room or the pilots could call for the maneuver to be terminated, with the termination maneuver having been rehearsed in the flight simulator prior to the flight.

SIS/SEF improved the stability and control characteristics of the B-1B at the high AOA that it needed to generate sufficient lift for the higher maximum gross weight of the B-1B (477,000lbs) compared to the B-1A (395,000lbs). When conducting SIS/SEF testing, the B-1B made frequent air refuelings to top-off the fuel load to attain a heavy weight. (*Brad Purvis collection*)

SIS/SEF testing was highly successful, with no departures of the B-1B from controlled flight during the test program, which was completed in 1989. With SIS/SEF installed, the B-1B had improved stability and departure resistance at expanded gross weights and altitudes. The B-1B could safely perform TF flight at up to one-third heavier gross weight with SIS/SEF than without it, which meant that it could carry a heavier load of weapons at longer range. SIS/SEF were not perfect – gross mishandling at the edges of the AOA envelope could cause problems. Training and operational limitations proved sufficient to prevent operational pilots from getting into trouble.

For the second time, B-1 test pilots were given the Iven C. Kincheloe Award by the Society of Experimental Test Pilots, when Rockwell test pilot Addison S. Thompson and AFFTC test pilot Lieutenant Colonel Harold R. 'Randy' Gaston were recognized in 1989 for their work on SIS and SEF.

'Yahoo!'

The TF capability was essential to the B-1B concept of operations. TF could be modeled and simulated, but ultimately the TF capability of the B-1B needed to be tested with a real airplane flying over real terrain. TF was a mode of operation in the B-1B, not a dedicated system, so all the changes from B-1A that affected it, including the inertial navigation system, radar altimeter and ACUs, needed to be considered. The most significant TF changes from the B-1A to the B-1B were the ORS and the heavier weight of the B-1B. The B-1B was flying fast and low, and the risk during this kind of testing was collision with the ground.

The general approach to TF testing followed a build-up sequence:

1. Radar terrain evaluation, which involved hand-flying the B-1B over surveyed terrain at low altitude to evaluate the accuracy of the terrain profile created by the ORS and TF command processing. The usual geographic feature used for TF flight testing at Edwards AFB was Haystack Butte, which steeply rose approximately 250ft above flat terrain. Not only did Haystack Butte offer a prominent and isolated target free of clutter for the ORS, but the aircraft flight path was in sight of range instrumentation. The first TF flight test was Flight 4-97 (14 March 1985).
2. The fail-safe fly-up feature was tested on Flight 4-131 (5 December 1985). The fly-up feature caused the aircraft to execute a pull-up if the TF system had anomalies.
3. The automatic TF feature was then tested against Haystack Butte, starting with the highest clearance plane and working down to 200ft in an incremental fashion. The B-1B did not have a usable manual TF capability because the FDC did not have a fast enough response. Automatic TF with the TF commands being fed into the AFCS was the only approved kind of TF. Risk was mitigated during this testing because it was only done in good weather and during the day. The pilots could always resume manual control and avoid Haystack Butte if the TF system put the aircraft into a hazardous situation. The pilots could select soft, medium, and hard rides, which set how closely the aircraft followed the terrain. Lieutenant Colonel C. Wayne Staley led a crew on flight 4-133 (12 December 1985) which flew the first automatic TF flight.
4. Major William J. Moran, Jr. and his crew conducted the first automatic let-down on Flight 4-161 (26 June 1986). Pitching down to a 10° flight path angle descent from 20,000ft altitude, B-1A Ship 4 screamed down at nearly 10,000ft per minute until the TF system engaged and brought the aircraft to TF flight.
5. The next step was to fly TF off-range on military low-level routes, which offered a more diverse set of terrain than just Haystack Butte. The off-range route started over the Pacific Ocean and crossed the California coast north of Morrow Bay and wound around south of Bakersfield to enter the AFFTC range complex. The route offered many interesting TF terrain profiles: over water, land/water contrast, flat terrain, rolling hills, and then the very rugged terrain of the Sierra Nevada mountains north of Edwards AFB, along with desert and sand dunes. The off-range testing followed a progression from high to low clearance planes.
6. The TF envelope was expanded in terms of wing sweep angle, CG location, and airspeed from the initial test condition of 0.85 Mach and 67.5° of wing sweep.
7. TF was conducted in degraded visual conditions of weather and darkness to evaluate controls and displays and associated human factors.

As might have been expected when a complex system operates in a complex environment, TF testing revealed numerous problems. Just as the Rockwell engineering flight simulator operated in a synergistic fashion with SIS/SEF flight testing at high-AOA, the Boeing systems integration laboratory played the same role for TF. The Westinghouse BAC 1-11 was also a useful tool to refine the ORS and it was a frequent visitor to Edwards AFB. Because OAS and ORS were based on software, the potential solutions to problems revealed in flight testing could be rapidly implemented in code, tested in the Boeing systems integration laboratory and possibly the BAC 1-11, then evaluated on the B-1B.

Radar terrain evaluation and fly-up testing revealed some issues; in particular there were too many spurious fly-ups. These problems were resolved before moving to the next step of automatic TF over Haystack Butte.

The early automatic TF runs against Haystack Butte revealed what test pilots described as 'abrupt nose-down transitions from scan to scan in hard ride'. The professional and understated tone of the description belied what it felt like to be in the B-1B during these tests. The automatic TF feature would violently jerk the aircraft nose-down, followed by a maximum-performance fly-up. These excursions were named 'yahoos' by Rockwell test pilot Norman 'Ken' Dyson, and they occurred frequently (at worst, every few seconds). Selecting the soft ride mode reduced the magnitude of the unpleasant and potentially dangerous 'yahoos' while the problem was analyzed and solved. The B-1B CTF first flew automatic TF at the 200ft clearance plane with soft ride over flat and rolling terrain on Flight 4-174 (25 September 1986).

AFFTC flight test engineer Captain Jaime R. Silva played a key role working with Boeing and Westinghouse on the 'yahoo' problem. Other important contributors included test pilot Major Perry L. Lamy, OSO Major Stephen A. Henry, and Boeing engineer Dale Schellhorn. The contractors and USAF discovered that the root cause of the 'yahoos' was the multi-mode scan pattern used by the ORS. With only one antenna, the ORS adaptively interleaved TF scans and other scans such as ground mapping with periods of silence to reduce radar emissions from the aircraft and make it more difficult to detect. The intermittent scans created a vertical disparity between the previously generated TF desired flight path and the new desired flight path. The solution was to use software to smooth the transition between the previous and new desired flight paths. With the desired flight path smoothing, 200ft clearance plane TF with the hard ride was successfully accomplished on Flight B1-099 (21 July 1987).

Off-range testing exposed the TF system to a broader set of topography and generated more deficiency reports, resulting in further changes to aircraft systems. Testing of automatic TF at the 200ft clearance plane and a soft ride in mountainous terrain was first accomplished on Flight B9-28 (16 July 1987). After the resolution of the 'yahoo' problem, the TF testing in mountainous terrain was repeated at clearance planes down to 200ft with hard ride. More problems were discovered with the radar scan, which led to a temporary halt in TF testing while they were addressed with a more sophisticated smoothing of the type that had been used to solve the 'yahoo' problem. It took until Flight B9-085 (8 September 1988) for the 200ft TF flight with hard ride to be successfully flown over mountains.

The pilots monitored automatic TF with a combination of symbology on their VSD and aural tones. In the initial design, the VSD steering cross was constantly moving during TF and the tones were constantly sounding, with no good indication of proper aircraft response to TF system commands. The solution was to drive the VSD steering cross and the aural tones with flight path errors signals. When the aircraft was on the TF desired flight path, the VSD steering cross was stationary and the aural tone was silent. When the VSD steering cross moved or the aural tone sounded with a high–pitch 2,500Hz tone to pull up or a low–pitch 500Hz tone to push down, that was the indication to the pilots that the aircraft had deviated from the TF desired flight path.

The repeated cycle of test, fix, and re-test should not be regarded as an indication of failure but rather as an integral part of the development process working as intended. For TF, the development process was more protracted than anticipated. Consequently, when SAC achieved B-1B IOC, the B-1B did not have a TF capability cleared for operational use. To accelerate progress, IOT&E pilots such as Major William J. Moran, Jr. from the 4200th TES participated in the DT&E of the TF capability.

As SIS/SEF testing cleared the envelope for high–AOA and therefore higher gross weights, TF testing at these higher gross weights followed. Final clearance of full TF capability for SAC required operational testing that stretched into 1992. The 31st TES (as the 4200th TES was redesignated in 1986) brought in experienced B-1B pilots including Major Theodore 'Brad' Purvis to give TF its final round of testing before it was released to operational SAC units.

Weapons Testing

The B-1B could fly heavy, fast, and low but none of those things mattered if it could not effectively deliver weapons, the purpose of a bomber. The required capabilities for IOC were the initial priority for weapons testing. B-1A Ship 2 had demonstrated the basic ability of the B-1B to carry and separate weapons, but the full weapons delivery test program using an actual B-1B (B-1B #1) began on Flight B1-013 (18 June 1985). The B-1B weapons test program established a delivery envelope from 0.55 to 0.90 Mach and 200ft AGL to 27,000ft altitude. The B-1B CTF tested the B61, B83 and AGM-69A SRAM nuclear weapons and also evaluated a limited conventional capability with Mk 82 bombs and Mk 36 mines.

Weapons separation might be considered a trivial matter (don't objects fall when dropped?) but actually it posed a difficult aerodynamic problem. The B-1B generates a powerful flow field around its airframe, particularly in the area of the aft weapons bay where the venturi effect accelerates the local airflow to supersonic speeds. The flow field could direct the weapons to separate in an undesired direction. Poor separation characteristics could prevent the weapons from arming and might degrade their accuracy. In the case of the SRAM, during a low altitude launch the missile might fire its engine with the missile pointed down, leading to a ground impact soon afterwards.

The general approach was to use a wind tunnel to measure the flow field around a model of the B-1B. Aerodynamicists used the wind tunnel data to generate a mathematical model of the flow field. Ground tests using B-1A Ship 3 measured the dynamics of initial weapon separation using a technique called a 'box drop'. During a box drop, the aircraft was positioned over a large container filled with rubber foam. A weapon shape was loaded on the ejector rack. When the pyrotechnic cartridges in the ejector rack were fired, the ejector rack released the weapons shape and pushed it into the box. High-speed motion picture cameras captured the motion of the weapon shape.

Test planning was based on the prediction that the forward and intermediate weapons bay flow fields were nearly identical, so little forward weapons bay testing needed to be conducted.

The aft weapon bay appeared to have the most challenging conditions for weapons separation, so that bay was the focus of testing. As with all potentially hazardous testing, there was an incremental build-up from the most benign test point to the most challenging.

During the flight tests, B61 results were good and B83 results were excellent. The B83 was helped by its high weight, which reduced its sensitivity to flow field effects. There were nineteen B61 separations and twenty-five B83 separations during the B-1B test program.

SRAM separation from the forward and intermediate weapons bays was good. On Flight B1-045, a SRAM shape exhibited poor separation characteristics from the aft weapons bay, reaching 50° nose down in 0.62 seconds. One solution was to lower the aft weapons bay spoiler only halfway when the SRAM was launched from that bay. This solution was successfully tested on Flight B1-124. On Flight B1-125, the alternative solution of opening the intermediate weapons bay doors when launching the SRAM from the aft weapons bay was successfully demonstrated. B-1B #1 successfully fired a live (powered and guided flight, not just a shape) SRAM on the Tonapah Test Range on Flight B1-077 (16 January 1987), with the launch parameters being 0.9 Mach, 500ft AGL and intermediate weapons bay.

Although intended primarily for the nuclear mission, the B-1B was designed from the start with a conventional bombing capability using the Mk 82 bomb carried internally. The B-1B was also designed to carry the Mk 36 mine, which was just a Mk 82 bomb with a kit. Mk 82 testing was challenging, because the Mk 82 bomb was lighter than any of the nuclear weapons

On Flight B1-013 on 18 June 1985, B-1B #1 conducted the first separation of a B83 shape from a B-1B. The B83 was optimized for low-altitude high-speed delivery. The B83's parachute decreased the shock of impact, prevented the bomb from skipping along the ground, and allowed the B-1B to escape the blast of the weapon. (*Stephen Henry collection*)

Above: Photo chase was an essential part of each weapons separation test. The cameras carried by the photographer in the rear seat of the T-38A Talon complemented the high-speed movie cameras carried on the B-1B and operated by the OSO. (*Stephen Henry collection*)

Right: Flight B1-025 on 17 January 1986 had multiple objectives but was focused on weapons testing including a B61 shape separation and a weapons bay vibration and acoustics survey. (*Paul Reynolds/US Air Force*)

and was blown around more by the B-1B flow field. Under some conditions from the aft bay, the Mk 82 shapes would pitch nearly straight down. It took several years before release sequences and other system setting were determined to ripple-fire a full load of eighty-four Mk 82 shapes from the three weapons bays in less than two seconds. After the first mass drop of eighty-four Mk 82 shapes in 1989, Rockwell test pilot Addison S. Thompson remarked that inside the bomber, the firing of pyrotechnic cartridges on the ejector racks felt like a Gatling gun was firing. With the B-1B losing approximately 20 tons of weight in few seconds, the aircraft wanted to rapidly climb.

At the time of its loss, B-1A Ship 2 had been scheduled for five more test flights and then would have entered a lay-up from November 1984 to July 1985 to be modified to conduct ALCM carriage and separation tests. With the loss of Ship 2, the entire ALCM test program was moved to B-1B #9 (tail number 84-0049). B-1B #9 was the first B-1B with the movable bulkhead between the forward and intermediate weapons bays, so that it could carry the ALCM internally. It also was the first B-1B with full external stores capability. B-1B #9 joined the

B-1B #9 was the primary test aircraft for ALCM integration on the B-1B. It also was used for SRAM II testing, although that missile was cancelled before it ever had a powered flight. Flight B9-150 (25 September 1990) featured the release of a SRAM II JTV. From left to right, the B9-150 crew was Steven G. Schmidt (Rockwell flight test engineer), Major Keith Otsuka (AFFTC test pilot), Major Theodore B. 'Brad' Purvis (SAC 31st TES pilot), and Major James E. Meier (AFOTEC OSO). The composition of this crew illustrated the truly combined nature of the B-1B CTF. Meier and Purvis had completed tours as an operational B-1B aircrew members prior to coming to the B-1B CTF, bringing valuable perspective to it. (*Brad Purvis collection*)

B-1B CTF in May 1986. B-1B #28 (85-0068) became a B-1B CTF test asset in November 1986. Originally intended to be the primary platform for B-1B/ACM integration testing, it eventually was used for a wide variety of testing. Like B-1Bs #1 and #9, B-1B #28 was instrumented for testing.

After the external ALCM capability for the B-1B was designed and fitted to B-1B #9 and #28, analysis showed that the engines produced a very hostile vibration and acoustics environment that would be detrimental to the health of the ALCM if it was carried externally. ALCM testing on the B-1B was limited to using the ALCM rotary launcher in the extended intermediate weapons bay. After four jettisons of inert ALCM shapes and several captive carries of live missiles, the first ALCM launch from the B-1B was on Flight B9-040 (24 November 1987). The second ALCM launch was on Flight B28-089 (7 April 1989). Both launches were conducted over the Utah Test and Training Range.

B-1B #28 conducted thirteen separation tests of ACM shapes and ten captive carries with live missiles. Because ACM could survive higher levels of vibration and acoustic energy than the ALCM, it was tested on the external stations. During the testing of ACM on the B-1B, the ACM was 'sight sensitive', which is to say that the external appearance was classified and viewing the missile was restricted to personnel with special access security clearances. On the ground at Edwards AFB, the ACMs were covered in loose bags which concealed their shape from random onlookers. Ground crew removed the bags as late as possible before the B-1B taxied for take-off and covered the missiles as soon as possible after the B-1B landed. A vehicle or other large object was placed to block view of the underside of the B-1B during ACM loading, ground testing and operations.

The Autry Hop

System testing identifies development issues and matures technology. When testing the complex integrated systems of the B-1B, there were a myriad of issues to be addressed. Here are a few of the more interesting ones.

One problem that seemed almost trivial, but was actually quite significant, was that boom operators on tankers had difficulty at night locating the right place to place the aerial refueling boom and judging depth. For the B-1B, which required aerial refueling under all conditions to accomplish its mission, this was a deficiency with major operational implications. Not only might the B-1B not be able to refuel, but a boom operator might slam the end of the boom into the windshield of the B-1B. The original aerial refueling markings on the forward fuselage of the B-1B were black, which did not contrast well with the dark green and gray paint on the B-1B. B-1A Ship 1 had been sitting in a hangar since 1978, when it last flew. Slowly being cannibalized for parts, Ship 1 was painted like a B-1B and used to ground test white aerial refueling markings, which had better contrast with the dark green and gray camouflage paint than black markings. After the ground tests on B-1A Ship #1, the white markings were tested in flight.

Lieutenant Colonel C. Wayne Staley and other CTF pilots tested the feasibility of air refueling the B-1B with the TFPE shields erected. Staley reported that it was possible to fly the maneuver by looking only through the PZLT portholes, but difficult because of the limited field of view and lack of peripheral vision cues.

Once the star of the show, B-1A Ship 1 sat nearly forgotten in this picture taken on 24 October 1982. At this time, its remaining role was to be cannibalized for parts to keep Ships 2 and 4 flying. B-1A Ship 1 would be used for one more test. Painted green and two-tone gray like the B-1B, it would be used for ground testing of the markings around the UARSSI. (*Ian Tate*)

This B-1B has white markings around the UARSSI, which make the job of tanker boom operators easier at night. Ground tests with B-1A Ship 1 helped develop these markings. (*Brad Purvis*)

The minimum unstick speed test determined the lowest speed that a B–1B could take off at. In such a test, the risk was that the aft end of the fuselage would contact the ground during rotation. For the minimum unstick speed test, Rockwell fitted B–1B #9 with a proximity wand on its aft fuselage and a cockpit indicator. On one test, B–1B #9 dragged its aft fuselage on the runway, requiring the structure to be repaired with a patch.

Another performance test was the maximum gross weight abort. At full thrust, the pilot accelerated on the runway until reaching take-off abort speed, at which time he retarded the throttles to idle and applied maximum breaking. The 15,000ft long runway as Edwards AFB was ideal for maximum gross weight abort testing and it was used for that purpose not only by military aircraft but also by Boeing for their airliners. In this ultimate test of the wheels and brakes, the brakes of the B–1B glowed white hot. The thermal relief plugs in the wheels blew as intended. The tires flattened but they did not explode, because of the relief plugs. The heat from the brakes was so intense that the wheels actually melted. Amazingly, after they cooled, the brake pads appeared to be in fine condition. The aircraft had to be jacked up to replace its wheels and tires before it could be towed off the runway.

AFFTC operated a modified KC-135 tanker which carried tanks of water instead of jet fuel. At the end of its aerial refueling boom, it had a spray head which created a stream of tiny droplets representative of the liquid moisture inside a cloud. The water was colored with yellow dye. At altitude where the temperature was ideal for icing, generally slightly lower than the freezing point of water, the B–1B flew behind the icing tanker. Cameras documented the build-up and removal of the yellow-tinted ice on the B–1B. The 'potato chips' in the inlets proved to be particularly prone to ice accumulation. On three of four icing test flights, chunks of ice broke off in the inlets and damaged engines, leading to operational limitations for the B–1B in icing conditions.

East-west navigation legs from California to Texas and back and north-south legs from Edwards AFB to Oregon and back tested long-range OAS navigation performance. Of particular interest was the use of position fixes obtained using the ORS high-resolution ground mapping capability to align the inertial navigation system in the air. Testing was conducted using operationally relevant targets and geo-location accuracies. Navigation accuracy was also a critical factor in the transfer alignment of the inertial systems on the SRAM, ALCM and ACM.

B–1B #17 (tail number 84-0057) was the subject of RCS measurement tests. RCS measurement didn't require any particular instrumentation on the aircraft or flight test techniques. The B–1B did need to precisely follow a ground track to present the specified aspect to the radars measuring the RCS, because RCS is sensitive to target orientation. The RCS measurement tests did experiment with the use of copper tape applied to panel edges and structural seams in an attempt to reduce RCS.

Human factors testing included fire escape and rescue procedures. The B–1B CTF built a giant wooden mockup of the crew cabin in a hangar. Crew members had to play 'dummies' to be rescued by the fire department in the event of a ground fire or mishap. Such duty was important, but it did not endear the human factors engineers to the crew members.

One of the most interesting discoveries during the B–1A flight test program was the 'Autry hop', named after 4200th TES pilot Captain L. Dale Autry. When landing and applying the wheel brakes after the nose landing gear contacted the ground, occasionally there was a disconcerting high-amplitude vertical oscillation felt in the cockpit, which disappeared

Above: Another new USAF aircraft in the 1980s was the KC-10A Extender, a tanker based on the McDonnell Douglas DC-10 airliner. Flight 4-128 (14 November 1985) brought B-1A Ship 4 and the KC-10A together for the first time. (*Brad Purvis collection*)

Left: This B-1B has a more elaborate set of markings around the UARSSI, which were used early in the program. The configuration of the aerodynamics surfaces on the boom identifies the tanker as a KC-10A. (*US Air Force*)

Testing a new aircraft required a vast number of test points. This B-1B is testing the fuel dump capability with the wings, flaps, slats and landing gear in the landing configuration. (*Brad Purvis collection*)

when the brakes were released. An unusual thing about this phenomenon was that it seemed to affect some pilots but not others. In the B-1B flight test program, Major Perry L. Lamy experienced the same problem. Captain Scott M. Dayton, the B-1B SPO engineer responsible for the landing gear, wheels, brakes, and tires, investigated the oscillations. More than thirty years later, Dayton recalls the issue: 'Major Lamy and I had some pretty heated conversations about that problem. I remember them well – he outranked me and was a patch wearer [USAF Test Pilot School graduates wore a distinctive patch], so you can imagine who was heated and who was sitting there taking the verbal beating.' It is easy to fall into the trap of thinking that the development, test, manufacture, and deployment of the B-1B was about large impersonal organizations. Those organizations mattered, but at the working level where things actually got done, it was about hard-working and highly competent individuals working as a team to make things happen.

AFFTC civilian engineer Michael Garland solved the problem. The long fuselage of the B-1B was flexible and had a 3Hertz fuselage bending mode. Pilots of shorter stature, like Autry and Lamy, placed their feet on the pedals in a way that activated the wheel brakes slightly differently than taller pilots. Once the oscillation was excited, the pilot flying the aircraft tended

Flight B1-25 (17 January 1986) illustrated the diverse tests that the B-1B carried out. B-1B CTF conducted weapons separation, weapons bays vibration and acoustics, engine, inlet, flutter, SMCS, ORS, and SIS on this 5.6-hour flight. (*Paul Reynolds/US Air Force*)

to sustain the motion because his feet were oscillating on the pedals in phase with the structural oscillation. The 'Autry hop' was solved by adding a note in the B-1B flight manual for the pilot handling the flight controls to temporarily relieve foot pressure on the pedals or pull the stick full aft should the oscillations occur.

Dastardly DAS

'Yahoos', weapons separating from the B-1B at weird angles, and the 'Autry hop' were the sort of normal problems that aircraft test programs discovered and engineers solved. Problems with the maturation of the DAS were of a more serious nature and threatened the viability of the entire B-1B program.

The B-1A test program thoroughly tested the airframe, flight controls, and engines. During the B-1B test program, new features like the inlets with RCS reduction vanes, HML, increased gross weight, SIS/SEF, graphite/epoxy composite weapons bay doors, and new weapons (Mk 82/Mk 36, ALCM, ACM) had to be tested. These features were significant but not major changes to a generally well-proven airplane. OAS built on the proven foundation of the OAS used by the B-1A and B-52G/H. ORS was the one major change in the B-1B OAS, and the TF capability using ORS took several years to meet requirements.

In contrast, the BPE using B-1A Ship 4 had been useful in defining the requirements for the B-1B and its AN/ALQ-161A, but the BPE had never been intended to be a thorough test of the DAS. The most advanced element of the B-1B weapon system was also the least tested and most technically immature. The situation was aggravated by the shortage of test resources. Between the return of B-1A Ship 4 to flight and the first flight of B-1B #1 in the 1984 and the arrival of B-1B #9 in 1986, there were only two test aircraft in the B-1B CTF and they were kept fully occupied with a wide range of tests, among which DAS was only one of many systems tested.

Like the flight control system and OAS, flight testing was coordinated with ground test facilities. In the case of DAS, AIL had the Defense System Integration Facility (DSIF) at its home base in Deer Park, New York. A full AN/ALQ-161A system was installed in the DSIF, which included a threat emitter that could simulate more than seventy threat radars. AIL also delivered a partial system to Rockwell for installation on a full-scale B-1B mockup to measure antenna patterns. Another partial system went to the Integration Facility for Avionics System Test (IFAST) at Edwards AFB. IFAST was a major USAF investment in AFFTC avionics testing capability, driven by the understanding that the cost and time required to evaluate complex integrated avionics systems could be reduced by substituting computer simulations with actual avionics hardware for some time flight tests. IFAST had four bays with radomes oriented towards the Edwards AFB runway, which provided a steady stream of targets. The B-1B OAS occupied one bay and the DAS occupied another bay. In effect, IFAST was another B-1B, only this B-1B didn't burn fuel or require the maintenance or other downtime of an aircraft.

IFAST effectively was another test airplane from the perspective of those working on OAS and DAS. The white radomes on the side of IFAST covered antennas which used aircraft in the traffic pattern at Edwards AFB as radar targets. (*Stephen Henry collection*)

By February 1986, flight test reports were indicating problems with DAS. DAS performance was inconsistent. On some flights DAS worked well, but then on a subsequent flight it did not even detect the emitter. The problem was that the transmitters were sometimes jamming the receivers on the system. Furthermore, a prototype of the DAS tail warning function had been installed on an NC-141A (tail number 61-2777) testbed. The first iteration of the DAS tail warning function generated a large number of false alerts. The second iteration of the design reduced the number of false alerts, but it was insufficiently sensitive to detect targets with low relative motion, such as a fighter closing on the tail of the B-1B. Tail warning function tests used a special test technique. As the NC-141A or B-1B flew over the range at Eglin AFB in Florida, an F-4 Phantom II fighter flew behind the test aircraft and launched an actual air-to-air missile at it. The missile had a reduced load of propellant in its rocket motor, so the test aircraft was never actually in danger of being shot down. While the missile closed in on the test aircraft, it provided a realistic target for the DAS tail warning function.

In 1987, the Rome Air Development Center (RADC), a USAF laboratory specializing in electronic warfare, received authorization for a B-1A airframe to be used as a ground-based antenna measurement testbed. B-1A Ship 1, the very first B-1, was disassembled at Edwards AFB and trucked in pieces across the country to RADC. The pointed tail cone of Ship 1 was inappropriate for antenna testing, so the aft radome of B-1A Ship 4, now on display at the National Museum of the US Air Force, was cannibalized for Ship 1 at RADC. That swap is how Ship 4, which always flew with an aft radome with its distinctive rounded shape, ended up on display with the pointed tail cone with which it never flew.

Flight 4-92 (18 January 1985) was one of the early evaluation missions for DAS. It became evident that DAS had serious problems. (*Brad Purvis collection*)

[Author's note: Another source indicates that B-1A Ship 4 actually is displayed with the tail cone of Ship 3, not Ship 1.]

AIL supplied so-called Mod packages for the DAS. Mod-0 brought all the B-1B aircraft to a common DAS configuration. Mod-1 changed mostly software to improve system performance. In the Mod-1 configuration, DAS wasn't totally ineffective, but it had major deficiencies that were revealed by tests conducted in March through May 1988. When the B-1B was at very low altitudes overflying an emitter, the power level of the simulated threat radars was greater than expected. The high-power signals produced harmonics in the receivers that exceeded their dynamic range and became noisy; this generated extra signals and overloaded the receiver processor. The jamming function of the DAS did work well. With increased operator workload DAS had considerable capabilities, although this operational mode negated the advantages of the automation-centric DAS architecture.

Mod-2 was intended to bring the DAS into compliance with its requirements, but in July 1988 the SPO directed AIL to stop work on Mod-2. It was determined that Mod-2 would be unable to meet its objectives because of fundamental problems in DAS architecture and hardware. John E. Krings, the Director of Operational Test and Evaluation in the Department of Defense, reported to Congress: 'The system, as originally designed, does not have the inherent capability to process information to handle all the threats. It doesn't have the capacity, the speed, the processing capability or the architecture.' An operational test of Mod-1 began in November to better determine Mod-1 capabilities and limitations. It was a period of crisis for the B-1B program. The B-1B had been justified as an interim bomber which could rapidly

Ground testing of DAS on the aircraft preceded and complemented flight testing. A 'hat' covers the radome which protects the right and front of the B-1B while AIL personnel troubleshoot DAS. (*Chuck Klein collection*)

bolster the airborne leg of the strategic triad. Seven years after President Reagan decided to move forward with the B-1B, one of the most important systems of the aircraft was judged to have only 50 per cent of its intended capability against Soviet air defense systems, with no resolution of the issues in sight and an increasing belief that DAS was fundamentally flawed.

To further aggravate the situation, the B-1B attracted the ire of Representative Les Aspin, the chairman of the House Armed Services Committee. Aspin had never been a B-1B supporter, and now DAS appeared to be going to be an undetermined drain on the defense budget for some indefinite time. That Aspin was a Democrat and the B-1B was deeply identified with the Republicans did not help the situation.

Through 1988 and into 1989, the USAF and industry wrestled with the next step. AIL proposed an ambitious and expensive program to upgrade the AN/ALQ-161A. The SPO investigated the feasibility of installing a stand-alone AN/ALR-56M or AN/ALR-74 radar warning receiver on the B-1B to supplement the receivers on DAS. The USAF chose the AN/ALR-56M but it was never actually retrofitted to the B-1B

The B-1B program funded the construction of BAF, the world's largest anechoic chamber, at Edwards AFB. BAF joined IFAST in AFFTC's growing avionics test capability. BAF was a large hangar that could easily fit the B-1B. Inside BAF, the test aircraft was towed onto a large turntable, raised on jacks, and had its landing gear retracted. The walls, floor, and ceiling were covered with thousands pieces of pyramid-shaped radio wave-absorbing foam. From an electromagnetic perspective, the test aircraft was in an open-air environment. Three walls of BAF contained emitters. Rotating on the turntable, receiving signals from the emitters, and operating its transmitters whose output was absorbed by the foam pyramids, the test aircraft tested its electronic warfare systems as if it were in the air. Compared to flight testing, testing in BAF was less expensive, more controlled, and allowed highly classified waveforms to be transmitted without any chance of them being received by a hostile intelligence service. As with all other forms of ground testing, ultimately the system had to be verified in flight. B-1B #40 (tail number 85-0080) was the first occupant of BAF.

By 1990, the DAS was in better shape. AIL had designed improvements and proved them in a system qualification test in August 1990. The B-1B CTF ran a short DAS flight test effort in September 1990 to get an early look at the improved DAS in flight. Additional tests at AIL's DSIF and on the ground at AFFTC in September and October 1990 showed positive results. Meanwhile, testing in BAF generated eighteen problem reports, but none were showstoppers. In addition to functional testing to improve performance, the DAS was finally integrated with CITS, improving the maintainability of the complex system. By this time, the idea of installing a stand-alone radar warning receiver was receding, with Congress directing that the USAF spend no more funds on it.

The extensive ground testing of the improved AN/ALQ-161A led to a DAS graduation exercise. A flight test program by the B-1B CTF began in October 1990 but was halted by an unrelated engine problem that grounded the entire B-1B fleet between 19 December 1990 and 6 February 1991. Flight testing resumed when the grounding was lifted and was completed in late February 1991. Electronic warfare testing used the electronic warfare ranges at Eglin AFB and the Naval Weapons Center China Lake in California. The testing did uncover a problem. On the DSO's TSF display format, the depiction of threat location jumped around in a disconcerting way because the EDU did not update as often as the DAS did. Both problems were considered reasonably simple to fix. AIL also discovered the root cause of the problem

The BAF was a valuable facility for testing DAS. Notice how the B-1B landing gear is draped in radar-absorbing material. (*Air Force Test Center History Office*)

with the DAS tail warning function. An oscillation in an antenna filter was generating noise in the receiver. It had taken more time and money than planned, and DAS still did not meet its full set of requirements, but by 1991 the B-1B had a fairly effective DAS.

Fire and Ice

The global nature of the Second World War educated the US military about the need to have equipment that could operate in the arctic tundra of Alaska, the steaming jungles of the Solomon Islands and New Guinea, and intense heat and dust of the Sahara Desert. During the war, Lieutenant Colonel Ashley C. McKinley commanded the cold weather testing operation in Alaska. He realized that it would be quicker and more efficient to have a laboratory in which the full range of extreme climates could be created on demand at one location for testing, rather than have new aircraft go to multiple locations and wait for the desired ambient conditions. That facility, later named the McKinley Climatic Laboratory in his honor, was located at Eglin AFB in Florida. It was an enormous hangar with the equipment to generate hot, cold, simulated sunlight, rain, snow, wind and dust.

The McKinley Climatic Laboratory exposed the B-1B to an extreme range of conditions in a controlled environment. (*Technical Sergeant Kit Thompson/US Air Force*)

In the McKinley Climatic Laboratory, the B-1B was placed on jacks so that the landing gear could be retracted during the tests. Cables restrained the B-1B when the engines were run. (*Technical Sergeant Kit Thompson/US Air Force*)

Drenching rain from an array of spray nozzles suspended from the roof of the McKinley Climatic Laboratory tested the resistance of the B-1B to water intrusion. (*Stephen Henry collection*)

AFFTC borrowed B-1B #10 (84-0050) from SAC to bring to the McKinley Climatic Library in July and August 1986. Inside the hangar, the aircraft was put on jacks so that its landing gear could be raised and lowered. Restraints secured the B-1B to the floor to oppose the thrust of its engines. Ducts fitted to the engines and APUs removed their exhaust gases. Inside the facility, the aircraft 'flew' simulated missions at temperatures between -65°F and +125°F. The climatic testing was a critical step in proving that the B-1B could be kept at a high degree of readiness on alert during a North Dakota winter and later be based on the Arabian peninsula, one of the hottest places on the planet.

From November 1987 through September 1989, the B-1B underwent EMP testing at the Sandia National Laboratories adjacent to Kirtland AFB in New Mexico. The B-1B was towed onto Trestle, the largest non-metallic structure in the world. Being constructed entirely of wood and glue, Trestle was transparent to EMP. High above the ground on Trestle, the B-1B was blasted by high-powered EMP generators, demonstrating that the aircraft systems could survive the EMP effects of nuclear weapons. The test set-up shakedown in November and December 1987 used B-1B #66 (tail number 86-0106). The actual testing in July through December 1988 and July through September 1989 used B-1B #100 (tail number 86-0140).

The ground and flight testing of the B-1B validated the design, demonstrated system performance, and identified features that needed further development.

Chapter 8

Building the B-1B

'We worked like we were on the front lines of the Cold War.'

Sam F. Iacobellis
B-1B General Manager, Executive Vice President and Chief Operating
Officer, North American Aircraft Operations, Rockwell International

Concurrency

Congress had set a firm cost cap of $20.5 billion in 1981 dollars and an IOC date when it authorized the B-1B program. To meet the IOC date, the USAF and its contractors implemented a high degree of concurrency.

The USAF and its contractors had implemented the B-1A program using Packard's 'fly-before-buy' strategy. 'Fly-before-buy' is a systematic approach to mitigating risk. In this approach the weapons system does not enter production until it is developed and tested. The advantage of 'fly-before-buy' is that the weapon system is technically matured before it is produced in quantity. Being fully tested, it is less likely to enter service with major problems or require expensive post-production retrofits to resolve those problems.

By design, the B-1B was an interim bomber intended to fill a gap in American strategic nuclear capability while the longer-term solution to the bomber requirement, the B-2A, was developed. The Congressionally-mandated IOC date reflected the urgency of equipping SAC with the B-1B. The B-1B program had only five years between program initiation and IOC – achieving IOC required concurrency between development, testing, and production. Rockwell and the other contractors would start full-rate production before testing of new B-1B capabilities was completed or, in some cases, even started. Essentially 'fly-before-buy' was replaced by 'fly-fix-fly'.

While concurrency introduced risk to the program, it also had advantages. The obvious benefit of concurrency was that it got the B-1B into service with SAC as soon as possible. Less appreciated was that concurrency relieved the contractors of the dreaded break between development and production. Contractors build facilities and hire skilled personnel to build the prototypes for testing, but after building these prototypes, they often have no revenue stream to pay for these facilities and people until they receive a production contract.

Two factors mitigated the risks that concurrency imposed on the B-1B program. First, the B-1B program was built on the extensive work done on the B-1A. The B-1B improvements relative to B-1A were judged to have low technical risk. Second, the software-intensive nature of the B-1B systems such as EMUX, CITS, OAS, and DAS made it likely that problems discovered in testing those systems could be resolved with new software releases instead of reworking and retrofitting hardware. The frequent stream of software patches and releases introduced its own complications.

In practice, the assumption of low technical risk had a mixed record on the B-1B program. The B-1A certainly did provide a solid basis for the B-1B. The use of two B-1A aircraft to test B-1B systems before B-1B #1 was available was most useful. Several systems proved to be less technically mature than expected. The AN/ASQ-184 OAS in the B-1B benefited from its similarity to the AN/ASQ-176 on the B-52G/H, but the ORS and TF capability required several years after IOC to complete their development and testing. The availability of SIS/SEF in the operational fleet also lagged IOC. SEF would not be fully fielded until 1992 with attendant limitations imposed on the aircraft that had not been retrofitted with it. The AN/ALQ-161A DAS was the most problematic and immature system on the B-1B.

Major General Peter W. Odgers succeeded Major General Thurman as the B-1B System Program Director in May 1985. Before coming to the B-1B SPO, Odgers had commanded AFFTC. Already deeply involved in the B-1B program, he was well positioned to take the program forward during a period of intensive flight testing.

B-1B Production Program

The B-1B industry team would manufacture the aircraft in five lots.

Lot	Aircraft in Lot	Line Numbers	Tail Numbers
I	1	#1	82-0001
II	7	#2 through #8	83-0065 through 83-0071
III	10	#9 through #18	84-0049 through 84-0058
IV	34	#19 through #52	85-0059 through 85-0092
V	48	#53 through #100	86-0093 through 86-0140

The first two digits of the tail number indicate the fiscal year in which the SPO contracted for the aircraft; for example 84-0049 and the other aircraft in Lot III were manufactured under a Fiscal Year 1984 contract. The Lot I airplane (82-0001) was built with some parts from the never-completed B-1A #5; it was a unique configuration that could be built quickly and was useful for testing but never entered operational service. The Lot II aircraft were well along in manufacturing before B-1B #1 had its first flight. Their configuration was not able to take advantage of any lessons from flight test and in various ways they had limitations. Despite their limitations, the Lot II aircraft were useful for standing up the first SAC wing and training the initial cadre of aircrew and maintainers.

Because of early supply and reliability issues, the B-1B program used production parts for future planes to fill operational shortfalls of fielded aircraft. As the program and supply chain matured towards the end of production, parts were recovered from the operational bases and returned to Palmdale under what was informally called Project 100.

By 1986, Rockwell was completing and delivering four aircraft each month in Palmdale. The industry team faced an impending decrease in production from a full rate of four aircraft each month to zero with the completion of the last Lot V aircraft. In 1986, Rockwell submitted an unsolicited proposal to the USAF for an additional forty-eight B-1B aircraft. With the production line and supply chain running at full speed, the additional aircraft would have been able to be produced at a relatively low cost if the production program could be extended before the process was shut down. Unfortunately, by 1986 American defense spending had peaked and USAF focus had shifted beyond the B-1B to the B-2A. The USAF did not accept the Rockwell proposal, and B-1B ended production with B-1B #100.

All Roads Lead To Palmdale

Rockwell managed its part of the B-1B program at its El Segundo, California facility. El Segundo was the location of most engineering, planning, purchasing, contracts and finance work. The plant in El Segundo manufactured parts and tooling for Palmdale.

The most visible location for B-1B production was at the Rockwell facility in Palmdale, California. But as in an iceberg, Palmdale was only the tip of an enormous industrial effort spread across more than 5,000 contractors and subcontractors in forty-eight states. The broad inclusion of firms and locations served not only to facilitate the maximum participation of talent, expertise and capabilities but also to create the largest possible base of Congressional

Rockwell workers build a B-1B in Palmdale. With the exception of the Palmdale-built forward fuselage, the systems and other structural modules were built elsewhere and transported to Palmdale for assembly. (*Stephen Henry collection*)

support for the B-1B program. Members of Congress who might have opposed the B-1B understood that the cancellation of the program would cost jobs in their district, something for which they would be held personally responsible at the next election. The B-1B was a creation of the political process as much as it was an engineering marvel.

B-1B systems came from suppliers like Hamilton Standard in Windsor Locks, Connecticut for the environmental control system, pressurization controls, and air conditioning units, Sundstrand in Rockford, Illinois for the wing sweep actuators, Simmonds Precision in Vergennes, Vermont for the FCGMS, Rockwell Collins in Cedar Rapids, Iowa for the FDC, and Cleveland Pneumatic in Cleveland, Ohio for the main landing gear struts. In turn, these suppliers relied on vendors who supplied parts including castings, forgings, fasteners, electrical and electronic components, and printed circuit boards. Managing the requirements, technical interfaces, and production deliveries of all these suppliers itself was a massive effort. Late delivery would halt assembly of the aircraft, but excessively early delivery would leave Palmdale clogged in inventory.

The B-1B SPO used technology modernization (techmod) funding to lower costs. Companies applied to the USAF for techmod funding to improve manufacturing processes. The idea behind techmod was that up-front investments would save on recurring costs during production. Multi-year contracts were another tool to reduce costs. Since the B-1B production program was well defined and stable in terms of numbers of units and schedule, a multi-year contract allowed suppliers to invest in efficient production without the risk that their funding would be cut in the future before they could obtain a return on investment.

Avco Aerostructures built the movable portions of the B-1B wings in a renovated plant in Nashville, Tennessee. The majority of the wing was manufactured out of aluminum, with

General Electric built the F101-GE-102 engines. Rockwell workers are installing engine #1 in the left nacelle. (*Master Sergeant Mark Dial/US Air Force*)

Platforms on wheels surround the B-1B, giving the workers access to the aircraft. Tooling for B-1B manufacturing was a major investment. (*Staff Sergeant T.L. Viada/US Air Force*)

titanium wing pivot points. Throughout the facility, the company used advanced machine tools with computer numerical control. In general, the B-1B program arrived at a time when it could take advantage of recent advances in computer-aided manufacturing technology. Avco Aerostructures cryogenically cooled stainless steel bushings and forced them into the wing pivot points. When the bushings warmed they expanded, which permanently and tightly fit them into the wing pivot points.

The Columbus Division of Rockwell in Columbus, Ohio built the forward intermediate fuselage, WCT structure, and nacelles of the B-1B. One of the largest B-1B production sites, the Columbus Division alone employed 6,500 workers at peak production rates in 1986. Rockwell's Tulsa Division in Oklahoma built the landing gear doors, flaps, OWF, rotary weapon launcher, and other smaller items.

Vought Corporation was another major supplier of B-1B structure, producing the aft intermediate and aft fuselage sections in Dallas, Texas. Vought developed the Voughtmatics automated riveting system, which it not only used in Dallas for B-1B production, but also sold to Rockwell. Vought also used techmod funding to implement a flexible automated machining system. Like the other structure suppliers, Vought did not just provide pieces of structure. It assembled the structures with plumbing, wiring, and systems, which meant that Palmdale only needed to conduct final assembly. The aft intermediate fuselage was too large to ship by rail in one piece, so Vought shipped the two halves of the aft intermediate fuselage to a facility that it built in Palmdale across the street from Rockwell. At Vought's Palmdale factory, workers joined the two halves of the aft intermediate fuselage before delivery to Rockwell. Martin Marietta was another major subcontractor for the structure of the B-1B, building the vertical stabilizer and horizontal stabilators. Brunswick built the nose and tail radomes.

GE, Boeing and AIL had their own supply chains for the F101-GE-102 engine, OAS, and DAS respectively. In general, GE and Boeing did well with production deliveries. The same could not be said for AIL, which had production woes to complement the major development issues that it was facing on the DAS. AIL had turned out to be an unusual choice for a large production program like the B-1B. The company was greatly respected for its innovation and had cultivated its reputation in the secretive world of electronic warfare for work on classified programs like the SR-71A Blackbird reconnaissance aircraft. Unfortunately for AIL and the B-1B program, there were considerable differences between delivering a few hand-built systems for specialized use and large-scale production of standardized equipment. AIL's program management, manufacturing, purchasing, and configuration management capabilities were not up to the task. At one point, Rockwell was delivering B-1B aircraft to the USAF without the DAS installed. They would need to be fitted after delivery at the operational bases. Eaton, the corporate parent of AIL, stepped in and reassigned AIL's B-1B DAS program manager, John L. Canfalone. Eaton executive Herman R. Staudt replaced Canfalone and also took over running AIL. James R. Smith, an AIL executive, would assist Staudt as his principal deputy.

Problems with DAS also cost Major General Odgers, B-1B System Program Director, his position. In a 1987 meeting with Secretary of Defense Caspar W. Weinberger and USAF Chief of Staff Larry D. Welch about the B-1B, Odgers was candid that the causes of the DAS problems were not understood and so there was not yet a plan to solve them. Although it was truthful, General Welch was embarrassed by the answer and had Odgers relieved. It was a poor way to treat a well-regarded officer who had spoken with courage and integrity. Major General Elbert E. Harbour replaced Odgers as B-1B System Program Director and served in that role from January 1987 to July 1988. Colonel John Madia followed Harbour in leading the B-1B SPO.

Palmdale, California was familiar turf for Rockwell, having been the final assembly facility for the XB-70A and B-1A. For B-1B production, it underwent a major upgrade. Some parts for the B-1B were delivered by truck or air, but the major assemblies arrived by rail at a new unloading facility, which enabled even the largest B-1B structural modules to be unloaded for their railcars inside an enclosed space. A large warehouse was next to the rail terminal.

At a 256,000 square foot fabrication building, Rockwell workers fabricated and tested wiring harnesses and tubing. With its vast array of systems, the B-1B had an enormous amount of wiring and tubing. Some of this was already installed by the subcontractors inside the structural modules, but much of it was built in Palmdale.

Rockwell built the forward fuselage module in Palmdale with parts fabricated in El Segundo. All the pieces of the B-1B came together in the 264,000 square foot assembly building. At full production rate, nine aircraft were in the final assembly building: five in fuselage mate stations, where the fuselage including vertical stabilizer was built up around the WCT, two in aircraft mate stations, where the VG wings were installed, and two in final assembly stations. Mating the different structural modules in the assembly building was the ultimate test of precision manufacturing, in which two large sections built hundreds or thousands of miles apart needed to fit together with tolerances measured in fractions of an inch. Rockwell made extensive use of air-glide pads to move and precisely position the massive structural modules.

The most difficult assembly operation was mating the VG wings to the fuselage. The titanium pins around which the wings were pivoted were cooled in liquid nitrogen to reduce their diameter. The WCT wing attach fittings were heated to enlarge them. The heating and cooling provided clearance to insert the pins. As the pins heated and the fittings cooled, the pins were permanently fixed in place. On B-1B #9, a pin was somehow installed upside down. If Rockwell couldn't figure out how to remove it and reinstall it correctly, the wing and WCT

A work platform specially designed to rest on the top of the aircraft accommodates the workers in this area. This B-1B is approaching the completion of assembly. The engines, OWF, and all wing control surfaces are in place. (*Staff Sergeant T.L. Viada/US Air Force*)

This B-1B is being checked out on the ramp at Palmdale. Red 'hats' cover some DAS antennas on the aft fuselage, but not the aft radome. The aircraft is still unpainted. (*Technical Sergeant Michael J. Haggerty/US Air Force*)

would have needed to be scrapped. It was quite an operation in the assembly building, but Rockwell removed the 'permanently' installed pin and reinserted it correctly.

Sometimes a component was unavailable when the aircraft was at the assembly station where the component was supposed to be installed. Instead of halting production and waiting for the component, which would propagate the delay to all following aircraft undergoing assembly, the aircraft continued through assembly and checkout without that component, as long as the system was not essential for safe flight. The USAF would accept the aircraft with a waiver, and then a Rockwell team would install the missing system at the aircraft's operational base when the component became available.

A tug towed the B-1B from the assembly building to the 160,000 square foot checkout building. The utilities in the checkout building supplied air and liquid cooling, hydraulics, pneumatics, and AC power to the B-1B. After being positioned in the building, technicians connected the utilities to the aircraft. With these inputs, every B-1B mechanical system operated as if the engines or APUs were running. A computer automatically controlled the tests, with test status and system failures being recorded. The checkout building handled up to four aircraft simultaneously. At the time, it was the most advanced facility of its type in the world, with higher repeatability and faster checkout execution than manual system checkout.

A tug tows B-1B #1 from one of four stations in the checkout building. In general, the B-1B production flow had the aircraft undergo checkout before they were painted. B-1B #1 was painted first for the ceremonial rollout before completing checkout. (*Master Sergeant Mike Dial/US Air Force*)

Having emerged from the paint shop, this B-1B is undergoing a few final checks before it flies. (*Technical Sergeant Michael J. Haggerty/US Air Force*)

Following checkout, the next stop for the B-1B was the paint hangar. To protect both the workers and the environment, the paint hangar had below-floor air plenums that pulled air contaminated with paint fumes and droplets into filters that removed them. The final stop for the B-1B was the ramp. In the open air, Rockwell tested ORS and DAS, fueled the aircraft and calibrated the fuel measurement probes, and ran the engines and APU.

Production Acceptance and Delivery

Production flight tests used Palmdale's two 12,000ft long runways. The B-1B CTF conducted the production checkout, acceptance, and delivery of the first few aircraft. Detachment 15, Contract Management Division was onsite at Palmdale. It was responsible for production oversight by the USAF. After Detachment 15 crews got qualified in the B-1B, they conducted acceptance test flights with Rockwell production test pilots and Boeing OSOs.

A typical production test flight lasted three to four hours. After take-off, the crew did flight control checks. Wind-up turns and wing sweeps at 5,000, 10,000 and 15,000ft verified proper operation of the air data and flight control systems. The crew dumped crew compartment pressure and then repressurized to check out the crew compartment air-cycle refrigeration unit and pressurization controls and valves. Climbing to 25,000ft, the pilots conducted throttle transients on the engines. The B-1B then descended to 20,000ft where, one at a time, the engines were shut down and restarted. The engine shutdowns and restarts exercised the hydraulic, electrical, and pneumatic systems.

OAS, DAS, and TF checkout followed, including opening and closing the weapons bay doors. The B-1B refueled from a tanker, checking the UARRSI and the fuel system. Returning to Palmdale, the pilots operated the wing sweep, flaps, slats, and landing gear. Several trips around the landing pattern at Palmdale checked out the proper operation of the wheels, brakes and tires.

It was desirable to 'sell' the airplane with only one production test flight. Once the production process stabilized, it took an average to three flights to work out problems before Detachment 15, Contract Management Division accepted the aircraft. Usually, it was an operational crew that flew the B-1B to its assigned base.

On 2 May 1988, B-1B #100 (tail number 86-0140) departed Palmdale for McConnell AFB, concluding B-1B production. The one hundredth B-1B aircraft had been delivered ahead of schedule and below budget.

Right: B-1B #81 (tail number 86-121) climbs dramatically over the Sierra Nevada mountains during an acceptance test flight. During the flight, a variety of tests verified that the aircraft was ready to be accepted by Detachment 15, Contract Management Division. (*Technical Sergeant Michael J. Haggerty/US Air Force*)

Below: With its wings swept back, B-1B #81 does a high-speed run. It would be delivered to Grand Forks AFB. In a few years, this aircraft would set world records for performance. (*Technical Sergeant Michael J. Haggerty/US Air Force*)

The second shift worked to repair problems found during the production test flights. Pressure to deliver high-quality aircraft on schedule was unrelenting. (*Erik Simonsen*)

Detachment 15, Contract Management Division used F-106A (single-seat) and F-106B (two-seat) Delta Darts for chasing B-1B acceptance test flights. Having been replaced in the fighter-interceptor role, they were available and they were fast. Chasing the B-1B was the penultimate use for this fine aircraft by the USAF. After a few were used in this role, the F-106 fleet was converted to remote control and expended as full-scale aerial targets. (*Staff Sergeant John K. Mcdowell/US Air Force*)

World Records

The USAF wanted to demonstrate the performance of its new bomber. As part of its acceptance test flights, Detachment 15, Contact Management Division used the B-1B to set world records. On 4 July 1987, a Detachment 15 crew of Lieutenant Colonel Robert Chamberlain (pilot), Captain Michael Waters (co-pilot), Major Richard Fisher (OSO), and Captain Nathan Gray (DSO) flew B-1B #58 (tail number 86-0098). The world record was for speed over a 2,000km closed course over the Pacific Ocean carrying a 30,000lb payload, in this case water carried in fuel tanks in the weapons bays. B-1B #58 and its crew flew at an average speed of 1,077kph.

The Detachment 15 record-setting continued on 17 September 1987. Again Chamberlain was the pilot. For this flight, his crew was Major Brent Hedgpeth (co-pilot), Captain Alexander F. J. Ivanchishin (OSO), and Captain Daniel J. Novick (DSO). Flying a 5,000km closed course of approximately triangular shape up the west coast of the United States abeam Seattle, then turning southeast to Colorado, then returning to California, B-1B #70 (tail number 86-0110) averaged 1,054kph.

USAF Chief of Staff General Larry D. Welch presented the 1988 Mackay Trophy to Detachment 15 for the most meritorious flight or flights of the year.

Captain Alexander F. J. Ivanchishin (left) and Lieutenant Colonel Robert Chamberlain prepare for a B-IB acceptance flight. On 4 July 1987, they were part of a crew that set world records in B-IB #58, demonstrating the high performance of the B-IB. (*Technical Sergeant Michael J. Haggerty/US Air Force*)

Chapter 9

SAC Service

Now the day I was born
The nurses all gathered 'round
And they gazed in wide wonder
At the joy they had found.
The head nurse spoke up
Said, 'Leave this one alone.'
She could tell right away
That I was bad to the bone.

Bad to the bone
Bad to the bone
B–B–B–B–Bad
B–B–B–B–Bad
B–B–B–B–Bad
Bad to the bone.

'Bad to the Bone' by George Thorogood & The Destroyers, 1982.
A popular song in the 1980s at B-1B bases.

Always at War

Developing, testing, and building the BONE were not ends in themselves, but necessary steps before it entered service with SAC. Making the B-1B an operational SAC weapon system by the target IOC date was an effort whose complexity and challenge rivaled that of bringing the machine itself into existence.

SAC was a unique military organization – almost a separate service within the USAF. Historian and retired SAC bomber pilot Colonel Melvin G. Deaile, in his insightful book *Always at War: Organizational Culture in Strategic Air Command, 1946–62*, described a command that was shaped by its unique mission. SAC was constantly ready to go to war at a moment's notice. It had the awesome responsibility of controlling and delivering a massive arsenal of nuclear weapons. SAC personnel had the satisfaction of knowing their critical role in national defense, but SAC was not a high-spirited and fun-loving command. Day-to-day operations centered around the imperative to maintain a force on alert no matter the conditions of weather or machines. Procedures to maintain security, nuclear surety, and positive control were omnipresent and strictly enforced. As SAC personnel liked to say, 'To err is human, to forgive is divine, but neither is SAC policy.'

For the B-1B to become operational in SAC, the following tasks needed to be accomplished:

- Select main operating bases.
- Deliver aircraft and support equipment to the units to be equipped with the B-1B.
- Construct facilities for the B-1B at the main operating bases.
- Train personnel, both aircrew and maintainers.
- Implement the support infrastructure for a complex machine.
- Integrate the B-1B into SAC war plans.

The B-1B would be based at existing SAC bases. Although SAC had reduced its footprint by the 1980s, it still had bases throughout the United States. As SAC entered the B-1B era, the general trend was to base those aircraft whose primary focus was standing alert in the central United States, away from the coasts. Bases on the coast were more vulnerable to a surprise attack by submarine-launched missiles. Aircraft in the central United States would have a few minutes more time between when early warning sensors detected missile launches from submarines and when the missiles hit the bases, permitting the alert force to launch and escape. SAC bases on the coasts, such as Castle AFB and Mather AFB in California and Loring AFB in Maine, tended to be assigned a primary training or conventional role, although they still generated nuclear alert forces. Aside from military considerations, there was a political dimension to B-1B basing decisions. To be selected as a B-1B base meant jobs and funding, and the Reagan administration used its basing decisions to obtain and reward legislative support for the B-1B program.

In order of transition from their previous aircraft, the main operating bases and units for the B-1B were:

1. 4018th Combat Crew Training Squadron (CCTS) and 337th Bombardment Squadron (BMS), 96th Bombardment Wing (BMW), Dyess AFB, Texas
2. 37th BMS and 77th BMS, 28th BMW, Ellsworth AFB, South Dakota
3. 46th BMS, 319th BMW, Grand Forks AFB, North Dakota
4. 28th BMS, 384th BMW, McConnell AFB, Kansas

The B-1B crew members of the BMS were the most visible members of a SAC BMW, but in fact they were only a small fraction of the personnel in the BMW. The BMW consisted of a wing headquarters and three main elements of the wing: support, maintenance and operations, plus a medical group. The combat support group, under the base commander, included civil engineering (facilities), services, personnel, supply, transportation, and security police squadrons. The wing deputy commander for maintenance controlled the organizational (flight line), field (second-line maintenance in the specialized shops), avionics, and munitions maintenance squadrons. His job was to keep the aircraft on alert and serviceable for training missions. The deputy commander for operations and his squadrons executed the flying mission. Each BMW had one or two BMS with B-1B bombers and an Air Refueling Squadron (ARS) with KC-135 tankers.

The arrival of the B-1B also led to an elaborate shuffling of SAC resources. The B-1B displaced other aircraft that had previously been assigned to its main operating bases. It also allowed SAC to retire part of the B-52G fleet. B-52H aircraft that had previously been stationed at B-1B main operating bases went to new bases.

An SAC bombardment wing had one or two bomber squadrons and an air refueling squadron with tanker aircraft. One element of SIOP was coordinating that each bomber and its tanker would meet at the correct time and place if the EWO was executed. This B-1B is refueling from a KC-135R, which was a KC-135A re-engined with four CFM56 (military designation F108) engines that used the gas generator core of the YF101-GE-100 engine. (*Staff Sergeant Michael J. Haggerty/US Air Force*)

The Joint Strategic Target Planning Staff (JSTPS) was collocated at Offutt AFB with SAC headquarters. JSTPS was commanded by the SAC commander with a US Navy admiral as his deputy. JSTPS created the Single Integrated Operational Plan (SIOP), the plan for nuclear war, which needed to coordinate the actions of all American bombers, ICBMs and SLBMs when conducting nuclear strikes. The SIOP was extraordinarily elaborate, to ensure coverage of targets, coordination of forces such as having tankers and bombers arrive at the same time at air refueling control points and avoid fratricide. It was also dynamic. If a base was rendered non-operational by a blizzard, a missile silo was out of service due to maintenance, or a submarine needed to return to port early, the highest priority targets needed to be reassigned

Construction projects were part of the B-1B deployment plan. In this 1986 photograph, construction workers are excavating trenches into which will be laid the lines for CASS at Grand Forks AFB. Located on parking spots, CASS supplied utilities to the B-1B instead of AGE carts. While Grand Forks AFB prepares for the B-1B, the 319th BMW is still using its predecessor, the B-52G. (*Sergeant Rockwell Jackson/US Air Force*)

to other forces. When it entered service, the B–1B had new capabilities and also operational limitations. As a result, JSTPS needed to revise the SIOP for the B–1B.

To support activation of the B–1B force, the B–1B SPO created branch offices. There was one of these offices, called a Site Activation Task Force (SATAF), at each B–1B main operating base. The SATAF represented the SPO on-site at the base.

Construction crews also went to work on future B–1B bases. Hangars needed modification for the B–1B. Parking spots for the BONEs included the Consolidated Aircraft Support System (CASS), which supplied utilities instead of AGE carts.

While SAC prepared the B–1B for operations, Oklahoma City Air Logistics Center (OC-ALC) at Tinker AFB prepared to become the B–1B maintenance depot. Like other USAF aircraft, the B–1B had a three-level maintenance concept. The first level was servicing the aircraft on the flight line and removing and replacing components. The second level entailed repair of components in maintenance shops. Both of these levels of maintenance were conducted by the maintenance squadrons of the BMW. OC-ALC did third-level maintenance, which included periodic depot maintenance, heavy repairs, and major modifications and upgrades.

The Star of Abilene

Production was not the only facet of the B–1B program that was concurrent with development and test. In order to meet the target IOC date, SAC needed the 96th BMW to receive B–1B aircraft for training as early as possible. Ideally, the Lot II aircraft would have augmented the fleet at the B–1B CTF to accelerate testing. Instead, the Lot II aircraft, starting with B–1B #2 (tail number 83-0065) would go to the 96th BMW. At delivery, the Lot II aircraft had little operational capability – TF, weapons delivery, SIS/SEF, and DAS were either incompletely tested, not yet cleared for operational service, or in some cases not even yet installed. Despite their limitations, the Lot II aircraft were useful for training.

USAF airmen needed to maintain the B–1B by themselves without contractor assistance for the aircraft to become operational. To guide operation and maintenance of this complicated and expensive aircraft, the USAF uses publications called Technical Orders (TOs) to guide

B-1B #2 (tail number 83-0065), the first Lot II aircraft, is being assembled in Palmdale. This aircraft was destined to become the 'The Star of Abilene', the first B-1B delivered to SAC. (*Master Sergeant Mike Dial/US Air Force*)

the actions of its personnel. The aircrew flight manual was the most well-known TO, but there were thousands of others. TOs covered everything from towing the B-1B, servicing systems, conducting inspections, installing and removing items ranging from engines to avionics units to tires, loading and unloading weapons, to troubleshooting and repairing components in the shops.

B-1B #2 first flew on 4 May 1985. After USAF acceptance, its first stop was Edwards AFB, but not for flight testing. Maintainers from AFFTC and 4200th TES used it for TO Validation and Verification (TOV&V). For example, there was a TO for removing the APU. Following the step-by-step procedure in the TO, the TOV&V team members would remove the APU, noting errors and ambiguities in the TO. These problems were sent to the TO writers, who would revise the TO. TOV&V lacked the drama and glamor of flight testing, but it was every bit as essential to entry of the B-1B into SAC service.

The arrival of B-1B #2 at Dyess AFB was an important program milestone. As a highly visible symbol of President's Reagan's defense build-up, the first SAC B-1B sent political and international messages. After a shakedown at Edwards, B-1B #2 was christened the 'Star of Abilene', in honor of the Texas city in which Dyess AFB was located.

B-1B #2 flew from Edwards AFB to Offutt AFB. After landing at Offutt AFB, the maintainers performed a routine post-flight inspection and discovered that the ingestion of foreign objects had damaged its engines. There are hinged EBADS flapper doors in the engine inlets. Vibration had worked the hinge pins and other hardware loose, which then entered the #1 and #2 engines and damaged them. Heroic efforts to quickly repair the aircraft, including the use of F-111 aircraft for the world's fastest and most expensive package delivery service, failed to fix B-1B #2 in time. A C-130 brought two replacement engines from Edwards AFB. After installation, all four engines were further damaged. There was a grand party planned for 29 June 1985, at which Dyess AFB and the Abilene community would welcome the arrival of the B-1B, and the guest of honor was unable to attend. Since one B-1B looked like another except to the most knowledgeable observers, a crew including SAC commander General Bennie L. Davis flew B-1B #1 to Abilene. It was a suitable replacement for B-1B #2, and party attendees enjoyed the festive occasion none the wiser about the last-minute substitution.

The 'Star of Abilene' flies over the picturesque landscape of the American West. All B-1B aircraft were delivered in the Strategic camouflage scheme, with FS34086 Dark Green and FS36081 Dark Gray on the top. The bottom was painted FS36081 Dark Gray and FS36118 Gunship Gray. (US Air Force)

IOC

Training was a major task during the rush to IOC. The 436th Strategic Training Squadron provided support through classroom instruction and the production of training material production and aids. Experienced aircraft maintainers like Technical Sergeant Lonnie Williams brought their expertise gained on the flight line and in shops to that squadron. Aircrew from the B-1B CTF trained the initial cadre of 4018th CCTS (later redesignated the 338th CCTS) instructors. Some aircrew and maintainers transferred from the 4200th TES at Edwards AFB to the 96th BMW to give it a core of people experienced with the B-1B.

The B-1B's arrival coincided with the advent of the Computer Age. Digital computers had existed for decades but now they were becoming pervasive. The B-1B was itself a flying network of computers: CITS, DAS, EMUX, and OAS. Computers played essential roles in B-1B development, testing, and manufacturing. The impact of computers extended into training. Computer-Based Instruction (CBI) introduced future B-1B aircrew in the 4018th CCTS to aircraft systems. The CBI included extensive graphics, reviews and tests. Because of the concurrency in the program, the CBI was updated frequently as the aircraft systems evolved.

After CBI, 4018th students advanced to the simulators. The Cockpit Procedures Trainers (CPT) were non-functioning low-fidelity trainers. Students used the CPTs to learn the location of instruments and controls and practice checklist procedures. Initially, the students advanced from the CPT to the Engineering Research Simulator (ERS). The ERS was lent to the 4018th CCTS while the definitive Weapon System Trainer (WST) was completed. The WST was a high-fidelity moving base simulator which allowed a full crew to simulate the full range of B-1B capabilities.

With the training program in place, the next step was to train the aircrew of the first operational B-1B squadron (the 337th BMS) and also the maintainers. The 96th BMW had more than its fair share of experienced people assigned to it. Not only would these people bring the B-1B to operational status, they would also be able to provide critiques and feedback of the training so it could be improved.

The qualifications for the initial complement of 337th BMS aircrew were high. Once the B-1B had matured as a weapon system, graduates fresh out of flying training could be assigned to the B-1B, but at first the minimum qualifications were:

- Aircraft Commander: 1,800 total flying hours, three years in a SAC weapon system (B-52, FB-111, KC-135, EC-135, RC-135), eighteen months as an aircraft commander.
- Co-pilot: 750 total flying hours, one year in a SAC weapon system.
- OSO: 1,500 total flying hours, three years in a SAC weapon system.
- DSO: 1,000 total flying hours, one year in a SAC weapon system.

As people streamed into Dyess AFB and were trained, the flow of aircraft from Palmdale also began. After repair, B-1B #2 finally arrived at Dyess AFB in July 1985. The 96th BMW would get all the Lot II and Lot III aircraft and some of the Lot IV aircraft to equip the 4018th CCTS and 337th BMS.

In parallel with training, a Follow-on Operational Test & Evaluation (FOT&E) program started at Dyess AFB. The flight testing at the B-1B CTF was DT&E (does the B-1B work and meet requirements?) and IOT&E (can the B-1B be an operationally effective and logistically supportable weapon system?). Building on DT&E/IOT&E, FOT&E evaluated training, procedures, and tactics. Several members of the B-1B CTF, including AFFTC flight test engineer Captain Otto J. Waniczek Jr., travelled to Dyess AFB to lend their experience to help set up the B-1B FOT&E. Detachment 1, 4201st TES conducted B-1B FOT&E for SAC.

The 96th BMW achieved IOC on 1 October 1986, under the command of Colonel Alan V. Rogers. It had fifteen B-1B aircraft on station and trained crews for those aircraft. B-1B #12 (tail number 84-0052) was the first airplane on alert, loaded with live nuclear weapons. Pilot Captain John Chilstrom, co-pilot Captain Rick Davis, OSO Captain Steve Clark, and DSO Captain Tim Young of the 337th BMS composed the first alert crew. Master Sergeant Walter Martin and Staff Sergeant Tim Coffey of the 96th Organization Maintenance Squadron were the first crew chiefs on alert. Staff Sergeant Joseph Cooper and Sergeant Glenn Breaux relieved Martin and Coffey at shift change. IOC was a major milestone for the program. The B-1B was now an operational weapon system and part of the SIOP.

B-1B 86-0109 'Spectre' was originally assigned to the 319th BMW at Grand Forks AFB. When this photograph was taken on 6 July 1988, it was in the inventory of the 28th BMW at Ellsworth AFB. (*Technical Sergeant Michael J. Haggerty/US Air Force*)

Nose art was a part of the culture of US Army Air Forces bomber units in the Second World War, but until the 1980s SAC did not permit it. In an attempt to raise morale and reach back to the heritage of the service, SAC then authorized it. Compared to Second World War nose art, SAC's in the 1980s was tame, with nothing too risqué. Considering the rising number of women in the ranks of the USAF during that period, overtly sexual nose art would have caused offense. B-1B 86-0109 was nicknamed 'Spectre'. (*Master Sergeant Jose Lopez, Jr./US Air Force*)

As B-1B production increased to the rate of four aircraft per month, the other SAC main operating bases rapidly filled their ramps with B-1B aircraft. On 21 January 1987, B-1B #33 (tail number 85-0073) arrived at Ellsworth AFB for the 28th BMW, beginning the equipage of that unit. B-1B #70 (tail number 86-0110) was the first B-1B for Grand Forks AFB for the 319th BMW, arriving on 19 September 1987. McConnell AFB received the B-1B last, with B-1B #84 (tail number 86-0124) arriving on 5 January 1988 for the 384th BMW.

Alert

SAC proudly proclaimed its motto: 'Peace is our Profession'. As ironic as that motto seemed for a military unit capable of unleashing death and destruction on an unimaginable scale, it happened to be true. At the core of SAC's capabilities was the alert force of bombers and ICBMs able to survive a first strike and retaliate, thus making that first strike an unthinkable choice. Putting the B-1B on alert was the culmination of a three-decade pursuit of SAC's next bomber.

An operational B-1B squadron in SAC had approximately seventeen aircraft. On a routine basis, four were on alert at any one time. The remainder were undergoing maintenance or used for training. In a crisis, every aircraft in a condition to accomplish the mission could be put on alert, but that was not a sustainable force posture for long periods. A similar number of KC-135 tankers would also stand alert at the base.

Each SAC bomber base had an alert pad on which the alert aircraft were parked. The alert pad was laid out to facilitate the rapid exit of the aircraft, with no aircraft positioned to block others if it could not be started. An alert facility near the alert pad housed the personnel on alert, with quarters, food service, dining area, offices, and recreation rooms. Fences and security police secured the alert area, with entry restricted to those authorized to be there.

Aircrew members served seven-day alert tours, generally from Thursday to Thursday. After turning over alert responsibility to the following crew, the aircrew members enjoyed Combat Crew Rest and Relaxation (C²R²) through the following Sunday. The crew chiefs assigned to

The Ellsworth AFB alert pad can be seen underneath B-1B 86-0097 'Iron Eagle'. The parking spots on the alert pad were arranged in what was called a 'Christmas tree' to facilitate rapid scrambling of the alert force. (*Technical Sergeant Michael J. Haggerty/US Air Force*)

maintain the alert aircraft either served a seven-day alert tour like the aircrews or rotated on shorter shifts, with different units having different policies. Depending on the manning levels in the unit, aircrew members pulled an alert tour every three to five weeks. Crew chiefs were on alert when their aircraft was on alert.

SAC used 'hard' crews for its combat units, which meant that the crews kept the same members for alert and flying. 'Hard' crews worked and trained together, and their superior teamwork led to better performance. On an annual basis, each crew demonstrated its mastery of its Emergency War Order (EWO) mission to the satisfaction of the BMW commander. Crews needed to be re-certified on their EWO when the SIOP changed. On assumption of alert status, the incoming crew conducted a turnover with the departing crew, verifying all classified documents and cryptological material and conducting an inventory of the weapons loaded on the aircraft by serial number. Afterwards crew members needed to pass quizzes on both emergency procedures and nuclear command and control procedures. The passing grades on both quizzes were 100 per cent. The crew studied their EWO. Each morning there was a briefing for all personnel on alert, covering aircraft status, weather, and intelligence. After the daily briefing, the aircrew and crew chiefs inspected the alert aircraft.

The restrictions on movement of personnel on alert depended on the threat assessment. Depending on that assessment, alert personnel would be limited to the alert area or allowed to leave the area for other parts of the base that were close enough to return there quickly. In the event of a very high threat assessment, crews could be required to be onboard the aircraft at all times.

At least once per alert tour, the klaxon sounded and the alert force sprang into action. The personnel in the alert force did not know if this was only a drill or the beginning of a war, so every klaxon was treated with deadly seriousness. Depending on the location of their aircraft, the aircrew and crew chiefs ran to their aircraft or jumped in a truck to drive to it. The first person to reach the aircraft dropped the entry ladder and started the APU using a start switch located on the nose gear strut. The aircrew entered the B-1B, while crew chiefs such as Master Sergeant George A. Gilbert, Technical Sergeant Jerry Densmore and Staff Sergeant Henry Miller of the 96th Organizational Maintenance Squadron, Sergeant Anthony B. 'Blaine' Cason of the 28th Organizational Maintenance Squadron, and Sergeant Kyle C. Fagin of the 384th Organizational Maintenance Squadron removed any covers, supported engine starts, and pulled the nose landing gear chocks. Onboard the aircraft, the aircrew decoded instructions that could range from shutting down the aircraft, to taxiing only, to take-off. By the time that the B-1B entered service, SAC aircraft did not fly for training when loaded with live nuclear weapons. If the aircraft were directed to take-off, the take-off interval between B-1B aircraft was twelve seconds. From the klaxon sounding to all bombers getting airborne only took a few minutes. Orchestrating this process took SAC years to perfect, and the B-1B was designed around it.

SAC insisted on a high level of security. Fences around areas containing nuclear weapons had signs attached to them that warned it was a restricted area and included the memorable phrase 'Use of deadly force authorized'. Not only was access to the entire alert area controlled, but each aircraft was also a secure zone. Painted red lines on the alert pad were inviolate. The consequence of crossing that red line was to end up face down on the ramp at the direction of a young security policeman aggressively pointing his M16 rifle at the trespasser. Rank was no protection; the security policemen took special delight in 'jacking up' senior officers who did not watch where they walked. An entry control point at the nose of each aircraft manned by an armed security police airman was the only authorized way to enter the 'no lone zone' enclosed by the red line. The zone was so named because no person was allowed to be in proximity to a nuclear weapon by himself. The security police airman checked the identification of anyone attempting to enter the zone against an access authorization list but was himself not permitted to enter the zone. Any visitors to the zone such as maintenance specialists needed to be vouched for by the aircrew or a crew chief.

The security included roving patrols of security police airmen in and around the alert area. Heavily armed security police airman also escorted convoys transporting nuclear weapons between the Weapon Storage Area and the alert area. SAC perfected snow removal. Northern tier SAC bases like Grand Forks AFB often experienced severe winter weather, but the alert force needed to remain ready to go despite the inclement weather. While the civil engineer squadron plowed the snow on the ground, the crew chiefs removed snow and ice from the alert aircraft.

The Operational Readiness Inspection (ORI), conducted by the SAC Inspector General, was the most critical event in the career of every SAC unit commander. Periodically, the SAC Inspector General would visit each BMW for a no-notice ORI. The ORI exercised every element of the BMW, on the ground and in the air, to evaluate its ability to execute its EWO mission. ORI failure ended the career of a SAC unit commander, who would be immediately relieved of his position. Service in SAC was often meaningful and professionally challenging but it was always stressful.

Problems

When the B-1B entered service with SAC, it was still a work in progress. Because of its immature state, critics of the B-1B lambasted it. Most of the problems would eventually be solved, but at IOC the B-1B operated with serious limitations.

At IOC, the B-1B lacked an operational TF capability. DAS had major deficiencies. With SIS/SEF still under test, SAC was not permitted to fly the B-1B at its maximum gross weight. The B-1B had yet to launch a SRAM. To keep B-1B production on schedule, systems and components in short supply were removed from operational aircraft at Dyess AFB and returned to Palmdale for installation in other aircraft.

Colonel James L. Wakefield, the 96th BMW deputy commander for maintenance, his team, and their counterparts at the other B-1B wings faced major challenges in keeping their growing fleet of B-1B bombers in the air. Reliability and maintainability were a huge challenge for the B-1B. As with the other aspects of the program, B-1B maintenance was designed around computers. CITS detected faults. After each flight, maintainers downloaded faults data from CITS and fed it to the Core Automated Maintenance System (CAMS). CAMS was the new base-level automated maintenance management information system. It replaced traditional USAF aircraft maintenance paperwork with a computerized system. In theory, the combination of CITS in the B-1B and CAMS on the ground made aircraft maintenance more efficient and responsive.

In practice, B-1B maintenance at the time of IOC was problematic. The B-1B was a new aircraft and experienced its share of the problems inherent to any new system. CITS development lagged behind the development of other aircraft systems. It needed several years of additional programming to tune its problem detection and isolation algorithms and reduce false alarms. In 1985, CITS generated as many as 200 false failure indications per flight. CITS improved in 1987 and 1988, but AFOTEC still expressed concern that it was unsatisfactory.

Dyess AFB was the first base at which CAMS was deployed. Like CITS, it was not fully debugged. The combination of a new aircraft, an immature CITS, an immature CAMS, and maintenance personnel who were still adjusting to computerized maintenance cast the B-1B in a bad light.

Despite all the work on TOs, writing them and conducting TOV&V did not keep up with demand. USAF maintainers were forced to use Engineering Dispositions, which was not standard procedure for USAF maintenance. Rockwell technical representatives onsite at the main operating bases played a large part in getting the Engineering Dispositions approved until the TOs caught up with the need for them.

Another serious problem was the lack of adequate stocks of spare parts. In some cases, the service lives of parts had been overestimated, leading to more demand than predicted. Some suppliers were late in delivering spare parts. Concurrency also was a factor in the problem. With simultaneous testing, production and fielding, the design of parts was being frequently revised. The instability in design made it difficult to produce parts in the proper configuration.

The lack of spare parts degraded the operational readiness of the B-1B fleet. In early 1987, between six and fourteen aircraft were not mission-capable because of supply issues. B-1B maintainers needed to resort to the dreaded practice of cannibalization, in which parts were removed from one aircraft to repair another. In theory, cannibalization tripled the maintenance workload, because the part now had to be removed from and then replaced on the donor aircraft, as well as installed on the recipient. Cannibalization actually caused maintenance workloads to be more than tripled, since every maintenance action had the potential to cause further damage in the form of stripped and cross-threaded fasteners, broken wires, and other maintenance-induced damage. The large number of B-1B aircraft grounded for lack of spare parts and needing maintenance reduced the availability of aircraft for training flights. The FOT&E team reported that 40 per cent of the B-1B fleet at Dyess AFB was not mission-capable because of supply between September 1987 and January 1988. Between broken airplanes and lack of fully trained crews, the B-1B wings could not meet their full commitments to put aircraft on alert.

The B-1B was plagued with fuel leaks. Because the fuel system used integral tanks with no bladders, the structure itself needed to be sealed tight. As training flights became more frequent, the stress and strains in the airframes increased, which aggravated the problem. The contractors sent teams to the B-1B main operating bases to find the source of the leaks, remove all fuel from the tanks, remove old sealant, prepare surfaces, and then reapply the sealant to them. The fuel leakage problem was annoying rather than indicative of a fundamental deficiency in the B-1B, but it did contribute to the B-1B's growing image problem. DAS, SIS/SEF and TF might be difficult for those outside the aerospace community to understand, but anybody – and that would certainly include members of Congress and newspaper editorial writers – could appreciate the importance of fuel leaks.

On 10 March 1986, B-1B #2 was on a 4018th CCTS training flight from Dyess AFB. While being swept forward, the VG wings halted at a 55° sweep angle. To complicate the situation, the aircrew shut down engine #3, which had indications of problems. After consultation with the 96th BMW command post, the B-1B headed to Edwards AFB, which had the Rogers Dry Lake, the landing strip of choice for high-speed landings. On the way to Edwards, the B-1B refueled from a KC-135A. Air refueling a B-1B with the wings swept at 55° was a decidedly non-standard maneuver and was never flight tested, but the B-1B crew did a fine job, considering they had one engine shutdown.

An F-111 from the B-1B CTF launched to chase B-1B #2. Rogers Dry Lake did not live up to its name, for it was wet and muddy after some recent rain. The B-1B would land on 15,000ft long Runway 04. After two practice low passes, the B-1B set up for landing. Because of the 55° wing sweep angle, the B-1B could not extend its flaps and slats. Normally, a B-1B at light weight would fly an approach at 150 KIAS. With the wings swept at 55° and the flaps and slats retracted, B-1B #2 flew its approach at a blisteringly fast 238 KIAS. The landing used up all but the last 2,000ft of runway. Firefighters doused a small brake fire while the aircrew rapidly egressed the aircraft. The USAF decorated Major David Holmes, Major Dean Hodgson, Major William Fier, Major James LaSalvia, and Major Fred Strain with the Air Medal for their cool and competent handling of this emergency. Post-flight investigation discovered a kink in a mechanical interconnect cable that ensures both wings move together to prevent asymmetrical wing sweep. Engineers revised the drawing for the cable installation to ensure it would not kink.

Tragedy struck the 338th CCTS on 28 September 1987. B-1B #12 (tail number 84-0052) with the callsign TAUPE 52 was flying on low-level training route IR-177 near La Junta, Colorado at 560 KIAS and 600ft AGL altitude. Captain Lawrence H. 'Larry' Haskell, an experienced B-52 pilot transitioning to the B-1B, was sitting in the pilot's seat and controlling the aircraft. He noticed a white or gray blur slightly to the left of the nose and moving left to right. A moment later, Haskell felt a powerful impact, with the aircraft shaking and rattling. Haskell described the aircraft as feeling like 'gears grinding without oil'. Haskell passed control to instructor pilot Major James T. Acklin, Sr., sitting in the co-pilot seat. Acklin started to slow the aircraft down while Haskell focused on the checklist and emergency procedures. After receiving indications

'The Star of Abilene' made an emergency diversion to Edwards AFB on 10 March 1986 to land on its 15,000ft long runway when the wings could not be swept forward. The high-speed landing stressed the wheels, brakes, and tires beyond their limits, and fire crews responded to the small fires that resulted. The aircraft did not suffer any serious damage in the incident. (*Air Force Test Center History Office*)

of fires in engines #3 and #4, Haskell activated the fire suppression system for those engines. Captain Ricky M. Bean was another pilot transitioning to the B-1B, and he was sitting in the forward jump seat between Haskell and Acklin. It was a tight fit in the jump seat, and occupants didn't normally wear a parachute. Haskell told Bean to get a parachute on. Presumably Major Wayne D. Whitlock in the aft jump seat between the DSO and OSO was doing the same thing. Haskell used a radio to contact the nearest air traffic control facility, Denver Air Route Traffic Control Center and reported an emergency: 'TAUPE 52, emergency aircraft, aborting IR-177, bird strike, engine fire, request 10,000 feet.'

A large bird had hit the B-1B where the right nacelle mated with the fuselage. The bird entered a small gap between the top of the nacelle and the bottom of the fuselage, shattering a fuel line which then sprayed fuel onto hot ducts, igniting a fire in the OWF area. The right OWF departed the aircraft, and the hydraulic systems in the zone failed. Acklin lost control as the B-1B rolled to the right. Haskell initiated a crew ejection. Haskell, Major William Price, and Captain Joseph S. (Sloan) Butler successfully ejected. During the mishap investigation, calculations showed the aircraft was within two seconds of being out of the safe ejection envelope. Major Acklin, sitting in the co-pilot seat, was unable to eject because of a system failure and perished. Major Wayne D. Whitlock and Captain Ricky M. Bean occupied the jump seats. They attempted a bottom bailout but were unable to accomplish it and also died in the mishap. The B-1B crashed eight seconds after the crew ejected. For Bean and Haskell, it had been their first flight in the B-1B.

The root cause of the failure in Acklin's ejection seat was an AND gate in the pyrotechnic ejection sequence. The AND gate was a valve that prevented the ejection seat from firing until the overhead hatch had been jettisoned. It should have repositioned after the overhead hatch separated but did not.

Investigators discovered the right OWF along the flight path 17 miles before the aircraft impact point. The OWF provided evidence of the extent of damage to the aircraft near the area of the bird impact. In the aftermath of this accident, the juncture between the nacelles and the fuselage was hardened with Kevlar and steel. Maintainers inspected the ejection seats on all other B-1B aircraft and found other aircraft with AND gate defects that needed to be fixed. Also, there were many airplanes in which the bottom bailout interlock was improperly rigged. This interlock prevented the bottom bailout handle from being pulled before the inner pressure hatch was opened. The suction from venturi effect when the entry hatch was jettisoned was strong enough that the interior pressure hatch could not be opened. Henceforth, the crew compartment jump seats were restricted from use during low-level flight. Eventually they were removed.

B-1B #23 (tail number 85-0063) experienced a major fire in the left OWF area while in the traffic pattern at Dyess AFB on 8 November 1988. The exact origin of the fire was never discovered, but there were several fuel lines in that area and mostly likely one of them was leaking. Captain Michael E. 'Muddy' Waters, Captain George M. Gover, Captain Charles M. Zarza and 1Lt Anton Eret, Jr. of the 337th BMS ejected before the aircraft crashed. After his three crewmates ejected, Captain Waters, the pilot, stayed onboard the aircraft to steer it away from populated areas before ejecting himself. In the aftermath of the mishap, the B-1B got an OWF fire detection and suppression system.

Only a few days later, B-1B #36 (tail number 85-0076) crashed at Ellsworth AFB during an instrument approach on a foggy night on 17 November 1988. The aircraft was below the minimum descent altitude for a non-precision approach procedure and hit a utility pole. Major Thomas C. Skilman, Captain Mick R. Guthals, Major Dean C. Spraggins, and Captain Grover M. Gossett of the 77th BMS, 28th BMW ejected at a very low altitude and with the aircraft at a steep bank angle, with two men suffering injuries. Investigators cited deficiencies in the VSD and FDC which caused precision approaches to be prohibited in the B-1B to be a contributing factor to this mishap. System improvements implemented after this mishap led to precision approaches being permitted in the B-1B.

Although there was no pattern to the accidents, SAC had lost three expensive B-1B bombers and three crew members in slightly more than one year. The combination of accidents, reliability and maintainability problems and immature aircraft systems painted an unflattering picture of the program.

B-1B #30 (tail number 85-0070) from the 337th BMS, 96th BMW was on a training mission on 4 October 1989 when the nose landing gear did not extend and the alternative extension system did not work. The aircrew pulled Gs in an attempt to extend the nose landing gear. When those maneuvers failed to extend it, they tried two touch and go landings on the theory that setting down the aircraft on the main landing gears would jar the nose landing gear into position; again, the landing gear remained in its bay. B-1B #30 flew to Edwards AFB where it was met by an F-111 from the B-1B CTF. Unlike B-1B #2's unplanned landing at Edwards AFB in 1986, this time Rogers Dry Lake was indeed dry and hard. After a practice touch and go landing and dumping fuel to achieve a lighter weight, B-1B #30 landed on Lakebed Runway 33 with minimal damage to the aircraft. Captain Jeffrey K. Beene, Captain Vernon B. Benton, Captain Robert H. Hendricks, and Lieutenant Colonel Joseph G. Day received the Mackay Trophy in 1989 for their superb airmanship, which saved a valuable B-1B bomber. After the incident, investigators discovered that the nose landing gear failed to extend because a maintainer had failed to fully seat a connector when changing the nose landing gear selector valve.

B-1B #88 (tail number 86-0128) from the 28th BMS, 384th BMW was flying a night TF training flight on 4 October 1990 when the aircrew felt an explosion and the aircraft yawed to the left. Captain Greg Buelt, in the pilot's seat, looked out his left side window and saw a flame.

B-1B 85-0076 'Black Jack' crashed at Ellsworth AFB during an instrument approach on a foggy night on 17 November 1988. (*Master Sergeant Jose Lopez, Jr./US Air Force*)

B-1B 85-0070 'Excalibur' of the 96th BMW diverted to Edwards AFB on 4 October 1989 to land on the dry lakebed when the nose landing gear could not be lowered. The crew egressed the aircraft through the opened overhead ejection hatch. The damage was minimal and quickly repaired. (*US Air Force*)

Instructor pilot Major Bill Clift, seeing instruments for the #1 engine trending to zero, shut down that engine. OSO Major John Howe and DSO Captain Sean Yeronick assisted the pilots with setting up for an approach to Pueblo Memorial Airport in Pueblo, Colorado. After landing, the aircrew performed an emergency ground egress. Upon inspecting the aircraft, they discovered that the #1 engine had completely separated from the B-1B, along with the engine bay doors and part of the nacelle. The left horizontal stabilator, left wing, fuselage aft of the #1 engine, and aft radome also suffered damage. A tough structure and systems redundancy enabled the B-1B to survive this serious emergency.

Repairing the B-1B #88 at Pueblo was impractical. Rockwell personnel designed and applied temporary fixes to the aircraft structure and systems so it could be ferried. Rockwell test pilot Addison S. Thompson calculated performance, stability, and control parameters for the unprecedented three-engine take-off, including information if the critical (#2 engine) failed. At a light take-off gross weight of 255,000lbs, the performance calculations showed the flight was feasible. Precautions included taking off away from the city of Pueblo. On 17 November 1990, a B-1B CTF crew consisting of Addison S. Thompson, Lieutenant Colonel Harold R. 'Randy' Gaston, Major Mark E. Hobba and Jim A. Nelson flew B-1B #88 without incident from Pueblo to Tinker AFB in Oklahoma for repair.

More engine trouble dogged the B-1B. B-1B #8 (83-0071) from the 96th BMW experienced an inflight engine fire on 19 December 1990. The following day, SAC grounded the B-1B and prohibited ground engine runs, although it remained on alert. Examination of the recovered #1 engine from the Pueblo incident and the failed engine from the Dyess AFB emergency both showed failure of a first stage fan blade retainer ring. GE redesigned and tested the component. New inspection procedures for the engines were subsequently developed. SAC lifted the grounding on 5 February 1991, with individual aircraft being released for flight when their engines were retrofitted with the new component and inspected. B-1B #8 flew on three engines from Dyess AFB to Palmdale for repairs at Rockwell, again with Addison S. Thompson in the pilot's seat.

SAC maintainers discovered cracks in the upper mount for the main landing gear actuators. Captain Scott M. Dayton, who transferred from the B-1B SPO to OC-ALC, was supporting the

B-1B 83-0071 'Grand Illusion' suffered an inflight engine fire on 19 December 1990. (*Staff Sergeant Roach/ US Air Force*)

B-1B in his new assignment and working to analyze and solve this problem. Engineers redesigned the mount and changed the material from titanium to steel. OC-ALC installed the new mounts in the field at the B-1B main operating bases. During its period of SAC service, the B-1B was also the subject of numerous other upgrades in response to incidents that fortunately did not cost lives or destroy aircraft. Kenneth V. Decker and his crew of Rockwell employees played an important role in improving the B-1B by visiting the bases to install changes to the aircraft.

Becoming an Effective Weapon System

To personnel in the middle of the effort to bring the B-1B into operational status with SAC, the period leading up to IOC and the several years thereafter were filled with frustration. As exciting as it was to work with the beautiful and sophisticated BONE, it had numerous problems and limitations. The situation looked more promising when viewed in perspective and with hindsight. The diligent efforts of the SPO, the contractors, the B-1B CTF, and SAC were showing progress.

As the B-1B CTF tested the TF capabilities, operational SAC units began to get limited clearance to fly TF. The first SAC TF flight was on 9 March 1987, flown by the 337th BMS.

B-1B #32 (tail number 85-0072) carried additional instrumentation. It was the aircraft of choice for several interesting missions. On 14 April 1987, it flew a 21.7-hour, 9,411-mile mission over the North Pole and within 160 miles of the Soviet Union. Flying over the North Pole was not just a means of getting a headline. Due to the nature of certain trigonometric functions, navigation calculations had been known to fail when flying over a pole, and this flight proved the OAS did not have this problem.

During 10–22 May 1987, B-1B #32 deployed across the Pacific Ocean to Hickam AFB, Hawaii and Andersen AFB, Guam for the Distant Mariner exercise. Distant Mariner included flights across the 180° meridian and the equator to verify the robustness of navigation calculations in the same way the North Pole flight did. On 3 June 1987, B-1B #32 conducted

B-1B 85-0072 'Polarized' got its name because of its navigation test flight to the North Pole. (*Master Sergeant Stephen Jones/US Air Force*)

the first operational test launch of a SRAM. Later that month, it flew four sorties during the Red Flag exercise at Nellis AFB, Nevada.

The B-1B #24 (tail number 85-0061) appeared at the Paris Air Show in June 1987. The flying display impressed the air show attendees. Less impressively, the aircraft broke when it attempted to leave and was stranded in France until it was repaired. The reliability problems that haunted the B-1B at this time had followed it overseas.

SAC wings competed annually to display their proficiency in the skills they needed to complete their mission. Olympic Arena was the name of the ICBM competition. The SAC Bombing and Navigation Competition, universally known as 'Bomb Comp', was called Giant Voice through 1987 and Proud Shield starting in 1988. The B-1B wings first competed in

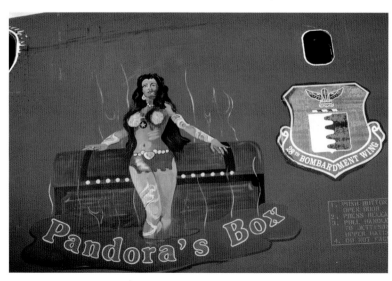

B-1B 85-0084 'Pandora's Box' was assigned to the 28th BMW when this photograph was taken in 1988. (*Master Sergeant Jose Lopez, Jr./US Air Force*)

Bomb Comp at Proud Shield 88 and excelled in the bombing and SRAM events, a testament to the outstanding navigation performance of the B-1B OAS. The following year, at Proud Shield 89, the 96th BMW won the Fairchild Award for the best bomber/tanker team.

As the B-1B matured and confidence in it grew, exercises became more demanding. The Mighty Warrior exercise in 1989 featured seven B-1B aircraft and a contingent of maintainers from the 319th BMW at Grand Forks AFB deploying to Mountain Home AFB, Idaho. The aircraft flew all forty scheduled sorties from Mountain Home AFB, demonstrating much better reliability than a few years earlier.

The 46th BMS, 319th BMW also conducted the Bold Crusade exercise in 1989, which simulated a EWO mission. Three B-1B bombers departed from Grand Forks AFB on 20 April 1989. First flying west until reaching the Pacific Ocean, the aircraft then proceeded to circumnavigate most of the continental United States. Along the way, the B-1B conducted air refueling, simulated low-level bomb attacks, practiced ECM techniques, and evaded fighters from the Air National Guard. After fourteen hours of flying, the B-1B aircraft landed at Plattsburgh AFB, New York.

B-1B 85-0092 'Enforcer' was yet another Lot IV airplane in the 28th BMW. Because the wings sequentially transitioned to the B-1B, aircraft in a wing usually were from the same or adjacent lots. (*Master Sergeant Jose Lopez, Jr./US Air Force*)

B-1B 86-0095 'Mystique' was built as part of Lot V. (*Master Sergeant Jose Lopez, Jr./US Air Force*)

In 1990, the B–1B was officially named the Lancer. Unofficially, the B–1B community used BONE and ignored the official name. Interestingly, Lancer applied only to the B–1B. The B–1A never received an official name.

USAF Chief of Staff General Merrill A. 'Tony' McPeak wanted to set some aviation records, and the B–1B offered the performance to satisfy McPeak's ambition. The 46th BMS under the command of Lieutenant Colonel William J. Moran, Jr. would put the B–1B into the record books for time-to-climb in three weight classes. Rockwell engineers designed the profiles with the assistance of the 46th BMS, in particular Captain Scott A. Neuman, a pilot and aeronautical engineer. Moran and his crews practiced them in the simulator. The flight profiles were demanding. The engines would be in maximum afterburner, burning fuel at an astounding rate. In the lightest weight class, the aircraft would be on the edge of exhausting its fuel after the record run. At the top of the profiles, the pilots would be pulling the nose up very close to the AOA limit to turn energy into climb rate – exceeding the AOA limit would have made the aircraft unstable. The B–1B set records for the *Fédération Aéronautique Internationale* categories of Class C-1 (landplane) Group III (jet propulsion), in the weight classifications of o (80,000kg to less than 100,000kg), p (100,000kg to less than 150,000kg), and q (150,000kg to less than 200,000kg).

Saturday, 29 February 1992 was an unusually warm day in the normally frigid North Dakota winter. On the first heavy weight (weight classification q) flight to 12,000 meters, MEC and AFT controllers on the F101-GE-102 engines commanded an augmenter fuel flow cutback as the aircraft climbed to prevent combustion instabilities at certain temperature and altitude combinations. The B–1B ended its climb short of the target altitude. Another crew repeated the attempt on 18 March 1992, setting the record.

Lieutenant Colonel William J. Moran, Jr. commanded the 46th BMS when it used the B-1B to set twelve world records for time-to-climb. He also was the pilot on several of those flights. In this picture taken several years earlier when he was a Major, he was a pilot assigned to the 4200th TES and flying with the B-1B CTF. Before his work on the B-1B, Moran flew the B-52G and FB-111A operationally. (*William Moran collection*)

Record	Class	Date	Tail number	Pilot	Co-pilot	OSO	Time (minutes: seconds)
Time to climb to 3,000 meters altitude	C-1, o, III	28-Feb-92	86-0111	Lieutenant Colonel William J. Moran Jr.	Captain Mark L. Eby	Captain Richard M. Nehls	1:13.06
Time to climb to 6,000 meters altitude	C-1, o, III	28-Feb-92	86-0111	Lieutenant Colonel William J. Moran Jr.	Captain Mark L. Eby	Captain Richard M. Nehls	1:42.23
Time to climb to 9,000 meters altitude	C-1, o, III	28-Feb-92	86-0111	Lieutenant Colonel William J. Moran Jr.	Captain Mark L. Eby	Captain Richard M. Nehls	2:10.98
Time to climb to 12,000 meters altitude	C-1, o, III	28-Feb-92	86-0121	Lieutenant Colonel James P. Robinson	Captain Scott A. Neuman	Captain Dennis J. Murphy	5:01.66
Time to climb to 3,000 meters altitude	C-1, p, III	29-Feb-92	86-0121	Lieutenant Colonel James P. Robinson	Captain Scott A. Neuman	Captain Dennis J. Murphy	1:19.28
Time to climb to 6,000 meters altitude	C-1, p, III	29-Feb-92	86-0121	Lieutenant Colonel James P. Robinson	Captain Scott A. Neuman	Captain Dennis J. Murphy	1:54.95
Time to climb to 9,000 meters altitude	C-1, p, III	29-Feb-92	86-0121	Lieutenant Colonel James P. Robinson	Captain Scott A. Neuman	Captain Dennis J. Murphy	2:22.77
Time to climb to 12,000 meters altitude	C-1, p, III	29-Feb-92	86-0121	Lieutenant Colonel James P. Robinson	Captain Scott A. Neuman	Captain Dennis J. Murphy	6:09.35
Time to climb to 3,000 meters altitude	C-1, q, III	29-Feb-92	86-0121	Captain Jeffry F. Smith	Captain Tracy A. Sharp	Captain Bryan S. Ferguson	1:59.97
Time to climb to 6,000 meters altitude	C-1, q, III	29-Feb-92	86-0111	Captain Jeffry F. Smith	Captain Tracy A. Sharp	Captain Bryan S. Ferguson	2:39.27
Time to climb to 9,000 meters altitude	C-1, q, III	29-Feb-92	86-0111	Captain Jeffry F. Smith	Captain Tracy A. Sharp	Captain Bryan S. Ferguson	3:47.75
Time to climb to 12,000 meters altitude	C-1, q, III	18-Mar-92	86-0121	Captain Jeffry F. Smith	Major John E. Alexander	Captain Paul S. Ellia	9:42.85

In addition to the 46th BMS crew members, a National Aeronautic Association official rode in the DSO seat for all the record-setting flights to certify the times.

B-1B 84-0051 'Lucky Lady' was the third Lot III aircraft. The nose art was an example of the more modest and fully-clothed pin-up art permitted under SAC regulations. In 1991, this aircraft was renamed 'Boss Hawg'. It is now on display at the National Museum of the United States Air Force. (*Staff Sergeant Roach/ US Air Force*)

Unsurprisingly, B-1B 84-0056 'Sweet Sixteen' was the sixteenth B-1B built. Master Sergeant David Gallentine of the 96th Organizational Maintenance Squadron 'owned' this aircraft in 1996. He was assisted by Staff Sergeant David Walraven, Staff Sergeant Jerry Rader, Sergeant Jack 'Willie' Burnell, Sergeant Henry Miller and Airman 1st Class Tracy Brouillard. A team of this size could cover 'round-the-clock' shifts if needed. (*Staff Sergeant Roach/ US Air Force*)

B-1B 85-0062 'Sky Dancer' with nose art of a girl riding a winged horse. Technical Sergeant Jerry Densmore was the crew chief of 'Sky Dancer' in 1986-1988. (*Staff Sergeant Roach/ US Air Force*)

The Cold War Ends

The B-52G was a workhorse during Operation Desert Storm in 1991. Seven B-52G bombers launched some of the first air attacks against Iraq, using a highly classified conventional-armed variant of the ALCM. The major contribution of the B-52G in the war was devastating area attacks against Iraqi ground forces. While part of the B-52G force participated in the war, the remainder of the B-52G bombers, all of the B-52H bombers and the B-1B force remained on alert. SAC commander General John T. Chain, Jr. directed SAC to plan a mission with four B-1B bombers from the 28th BMW that would fly directly from the United States to Iraq and back. But a spate of severe engine problems in late 1990 grounded the B-1B fleet, even though it remained on alert. The capability of the B-1B to deliver a full load of Mk 82 conventional bombs was also not fully tested at this time. Chain's successor, General George L. Butler, cancelled the plans. The B-1B would eventually see plenty of action in the skies over Iraq, but not in 1991.

Cold War tensions dramatically lessened in the aftermath of the fall of the Berlin Wall in 1989. The Cold War ended for SAC on 28 September 1991. In an unclassified message transmitted that day to SAC units:

THE SECRETARY OF DEFENSE HAS DIRECTED, EFFECTIVE IMMEDIATELY, ALL SIOP BOMBERS, THEIR SUPPORTING TANKERS, AND MINUTEMAN II ICBMS ARE RELEASED FROM THEIR IMMEDIATE/MODIFIED RESPONSE SIOP ALERT COMMITMENT.

A subsequent paragraph of the message directed the units to download weapons, return them to the WSA, and remove aircraft from the alert pads. SAC had lived up to its motto: 'Peace is our Profession'. Considering the consequences of nuclear war between the United States and the Soviet Union, it may have been the most important military victory in American and even world history.

When this picture was taken on 23 December 1991, the SAC bomber and tanker force had been taken off alert and the Soviet Union was in the process of dissolving into its constituent republics. (*B. Thompson/US Air Force*)

Retrospective

The Cold War gave birth to the B-1. Its maturation as an effective strategic weapon system coincided with the end of that war. With the benefit of hindsight, did the policy decisions concerning the B-1 appear to be correct? How did the B-1B contribute to the end of Cold War and its favorable resolution from an American perspective?

The political context of President Carter's decision to cancel B-1A production was a post-Vietnam weariness with high levels of military spending and a belief that détente and arms control treaties were the best ways to manage Cold War tensions and reduce the threat of nuclear war. When Carter chose the ALCM over the B-1A, the two systems were at a similar

While its military effect on the Cold War was probably minor, the B-1B was a powerful statement of American determination. (*Staff Sergeant Michael J. Haggerty/US Air Force*)

level of technical maturity. At the time of the decision, the critical guidance and navigation, nuclear warhead, and turbofan engine technologies for ALCM had all been demonstrated, but ALCM in a production configuration had not yet flown. The B-1A had been flying for nearly three years at the time of the decision, but never with the critical DAS. Depending on what assumptions were used, either the B-1A or B-52/ALCM could be shown to be superior. There were such great uncertainties in the assumptions and calculations that drawing conclusions from the studies of relative effectiveness was questionable. Both alternatives undoubtedly posed a significant threat to the Soviet Union, and the B-52/ALCM choice was less expensive.

On the other hand, it is undeniable the Soviet Union felt free to exhibit its predatory and aggressive nature during the years of the Carter presidency. Its military build-up during this period was also vast. In theory, the Soviet Union attained the ability to preemptively destroy the American ICBM force in its silos, and intercept and destroy the bombers that escaped a surprise first strike. The submarines with their SLBMs were largely invulnerable to a first strike, but this invulnerability did not necessarily extend to the communications links over which their launch orders would be transmitted. The threat was less that the Soviet Union would actually carry out a nuclear first strike than that it would translate nuclear superiority into coercive power to intimidate American allies into neutrality and force the United States to retreat during confrontations.

The reality of the adverse trends in the strategic balance was overstated. Even a 95 per cent effective Soviet first strike, which would have been extraordinary for an unprecedented military operation that could never be rehearsed in any realistic way, would have resulted in several

Mount Rushmore National Memorial is carved into a granite hill near Ellsworth AFB. It is a favorite backdrop for photographs of aircraft from that base. (*Technical Sergeant Michael J. Haggerty/US Air Force*)

hundred thermonuclear weapons hitting the Soviet Union. It is inconceivable the Soviet Union could have emerged from nuclear retaliation as a functioning state. The Soviet leadership of the era was ruthless but most of all it craved power. The basis of its power would no longer exist even after a greatly weakened American strike.

Even if American vulnerability was overstated, the issue was real. Merely the perception of strategic vulnerability increased the probability of starting a chain of events which ended in nuclear war. The consequences of nuclear war were so catastrophic it was worth literally anything and everything to avoid it. Détente and arms control had proven to be disappointing, but deterrence and achieving peace through strength were effective. It was in such an environment that President Reagan decided to build the B-1B as an interim bomber while the B-2A was developed.

At IOC, the B-1B was incompletely developed. From a purely military perspective, its importance at IOC was negligible. One combat-loaded B-1B on the alert pad at Dyess AFB had more firepower than the United States had inflicted on its enemies from the first shot at Lexington Green in 1775 up until that time, but its effect at the margin was negligible considering the totality of American strategic forces at the time. At a symbolic level, B-1B IOC provided a tangible expression of American determination.

By the time the B-1B matured as a nuclear weapons system several years later, the end of the Cold War marked by the fall of the Berlin Wall in 1989 and the collapse and dissolution of the Soviet Union in 1991 rendered its capabilities less relevant, but in a broader sense the B-1B affected these events. To maintain its status as a superpower, the Soviet Union needed to respond to each American weapon system with corresponding efforts. The threat of the B-1B and ALCM led the Soviet Union to spend lavishly on upgrading its air defense system. The United States could fund even extravagant military expenditures with a small fraction of its highly productive and innovative economy. The Soviet Union, on the other hand, was a corrupt and inefficient dictatorship. Its attempt to match American military modernization was one factor that drove it to economic and political collapse. In that real albeit indirect way, the B-1B contributed to the American victory in the Cold War.

To save money, the early production B-1B aircraft were the first to be retired. 'The Star of Abilene' is now on display at Dyess AFB. (*Author*)

Chapter 10

After the Cold War

'Pete, we just won the Cold War.'
Lieutenant Colonel Gary H. Flynt, Commander,
337th Bombardment Squadron, talking to
Lieutenant Colonel Peter Kippie,
his operations officer, 28 September 1991.

'What Now?'

The BONE was a creation of the Cold War – designed, built, and deployed to deter the Soviet Union. Five years after it became operational, the world's best operational bomber, the pride of the USAF, no longer had a mission. Was the B–1B relevant in the aftermath of the Cold War? Lieutenant Colonel Kippie responded to his commander's observation that the Cold War was over by saying, 'Yeah. What now?'

Operation Desert Storm, conducted earlier that year against Saddam Hussein's Iraq, provided a hint of the answer to Kippie's question. The demise of the Soviet Union had brought a great promise of freedom and democracy, but new threats to peace and stability emerged. The combat results of Desert Storm were stunning. Airpower hadn't just improved in the previous decades; it had been revolutionized by advances in stealth, precision-guided munitions, sensors, space technology, and realistic training.

The end of the Cold War and Desert Storm led to a reorganization of the USAF. Tactical airpower was defined as airpower that worked with other types of military forces to achieve classical battlefield victories against enemy forces. In contrast, strategic airpower worked alone to directly attack the enemy homeland. In the USAF of the Cold War era, strategic airpower was synonymous with SAC and its nuclear-armed bombers and ICBMs.

The situation was different in the post-Cold War era. A residual nuclear deterrent mission remained as long as countries like Russia and China retained nuclear arsenals, but that mission was no longer the undisputed focus of American national security strategy. Desert Storm blurred the relationship between missions and types of aircraft. Fighters flew strategic missions against Iraq. B–52G bombers performed battlefield interdiction attacks against Iraqi troops. SAC in its Cold War form didn't match the reality of the new situation. The 31 May 1992 reorganization of the USAF disestablished SAC, moving its bomber, reconnaissance and aerial command post aircraft, and ICBMs, along with all TAC aircraft, to the newly established Air Combat Command (ACC). SAC tankers joined Military Airlift Command transport aircraft in the new Air Mobility Command. In practice, ACC was essentially an expanded TAC that added parts of SAC. The SAC bomber, reconnaissance, and ICBM communities now had the challenge of finding a place in a command dominated by fighter pilots, a tribe not renowned for valuing the contributions of those who are not fighter pilots.

The transition from SAC to ACC caused changes to the markings on B-1B aircraft. From top down, this vertical stabilizer has a squadron tail stripe, an ACC emblem, and a two-letter code that indicates the wing to which the aircraft was assigned. In this case EL stands for the 28th BW at Ellsworth AFB. This aircraft, B-1B 86-0134, has the 'Thunderbirds' tail stripe of the 34th BS. It also has white highlights on the EL which indicate that it is the flagship of the 34th BS. (*Author*)

SAC had a centralized, top-down style of command, control, and operations which made perfect sense for its mission. The exercise of initiative in the delivery of nuclear weapons was not something to be encouraged. The successful execution of the highly synchronized and coordinated SIOP put a premium on rigorously following a plan. The SAC way of war had proven to be unsuitable for conventional conflicts going back to the use of B-52 bombers in the Vietnam War. If the bomber force, including the B-1B, was going to be a useful component of ACC, it would need to adapt to a more flexible tactical doctrine.

The United States lavishly funded its military during the years of the Reagan administration, with high expenditure on modernization, readiness, and training. Reagan's successor, President George H. W. Bush, presided over Desert Storm and the end of the Cold War. President Bush supported a strong military but he was also a fiscal conservative. Politically, it was impossible to justify Cold War levels of defense spending in the post-Cold War era. Budgets plummeted, and the SAC (later ACC) bomber force keenly felt those cuts. There had been a plan to modernize part of the B-52G fleet, but instead it was retired in entirety. Production of the B-2A Spirit was halted at twenty-one aircraft. The mainstays of the ACC bomber force would be the aging B-52H and the new B-1B. The cancellation of the SRAM 2 program left the B-1B armed only with the B61 and B83 bombs for its nuclear mission, since SRAM had aged out and ALCM and ACM were never deployed on the B-1B. Mk 82 bombs and Mk 36 mines were the only conventional weapons certified on the B-1B. The B-1B community touted its conventional capabilities with these weapons, but with the ever-increasing prominence of precision-guided munitions the B-1B had highly limited value.

Despite its dearth of immediately relevant capabilities in the early post-Cold War era, the B-1B held enormous potential. It was a fast, long-range platform with a large payload, an excellent OAS based on digital computers that could be reprogrammed for new uses, and a DAS that was finally effective. It did not take a great stretch of the imagination to see that the B-1B could be modernized in ways that would make it highly capable in the new environment.

Two B-1B aircraft fly in formation. The DY code indicates that they are assigned to the 7th BW at Dyess AFB. The aircraft in the foreground, 86-0112, has the tail stripe of the 9th BS 'Bats'. The aircraft to its left, 86-0107, has the checkered tail stripe of the 28th BS 'Mohawks'. The B-1B aircraft were repainted FS 36118 Gunship Gray to replace the Strategic camouflage scheme. (*Master Sergeant Kevin J. Gruenwald/US Air Force*)

A Changing Air Force for a Changing World

The organizational structure of the B-1B community changed after the transfer to ACC. The 319th BMW and 384th BMW were deactivated. ACC created the 366th Wing at Mountain Home AFB, Idaho. The mission of the 366th Wing was to be a high-readiness expeditionary force that could rapidly deploy to respond to a crisis like the Iraqi invasion of Kuwait in 1990. Departing from traditional USAF organization, the 366th Wing had squadrons of bombers, fighters, and tankers in the same wing. Originally the 34th Bomb Squadron of the 366th Wing had the B-52G, but it relocated to Ellsworth AFB on 31 March 1994, when it reequipped with the B-1B to take advantage of the B-1B infrastructure at that base. Once Mountain Home AFB had B-1B facilities, the 34th BS joined the rest of the 366th Wing at Mountain Home AFB on 1 April 1997. The 366th Wing was a laboratory for the integration of bombers and fighters, as well as a means of infusing fighter-style doctrine into the B-1B community.

The USAF had always had a portion of its capabilities in its reserve components: the Air Force Reserve and the Air National Guard. Primarily staffed by 'weekend warriors' with full-time civilian careers who drilled with their units periodically, reserve component units would be recalled to active duty to reinforce the regular USAF in time of crisis or war. During the Cold War, it made no sense to have reserve component units as part of the SAC bomber force, since SAC maintained its forces on round-the-clock alert. After the Cold War the time was right to assign part of the bomber mission to the reserve component. The pay and benefits of military personnel were the most expensive aspect of a military unit. Reserve component units were less expensive because their members only received pay when they were drilling or recalled to active duty. B-1B bombers went to the Kansas and Georgia Air National Guards. In 1997, the organization of the operational B-1B force was:

- 9th Bomb Squadron (BS) ('Bats') and 28th BS ('Mohawks'), 7th Bomb Wing (BW), Dyess AFB, Texas
- 37th BS ('Tigers') and 77th BS ('War Eagles'), 28th BW, Ellsworth AFB, South Dakota
- 34th BS ('Thunderbirds'), 366th Wing, Mountain Home AFB, Idaho
- 128th BS, 116th BW, Robbins AFB, Georgia (Georgia Air National Guard)
- 127th BS ('Jayhawks'), 184th BW, McConnell AFB, Kansas (Kansas Air National Guard)

One subtlety of the transition from SAC to ACC was that Bombardment Squadrons (BMS) became Bomb Squadron (BS) and Bombardment Wings (BMW) became Bomb Wings (BW). The practical implication of this change in unit names was to bring the formal names into alignment with common usage. Whereas each SAC BMW had previous had a tanker squadron, the ACC BW did not, with the exception of the unique composite 366th Wing.

B-1B 85-0059 is marked as the flagship of the 9th BS. '9th BS/CC' is USAF shorthand for the commander of the squadron, although any crew can fly an airplane so marked. The WA tail code and yellow/black checkerboard tail stripe are used by the 57th Wing, the parent organization of the USAF Weapons School and its 77th Weapons Squadron. B-1B 85-0061 is assigned to the 28th BS. B-1B aircraft assigned to Grand Forks AFB and McConnell AFB had GF and OZ tail codes respectively for the short period between the activation of ACC and the deactivation of those wings. (*Senior Airman Brett Clashman/ US Air Force*)

B-1B 86-0104 has the yellow and black tiger stripe of the 37th BS 'Tigers' and the EL tail code of the 28th BW. (*Senior Airman Corey Hook/US Air Force*)

The USAF has an elaborate system to preserve the heritage of its most distinguished units, based on their longevity and combat record. For example, under SAC the 9th BMS, 7th BMW had been a B-52H unit under SAC at Carswell AFB, Texas. In the post-Cold War force reduction and base realignment and closure, Carswell AFB lost its bomber mission. Similarly, the active duty 28th BMS no longer had a place at McConnell AFB with the deactivation of the 384th BMW. Because of the order of precedence of USAF units, the 96th BMW was reflagged at the 7th BW, the 337th BMS ('Dragons') as the 9th BS, and the 338th CCTS as the 28th BS. These redesignation exercises were administrative actions – no people or equipment actually moved.

BONEs of the 34th BS 'Thunderbirds' and 37th BS 'Tigers of the 28th BW share the ramp at Eielson AFB Alaska with KC-10A tankers. They are participating in Red Flag-Alaska 07-1. Red Flag exercises are an important element of the integration of the B-1B with other types of airpower. (*Staff Sergeant Joshua Strong/US Air Force*)

B-1B 86-0118 was assigned to the 34th BS when this photograph was taken in 1995. At the time, the 34th BS was part of the 366th Wing at Mountain Home AFB, which is why it had a MO tail code. In 2002, the 34th Bomb Squadron transferred to the 28th BW and its aircraft got the EL tail code. (*Staff Sergeant Lem Robson/US Air Force*)

The USAF Fighter Weapons School, part of the 57th Wing at Nellis AFB, Nevada, had been the foremost institution within TAC for the development of fighter tactics and the education of tactical experts within the ranks of fighter pilots. USAF Fighter Weapon School graduates wore a patch on the left shoulder of their flight suits and formed an elite cadre. With the creation of ACC, the USAF Fighter Weapons School expanded its scope and was renamed the USAF Weapons School. It added sections for non–fighter aircraft (bombers, tankers, transports, reconnaissance, special operations, rescue) and also cyber warfare, intelligence, air battle managers, space operations, remotely piloted aircraft, joint terminal attack controllers and ICBMs.

The inclusion of the B-1B in the USAF Weapons School marked a significant cultural change in the B-1B community from a stand–alone nuclear/SIOP orientation to being part of an integrated conventional force. The activation of Detachment 4, 57th Wing at Ellsworth AFB commenced the B-1B course at the USAF Weapons School. Commanded by Lieutenant Colonel Fred Weiners, the initial staff of Detachment 4 was Major Dan Walker, Major Terry Gribben, Captain Mark Eby, Captain Jim Hutto, Captain Lenny Moskal, Captain Brian Ferguson, and Captain Fred Swan.

In a 2003 reshuffling of B-1B units, the 34th BS relocated from Mountain Home AFB to Ellsworth AFB, becoming the second operational B-1B squadron in the 28th BW. To maintain the heritage of the 77th BS, Detachment 4 was reflagged as the 77th Weapons Squadron and relocated to Dyess AFB.

During the SAC era, the B-1B occasionally participated in Red Flag exercises. Red Flag had started in the 1970s as a result of lessons learned from USAF participation in the Vietnam War. That war revealed major deficiencies in USAF combat training. Red Flag rectified those

B-1B 85-0077 is marked as the 77th Weapons Squadron flagship and had previously been the 77th BS flagship. There is nothing substantively different about flagships, and they are marked that way only to boost squadron morale and identity. (*Staff Sergeant David Owsianka/US Air Force*)

shortfalls with large-scale, highly realistic aerial combat exercises over the Nellis AFB ranges. The benefits of Red Flag were confirmed by the spectacularly successful USAF performance during Operation Desert Storm. In the ACC era, B-1B participation in Red Flag became a regular event.

The USAF maintained a B-1B test capability in the post-Cold War era because the B-1B was the beneficiary of a modernization program associated with its new roles. The B-1B CTF at AFFTC became a USAF squadron in 1989, designated the 6510th Test Squadron. As B-1B test activity decreased, the 6510th Test Squadron folded into the 6519th Test Squadron (which conducted B-52 and cruise missile test programs at AFFTC) in 1991. The 6519th Test Squadron was redesignated at the 419th Flight Test Squadron in 1992. B-2A flight test work subsequently also moved under the 419th Flight Test Squadron. The 419th Flight Test Squadron was also called the Global Power CTF and was responsible for bomber DT&E.

ACC had its own OT&E capability for the B-1B. The B-1B OT&E unit had frequent changes in designation associated with reorganizations internal to ACC, until the designation stabilized in 2004 as the 337th TES ('Slayers'), 53rd Test Management Group, 53rd Wing based at Dyess AFB. The designation of the 337th TES continued the heritage of the first operational

B-1B 86-0132 is marked as the flagship of the 337th TES. It has the tail stripe and OT tail code of the 53th Wing, which is the ACC wing that conducts OT&E and to which the 337th TES is assigned. (*Airman 1st Class Jonathan Stefanko/US Air Force*)

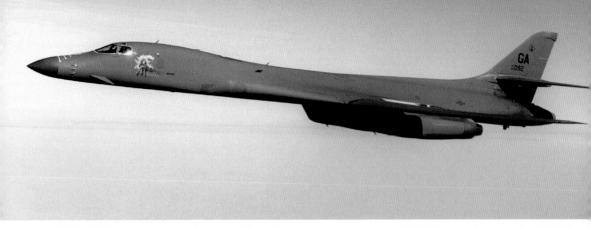

B-1B 85-0092 was the last Lot IV aircraft. When this photograph was taken in 2000, it was assigned to the 127th BS, 116th BW, Georgia Air National Guard. It had a GA tail code and the Air National Guard symbol on its tail instead of an ACC symbol. (*Chief Master Sergeant Betsy Winn/US Air Force*)

B-1B 85-0092 was assigned to the 127th BS, 116th BW, Georgia Air National Guard. B-1B 85-0084 is behind it. The National Guard is a uniquely American military institution that traces its origin back to the militias of the colonial era. Air National Guard units are both a reserve component of the USAF and the military force of their state, providing services such as disaster assistance under the command of the state's governor. Supersonic bombers are not useful for the state role, but the logistics and medical capabilities and trained, disciplined manpower of Air National Guard units most certainly are. (*Technical Sergeant Rick Cowan/US Air Force*)

B-1B 86-0129 of the 128th BS, 184th BW, Kansas Air National Guard shares the ramp at McConnell AFB with KC-135R tankers of the 22nd Air Refueling Wing. The assignment of aircraft to Air National Guard units is an intensely political process, but since McConnell AFB had infrastructure and facilities for the B-1B that had been built for the deactivated 384th BMW, it was a logical assignment. (*Master Sergeant Danny R. Walker/US Air Force*)

A B-1B of the 128th BS, 184th BW, Kansas Air National Guard is refueled by a KC-135E of the 141st Air Refueling Squadron, 108th Air Refueling Wing, New Jersey Air National Guard. Air National Guardsmen often have decades of experience and the turnover of personnel in the units is low, so these units of 'weekend warriors' are highly proficient members of the USAF total force. (*Master Sergeant Kenneth Fidler/US Air Force*)

B-1B squadron, the 337th BMS. Detachment 3, 53rd Test Management Group, 53rd Wing was collocated with the 337th TES and provided engineering and operations analysis support for B-1B OT&E.

The B-1B in ACC

Removing the B-1B from standing regular nuclear alert was the first step in the total loss of the nuclear mission. At first, the B-1B wings retained their nuclear capabilities and weapons. They could return to an alert posture within 24-hours. As the decade proceeded, the B-1B wings progressively lost their nuclear tasking. The last B-1B wing to have a nuclear ORI was the 7th BW in 1996. The B-1B nuclear era officially ended on 1 October 1997. For a while afterwards, there was contingency planning to reconstitute the nuclear capability if needed in a crisis, but those plans were never implemented. As the B-1B was modified for a conventional role, its systems lost their nuclear certification, which made reconstitution of nuclear capability impossible without a major development and test effort.

The B-1B community began promoting its conventional bombing capability soon after the nuclear mission began to fade away. An early convert was General John M. Loh, the first commander of ACC. Loh was a career fighter pilot and therefore not necessarily a natural advocate for the B-1B. But he recognized the potential of the B-1B to serve in new roles and became a supporter of upgrading the BONE. He persuaded USAF Chief of Staff General Merrill A. McPeak of the case for the B-1B.

Aviation Week & Space Technology editor William B. Scott went along on a conventional training mission in the DSO seat of a B-1B. He was a USAF Test Pilot School graduate and former flight test engineer. *Aviation Week & Space Technology* was highly regarded in the aerospace and defense industry and the policy community in Washington, DC. Scott highlighted the high-speed TF capability at 400ft AGL altitude, smooth ride, ORS high-resolution ground mapping, and accurate navigational capability. Scott's positive report on his flight sent a message about the viability of the B-1B in the post-Cold War world to a broad audience.

One lingering concern with the B-1B was its low mission-capable rate. The USAF claimed that the low availability of the B-1B fleet was because the operational units were understaffed and had insufficient spare parts. Congress directed the USAF to conduct an Operational Readiness Assessment (ORA) in 1994. The objective of the ORA was to test the mission-capable rate of the B-1B if proper resources were available. The 28th BW was the test unit for the ORA – it was brought up to full strength with personnel temporarily detailed from the other B-1B wings. The 28th BW also got all the parts that it needed and full support from OC-ALC. Monitored by AFOTEC, the ORA was named Dakota Challenge. It started at Ellsworth AFB in June 1994. In November 1994, the 77th BS deployed nine B-1B aircraft, its personnel, AGE, other tools and equipment, and a flyaway kit of spare parts for two weeks to the civilian airport in Roswell, New Mexico. The 77th BS was under the command of Lieutenant Colonel John S. Chilstrom, who as a captain had been the aircraft commander of the very first B-1B on alert at Dyess AFB. Chilstrom remained at Ellsworth AFB for the deployment. The deployed 77th BS commander was Major Jim Roland, with Captain Ernie Tavares as his operations officer. For fourteen days, the 77th BS simulated combat missions operating out of a bare base at the end of a long supply line. The unit completed 109 missions out of 109 scheduled, proving that the airplane and the people could operate in a sustained wartime environment. Dakota Challenge concluded in December 1994, having proven that the B-1B was a reliable aircraft if properly supported.

Technical Sergeant Alana Hasting, Senior Airman Jeremy Harper and Airman 1st Class Jacob Kobielusz change the bleed air precooler in the left nacelle. The ORA demonstrated that the B-1B could have a high readiness rate if adequate spare parts and maintenance personnel were available. (*Staff Sergeant Joanna E. Hensley/US Air Force*)

A role for which the B-1B was well suited was direct flights from bases in the continental United States to targets in Europe, the Middle East and Asia. Such attacks could provide decisive action against an aggressor in the first hours of a conflict. The 7th BW and 28th BW conducted Global Power exercises which demonstrated this capability. Vigilant Warrior 94 was a typical Global Power mission. Four B-1Bs from the 37th BS launched from Ellsworth AFB on 31 October 1994 and headed east. Each jet carried a fuel tank in the forward weapons bay and fourteen Mk 82 bombs each in the intermediate and aft weapons bays. Over the Atlantic Ocean, the two primary aircraft successfully refueled from tankers and the two spare aircraft returned to Ellsworth AFB. The two aircraft continued to cross the Atlantic Ocean and refueled again over the Mediterranean Sea. Overflying Egypt, the Red Sea and Saudi Arabia, the flight of two bombers descended to TF at 500ft AGL after reaching Kuwait. After updating their navigation with radar position fixes, the bombers accurately delivered their bombs to targets on a range in Kuwait. The jets turned west and refueled over Saudi Arabia and the Mediterranean. After 24.9 hours of flying, the aircraft landed at Lajes Field in the Azores. Relief crews prepositioned at Lajes Field returned the aircraft to Ellsworth AFB.

Global Power missions tested both the reliability of the aircraft and the endurance of the crews. The Armstrong Laboratory, the USAF unit devoted to human factors and aeromedical research, developed nutrition, hydration, rest, and activity guidelines to keep Global Power crews able to do their jobs on the long flights. Crew members placed a foam pad or air mattress on floor in the aisle between the pilots' seats and the DSO/OSO seats so that they could use it as a bunk. Wearing a helmet to keep out noise and lowering the tinted visor to keep out light, crew members could take naps one at a time.

Global Power missions demonstrated the long-range power projection capabilities of ACC bombers. This B-1B is approaching a tanker near Iceland during the Northern Viking 95 exercise. (*Senior Airman Richard T. Kaminsky/ US Air Force*)

Missions like Vigilant Warrior 94 sent messages to multiple audiences. To Saddam Hussein, the dictator who ruled Iraq, the message was that the United States could act to stop aggression within hours from bases in the United States. The B-1B also showed that it was an important asset in the post-Cold War USAF, worthy of investment in upgraded capabilities.

Coronet Bat

The USAF had traditionally demonstrated its ability to strike anywhere on the planet with non-stop round-the-world flights. The first non-stop round-the-world flight occurred on 25 February–2 March 1949, when B-50A 46-0010 'Lucky Lady II' of the 43rd Bombardment Group supported by multiple KB-29M tankers achieved this milestone. On 16–18 January 1957, RB-52B 53-0394 'Lucky Lady III' of the 93rd BMW repeated the feat at jet speeds, using KC-97 tankers.

In 1995, the B-1B made a similar non-stop circling of the globe during the Coronet Bat exercise. Four B-1B aircraft from the 9th BS departed Dyess AFB on 2 June 1995 at 0258 local time. One of the airborne spares left the formation as planned over the Atlantic Ocean and recovered at Langley AFB, Virginia. Three jets crossed the Atlantic Ocean and conducted a bombing run at the Pachino Range in Sicily, Italy. The second spare B-1B then recovered to Lajes Field in the Azores as the two primary aircraft continued east across the Mediterranean Sea, over Egypt, Saudi Arabia, and Oman, through southern Asia to east of Japan to south-west of Alaska and finally back to Dyess AFB. The aircraft cruised with the wings at 55° sweep angle, Mach 0.92 generally at 16,000ft altitude. This flight condition was chosen for speed, not fuel efficiency, because one of the objectives of the mission was to set a world record.

Ensuring that tankers were deployed to support the Coronet Bat was the critical consideration during mission planning. During the 36.2-hour flight, the two aircraft each refueled multiple

A row of 7th BW B-1B bombers are on the flight line at Dyess AFB on 1 June 1995 undergoing final preparations for the historic Coronet Bat mission. B-1B 84-0057 'Hellion' in the foreground is the 9th BS flagship. B-1B 85-0082 'Global Power' behind it is the other primary jet for the mission. Both aircraft are decorated with the 9th BS tail stripe. (*Staff Sergeant Lance Cheung/US Air Force*)

Above: Senior Airman Brian Bower attaches a refueling nozzle to the receptacle of a B-1B to fill it with fuel for the Coronet Bat mission. (*Staff Sergeant Lance Cheung/US Air Force*)

Right: Not just a record-setting flight, Coronet Bat also was the ultimate Global Power mission. Master Sergeant Jorge Olvera inspects the bomb drop system in the aft weapons bay of one of the B-1B bombers that will fly the mission. (*Staff Sergeant Lance Cheung/ US Air Force*)

times on six different air refueling tracks. Typical fuel onload per aircraft was 160,000lbs at each track with the largest being 220,000lbs. In total, Coronet Bat required twenty-six tanker aircraft (twenty KC-135, six KC-10A) that transferred more than 2.4 million lbs of fuel. In addition to Pachino Range, the B-1B bombers dropped bombs on a range on Tori Shima, an island that is Japanese territory, and the Utah Test and Training Range in the western United States. The Coronet Bat aircraft and aircrew were:

B-1B 85-0057 'Hellion'
Captain Ricky W. Carver (pilot)
Lieutenant Colonel Douglas L. Raaberg (co-pilot)
Captain Kevin D. Clotfelter (DSO)
Captain Gerald V. Goodfellow (OSO)

B-1B 85-0082 'Global Power'
Captain Christopher D. Stewart (pilot)
Captain Steven G. Adams (co-pilot)
Captain Steven B. Reeves (DSO)
Captain Kevin R. Houdek (OSO)

[Author's note: During ACC era, there was no longer a progression from co-pilot to pilot. All B-1B pilots were qualified to fly in either seat. The pilot responsible for the safe conduct of the flight is designated as the Aircraft Commander. For reasons of simplicity, in this book the convention is that the pilot in the left front seat is referred to the pilot and the pilot in the right

B-1B 84-0057 'Hellion' was one of the two primary Coronet Bat aircraft. Its crew chief was Staff Sergeant Kenneth Kisner, who was assisted by Senior Airman Raymond Gonzalez, Senior Airman Mari Wilson, Airman 1st Class Richard Katona and Airman 1st Class Robert Kauff. Their diligence was a critical component of the success of Coronet Bat. Senior Airman Wilson missed the landing at Dyess AFB because 3 June 1995 was his wedding day. *(Staff Sergeant Lance Cheung/US Air Force)*

The team of Staff Sergeant Michael D. DeWitt, Senior Airman Derrick Gross, Airman 1st Class Bill Boyd, Airman Garrett Schomberg and Airman Eric McCumbee took care of B-1B 85-0082 'Global Power'. The nation entrusted an extraordinarily expensive machine and the lives of its aircrew to these young men. (*Staff Sergeant Lance Cheung/ US Air Force*)

seat is the co-pilot. The Aircraft Commander might sit in either seat. During Coronet Bat, Lieutenant Colonel Raaberg and Captain Adams were both instructor pilots.]

The two B-1B aircraft landed at Dyess AFB on 3 June 1995 to complete their circumnavigation of the earth. After landing, Captain Kevin R. 'Hooter' Houdek sought out Master Sergeant Joe Lansdell, a flight line maintenance supervisor, to return something to him. Houdek and Lansdell had more than just a professional relationship. They were brother-in-laws. Before take-off, Lansdell had given Houdek a small item wrapped in paper. Houdek put it in his pocket and proceeded to forget about it because he was busy navigating the B-1B. About fifteen hours into the flight, Houdek remembered that Landsell had given him something, retrieved it from his pocket, and unwrapped the paper. The object in the paper was Lansdell's wedding ring, and the paper was a note:

> Kevin:
>
> There is no greater confidence than a crew chief lending his wedding ring to a crew dawg.
>
> > Good luck
> > Joe

The aircrew were the most visible members of the Coronet Bat team, but the aircraft maintainers, ground mission commanders, airspace specialists, air refueling coordinators, foreign range experts, communications specialists and meteorologists all had important roles. Every air refueling went flawlessly, a testimony to the professionalism of the air refueling units. In his after-action report, Captain Christopher D. Stewart summarized the accomplishments of Coronet Bat:

> This mission was a remarkable success. It was a classic illustration of the concept that 90% of success is a result of meticulous and careful preparation. It was also an important illustration of the value of team work, not only within the 7th Wing, but other far reaching units as well.

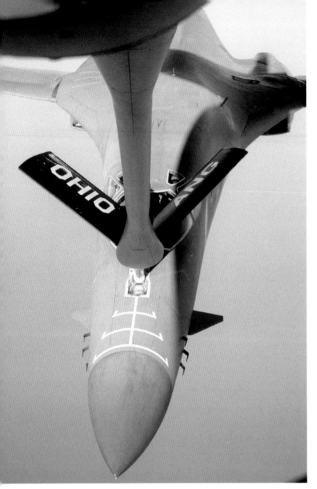

Left: A KC-135R of the 166th Air Refueling Squadron, 121st Air Refueling Wing, Ohio Air National Guard conducts the first refueling of B-1B 84-0057 'Hellion' over the Atlantic Ocean. Each Coronet Bat refueling was critical. If a jet could not refuel it needed to land. After 'Hellion' successfully completed this refueling, one of the airborne spares departed the formation and landed at Langley AFB, Virginia. (*Staff Sergeant G. D. Robinson/US Air Force*)

Below: B-1B 84-0057 'Hellion' is above the clouds over the Bering Sea off the coast of Alaska as it approaches its last air refueling of Coronet Bat. After the refueling, the two jets will conduct a bombing run at the Utah Test and Training Range and then land at Dyess AFB. (*Technical Sergeant Marvin Krause/US Air Force*)

Coronet Bat sent a message about the reach and reliability of the B-1B in the conventional role. Brigadier General Charles R. Henderson, the commander of the 7th BW, noted in a letter of appreciation the significance of Coronet Bat:

> What a proud and exciting moment it was Saturday, 3 June 1995, when our crews passed overhead at the conclusion of their record-breaking, around-the-world mission. Simply put, it was a great team accomplishment on these individuals' part. They stretched the aircraft as well as their own capabilities to the very limit, making enormous personal sacrifices preparing for and then executing this flight, and the payoff is incalculable. They demonstrated to the entire world that Global Power/Global Reach isn't a catchy mission statement, it is reality.

In 1996, the eight Coronet Bat aircrew members won the Mackay Trophy for the most meritorious USAF flight of the previous year. The crew of B-1B 85-0057 was recognized by *Fédération Aéronautique Internationale* for a new record for Speed Around the World, Eastbound, with In-Flight Refueling in Class C-1 (landplane), Group III (jet propulsion), q (150,000kg to less than 200,000kg). The crew of B-1B 85-0082 also could have broken the record, but the instrumentation required to certify the record on their aircraft malfunctioned.

B-1B 85-0057 'Hellion' is in its parking spot after landing at Dyess AFB on 3 June 1995. Its crew chief, Staff Sergeant Kenneth Kisner, was quoted as saying: 'We felt great and experienced a sense of accomplishment and satisfaction, knowing of all the hard work invested by the crew chiefs and systems specialists. We were proud to receive them as they taxied in.' (*Staff Sergeant Lance Cheung/US Air Force*)

The WSO Arrives

In SAC, there were separate training curricula for the DSO and OSO. The former concentrated on ECM with DAS and the latter on navigation and weapons delivery with OAS. After a period of controversy that lasted for several years after the La Junta mishap in 1987, the B-1B ceased to carry supernumerary instructors in the jump seats. An instructor DSO would need to sit in the OSO seat, while the student DSO sat in the DSO seat, necessitating that instructor DSOs got trained as OSOs. The opposite was partially true for instructor OSOs. They had to learn how to use the communications equipment operated from the DSO position but did not use the DAS.

When the B-1B moved to ACC, ACC commander General Loh wondered why the Weapon System Officer (WSO) in the rear of a two-seat F-15E could navigate, operate the weapons system, and defend the aircraft electronically but the B-1B DSO and OSO were not cross-trained. Starting in 1995, the two rated navigators flying in the rear two seats of the B-1B were categorized as WSOs and trained to act as either the DSO or OSO depending on position at which they sat.

B-1B Mishaps in ACC

The B-1B has had a good safety record since the end of the Cold War, but flying military aircraft is inherently dangerous. ACC lost four B-1B aircraft and eight crew members in training mishaps.

On 30 November 1992, B-1B 86-0106 of the 337th BMS with call sign PYOTE 70 was conducting night TF training over western Texas near the Mexican border. The aircraft collided with steep terrain, killing Major Zenon C. Goc (pilot), 1st Lieutenant Paul S. Ziemba (co-pilot), Captain Scott D. Genal (OSO) and 1st Lieutenant Timothy A. Cookson (DSO).

Low-level tactical flying is dangerous. B-1B 85-0078 of the 37th BS with call sign FURY 02 crashed when it developed an excessive sink rate during a defensive maneuver. The 19 September 1997 mishap over Montana took the lives of Colonel Anthony M. Beat (pilot), Major Kirk L. Cakerice (co-pilot), Major Clay K. Culver (WSO), and Captain Gary M. Everett (WSO).

B-1B 84-0057 of the 9th BS with the call sign DARK 02, one of the Coronet Bat aircraft, crashed on 18 February 1998 in Kentucky, when a short circuit in a new fire warning panel shut down all four engines. Lieutenant Colonel Daniel J. Charchian (pilot), Captain Jeffrey T. Sabella (co-pilot), Captain Kevin J. Schields (WSO) and 1st Lieutenant Bert G. Winslow (WSO) ejected successfully.

While sweeping its wings aft, a fold-down baffle in the left OWF detached and cut a fuel line on B-1B 85-0091 with call sign THUNDER 21 while it was flying on a training mission over Montana on 19 August 2013. The resulting fuel leak contacted a hot surface, causing a fire which resulted in an explosion propagating through the fuel system. The 34th BS crew consisting of Major Frank Biancardi (pilot), Captain Curtis Michael (pilot), Captain Brandon Packard (WSO), and Captain Chad Nishizuka (WSO) ejected successfully.

Unguided Bombs

The Mk 82 bomb was the first conventional weapon for which the B-1B was armed. The Mk 82 contains 192lbs of explosive filler in a streamlined steel case. The Mk 82 can be fitted with

Airman Sidney Hering, 28th Aircraft Maintenance Squadron weapons load crew member, uses an MHU-83D/E to lift a bomb into position. The bomb body is blue, indicating that it is an inert BDU-50/B practice bomb. It has a BSU-49/B tail assembly for low-level delivery, which deploys a ballute after the bomb is dropped so that the B-1B can escape the fragmentation pattern of the bomb after it explodes. (*Airman 1st Class Rebecca Imwalle/ US Air Force*)

low-drag conical fins for medium-to-high altitude delivery in the Mk 82 Low Drag (LD) configuration. The Mk 82 LD weighs 531lbs. For low-altitude delivery, the Mk 82 AIR has the BSU-49/B tail assembly with a ballute so that the B-1B can escape the effects of the bomb. The Mk 82 AIR weighs 554lbs. The Mk 82 damages the target with blast and fragmentation. The BDU-50/B is an inert version of the Mk 82 with no explosives, which can be distinguished by the light blue paint applied to it. The Mk 36 and Mk 62 mines use the Mk 82 body and can also be carried by the B-1B.

The B-1B was designed to carry one Conventional Bomb Module (CBM) in each weapons bay which uses the same attach points in the weapons bays as the rotary launchers for nuclear weapons. Each CBM carries twenty-eight Mk 82 bombs, for a total of eighty-four Mk 82 bombs on the B-1B. To maximize the carriage of bombs, each CBM has two banks (forward and aft) of swing arms and fixed supports that hold the ejector racks for the Mk 82 bombs. When all the bombs on a swing arm are released, it moves out of the way and the bombs on the swing arm above it are released. The entire mechanism is computer-controlled for timing and to prevent bombs from being dropped on a swing arm that has not moved out of the way.

B-1B 84-0049 of the 6510th Test Squadron drops a load of bombs on the Edwards AFB PIRA on 17 July 1991. This photograph clearly illustrates ballute deployments from the BSU-49/B tail assemblies. The bomb bodies are blue and therefore BDU-50/B shapes. Had they been actual explosive-filled Mk 82 bombs, they would have been painted olive green with yellow rings around them. (*Air Force Test Center History Office*)

To rapidly release a full load of bombs is a highly engineered process involving aerodynamics and pyrotechnics. For low-altitude delivery of the Mk 82 AIR bomb from the B-1B, each bomb has a DTU-31A/B delay element that gives the bomb time to clear the aircraft before the BSU-49/A ballute is deployed and inflated. (*Author*)

The Mk 82 bomb body forms the basis of a modular family of munitions. From front to back, there is a GBU-54(V)1 Laser JDAM with a DSU-38/B laser-homing target detection device on its nose, a GBU-38(V)1 JDAM, an unguided 'dumb bomb' with a BSU-33/B conical fin section for medium-high altitude delivery, and an unguided bomb with a BSU-49/B tail assembly for low altitude delivery that has a DSU-33C/B radar proximity fuze on its nose. The small round object just forward of the guidance tail assembly on the two JDAMs is the connector for the MIL-STD-1760 interface over which the JDAM is targeted. (*Author*)

The new generation of cluster bombs had been extremely effective in Operation Desert Storm, dropped from the B-52G and other aircraft. Arming the B-1B with cluster bombs was the next logical step in increasing its conventional bombing capability. A cluster bomb consists of a dispenser, a fuze to initiate opening the container, and submunitions contained in the dispenser. A cluster bomb can cover a large area with submunitions.

The B-1B carries three types of cluster bombs, which look nearly identical externally but carry different submunitions. The CBU-87/B consists of a SUU-65/B dispenser filled with 202 BLU-97/B bomblets and weighs 960lbs. The BLU-87/B combined effects munition has shaped charge to penetrate armored vehicles, a scored case around its explosive charge for fragmentation, and a zirconium ring for incendiary effects. As demonstrated during Operation Desert Storm, the CBU-87/B is highly effective against troops in the open, artillery, air defenses, and formations of armored vehicles.

The CBU-89/B Gator uses a SUU-64/B dispenser loaded with 72 BLU-91/B anti-tank mines and 22 BLU-92/B anti-personnel mines. It weighs 696lbs. A B-1B dropping a string of CBU-89/B bombs will create a large minefield.

The CBU-97/B Sensor Fuzed Weapon is a SUU-66/B tactical munitions dispenser containing ten BLU-108/B submunitions. It weighs 920lbs. When the SUU-66/B opens it releases the ten BLU-108/B submunitions, which then descend on a parachute. Each BLU-108/B throws out four warheads. The warheads have infrared sensors that detect armored

The Mk 62 Quickstrike mine is another variant of the Mk 82 bomb that uses a specialized nose fuze and tail kit to convert the bomb into a sea mine. Using the Mk 62 Quickstrike, a B-1B can stop ships from safely using a port or naval base. (*Senior Airman Emily Copeland/US Air Force*)

The CBM is a complex mechanical device that densely packs twenty-eight Mk 82 bombs into a B-1B weapons bay. A B-1B can carry one CBM in each of its three weapons bays. The CBM has forward and aft banks of arms; each bank has fourteen bombs. In each bank, there are two movable arms and one fixed arm. The ejector racks that hold and release the bombs mount on the arms. (*Author*)

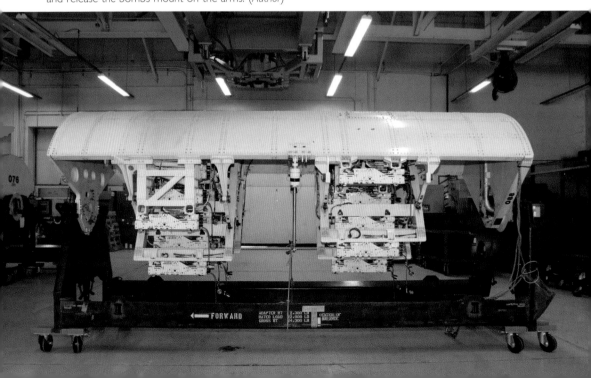

A weapons loader is moving a CBU-89/B cluster bomb to a B-1B. The CBU-89/B covers an area with minelets after opening, creating a large minefield to impede the movement of enemy forces. The blue band painted on the cluster bomb marks it as an inert training unit. A B-1B can carry thirty cluster bombs, ten in each weapons bay. (*Airman 1st Class Nathaniel G. Bevier/US Air Force*)

vehicles. When a warhead passes over a vehicle, it fires an explosively-formed penetrator into the top of the vehicle. Since the top of a tank is its most lightly armored aspect, the likely result is a turret penetration with the ammunition being ignited or hull penetration that disables the engine and sets the fuel on fire.

Rockwell modified some of the CBM inventory to carry ten cluster bombs instead of twenty-eight Mk 82 bombs. The modified CBM is called the Enhanced Conventional Bomb Module (ECBM). With one ECBM in each weapons bay, the B-1B carries thirty cluster bombs. B-1B delivery of cluster bombs was flight tested in 1994/5, with the first drop of a full load of thirty cluster bombs in December 1994.

In the aftermath of Operation Desert Storm, one of the greatest American national security concerns was a repetition of the kind of aggression that Iraq committed against Kuwait – a rogue state invading an American-allied neighbor. The B-1B armed with cluster bombs could have been a powerful way to oppose this kind of attack. With its speed, range, ability to penetrate air defenses, and large payload of highly effective area weapons, the B-1B could devastate an invading force, potentially flying directly from bases in the United States.

Smart Bombs and Stealthy Missiles

In theory, unguided bombing accuracy is related to how accurately the bomber measures its velocity, location, and wind, determines the location of the target, and calculates the trajectory of the bomb. The B-1B OAS excels in these three factors, approaching the limit of accuracy. Despite its capabilities, the B-1B cannot deliver an unguided bomb with perfect accuracy.

The aircraft may have a slight sideslip angle. There are always variations in the timing of the pyrotechnic cartridges in the ejector racks, the deployments of parachutes and ballutes from retarded bombs, and the alignment of the bomb fins. For bomb drops from medium or high altitudes, the wind direction and speed calculated by the OAS may be different to what the bomb experiences during its fall. Consequently, an unguided bomb dropped from a B–1B with even the most skilled crew is likely to miss the target by 100 or more feet. A miss distance of 100ft is unlikely to matter when using a nuclear weapon, but it certainly might decrease the effectiveness of a conventional attack against a bridge or bunker. It would also impose a high risk of unintended casualties if the target is in close proximity to friendly forces or innocent civilians.

The word 'revolution' is overused. Jet engines revolutionized airpower, as did radar and nuclear weapons. The Precision-Guided Munition (PGM) certainly falls into the category of revolutionary airpower technology. During the later years of the Vietnam War, certain targets in North Vietnam which had withstood multiple attacks conducted at a high cost in American aircraft and aircrew were quickly destroyed once the United States began to employ 'smart bombs'. PGMs truly came into their own during Operation Desert Storm. Guided by laser-homing, electro-optical (television) or infrared sensors, PGMs employed against strategic and battlefield targets increased the lethality of airpower by at least an order of magnitude. To function as a modern conventional bomber in the post-Cold War era, the B–1B needed to be able to deliver PGMs. Having the capability to deliver only the unguided 'dumb' bombs was inadequate.

The GBU-31(V)1/B uses the Mk 84 bomb body with a guidance tail assembly, strakes, and fuze. The bomb body in this GBU-31(V)1/B is blue, which means that it is a BDU-56/B inert shape with no explosive fill. Straps hold the strakes on the bomb body. (*Author*)

The most important PGM for the B-1B is the Joint Direct Attack Munition (JDAM). The JDAM is an unpowered launch-and-leave bomb autonomously guided by an onboard Global Positioning System (GPS)-aided inertial navigation system. Before release, the B-1B OAS programs the JDAM with target coordinates.

The JDAM consists of a bomb body, guidance tail assembly, strakes, and fuze. Depending on the specific version of JDAM, the bomb body is a Mk 82, a larger Mk 84, or a BLU–109/B. Whereas the Mk 82 and Mk 84 use blast and fragmentation as their destruction mechanisms, the BLU–109/B is a steel penetrator with thick walls and a small explosive fill. Popularly known as a 'bunker buster', the BLU–109/B is designed to destroyed hardened and buried targets such as fortifications, caves, and underground facilities.

The guidance tail assembly includes the guidance electronics, control actuation system, and control fins. The guidance electronics has a GPS receiver and an inertial navigation system. The GPS receiver uses signals from navigation satellites to determine a very precise position, velocity and time. As in the B-1B OAS, a Kalman filter running in the guidance electronics combines the data from the GPS with the inertial navigation system outputs to calculate an optimal estimate of JDAM position, velocity, and orientation. Because the GPS signals come from outside the JDAM, they can be interrupted or jammed. In the case of signal loss, the inertial navigation system alone continues to guide the JDAM while the GPS attempts to reacquire the satellite signals. The JDAM guidance electronics use the programmed target coordinates and the JDAM position, velocity, and orientation information to calculate the flight path to the target. The control actuation system moves the control fins so that the JDAM follows the computed flight path.

Staff Sergeant Kevin Rayburn (left) and Technical Sergeant Jeff Allen load a GBU-31(V)1/B JDAM on to an MPRL in a B-1B weapons bay. They are using an MJ-40 lift truck. (*Senior Airman Erik Hofmeyer/US Air Force*)

The strakes are aerodynamic surfaces that strap on to the bomb body. Working in concert with the control fins, they generate the lift that the JDAM uses to follow the calculated flight path to the target. The JDAM uses the lift to correct for unknown winds and ballistic variation in the bomb. The strakes also increase the Launch Acceptability Region (LAR) for the JDAM. The LAR is the region of conditions from which a weapon can be successfully launched to reach the target. The conditions are the range to the target, the altitude of the target, the velocity and altitude of the launching aircraft, and the kinematics of the weapon itself. If the launch aircraft is flying high and fast, the LAR for a JDAM may be as distant as 15 miles from the target. The LAR of a JDAM is larger than that of an unguided bomb, and the JDAM is more accurate than an unguided bomb. Because the JDAM doesn't use a laser-homing, electro-optical or infrared sensor, its operation is unaffected by cloud, fog, dust, or smoke.

The fuze arms the JDAM warhead when it is a safe distance away from the B-1B and initiates the detonation of the warhead based on impact, delay, or proximity. Delay fuzing improves lethality against hardened and buried targets, allowing the bomb to explode inside the target. Impact fuzing is more effective against a building or entrenchment but less effective against targets in the open because some of the blast and fragmentation is absorbed by the ground. A proximity fuze is a small radar in the nose of the bomb that senses when the bomb is a specified height above the ground. By having the warhead explode before the bomb impacts, blast and fragmentation cover a wider area. The JDAM uses the DSU-33A/B,

Airman 1st Class Timothy Foreman, 28th Aircraft Maintenance Squadron munitions load crew member, assists in lowering a GBU-31(V)1/B on to a bomb trailer during a 28th BW ORI at Ellsworth AFB. The guidance tail assembly has a GPS receiver, inertial navigation unit, digital guidance computer, fin actuators, and movable fins. A battery inside the guidance tail assembly powers it after launch. The connector for the MIL-STD-1760 interface is visible on the top of the JDAM, approximately at the aft end of the strakes. (*Airman 1st Class Anthony Sanchelli/US Air Force*)

–33B/B, –33C/B, and –33D/B radar proximity fuzes, the suffix letters A through D denoting improvements in the fuze.

At first, each JDAM needed to have its fuzing set on the ground before flight, which decreased weapons employment flexibility. A major improvement in the JDAM was the incorporation of the FMU-152A/B Joint Programable Fuze (JPF). The JPF mode and delays can be set during the weapons buildup or load, during ground operations, or while airborne. The JPF operating mode, including arming delay, delay time, and whether to use or not use the radar proximity fuse if installed, may be changed in flight by the B-1B OAS to correspond to changes in the mission or the target.

When it was initially armed with JDAM, the B-1B carried the GBU-31(V)1/B and GBU-31(V)3/B. The GBU-31(V)1 uses a Mk 84 bomb and weighs 2,065lbs. The GBU-31(V)3 is built around the BLU-109/B 'bunker buster' and weighs 2,165lbs. Eight JDAMS are carried on an LAU-144/A Multi-Purpose Rotary Launcher (MPRL). A MPRL is the rotary launcher that carried the B61 and B83 nuclear bombs, repurposed for conventional weapons and equipped with a MIL-STD-1760 capability. MIL-STD-1760 is a standardized protocol to interface PGMs with aircraft avionics. Using MIL-STD-1760, a JDAM is controlled, monitored, and receive target coordinates from a B-52H, B-1B, B-2A, F-15E or any other aircraft that has a MIL-STD-1760 capability and has digital avionics programmed to work with JDAM. Because MIL-STD-1760 is a standard, a different version of JDAM is not needed for each type of aircraft that carries it, simplifying development, testing, and logistics. A B-1B can carry one MPRL in each weapons bay for a total of twenty-four JDAMs.

The B-1B can also carry the Mk 84 bomb in an unguided configuration. The Mk 84 'dumb bomb' has a MAU-91/B conical fin assembly with fixed fins. Because these bombs are painted olive green with a yellow ring, they are filled with high explosives. The Mk 84 with MAU-91/B weights 1970 pounds. (*Airman 1st Class Corey Hook/US Air Force*)

Technical Sergeant Christopher L. Warren and Senior Airman Michael T. Whitlach, 7th Munitions Squadron, inspect a JDAM. The GBU-31(V)3/B is a JDAM variant that uses the BLU-109/B 'bunker buster' penetrating munition. Compared to the Mk 84, the BLU-109/B has much thicker steel in the nose and walls and carries less high explosives. The hardback that is part of the GBU-31(V)3/B strake assembly has hooks which are held by the ejector racks on the MPRL. The blue band marks this BLU-109/B is a training unit that has no high explosives. (Author)

The yellow bands mark these BLU-109/B penetrating bombs as live munitions. When the weapon is a GBU-31(V)3/B, neither cave, bunker, nor hardened aircraft shelter provides protection. When the bomb explodes inside the target, the devastation is intensified because the structure contains the blast. (Staff Sergeant Shane Cuomo/US Air Force)

The LAU-144/A MPRL has a graphite/epoxy composite tube which holds eight BRU-56/A bomb release units. The BRU-56/A has 30-inch hook spacing so it can hold larger and heavier weapons like the Mk 84, but not the Mk 82 or cluster bombs which have 14-inch lug spacing. The boxes of electronics on the MPRL power the weapons and control the data flow over the MIL-STD-1760 interface between the B-1B OAS and the weapons. (*Author*)

The spline on the forward end of the MPRL is engaged by the power drive, which rotates the MPRL. A weapon on the MPRL can only be launched when it is in the bottom position. The B-1B OAS controls the power drive and MPRL rotation. (*Author*)

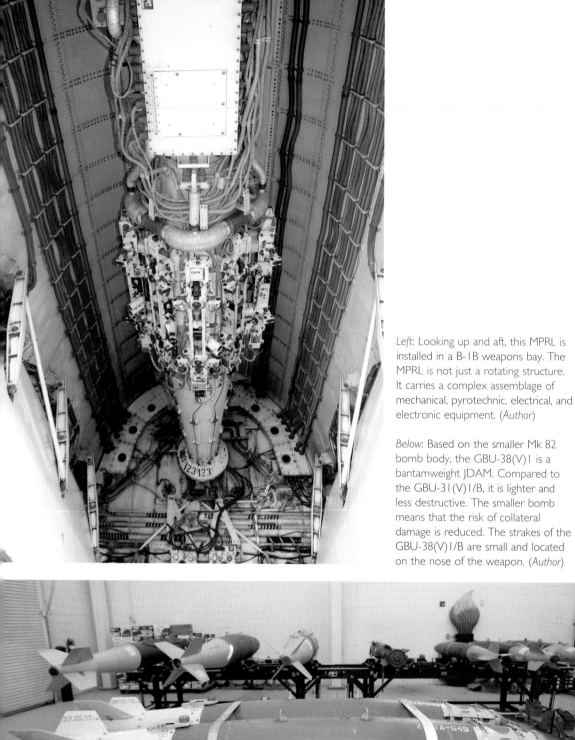

Left: Looking up and aft, this MPRL is installed in a B-1B weapons bay. The MPRL is not just a rotating structure. It carries a complex assemblage of mechanical, pyrotechnic, electrical, and electronic equipment. (*Author*)

Below: Based on the smaller Mk 82 bomb body, the GBU-38(V)1 is a bantamweight JDAM. Compared to the GBU-31(V)1/B, it is lighter and less destructive. The smaller bomb means that the risk of collateral damage is reduced. The strakes of the GBU-38(V)1/B are small and located on the nose of the weapon. (*Author*)

On 22 January 1998, a B-1B of the 419th Flight Test Squadron dropped a JDAM for the first time. This first JDAM delivery from a B-1B used inertial guidance only. On 11 February 1998, the B-1B dropped a JDAM using both inertial and GPS guidance. The 77th BS conducted the first JDAM drop by an operational B-1B unit on 24 November 1998.

Later, the B-1B was also armed with the GBU–38(V)1/B. The GBU–38(V)1/B is the smaller sibling of the GBU–31(V)1, built using a Mk 82 bomb body and weighing 552lbs. The advantage of the GBU–38(V)1/B is that it has a smaller lethal radius, which allows it to be used in closer proximity to friendly forces or against targets near innocent civilians. The GBU–38(V)1/B is carried on the 1760 Enhanced Conventional Bomb Module (SECBM), which is an ECBM further modified with MIL-STD-1760 interfaces for PGMs. Each SECBM carries six GBU–38(V)1/B weapons.

Because the JDAM flies towards a set of geographic coordinates, one JDAM limitation is that it cannot be used against moving targets. The GBU–54(V)1/B is a further development of the GBU–38(V)1/B that adds a DSU–38/B laser-homing target detection device. If it detects that the target has been designated with a coded laser beam, the DSU–38/B measures the angle to the laser spot and communicates it to the JDAM guidance electronics, which uses the data to update the coordinates of the target.

Cluster bombs suffer from the same problem as other bombs, which is that when dropped from medium altitude or higher, variations in wind direction and velocity between the launch altitude and the surface decrease the accuracy of the delivery. The Wind Corrected Munitions

The GBU-54(V)1/B Laser JDAM increases the accuracy of the weapons and adds the ability to engage moving targets. A gray conduit runs the length of the weapon on its bottom. The conduit contains wiring which runs between the DSU-38/B laser target detector device in the nose and the guidance tail assembly. (*Author*)

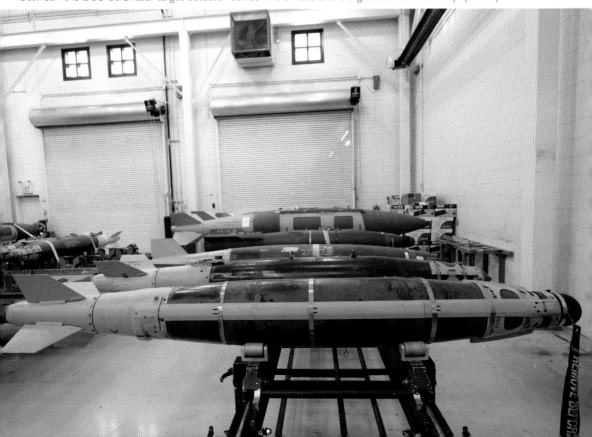

Dispenser (WCMD) adds a tail assembly to unguided cluster bombs. Like the JDAM tail kit, the WCMD has controllable fins and a MIL-STD-1760 interface. Because cluster bombs are area weapons with less demand for accuracy than a standard bomb, the WCMD has inertial guidance only and no GPS receiver. There are three versions of the WCMD: CBU-103/B (CBU-87/B with WCMD tail assembly, 961lbs), CBU-104/B (CBU-89/B with WCMD tail assembly, 738lbs), and CBU-105/B (CBU-97/B with WCMD tail assembly, 949lbs). Like the GBU-38(V)1/B, the SECBM carries the WCMD in the weapons bays.

Arming the B-1B with cluster bombs and PGMs dramatically increased its conventional lethality, but in many cases the B-1B still would need to fly in the engagement zone of enemy air defenses to deliver these weapons. Following the logic of the SRAM and cruise missile in the nuclear realm, the next step in increasing the conventional capability of the B-1B was to arm it with conventional standoff weapons. The JDAM was the first member of the family of so-called 'J-weapons'. The other 'J-weapons' were the Joint Stand-Off Weapon (JSOW) and Joint Air-Surface Stand-off Missile (JASSM).

The JSOW is a low-observable inertial/GPS-guided family of air-to-ground glide weapons. JSOW provides the B-1B and other aircraft with an all-weather, day/night, multiple kills per pass, launch-and-leave, and standoff capability. The JSOW is carried on the MPRL and controlled, monitored, and targeted with the standard MIL-STD-1760 interface. After launch, the JSOW wings unfold and the tail surfaces control it to the target. The JSOW range is up to 12 miles when launched from low altitude and up to 63 miles from high altitude.

The SECBM adds MIL-STD-1760 interfaces for smart weapons to the ECBM. Both the ECBM and SECBM are informally called the '10-carry', in contrast to the original CBM which is called the '28-carry'. Note the connectors for the MIL-STD-1760 interface which hang loose on the wire harnesses. (Author)

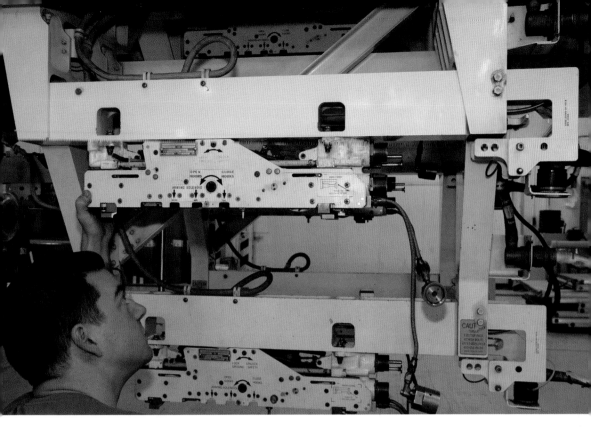

Above: Staff Sergeant Hunter J. Barto, a 7th Munitions Squadron armament floor supervisor, inspects an ejector rack on a SECBM. The ejector rack can carry a GBU-38(V)1/B, GBU-54(V)1/B or WCMD. (*Author*)

Right: The forward and intermediate weapons of bays of B-1B 86-0124 hold SECBMs which are carrying GBU-38(V)1/B JDAMs. Each bomb has a DSU-33C/B radar proximity fuze on its nose. The DSU-33C/B will cause the bomb to explode several feet over the ground, sending pieces of its steel case over a wide area. With its accuracy and the DSU-33C/B, the JDAM is exceptionally lethal against unarmored targets in the open. The maintainer under the aft intermediate fuselage is looking up at the aft weapons bay, the contents of which are not visible. (*Staff Sergeant Joshua Garcia/ US Air Force*)

A 34th BS B-1B delivers a GBU-38(V)1 from its forward weapons bay. This drop is over the Utah Test and Training Range. It is part of Combat Hammer, an FOT&E program that measures the reliability and accuracy of PGMs. The reliability and accuracy data obtained by Combat Hammer is used for mission planning and to identify problems with training, procedures, and stocks of fielded munitions. During the Vietnam War, the USAF discovered that its weapons were often much less effective in combat than had been predicted. Combat Hammer was launched to prevent a recurrence of that problem. (*US Air Force*)

The CBU-103/B is the WCMD version of the CBU-87/B cluster bomb. This particular item is a CBU-103(D-2)/B, a non-functional WCMD used for training. The CBU-103/B is carried on the SECBM. While extremely effective, cluster bombs have fallen into disfavor because the submunitions occasionally don't detonate on impact as expected. These duds then litter the ground, endangering friendly forces or civilians who traverse the area. (Author)

The AGM-154A version of the JSOW carries 145 BLU-97/B combined effects munitions and weighs 1,065lbs. Although the 419th Flight Test Squadron tested the AGM-154A from the B-1B in 2003, the USAF declined to acquire the weapon although the US Navy did. The AGM-154B carries six BLU-108/B submunitions. The AGM-154B was cancelled because attacking massed armored vehicles was a lesser concern at the time.

The most expensive member of the 'J-weapons' is the JASSM. It is a low-observable precision cruise missile designed for launch from outside area defenses. Like the JSOW, the MPRL carries eight JASSM weapons and the B-1B OAS uses the MIL-STD-1760 interface with JASSM. Wings are stowed in a folded location under the fuselage and are deployed after launch. A single vertical tail surface assists in steering control. The vertical tail surface is stowed in a folded position and is also deployed after launch. After the flight surface deployment, the jet engine in the JASSM starts and the missile flies under inertial/GPS guidance to the target. For area targets, the inertial/GPS guidance is sufficiently accurate by itself. For the most demanding point targets such as the entrance to a bunker, the JASSM has an infrared imaging sensor in its nose. By comparing the imagery from the sensor with a stored picture of target, the JASSM is accurate enough to literally fly through a door or window.

Right: A B-1B of the 419th Flight Test Squadron releases a JSOW. An F-16C of the AFFTC support fleet is the safety chase aircraft. The USAF never acquired the JSOW for operational use. (*US Air Force*)

Below: Technical Sergeant Christopher L. Warren uses an iPad tablet to carry an entire library of TOs with him. He is looking at a DATM-158A, the ground training version of the JASSM. (*Author*)

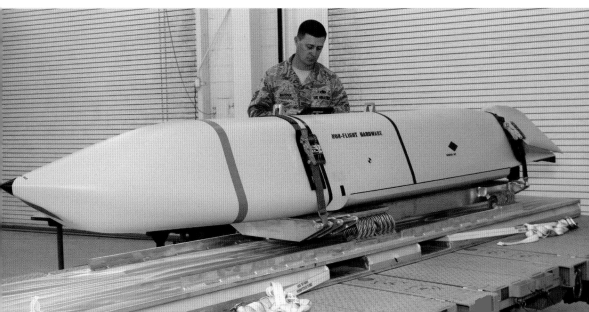

A 7th Aircraft Maintenance Squadron load crew member brings a JASSM to the jet. The actual missiles are very expensive and kept sealed in their storage containers until needed. Load training is done with ground training versions with a blue band. (*Airman 1st Class Austin Mayfield/US Air Force*)

The AGM-158A is the first version of the JASSM. It has a J402-CA-100 turbojet engine which gives it a range of approximately 200 nautical miles, a WDU-42/B unitary warhead with blast, fragmentation, and penetration effects, and weighs 2,250lbs. On its first flight on 19 January 2001, an F-16D launched the AGM-158A and the missile successfully flew to its target. The AGM-158A used the F-16C/D and B-52H as the carrier vehicles for the DT&E for the missile itself. The B-1B and B-2A followed those two aircraft, with integration work beginning on the B-1B even before the missile itself flew. Starting in 2000, engineers at AEDC used a wind tunnel to measure the separation aerodynamics of the JASSM from the B-1B. The 419th Flight Test Squadron began B-1B flight tests with JASSM in 2003. It achieved IOC with the 7th BW in 2005, with the 28th BW soon following. JASSM had a troubled infancy, with reliability problems and the unit cost more than doubling. The USAF considered cancelling it in 2007, but reliability improvements demonstrated in flight tests – fifteen of sixteen missiles fired between 10 September 2009 and 4 October 2009 destroyed their targets – saved the program.

The AGM-158B JASSM-ER (Extended Range) has a redesigned fuel system and an F107-WR-105 engine, but it is otherwise similar to the AGM-158A. The changes increase its range to approximately 500 miles. The first flight of the JASSM-ER was on 18 May 2006, when a B-1B fired it over the White Sands Missile Range. JASSM-ER achieved IOC in December 2014 with the B-1B being the initial launch platform. The long period between the first flight

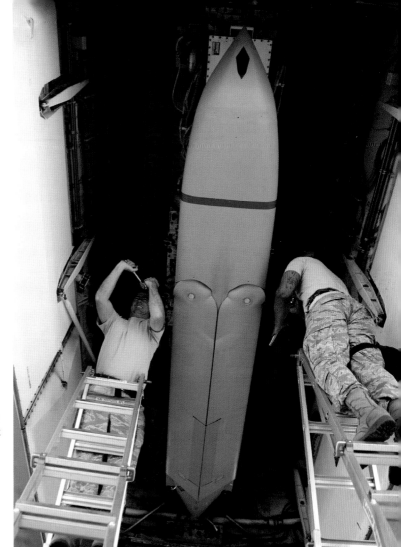

Right: Eight JASSMS are carried on an MPRL. The wings of the JASSM fold up for compact carriage and are extended after launch. The black polygon on the nose of the missile is a window for the imaging seeker that gives the missile its extraordinary terminal accuracy. (*Airman 1st Class Damon Kasberg/US Air Force*)

Below: A 419th Flight Test Squadron delivers a JASSM during a DT&E mission. The wings of the missile are in the process of extending. (*Ethan Wagner/US Air Force*)

and IOC of the AGM-158B was related to the time, resources, and effort required to improve the reliability in the AGM-158A before proceeding with the advanced version.

The next version of the JASSM is the AGM-158C Long Range Anti-Ship Missile (LRASM). LRASM is a JASSM-ER variant designed to sink enemy ships. Initially sponsored by the Defense Advanced Research Project Agency, the LRASM prototype underwent the first proof-of-concept flight tests against a target at sea on 27 August 2013. During the first flight test, a B-1B operated by the 337th TES launched the LRASM over the Point Mugu Sea Test Range off the coast of southern California. After launch, the missile navigated a pre-planned route towards the target. The LRASM autonomously detected the target and guided itself to hit it. Subsequent flight tests on 12 November 2013 and 4 February 2015 were also successful. After the LRASM concept was demonstrated, the missile was developed for production.

Above: The first LRASM prototype is delivered to B-1B 85-0075 of the 419th Flight Test Squadron. Based at Edwards AFB, this jet has an ED tailcode. *(Don Allen/US Air Force)*

Left: 'Missile away!' Chased by a US Navy F/A-18, B-1B 85-0075 releases a LRASM for a test flight over the Pacific Ocean *(US Air Force)*

A tactically-configured LRASM first flew in 17 August 2017. LRASM entered service with the 28th BW in December 2018. With LRASM, the long range of the B–1B, and its powerful ORS, the B–1B has excellent capabilities to work with the US Navy on the sea control mission.

The most recent version of the JASSM is the AGM-158D JASSM-XR (Extreme Range). JASSM-XR will have a range of approximately 1,000 nautical miles and deliveries will begin in 2024. The B–1B will be the first aircraft to carry JASSM-XR.

Upgrading the BONE

After the end of the Cold War, the American defense industry underwent a period of consolidation as revenues and programs shrank. Rockwell sold its military aircraft and space divisions to Boeing in 1996. NAR had defeated Boeing to win the B–1A contract in 1969. Twenty-seven years later, the Rockwell B–1B became the Boeing B–1B.

The B–1B systems needed upgrades to deliver the new weapons. The Conventional Mission Upgrade Program (CMUP) began in 1993 and was conducted in Phases. B–1B aircraft without CMUP improvements were called Block A aircraft. CMUP Block B improved the ORS by adding a Monopulse Ground Map mode. The operational fleet received Block B in late 1995.

CMUP Block C added the cluster bomb capability to the B–1B, including the modification of a portion of the CBM inventory to the ECBM configuration. Block C was the last configuration of the B–1B cleared to carry nuclear weapons. Since the cluster bomb capability needed to be added to the OAS software, the OAS needed to be tested to verify that the changes did not degrade other functions. Block C entered service in 1996.

CMUP Block D was the 'game-changer' for the B–1B. Block D added GPS to OAS, an AN/ARC-210 radio with secure and anti-jam capabilities, and the JDAM capability. The JDAM capability included the MPRL, the MIL-STD-1760 interface in the weapons bay for PGMs, and the addition of JDAM capabilities to the OAS software. In some ways, the new radio was as important as the JDAM. Now the B–1B could securely communicate with other aircraft in a tactical environment and also with forward air controllers on the ground. The operational B–1B force began to receive aircraft modified to the Block D configuration in late 1998, and all jets were modified by May 2002. Its nuclear mission now in the past, the BONE had become a state-of-the-art conventional bomber.

The round antennas on the B–1B are for GPS. The B–1B added GPS as part of CMUP Block D. (*Author*)

By the time Block D was fielded, the ACUs in the OAS were nearly two decades old, which meant that they were antiquated. The addition of new capabilities to the OAS like GPS navigation, cluster bombs, and JDAM had taxed the ACU memory and processing capacity to their limits. Not only was there no room for new weapons, but the B-1B could not carry mixed weapons loads. For example, the B-1B could physically carry JDAMs on an MPRL in weapons bay, a CBM with Mk 82 bombs in another weapons bay, and an ECBM with cluster bombs in the third, but OAS could not simultaneously handle the diverse weapons.

The core of Block E involved replacing legacy ACUs (but not the TF ACUs or the DAS preprocessor ACU) with new computers. The new computers have approximately 500 times more memory and processing speed than the ACUs, reflecting the dramatic advances in digital computer technology since the B-1B OAS was designed. The OAS software was completely rewritten for the new computers. Weapons software was modularized so that adding a new weapon did not entail testing the entire OAS software application. With Block E, the B-1B could carry a different kind of weapon in each weapons bay and drop patterns of PGMs, with each PGM having a different aim point. Block E added WCMD, JSOW, and JASSM to the B-1B, although JSOW was not fielded. GBU-38(V)1/B and the advanced versions of JASSM were not part of Block E, but the new computers and software made it a relatively fast and inexpensive effort to add those weapons when they became available. Block E upgrades to the fleet were completed in September 2006.

Block E dramatically increased the flexibility of the B-1B weapon system. In early May 2002, the 419th Flight Squadron attacked three targets, each with a different kind of weapon, on a single pass. The weapons were a Mk 84 bomb on a MPRL, three Mk 82 bombs on a CBM, and four CBU-89 cluster bombs on an ECBM. Prior to Block E, this attack would have required three different B-1B aircraft. The test on 10 August 2002 added PGMs to the capability, with two JDAMs, six Mk 82 bombs, and two WCMDs being dropped on a single pass.

Improving Defensive Systems

While the CMUP modernized the offensive capabilities of the B-1B, the defensive capabilities were also improved. In 1993, the USAF had proposals from industry to upgrade or replace the AN/ALQ-161A DAS hardware, but Congress forbade spending funds for that purpose. DAS was gradually improved through software releases. The greatest advance in defensive systems was the addition of the AN/ALE-50(V)1 Towed Decoy System (TDS). TDS was part of CMUP Block D.

TDS is contained in two magazines on each side of the B-1B aft fuselage, with a system controller inside the aircraft. Each magazine contains four decoys. In flight, a decoy is played out on a long tether from the magazine so that it trails the B-1B. The decoy emits signals that make it more attractive target to radar-homing missiles than the B-1B itself. If TDS works as intended, the missile will home in on the decoy instead of the aircraft.

The 419th Flight Test Squadron began flight testing TDS in March 1997. Flight testing included deploying the decoy, evaluating the interaction between the towed decoy and the aircraft (Does the tether rub against airframe? Do the engine exhaust plumes impinge on the tether?), and evaluating the effectiveness of TDS in protecting the aircraft. TDS was fielded from January 1999.

TDS is regarded as a highly successful modification to the B-1B and one major reason why no B-1B has ever been shot down in combat. A mission report from 21 March 2003 highlights the value of TDS:

Approximately 20 seconds from weapons release, an SA-6 Target Track indication was received on the jet's systems. The crew, now on its bomb run, ceased all maneuvering until

Right: The TDS magazines are located in fairings which were added to both sides of the aft fuselage. (*Author*)

Below: Viewed from the rear, the TDS fairing reveals the opening from which the decoys are deployed on tethers to trail the aircraft. A critical consideration during the design of the TDS installation on the B-1B was to avoid having the engine exhaust melt or burn the tether when it reeled out. (*Author*)

weapons release, while chaff was released to try and break lock with the target tracker.. The crew made a package advisory call to let all other aircraft aloft that REVAMP 67 was defensive with a surface to air missile system. Immediately after weapons release the OSO safed his weapons bay and called clear to maneuver. The Aircraft Commander broke hard left off target and pushed up his speed in his egress toward the Saudi Border. The crew was successful in evading the threat, as the missile passed aft and its explosion was seen behind the aircraft. Crew suspects a Towed Decoy save.

By 1996, the B-1B Defensive System Upgrade Program (DSUP) was one of ACC's highest priorities. The USAF and industry investigated how a variety of existing ECM systems could be integrated on the B-1B. CMUP Block F was intended to be a thorough revamping of the B-1B defense capabilities. Also called Defense System Upgrade Program (DSUP), it included the AN/ALR-56M radar warning receiver, the AN/ALE-55 fiber optic towed decoy, and AN/ALQ-214 receiver modulator processor. By 2001, the AN/ALE-55 had run into technical, cost and schedule problems. In December 2002, the USAF cancelled DSUP. The B-1B instead would get more incremental improvements to the AN/ALQ-161A.

A Decade of Change

The B-1B entered the 1990s as SAC's newest bomber, poised to fight a nuclear war against the Soviet Union. During the decade that followed, the transformation of organization, deployment, culture, employment doctrine, and weapon system capabilities converted the B-1B into a long-range conventional strike platform. The transformation of the B-1B was most timely, enabling it to become a valuable airpower asset in the new century.

CMUP didn't just add capabilities to the B-1B. It transformed the role of the BONE. (*Technical Sergeant Darcie L. Ibidapo/US Air Force*)

Chapter 11

Combat Debut

'Everybody in the B-1B community knows the capability of this weapons system, and now we have been given the opportunity to show the world the powerful tools we bring to the fight.'

Brigadier General Michael C. McMahan, commander, 7th BW,
remarking on Operation Desert Fox

Operation Desert Fox

Operation Desert Storm achieved a high degree of success on the battlefield, but military success did not translate into decisive results at the strategic level. Iraqi dictator Saddam Hussein and his regime remained in power. Under the terms of the ceasefire agreement and subsequent United Nations Security Council resolutions, United Nations inspectors verified that Iraq was not building or deploying weapons of mass destruction. Coalition airpower, primarily contributed by the United States, enforced no–fly zones over northern and southern Iraq to protect minority groups from the depredations of the regime's enforcers. Saddam Hussein proceeded to frequently test the coalition opposing him, resulting in airborne skirmishes and the occasionally punitive raid.

The tensions leading to Operation Desert Fox (called Operation Desert Thunder until 16 November 1998) had been building for years. In 1997, multiple B-1B squadron deployments to Sheikh Isa Air Base, Bahrain acted as a deterrent to Iraqi misbehavior. On 4 December 1997, two B-1B aircraft from the 37th Expeditionary Bomb Squadron (EBS) entered Iraqi airspace. No weapons were delivered on this mission (Operation Phoenix Scorpion), but it was the first time that the BONE and the aircrews that flew it logged combat time. [Author's note: An EBS was built around a BS with the same number, but often was augmented with personnel and aircraft from other squadrons.]

Operation Desert Fox was the most substantial of the punitive raids against Iraq. In response to Saddam Hussein's obstruction of the weapons inspectors, the United States and its coalition partner the United Kingdom launched Operation Desert Fox. The primary objective of Operation Desert Fox was to degrade the Iraqi weapons of mass destruction capability, with several secondary objectives. One secondary objective was to drive apart the regular Iraqi military and the Republican Guard. The latter was a separate armed force that was particularly loyal to the regime and acted as a counterbalance to the regular Iraqi military. The other secondary objectives were to diminish Iraq's capability to conduct aggression and to impress upon Saddam Hussein the consequences of violating international agreements, including denying United Nations inspectors access to Iraqi sites.

An advance team departed from Dyess AFB on 13 November in a C-17A transport to prepare for the arrival of the B-1B aircraft at Thumrait Air Base (AB), Oman. Oman was more favorably inclined towards military action against Iraq than the other Arab states in the region. The C-17A broke along the way, so the advance team did not arrive until after the first four B-1B aircraft arrived at Thumrait AB on 15 November 1998. Upon landing, the aircrew discovered that Thumrait AB was empty. They had the tent city all to themselves. The aircrews refueled the aircraft without assistance. Thumrait AB did not have CASS for the B-1B or an abundance of AGE. Fortunately, the B-1B had dual APUs and could power itself for ground maintenance. It also had CITS to checkout its systems. The full deployment of B-1B bombers was halted and restarted several times while Saddam Hussein pretended to cooperate with the weapons inspection and then reneged on his promises.

The distance from Oman to Iraq made it an undesirable base for fighters but an excellent place from which to launch long-range bomber missions. The runway at Thumrait AB was too narrow to accommodate the B-52 with its outrigger landing gear on its wing tips, but was adequate for the B-1B, providing a good example of how seemingly minor design features can have major operational implications.

Both the 7th BW and 28th BW contributed airplanes and personnel to the B-1B force at Thumrait AB, which was designated the 28th Air Expeditionary Group and commanded by Colonel Tim Bailey. Through late November and early December, training sorties familiarized the crews with the region and the joint force operating procedures. [Author's note: There is official documentation that calls this unit the 28th Air Operations Group, but that would have been an unusual unit designation and it contradicts other sources.]

A B-1B runs up its engines at Thumrait AB, Oman. When this photograph was taken on 14 December 1998, the 28th Air Expeditionary Group was conducting training flights in the run-up to Operation Desert Fox. *(Senior Airman Sean M. White/US Air Force)*

The political situation in the region complicated the planning of Operation Desert Fox. American military forces operated out of military bases in Saudi Arabia and several of the smaller emirates in the region. These countries had a complex and ambiguous relationship with the Iraqi regime. Simultaneously they feared it, felt solidarity with it as fellow Sunni Muslim Arabs, and appreciated it as a counterbalance to Iran, which is Shi'ite Muslim and predominantly Persian in ethnicity. Saudi Arabia, Kuwait and some other nominal American allies in the region would have been the ideal launch pads for Operation Desert Fox, but their rulers only permitted the United States and United Kingdom to use their bases for support missions such as aerial refueling. The strike aircraft would need to fly from more distant bases or from aircraft carriers. This was the environment in which the B-1B flew its first combat missions. The political constraints on basing meant that the US Navy aircraft flying from the aircraft carrier USS Enterprise would provide its escort. That the B-1B could be easily employed with US Navy aircraft was a testament to the value of Red Flag and other exercises which had a strong joint-service component. Captain Gordon 'Guv' Greaney, a WSO and Weapons School graduate, led the planning and coordination with the strike leader on USS *Enterprise*.

The United States and Great Britain launched Operation Desert Fox on 16 December 1998. For four days, the more than 650 strike and strike support sorties by manned aircraft and approximately 425 cruise missiles attacked targets in Iraq. The B-1B entered the action on 17 December 1998. A strike package of two B-1Bs, two F-14B Tomcats, eight F/A-18C Hornets, one EA-6B Prowler, and one E-3 Sentry AWACS hit the Republican Guard barracks at al-Kut in Iraq. The other aircraft in the package protected the B-1B from fighters and air defenses; the BONEs delivered the heavy firepower on the target. Each B-1B carried sixty-three Mk 82 LD bombs (twenty-one in each CBM), because PGMs were still unavailable at this time. The aircraft were crewed as follows:

SLAM 01
86-0096
Lieutenant Colonel Stephen Wolborsky (pilot)
Captain Chris Wright (co-pilot)
Captain Fred Bivetto (DSO)
Captain Peter G. Bailey (OSO)
37th BS, 28th BW

SLAM 02
86-0135
Captain Jeffrey Hoyt (pilot)
1st Lieutenant Bob Mankus (co-pilot)
Captain Jason Xiques (DSO)
Captain Gordon P. Greaney (OSO)
9th BS, 7th BW

While the maintainers conducted final checks on the two bombers, the aircrew met with mission planners, intelligence specialists, and the meteorologist. The aircrews were excited to fly on their first combat mission in the B-1B. The jets took off to the south on Runway 17 and made a left turn, slightly delaying their climb so as to overfly the tent city and go into full afterburner over it. They then flew north towards Iraq. To improve their situational awareness in the dark, the B-1B pilots wore night vision goggles, which enabled them to see the aircraft launched from USS *Enterprise* refuel from two KC-10A tankers. After a ten-minute delay to the original planned 'push time', the B-1B aircraft formed up with the naval jets. The strike package proceeded north and across Kuwait into Iraq. On the way to the target, the EA-6B shot an anti-radiation missile at an SA-6 surface-to-air missile site to suppress it. The ORS provided excellent high-resolution ground maps that the OSOs used to tighten up the OAS navigation and obtain fixes on offset aim points for the bombing. The two bombers attacked the al-Kut barracks using slightly different intersecting courses to place an X of bombs on the target. Iraqi anti-aircraft fire was plentiful but ineffective. Bombing accuracy from medium altitude was excellent, but the mechanical complexity and unreliability of the CBMs reduced the effectiveness of the weapons delivery. B-1B 86-0096 had twenty bombs remaining on the aircraft and B-1B 86-0135 had nineteen remaining. Some bombs 'hung' (did not release). When the bombs did not leave the CBM, the OAS inhibited other bombs from being released so that those bombs would not fall on the arms holding the hung bombs. The aircraft then flew to al-Jalaba Airfield to get rid of as many of the remaining bombs as possible on that secondary target. Maneuvering to return to Oman, the DSO on 86-0135 used the DAS to detect an SA-2 surface-to-air missile radar. Using their speed, the B-1B jets escaped the missile engagement zone. Because of the remaining hung bombs, the pilots declared an emergency before landing at Thumrait AB. Munitions loaders and explosive ordnance disposal specialists safed and unloaded the hung bombs after landing. The cause of bombs that did not release on al-Kut but did on al-Jalaba was a thin layer of desert dust on sensitive switches on the CBM arms.

The first B-1B combat mission of Operation Desert Fox was followed on 18 December 1998 by another B-1B attack on an oil refinery near Basra, Iraq and a return to the al-Kut barracks. SLAM 03 had some of the same kind of problems with hung bombs, but SLAM 04 released all sixty-three of its Mk 82 LD bombs in accordance with the plan.

Operation Desert Fox attacks continued into 19 December 1998 and were then halted, but with no B-1B combat sorties on the fourth day. Like during Operation Desert Storm, the airstrikes of Operation Desert Fox were technically impressive and operationally successful.

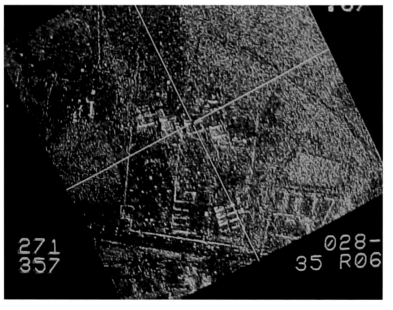

The ORS high-resolution ground mapping mode was an essential element of the highly accurate B-1B bombing capability. Captain Gordon Greaney on B-1B 86-0135 used this radar image of al-Kut to put weapons on target. Notice that the buildings in the center of the image can also be seen in the photograph that follows. (*Gordon Greaney collection*)

AL KUT BARRACKS WEST-NORTHWEST, IRAQ

Above: Bomb damage assessment photography of the first B-1B combat mission shows outstanding bombing accuracy. (*Department of Defense*)

Right: A munitions load team has brought a loaded CBM to B-1B 86-0109 'Spectre'. This aircraft flew as SLAM 03 on the second night of B-1B operations on 18 December 1998. Led by Lieutenant Colonel Garrett Harencak, the SLAM 03 crew came from 9th BS, 7th BW. (*Staff Sergeant Krista M. Foeller/US Air Force*)

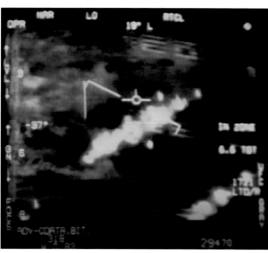

Above: (L to R) Captains John Martin (DSO), Joe Reidy (OSO), Jeffrey Taliaferro (pilot) and Randy Kaufman (co-pilot) stand in front of 37th BS B-1B 86-0102 during Operation Desert Fox on the flightline at Thumrait AB, Oman. Note mission marking under the pilot's side window. This aircraft was SLAM 04 on the 18 December 1998 mission. *(John Martin collection, via US Air Force)*

Left: A sensor pod on an escorting F-14B Tomcat captures strings of bombs from SLAM 03 and SLAM 04 as they inflict destruction on the target. The explosions can be seen in the center and lower right of the image. *(Randy Kaufman collection)*

The United Nations weapons inspectors returned to their posts. Regime change was not an objective of Operations Desert Fox, and so the Iraq situation persisted, but with some degradation in Iraqi capabilities.

The B-1B over Serbia and Kosovo

During the Cold War, Yugoslavia had been an anomaly in Europe. It was a collection of small and mutually hostile nationalities held together by the Communist dictatorship of Josip Broz Tito. Although a Communist, Tito was anything but a Soviet client and he maintained a neutral position in the Cold War. After Tito's death and the end of the Cold War, Yugoslavia disintegrated into multiple states amidst violence and ethnic cleansing. The North Atlantic Treaty Organization (NATO), with the United States as its leading member, gingerly involved itself in the wreckage of the former Yugoslavia to contain the disorder and mitigate the humanitarian disasters that resulted. By 1998, the focus of hostilities was the province of Kosovo. After the secession of many of the regions of Yugoslavia, what remained of Yugoslavia was largely Serbian. Although dominated by ethnic Serbs, the rump of Yugoslavia still contained other ethnic groups. In particular, the Kosovo region was regarded by Serbs as an integral part of their nation, but the majority of its population was ethnically Albanian. The Eastern Orthodox Christian Serbs and the Muslim Albanians had been mutually hostile for centuries. After failed diplomacy and an ineffective United Nations Security Council resolution, NATO launched Operation Allied Force to halt Yugolavian/Serbian attacks against ethnic Albanians. The American action within Operation Allied Force was called Operation Noble Anvil. It became the second combat employment of the B-1B.

Operation Allied Force/Noble Anvil was an exclusively air campaign. There were two aspects of the air war: a tactical campaign to oppose Serbian forces in Kosovo and a strategic campaign to coerce the Serbian regime of Slobodan Milošević into behaving in accordance with the United Nations Security Council resolution. CMUP Block D was just coming into service when the Kosovo actions began. The B-1B aircraft doing CMUP Block D tests were deployed for the action and modification of other jets to the Block D configuration was accelerated. Although equipped to deliver JDAMs, there were insufficient stocks of that PGM for it to be used by the B-1B. TDS was available and regarded as essential for safe penetration of defended airspace.

During Operation Allied Force/Noble Anvil, there were generally five or six B-1B aircraft at a time based at RAF Fairford in the United Kingdom, with individual aircraft being rotated out of the theater for maintenance and then replaced. The 77th EBS was the B-1B unit at RAF Fairford, commanded first by Lieutenant Colonel Robert B. Bush and then Lieutenant Colonel Steven P. Dickman.

B-1B aircrews had a useful new addition to their cockpits. The Combat Track II system was a laptop computer located between the DSO and OSO seats. It was wired into the aircraft GPS and SATCOM systems. With the laptop computer, the two WSOs could communicate with

B-1B 85-0091 is in the foreground and B-1B 85-0083 is in the background. Both have the tail stripes of the 77th BS 'War Eagles' and the EL tail code of the 28th BW. This photograph was taken at RAF Fairford on 1 April 1999. (*Staff Sergeant Randy Mallard/ US Air Force*)

Mk 82 LD bombs with DSU-33A/B radar proximity fuzes await being loaded on to the aircraft. Painted olive green with a yellow ring around the nose indicates that these bombs are filled with high explosives. (*Staff Sergeant Randy Mallard/US Air Force*)

mission planners or a command center by text chat and also had a moving map display with the aircraft location depicted on the map. Combat Track II increased the situational awareness of the aircrews in dynamic situations. Greg Van Swearingen, a civilian engineer, played a critical role in integrating Combat Track II into the B–1B.

The first B–1B attack of the conflict was on 1 April 1999. One particularly noteworthy B–1B action during the war was against the Novi Sad oil refinery, which was bombed by two B–1B aircraft on 1 May 1999. Two bombers, each with eighty-four Mk 82 LD bombs, devastated the refinery. Not only did the destruction of the Novi Sad oil refinery deprive Serbian forces of fuel, it also dealt a severe blow to the Serbian economy. With its excellent ORS, the B–1B remained highly capable in poor weather when fighters with laser-guided PGMs could not conduct attacks. TDS was one of the great successes of the war, saving several jets from surface-to-air missile engagements. By the cessation of hostilities in June 1999, the 77th EBS flew over 100 missions and had delivered 20 per cent of the total NATO weapons.

The BONE Enters the Twenty-first Century

The B–1B had been a success in combat, successfully penetrating defended airspace and accurately delivering 'dumb' bombs at night in poor weather. The CMUP Block D modifications were underway. Only a handful of JDAMs had been available during Operational Allied Force/Noble Anvil and they had been reserved for use by the B–2A Spirit, which saw combat for the first time in that conflict. JDAM was clearly a winner, and the USAF began to build up stocks of the weapon. With fortuitous timing, the B–1B was ready for its next challenge.

Chapter 12

The Global War on Terror

'The bomber's unique strengths of payload, range, and responsiveness coupled with precision attack are a cornerstone of America's airpower and force projection . . . The long-range capability provided by bombers could make them the first major U.S. weapon system on the scene in a rapidly developing crisis, particularly in regions where the United States does not routinely maintain forces or have basing rights.'

U.S. Air Force White Paper on Long Range Bombers, 1 March 1999

Does America Need the BONE?

The B-1B would become the bomber of choice in America's wars of the new century, but it began that century under existential threat. During his first tour as Secretary of Defense under President Gerald R. Ford, Donald H. Rumsfeld supported the B-1 and even took an orientation flight in one of the prototypes. In 2001, President George W. Bush nominated Rumsfeld to the same position in his administration. Rumsfeld regarded himself as an iconoclast who shook up calcified bureaucracies. The B-1B in its CMUP Block D configuration was highly capable, but Rumsfeld regarded it as fundamentally old technology and looked favorably on divesting it. The compromise was to retire thirty-three aircraft, leaving a fleet of sixty. The Air National Guard would lose its BONEs and the remaining fleet would be located at Dyess AFB and Ellsworth AFB, other than the aircraft assigned to the 419th Flight Test Squadron at Edwards AFB. The logic of the decision was that the funds saved by retiring some of the fleet would be used to modernize the remaining aircraft. The decision to reduce the size of the B-1B fleet was the swan song for the Lot II and III aircraft. The early production aircraft had some configuration differences with the later aircraft and they were more difficult to support, so they were the first to go.

Operation Enduring Freedom

It was the morning of 11 September 2001. Captain Kent L. Payne, a B-1B pilot assigned to the 34th BS, woke up, and as was his habit, turned on the news. Like other Americans, he was shocked by what he saw and heard. Calling into the squadron, he asked, 'Are you seeing what is going on?' The response from the squadron's deputy of operations was simple and direct: 'Get in here.'

After al-Qaeda launched its dramatic attacks on the United States on 11 September 2001, Americans thirsted for revenge against the terrorist group, and their government under President Bush sought to prevent future attacks. Attacking al-Qaeda was logistically daunting.

The group and its leader Osama bin Laden used Taliban-controlled Afghanistan as their headquarters. Afghanistan was distant, landlocked, and had formidable terrain. Out of this challenging situation was born a highly innovative and unconventional strategy. American and allied special operations forces working with Central Intelligence Agency (CIA) field officers would link up with anti-Taliban militias in Afghanistan. The militias would provide the manpower; the special operations forces and CIA would contribute money, communications, and intelligence. Perhaps the most valuable thing that the special operations forces would provide was air support. Equipped with GPS receivers for navigation, laser rangefinders to get target coordinates, satellite communications (SATCOM), and night vision sensors, combat controllers embedded within the special operations teams could bring down massive firepower from above on al-Qaeda and Taliban forces after the militiamen flushed them from hiding.

As with Operation Desert Fox, the expedition into Afghanistan, called Operation Enduring Freedom (OEF), had to operate in an extraordinarily complex and difficult diplomatic environment. Polite fictions aside, there were no countries adjacent to Afghanistan that could be regarded as American allies, so basing fighters and bombers in them was out of the question. At best, certain countries could be bribed or threatened into provide overflight rights or basing for low-key support activities. As occurred in Operation Desert Fox, a combination of naval airpower and long-range bombers provided the majority of airpower for OEF, until territory was captured and airbases set up within Afghanistan itself.

As special operations forces and CIA field officers infiltrated into Afghanistan, staff officers composed plans to attack al-Qaeda terrorists and their Taliban hosts. Diego Garcia played an important role in the plans. Known as 'DG' or 'DGar' to American service members, Diego Garcia had two outstanding characteristics. A small island located in the Indian Ocean, Diego Garcia was close enough to the Persian Gulf and Afghanistan to serve as a base. Even better, it was British territory and therefore controlled by a country that was the closest ally of the United States.

After the deployment order was issued on 19 September 2001, aircraft, support equipment, and personnel began to move to Diego Garcia to form the 28th Air Expeditionary Wing (AEW). The eight B-1B aircraft flew non-stop from Ellsworth AFB to Diego Garcia, arriving on 21 September 2001. Each jet was refueled four times in the air. After nearly a decade of Global Power missions, this impressive feat had become routine.

The commander of the 28th AEW was Colonel Edward A. Rice Jr. of the 28th BW. The vice commander was Colonel Anthony A. Imondi, the vice commander of the 2nd BW, the B-52H wing at Barksdale AFB, Louisiana. The 28th Expeditionary Mission Support Group, a component of 28th AEW, built Camp Justice to house the incoming 28th AEW personnel. The 28th AEW's flight operations were handled by the 28th Expeditionary Operations Group (EOG), commanded by Lieutenant Colonel Stephen W. 'Seve' Wilson. Within the 28th EOG, B-52H operations were organized into the 20th EBS commanded by Lieutenant Colonel Paul G. 'Taco' Bell, while B-1B operations fell under the 34th EBS, commanded by Lieutenant Colonel Thomas 'Bullet' Arko. At first, 28th AEW had eight B-52Hs and eight B-1Bs based on Diego Garcia. The B-1B aircraft sent to Diego Garcia had been upgraded to CMUP Block D. The 60th Air Expeditionary Group, commanded by Colonel Darren W. McDew and operating 12 KC-10A tankers, was also based on Diego Garcia.

The Combined Air Operations (CAOC) at Prince Sultan Air Base, Saudi Arabia was the nerve center of the OEF air war. The CAOC was a state-of-art facility with the latest communications and computing equipment.

Above: B-1B 85-0075 was one of the 34th EBS jets that deployed to Diego Garcia for OEF. A KC-10A Extender tanker from the 60th AEG is in the background. These tankers refueled the bombers on their transits to and from Afghanistan. (*US Air Force*)

Right: Colonel Edward A. Rice Jr. commanded the 28th AEW on Diego Garcia. (*US Air Force*)

MV *Major Bernard F. Fisher* is a ship dedicated to carrying munitions and other supplies to forward deployed bases. She is named after a USAF officer decorated with the Medal of Honor during the Vietnam War. On dock at Diego Garcia, containers of weapons have been unloaded from the ship and are being trucked to the weapons facility. (*Staff Sergeant Shane Cuomo/US Air Force*)

OEF combat operations began on 7 October 2001. The 28th AEW contribution was six B-52H and six B-1B sorties per day during the first two days, then settling into a sustained rate of four B-52H and four B-1B sorties per day. During the first two weeks of the operation, a variety of platforms attacked fixed targets in Afghanistan: 28th AEW B-1Bs and B-52Hs based on Diego Garcia, 509th BW B-2As flying to Afghanistan nonstop from their base in Missouri and then landing on Diego Garcia, carrier-based aircraft from the USS *Enterprise* and USS *Carl Vinson*, and cruise missiles fired from ships.

Planned first day targets for the three formations of two B-1B aircraft included an al-Qaeda training camp, the suspected headquarters of Osama bin Laden at Tora Gora (also called Tora Bora), and aircraft and airfields which might be used by Osama bin Laden to escape into hiding. Each formation had one B-1B armed with JDAMs and another with Mk 82 LD bombs. The sorties were typically eighteen hours long, with a six-hour transit from Diego Garcia over the Indian Ocean, Arabian Sea and Pakistan to Afghanistan, six hours over Afghanistan, and then the six-hour return flight. Tankers based on Diego Garcia provided fuel for the transit legs, while tankers based in some of the central Asian republics north of Afghanistan refueled the bombers over land.

The entire operation highlighted the pervasive influence of information and space technology on airpower. RQ-1 Predator remotely piloted aircraft fed full-motion video in real time by satellite data links to the CAOC. With the aircraft having SATCOM and GPS, the CAOC could direct the bombers to time-sensitive targets (TSTs), monitor their fuel state, and arrange for tankers to meet the bombers. Finally, GPS guided the JDAMs to their targets. The entire

A munitions load team member brings a GBU-31(V)1/B JDAM to an aircraft. The pace of combat during OEF consumed these weapons at a prodigious rate. (*Staff Sergeant Larry A. Simmons/US Air Force*)

arrangement was dynamic and responsive, the antithesis of the SAC fixed target, 'follow the mission plan' mentality.

Two B-1B bombers participated in a major attack on the villa of Mullah Omar, the Taliban leader, on 19 October 2001. The villa was heavily defended with machine guns in fighting positions, anti-aircraft guns, and man-portable surface-to-air missiles. The jets launched from Diego Garcia with a total of forty-eight JDAMs. After dropping twelve weapons on the Taliban targets near Kandahar, Afghanistan, they headed to the villa. Flying as high as possible to maximize the LAR, the two aircraft positioned themselves so that one could rain bombs down on the east side of the valley while the other covered the west side of the valley. In a matter of seconds, thirty-six GBU-31(V)1/B weapons with radar proximity fuzes hit the defensive positions, destroying them. Meanwhile, F/A-18 Hornets dropped laser-guided bombs on the anti-aircraft guns. In the words of B-1B pilot Captain Kent L. Payne, the 'whole sky lit up'. With the villa defenders either dead or stunned, an MC-130H Combat Talon II aircraft flew down the valley at low level to assess the remaining threat, followed by special operations forces who parachuted into the area. After a quick firefight, the special operations forces exploited the site to capture a treasure trove of maps, documents, computers, and prisoners, all exploited for their intelligence value.

Starting on 21 October 2001, the focus of the air offensive shifted from planned attacks on fixed targets to on-call close air support (XCAS) with special operations forces. With no American conventional ground forces yet in Afghanistan, American special operations teams from the CIA and the U.S. Army's 5th Special Forces Group (Airborne) linked up with anti-Taliban fighters of the Northern Alliance. The Northern Alliance fighters flushed out the Taliban and al-Qaeda from their hiding spots in Afghanistan's forbidding terrain. Then USAF

Above left: The forward weapon bay of this B-1B is loaded with a mix of GBU-31(V)1 and GBU-31(V)3 bombs. WSOs needed to keep track of which specific weapon types and fuze settings were on each MPRL station to match weapons to targets to get the desired effect. (*Staff Sergeant Larry A. Simmons/US Air Force*)

Above right: Writing messages to the enemy on bombs is a long-standing USAF tradition. This aircrew member has written, 'Osama, mess with the bull and you get the horns'. (*Staff Sergeant Shane Cuomo/US Air Force*)

combat controllers attached to the special operations teams used their GPS units and laser rangefinders to precisely determine the geographic coordinates of the enemy and call in strikes with AN/PRC-117F multiband digital radios.

The result of the previous decade of work by the B-1B community paid off in the skies of over Afghanistan. XCAS involved flying to Afghanistan with no defined target and orbiting in the airspace until a call from the CAOC directed them to the assistance of forces on the ground. B-1B aircrews now operated without strictly following a plan. Instead, they responded to the situation as it developed. With the new AN/ARC-210 radio, B-1B aircrews talked directly with personnel on the ground. That communications would often be followed shortly by a JDAM.

The mountainous terrain that covers much of Afghanistan presented significant challenges to B-1B operations. Communications between the forward air controller on the ground and the aircrew in the B-1B required line-of-sight between the two. If the forward air controller was in a valley, line-of-sight for air-ground communications only existed when the jet was nearly overhead. Because of this limitation, it often took several passes over the target for the B-1B to receive enough information to accurately deliver a weapon. On the first pass, the forward air

The Global War on Terror 287

controller gave the B-1B aircrew the target coordinates. Several aircrew members copied the coordinates and compared what they wrote down. As the B-1B moved beyond line-of-sight, the WSO in the OSO seat manually entered the coordinates into the OAS for download to the JDAM. The B-1B then circled around for a second pass. When the aircrew regained communications with the forward air controller, the aircrew read back the target coordinates to the forward air controller to verify them. Since the aircrew could not see the target and were dependent on information from the forward air controller, the readback and verification were essential to ensure accuracy and prevent fratricide. With the target coordinates verified, the jet circled again for the third pass to actually delivery the JDAM.

On 21 October 2001, American and indigenous forces started bringing units into place to take the key city of Mazar-i-Sharif. Major offensive action began on 28 October 2001, with accurate and lethal air support. The Americans and their local allies defeated the Taliban and captured Mazar-i-Sharif on 9 November 2001. On 13 November 2001, the Taliban fled Kabul, the capital of Afghanistan. The combination of special operations forces, indigenous troops, and airpower with PGMs was brilliantly effective. By the end of November 2001, the B-1B and B-52H bombers had delivered 72 per cent of the total bomb tonnage during OEF. Combat had validated the efforts of those who had advocated the transformation of the B-1B after the Cold War and implemented that transformation.

After the capture of Kabul, the action shifted to Kandahar, the last major city controlled by the Taliban. Kandahar fell to American and allied forces on 9 December 2001. The enemy then fled to the mountains and caves of Tora Bora. Despite efforts to surround them, Osama bin Laden and his entourage managed to escape Tora Bora and go into hiding.

On 12 December 2001, the 34th EBS suffered the first combat loss of a B-1B, although the cause of the mishap was a system failure, not enemy action. The aircrew of B-1B 86-0114 lost control of the aircraft at night. The root cause remains unknown, because the wreckage lies deep in the Indian Ocean, but it may have degraded the pilot's attitude information which would have been problematic, since in flying at night over the ocean there is no visual horizon. The aircrew declared an emergency and successfully ejected. A KC-10A tanker was departing Diego Garcia and diverted to the last known position of the B-1B. Using

B-1B 86-0114 crashed on 12 December 2001 into the Indian Ocean. The crew ejected successfully, but the wreckage was not recovered and there is no conclusive explanation of the root cause of the system failure that led to its demise. (*US Air Force*)

radio beacons, flares, and strobe lights, the B-1B aircrew drew the attention of the KC-10A, which located them and radioed the position to rescue forces. A US Navy P-3C Orion patrol aircraft joined the effort, and the destroyer USS *Russell* recovered Captains Allen Griffis, John Proietti, William Steele, and Jeffrey Strommer after they had spent approximately two hours in the water.

Oman finally decided to allow B-1B operations from its soil, which was beneficial because Oman was considerably closer than Diego Garcia to Afghanistan. The transit time from Oman to Afghanistan was less than three hours, compared to approximately six hours from Diego Garcia. Shorter flights reduced wear and tear on people and aircraft, saved fuel, and reduced the requirements for air refueling support. Starting on 23 December 2001, maintenance and support elements began to be airlifted from Diego Garcia to Thumrait AB, Oman. On 24 December 2001, two bombers flew a combat mission from Diego Garcia to Afghanistan and landed at Thumrait AB. Two more B-1B aircraft did this on 25 December 2001, and another two the following day. When the last B-1B departed Diego Garcia for Thumrait AB, the remainder of the ground contingent followed.

Shortly after the 34th EBS relocated the B-1B aircraft, support equipment, and spare parts to Thumrait, it was replaced by the 9th EBS, commanded by Lieutenant Colonel Eldon A. Woodie. The 9th EBS was in theater from 6 January 2002 to 16 May 2002. The 405th AEW was the overall USAF unit at Thumrait AB, commanded by Colonel Wendell L. Griffin. Colonel Griffin was promoted to the rank of brigadier general on 1 March 2002 and was the first general officer to fly the B-1B in combat. The 405th EOG controlled the flying operations of the 405th AEW. Commanded by Colonel Michael R. Moeller, the 405th EOG had KC-135, RC-135, and E-3 Sentry AWACS squadrons as well as the 9th EBS.

Three B-1B Lancers are on the flight line at Thumrait AB. When this photograph was taken on 3 January 2002, the 34th EBS had just relocated from Diego Garcia. It would hand off responsibility for B-1B operations to the 9th EBS in a few days. (*Staff Sergeant Shane Cuomo/US Air Force*)

As always, it was the vital work of the aircraft maintainers and support personnel that enabled the aircrews to execute their assigned missions. Deployed B-1B crew chiefs like Staff Sergeant Wesley T. 'Skip' Clark worked 12-hour shifts, six days a week, and more if needed. Oman was scorching hot, with temperatures reaching 50°Celsius. Nights were cooler, making that the desired time for heavy outdoors work.

Right: A 405th AEW weapons loader changes out the right TDS magazine on the aft fuselage. AGE like this maintenance stand needed to be pre-positioned in theater or else the deploying unit had to bring it with them. Logistics planning was one the myriad of support tasks that enabled the B-1B to fly combat missions. (*Staff Sergeant Shane Cuomo/ US Air Force*)

Below: B-1B 85-0085 has all engines running in preparation for launching from Thumrait AB on a combat mission. (*Technical Sergeant Cedric H. Rudisill/US Air Force*)

B-1B 85-0087 takes off from Thumrait AB. This 9th EBS jet has neither a tail code nor a squadron tail stripe. (*Staff Sergeant Matthew Hannen/US Air Force*)

This photograph of 405th AEW maintainers gives a good look at the OWF and its inflatable baffles that smooth the airflow and lower drag when the VG wing is at different sweep angles. (*Staff Sergeant Matthew Hannen/US Air Force*)

While CMUP Block D revolutionized the B-1B and was the foundation of its success during OEF, there was no denying that its then twenty-year-old computer technology greatly limited its capabilities in the fluid and dynamic environment of XCAS. Amongst the limitations of the OAS with CMUP Block D were:

- Frequently there was a need to deliver a pattern of JDAMs to cover an area or linear target that had not been planned before the flight. The only way to create a pattern 'on the fly' using CMUP Block D was to manually enter the coordinates for each impact point, a slow and error-prone procedure.
- The mountains of Afghanistan introduced additional complexity into the calculation of JDAM LAR. Not only did the LAR need to get to the JDAM target, it had to do it with a trajectory that did not fly through intervening high terrain.
- Until the OAS had the capability to set the JPF in flight, the B-1B was loaded before flight with weapons that had different fuze settings. Based on the situation, the OSO had to manually identify the weapons bay and MPRL station that held a JDAM with the appropriate fuze setting, then rotate the MPRL to place the selected JDAM was in the bottom position so that it was ready to drop when the aircraft entered the LAR.

Eventually, CMUP Block E would increase computational power to overcome those limitations, but OEF aircrews needed something immediately. Major James 'Grumpy' Weigle, a B-1B pilot and computer expert attending professional military education at the Air Command and Staff College, satisfied this immediate need. Named after its developer, the 'Grumpy Jet' laptop computer was the outstanding B-1B innovation during the early years of OEF. 'Grumpy Jet' was a laptop computer connected to a commercial GPS receiver whose antenna cable was spliced into the antenna cable installed as part of CMUP Block D. The laptop was loaded with navigation charts, satellite imagery, and custom applications to meet the aforementioned needs. The laptop was also tied into Beyond Line of Sight (BLOS) communications. Building on CMUP Block D with its GPS and JDAM capabilities, 'Grumpy Jet' and BLOS gave the B-1B and its aircrews the capabilities that they needed, when they needed them.

The primary 'Grumpy Jet' computer was attached between the DSO and OSO. The pilots had another computer that acted as a repeater display. (*Senior Airman Hannah Landeros/US Air Force*)

Three crew members pose for an inflight photograph during a mission while enjoying cups of espresso. Notice the laptop computer between the DSO (left) and OSO (right). Presumably the fourth crew member is flying the airplane! (*Lieutenant Colonel Chris Wachter*)

The 9th EBS faced a fairly quiet situation at first, but that ended when Operation Anaconda began on 2 March 2002. American intelligence determined that a large concentration of al-Qaeda forces was located in the Shah-i-Kot region. Operation Anaconda was the first action in Afghanistan in which conventional American ground forces played a large role. Unfortunately, the operation was poorly planned. The hallmark of Afghanistan operations in 2001 had been the close coordination of airpower, special operations forces and the indigenous irregulars. In contrast, the conventional US Army infantry and aviation units involved in Operation Anaconda were not integrated in a coordinated scheme of fire, maneuver, and communications with airpower and special operations forces, and there was no unity of command.

American ground forces that pushed into Shah-i-Kot found themselves under intense fire from skillful, highly motivated, and heavily armed al-Qaeda fighters. Intelligence had been correct that Shah-i-Kot contained a concentration of the enemy but had underestimated their numbers and capabilities. Air support was needed immediately. Without adequate planning, it had to be assembled 'on the fly'. By now, large numbers of land-based fighter and attack aircraft had moved into the theater, but the B-1B was still a mainstay.

Four B-1B aircrews who worked the Shah-i-Kot valley on 2 March 2002 carried out a range of missions. At mid-morning, one B-1B released JDAMs on troops and ridgeline targets for one forward air controller and then switched to another forward air controller to drop more JDAMs. In the early afternoon, another B-1B, over a two-hour period, delivered nineteen

JDAMs on ten different targets for multiple forward air controllers. A few hours later, a third B-1B delivered JDAMs on targets including a ZSU-23-4 self-propelled anti-aircraft artillery piece of Soviet design. Another B-1B dropped a total of fifteen JDAMs on six targets during six separate bomb runs.

For the next two weeks, the intensity of operations continued. Despite the lack of proper planning and coordination, the people at the 'sharp end' stepped up to improvise, adapt, and accomplish the mission, killing hundreds of al-Qaeda fighters.

OEF was a milestone in the history of the B-1B. Perhaps no weapon system was the object of more controversy during its development or had navigated a more circuitous path to prominence as its concept of operations was forced to adapt to changing circumstances. After OEF, there was no doubt that the B-1B was a cornerstone of American airpower and a highly capable combat aircraft in roles that its designers had never considered. By the spring of 2002, Afghanistan settled into a low-intensity counterinsurgency and nation-building situation.

The combat diary of Captain Daemon 'PBAR' Hobbs, a WSO with the 9th EBS, gives an insight into the variety of B-1B operations at this time. His 4 March 2002 flight was action-packed, with frequently changing targets and the prodigious expenditure of weapons. Hobbs wrote: '2 helos shot down before got there, several KIA & WIA and 1 POW. That put a damper on the day. I hope I killed some of the bastards responsible. Finally after ten years of military service – combat! The training pays off!' In another entry, he recounted an incident in which a low-altitude show of force using afterburners, sonic booms, and flares dispersed an angry crowd that was threatening a patrol from the Special Boat Squadron, a British special operations unit. It wasn't all action. Other flights had short and simple descriptions: 'Pretty routine', 'Boring nothing happened', 'Nothing exciting', and 'Very dull'. Such was the reality of providing air support to a counterinsurgency campaign.

The 9th EBS returned to Dyess AFB in May 2002. The exit of the B-1B from the region was only temporary, and this combat-proven weapon would soon return.

Operation Iraqi Freedom

President Bush and some of the most influential people in his administration, including Vice President Dick Cheney and Secretary of Defense Rumsfeld, perceived the war that began on 11 September 2001 had a broader scope than defeating Osama bin Laden and his al-Qaeda organization. They saw a dangerous nexus of terrorist groups, weapons of mass destruction, and rogue regimes in the Islamic world that needed to be defeated. Only after this nexus was vanquished could the threat of future terrorist attacks be diminished. At the top of the list of threats was Saddam Hussein and his regime in Iraq. Under this regime, Iraq had a record of regional aggression, sponsorship of terrorism (although not of al-Qaeda), and possession and use of weapons of mass destruction. Operation Desert Storm and the smaller operations in its aftermath such as Operation Desert Fox had contained Iraq. To Bush, the next step in his strategy was to remove the regime in Iraq, occupy the country, and reform it in a way that was analogous to what was done in Germany and Japan after the Second World War.

The attack on Iraq was named Operation Iraqi Freedom (OIF), its name implying that the objective of the war was to liberate Iraq from its oppressive ruler, not destroy it. In January 2003, the 34th EBS under the command of Lieutenant Colonel Richard M. 'Harpo' Clark deployed to Thumrait AB. It generally had twelve airplanes at Thumrait AB at any one time, all in the CMUP Block D configuration. The 34th EBS fell under the 405th EOG, commanded by Colonel Joe Brown, which in turn was part of the 405th AEW, which controlled all USAF units at Thumrait AB. Colonel James M. Kowalski commanded the 405th AEW.

Colonel Peter Kippie, vice commander of the 405th AEW, explained the characteristics of the B-1B that made it valuable for OIF: 'The B-1B was so flexible because of its long range and ability to carry more munitions than any other aircraft. We had a very dynamic capability to strike across the area of operations. There was no target within Iraq that was not at risk when we took off.'

JDAM supplies had been scarce during OEF. Since then, JDAM production had been put on a war footing. The 34th EBS would have plentiful supplies of the weapon for OIF.

Air operations against Iraq had never ceased after Operation Desert Storm. Punctuated by large raids, of which Operation Desert Fox was the most prominent, the now-routine patrols and occasional attacks seamlessly ramped up even before OIF officially began. Some of the flights focused on verifying routes into Iraq and the operation of DAS. DAS had never undergone a major upgrade, but a series of minor improvements made it highly capable against the aging but still dangerous Iraqi air defenses.

Other missions prior to the start of OIF were more lethal. One notable attack was on 14 March 2003. Two B-1B aircraft with the call signs TBIRD 61 and TBIRD 62 struck a communications and radar tower in western Iraq, a reinforced concrete structure. Five GBU-31(V)1/B munitions with a combination of airburst and delayed fuzes shredded the antennas on the tower and toppled it, rendering Iraqi forces in the region blinded and isolated after the 7.6-hour mission.

OIF formally began on 20 March 2003. For the next month, the 34th EBS was involved in high-intensity combat operations, flying multiple missions per day. A typical mission involved departing Thumrait AB, first attacking planned targets, then loitering over Iraq until needed

A B-1B from the 34th EBS takes off from Thumrait AB to fly a mission in support of operations in the Middle East on 16 March 2003. (*Staff Sergeant Cherie A. Thurlby/US Air Force*)

for XCAS missions in direct support of ground forces. That the jets departed with twenty-four JDAMs and often returned with empty launchers attests to the intensity of the combat.

The mission with B-1B 86-0121 and call sign WALLA 64 on 22 March 2003 illustrates the capabilities of the B-1B during OEF. The crew of WALLA 64 was Captain Lee Johnson (pilot), Colonel Joe Brown (co-pilot), Captain George Stone (DSO) and Captain Stephen G. Burgh (OSO). Only 15 minutes before take-off, the crew got a new tasking to attack six ground-based GPS jammers. The American military had become highly dependent on GPS, but like all radio signals it could be jammed. There was a two-and-a-half hour flight from Thumrait AB to Baghdad, the capital of Iraq and the location of the GPS jammers. During the outbound leg, the pilots refueled from a KC-10A while the WSOs targeted the JDAMs. The Baghdad Super MEZ (Missile Engagement Zone) surrounded the city and was defined by the lethal envelope of the surface-to-air missile systems that defended it. The B-1B needed to penetrate the Super MEZ to attack the GPS jammers, so it linked up with two F-16CJ Fighting Falcons and two EA-6B Prowlers to jam and suppress enemy air defenses. The B-1B flew at 27,000ft altitude, and there was a cloud deck beneath it. This was ideal weather for the attack since it meant that the Iraqis could not acquire and track the B-1B with visual means, only with radar, which could be detected, jammed and suppressed. Because the JDAMs used GPS and inertial navigation, their employment and accuracy was unaffected by the clouds.

Flying from target to target in Baghdad, the B-1B defeated four surface-to-air missiles with DAS, chaff, and TDS while evading heavy anti-aircraft fire. The jet delivered twenty-three JDAMs, completely destroying four jammers and damaging another one. The Iraqi GPS jamming capability was eliminated. One might think that GPS jammers would offer protection against the GPS-guided JDAM, but this turned out not to be the case. The GPS antenna in JDAM guidance tail assembly pointed up to the satellites, away from the ground-based jammers. Furthermore, the JDAM had a back-up mode that used inertial navigation only, further reducing its vulnerability to GPS jamming with some degradation in accuracy.

The B-1B was designed to penetrate heavily defended airspace and attack targets. WALLA 64 demonstrated that capability on its 22 March 2003 mission. The crew was decorated with the Distinguished Flying Cross for outstanding heroism while participating in aerial flight.

A 34th EBS jet lands at Thumrait AB. (*Staff Sergeant Matthew Hannen/US Air Force*)

Close Air Support at an-Najaf

An outstanding characteristic of the B-1B was the flexibility of the aircraft and its crews, who could quickly shift from one mission to another in response to tasking. On 25 March 2003, B-1B 86-0095 was engaged in a 'SCUD hunt' for Iraqi mobile missile launchers, when the crew of 'Lurch', 'Goon', 'Spot', and 'Von' got a message that an American ground force needed urgent close air support. Call signs were re-used and this aircraft also was using the WALLA 64 call sign.[Author's note: For security and privacy reasons, some B-1B crew members prefer to be referred to only by their personal call signs.]

Sweeping the wings back, the B-1B crew pushed the throttles up and sped towards the battle on the ground. 3rd Squadron, 7th Cavalry was the lead element of the 3rd Infantry Division as it advanced towards Baghdad.

Earlier in the day, Bravo ('Bone') Troop, 3rd Squadron, 7th Cavalry had reached the Abu Sukhayr bridge over the Euphrates River south-east of the city of an-Najaf. Designated Objective FLOYD, the bridge was important both for the 3rd Infantry Division's movement and to contain a potential Iraqi counterattack. Alpha ('Apache') Troop, 3rd Squadron, 7th Cavalry crossed the bridge to continue the advance. Charlie ('Crazy Horse') Troop, 3rd Squadron, 7th Cavalry remained in the vicinity of the bridge to secure it. Attempting to get some rest after previous actions, 'Crazy Horse' Troop found itself under attack by vehicles driven with suicidal determination by Fedayeen Saddam, irregulars fiercely committed to the regime. Fending off the paramilitaries, 'Crazy Horse' Troop was alerted that Iraqi troops with T-72 tanks and other armored vehicles were headed in its direction.

Under normal circumstances, 'Crazy Horse' Troop would have handily dispatched the Iraqis. Its M1A1 Abrams tanks and M3A2 Bradley cavalry fighting vehicles were superior to their enemy's equipment, and the cavalry troopers were far better trained. But these were not normal circumstances. A blinding sandstorm with driving winds and rain greatly reduced the range of the thermal sensors on the American vehicles. If the Iraqis infiltrated the 'Crazy Horse' perimeter under cover of the weather, the American soldiers would be desperately fighting for their lives and without the assistance of the other troops of 3rd Squadron, 7th Cavalry, which had continued north.

Fortunately for 'Crazy Horse' Troop, various elements of airpower were available. Staff Sergeant Michael S. Shropshire of the 20th Air Support Operations Squadron (ASOS), a USAF Joint Terminal Attack Controller (JTAC) with the call sign ADVANCE 57, was assigned to it. He had portable SATCOM to request close air support. The Iraqis shot up the antenna of the SATCOM unit, but Shropshire was able to patch it. There was also an E-8C JSTARS aircraft in the area which could use its powerful ground surveillance radar to detect and track the Iraqi vehicles.

The sandstorm prevented fighters and attack aircraft from coming to the assistance of 'Crazy Horse' Troop because they needed to put eyes on the target, either visually or with sensors. But the sandstorm was no problem for a B-1B with its weapons bays filled with JDAMs. JSTARS reported that forty tanks were coming out of an-Najaf toward the bridge and 'Crazy Horse' Troop. Using the data from JSTARS, Technical Sergeant Mike Keehan of the 20th ASOS, located at the 3rd Squadron, 7th Cavalry headquarters, plotted the location of the Iraqis and radioed to another B-1B, which made four passes to drop JDAMs. The Iraqi force was hit hard, but the survivors moved on to a populated area closer to

'Crazy Horse' Troop, knowing that the Americans would not call in an airstrike if civilians were in the vicinity.

At this time, scouts from 'Crazy Horse' Troop crossed the Abu Sukhayr bridge and located Iraqi T-72 tanks approximately 600 meters away. Scouts from both sides began shooting at each other. With the assistance of JSTARS, Shropshire plotted the location of the Iraqis and radioed the coordinates to WALLA 64. While the pilots 'Lurch' and 'Goon' maneuvered the B-1B for the attack, WSOs 'Spot' and 'Von' entered the target coordinates into OAS to download to the JDAMs. In multiple passes, WALLA 64 placed four JDAMs on the target coordinates that Shropshire radioed up, with JSTARS providing the location of the Iraqis.

All of a sudden, it was quiet. The next morning, 'Crazy Horse' Troop searched the bombing locations and found a scene of devastation, with smashed T-72 tanks and other vehicles and, in Shropshire's words, 'tons of bodies'. Thanks to the support of WALLA 64 and its JDAMs, the E-8C JSTARS, space technology (GPS and SATCOM), and Staff Sergeant Shropshire, 'Crazy Horse' Troop had held the Abu Sukhayr bridge without suffering any casualties. In his after-action report, Shropshire noted: 'The B-1 had effectively broken up their advance and essentially saved our position from being over-run by a numerically superior force. After we were finished, I passed the Aircraft off to another controller who employed the B-1's weapons on more armor.'

The first USAF member to be killed in action in OIF was a member of the BONE community, but he did not die in the air. Major Gregory L. 'Linus' Stone was a former B-1B WSO serving in the 124th ASOS, Idaho Air National Guard. His assignment was to coordinate air support for the 101st Airborne Division (Air Assault) as an Air Liaison Officer. A traitor murdered Stone and Army Captain Christopher S. Seifert on 25 March 2003.

A B-1B flies over a thick cloud layer on 25 March 2003. The tail number is not visible, but it is likely that this aircraft is B-1B 86-0095 using the WALLA 64 call sign. (*Staff Sergeant Cherie A. Thurlby/US Air Force*)

Going after Saddam

B-1B 86-0138 was orbiting over central Iraq. Using the call sign SWEDE 72, the crew on this 7 April 2003 sortie consisted of Captain Chris 'Wacky' Wachter (pilot), Captain Sloan 'Grimace' Hollis (co-pilot), 1st Lieutenant Joe 'Nads' Runci (OSO) and Lieutenant Colonel George F. 'Duck' Swan (DSO). Swan was mission commander on the aircraft and the deputy commander of the 405th Expeditionary Operations Group on the ground. Before entering its orbit, SWEDE 72 had taken off from Thumrait AB with a full load of GBU-31(V)1/B and GBU-31(V)3/B weapons and refueled over Saudi Arabia before entering the airspace over Iraq. The mission of SWEDE 72 was to perform a 'SCUD hunt', to find and destroy Iraqi missiles and also to bomb anti-aircraft guns and taxiways at al-Asad AB.

While orbiting, SWEDE 72 received new orders from an E-3 Sentry AWACS at 1350 local time: go direct to Baghdad and stand by for target coordinates for a TST. An intelligence asset had located Saddam Hussein and his two sons at a restaurant in Baghdad. Lieutenant General T. Michael Moseley, the commander of the American air component in the region, came on the radio and told the crew of SWEDE 72: 'This is the big one. Don't miss it.' Sweeping its wings fully back for high speed, SWEDE 72 began the 12-minute flight to Baghdad as the E-3 Sentry AWACS passed the target coordinates to it. The targets were inside the Baghdad Super MEZ. Normal procedure was for F-16CJ fighters to escort the B-1B, but there was no time to arrange the defense suppression support. SWEDE 72 would penetrate the Baghdad Super MEZ alone.

The crew did the weaponeering on the fly. Each target coordinate would get hit first by a GBU-31(V)3/B and then by a GBU-31(V)1/B, for a total of four weapons. Swan selected weapons with 25 millisecond delays programmed into their fuzes. The relatively long delays allowed the weapons to penetrate the ground before detonating; this would minimize collateral damage which was a consideration in an urban area. The appropriate weapons were blocked on the MPRL by others, so the crew jettisoned two JDAMs at 1356 Local time. The jet flew as high and fast as possible to maximize the range of the weapons. Approaching the targets, SWEDE 72 awaited approval to actually deliver the weapons. With two minutes to go, SWEDE 72 was cleared hot. Approval had reached all the way to President Bush for this TST. SWEDE 72 directly contacted the intelligence asset on the ground and instructed him to seek cover immediately. [Author's note: The B-1B with CMUP Block D in use at this time did not have the capability for the crew to program JPF fuze settings, which would have obviated the need to jettison two JDAMs.]

Upon reaching the LAR, SWEDE 72 released the four JDAMs, then made a hard left turn to the west and escaped the Baghdad Super MEZ at supersonic speed. The four weapons accurately hit their targets at 1400:40 local time. Somehow Saddam Hussein and his sons escaped at the last moment to survive the attacks.

Indicative of the range, payload, and versatility of the BONE, the TST attack in Baghdad was only the beginning of SWEDE 72's sortie. Heading west to al-Asad AB, SWEDE 72 pounded surface-to-air missile and anti-aircraft gun sites with six GBU-31(V)1/B weapons. The next target was in the city of Tikrit to the north-east of al-Asad. SWEDE 72 delivered nine GBU-31(V)1/B bombs on a surface-to-air missile site. Then SWEDE 72 returned to Thumrait AB, logging 10.6 hours for the sortie. The USAF decorated the SWEDE 72 crew

(L to R) Captain Chris 'Wacky' Wachter (pilot), Captain Sloan 'Grimace' Hollis (co-pilot), Lieutenant Colonel George F. 'Duck' Swan (OSO), and First Lieutenant Joe 'Nads' Runci (DSO) were the crew of SWEDE 72 that almost killed Iraqi dictator Saddam Hussein on 7 April 2003. (*US Air Force*)

members with the Distinguished Flying Cross. The citation stated: 'Swede 72's exemplary actions marked the beginning of the rapid collapse of the Iraqi regime and the fall of Baghdad to Coalition forces.'

Major combat operations in Iraq ended in April 2003. The 34th EBS returned home from Thumrait AB in May 2003. Unfortunately, the quiescent state of Iraq after the defeat of the regime did not last. Saddam Hussein remained on the loose and in hiding, an inspiration to die-hard regime loyalists. Various religious factions within Iraq vied for power and to settle scores. Islamic jihadists yearned to fight the Americans and their allies, and outside powers such as Iran and Syria facilitated them. Iraq descended into a combination of civil war and insurgency.

Meanwhile, the situation in Afghanistan was also worsening. The Taliban had been defeated but never decisively crushed; it renewed its insurgency with assistance from elements in the Pakistani government. Operation Anaconda had hurt al-Qaeda, but its leadership survived. The year 2003 brought not the decisive victory the United States sought but just the beginning of a long fight.

For the BONE, the performance of the 34th EBS in OIF further enhanced the reputation that the 9th EBS and it had built in OEF. Lieutenant General Moseley described the B-1B as his 'roving linebacker', using American football terminology to describe the fast and powerful player who quickly responds to the opposing team. It was an apt analogy.

For several months, there were no BONEs in the region. Starting in August 2003, the 37th EBS deployed to Diego Garcia, where it became part of the 40th AEG, and began a regular rotation of B-1B squadrons to that island:

37th EBS	August 2003–December 2003
34th EBS	December 2003–February 2004
9th EBS	March 2004–June 2004
37th EBS	June 2004–December 2004
34th EBS	September 2004–November 2004
9th EBS	December 2004–May 2005

B-1B 86-0113 of the 37th EBS has just arrived at Diego Garcia on 7 September 2003 from Ellsworth AFB. Aircraft were rotated out of the forward deployed units to undergo inspections and maintenance for which the forward bases were not equipped or staffed and replaced by other jets. Staff Sergeant Shane Swanson was the crew chief for this BONE, with Staff Sergeant Ryan Richards as his deputy. A KC-135R Stratotanker takes off in the background. (*Staff Sergeant Jocelyn Rich/US Air Force*)

A B-1B co-pilot's view of rolling out on final approach to Diego Garcia on 1 January 2004. (*Captain Chris Wachter*)

The deployed B-1B squadrons primarily flew missions to Afghanistan but could also go to Iraq. Starting in May 2005, B-52H squadrons (23rd EBS, 96th EBS, 20th EBS) operated from Diego Garcia, providing the 40th AEG with its bomber component:

23rd EBS	May 2005–September 2005
96th EBS	September 2005–January 2006
20th EBS	January 2006–May 2006

The B-1B returned to Diego Garcia when the 9th EBS arrived in May 2006. Starting in June 2006, the 9th EBS began to split its operations between Diego Garcia and al-Udeid AB, Qatar, departing Diego Garcia in August 2006.

The Dirty 'Deid

Finding bases for the B-1B and other airpower assets remained a challenge as operations in Afghanistan and Iraq continued. The Arab nations in the region had a complicated relationship with the United States. Allowing the United States to use bases stirred up resentment among Islamic radicals. But the ruling regimes generally regarded the United States as their ultimate source of protection, so they also wanted to maintain defense ties with the United States. This complex dance sent B-1B deployments from Thumrait AB to Diego Garcia to Thumrait AB to Diego Garcia. In January 2005, the 9th EBS sent a detachment of bombers and support to al-Udeid AB in Qatar. Of all the strange relationships in the region, that between the United States and Qatar was amongst the strangest. Qatar supported anti-American Islamists like the Muslim Brotherhood. It also worked with the United States to build a state-of-the-art facility at al-Udeid. The CAOC moved from Prince Sultan AB in Saudi Arabia to al-Udeid AB, and it also became home to the 379th Air Expeditionary Wing.

A B-1B prepares to connect with a KC-135R over the Indian Ocean on 7 July 2006. At this time, the 9th EBS was transitioning from Diego Garcia to al-Udeid AB. The advantage of al-Udeid AB was that it was closer to both Afghanistan and Iraq. The B-1B was flying a close-air-support mission in support of OEF. (*Senior Airman Brian Ferguson/US Air Force*)

Never missing the opportunity to use a sexual innuendo, American military personal called it 'The Dirty Deid' or simplified it to just 'The Deid'. Starting with the 9th EBS in June 2006, al-Udeid AB became the home for the B-1B squadrons that rotated into the region. As at Diego Garcia, there was a regular rotation: 9th EBS, then 37th EBS, then 34th EBS, then the 9th EBS again.

The CAOC moved from Prince Sultan AB, Saudi Arabia to al-Udeid AB, Qatar. Well equipped with communications and computers, the CAOC is the command and control center for American and coalition air forces in the region. (*Technical Sergeant Joshua Strang/US Air Force*)

B-1B 85-0084 flies over the rough and desolate terrain of Afghanistan on 27 May 2008. (*Master Sergeant Andy Dunaway/ US Air Force*)

An F/A-18F Super Hornet flies alongside B-1B 85-0080 after a close-air-support mission supporting coalition forces in Afghanistan. (*Lieutenant Marques Jackson/US Navy*)

During most of the al-Udeid era, the B-1B focused on close air support as part of counterinsurgency operations. Rarely would a jet return to al-Udeid with empty weapon bays. In this situation, the GBU-38(V)1/B now arming the B-1B was often the weapon of choice. Much smaller than the GBU-31(V)1/B, it could be employed closer to friendly forces and innocent civilians. CMUP Block E was a useful modification to the B-1B which was completed in September 2006. It enabled the carriage of the GBU-38(V)1/B. With CMUP Block E, the B-1B could carry a mixed load with the GBU-38(V)1/B on the SECBM in one weapons bay and the GBU-31(V)1/B on the MPRL in another weapons bay; this gave the WSOs the capability to program patterns of weapons without needing to target each individual JDAM, and enabled the WSO to set the JPF mode and delay timing using the OAS.

In 2006, the 37th EBS flew a mission over Afghanistan that illustrated the kind of operations in which the B-1B was involved and how its systems contributed to that mission. Loitering over Afghanistan, the 37th EBS crew was informed that a British ground unit needed their support. The B-1B flew to the British and contacted the JTAC assigned to it. The British unit had been traversing a desert area and had abandoned a broken-down vehicle. Not wishing the Taliban to capture it, allowing them to both use it and secure the minor propaganda victory of displaying a captured British vehicle, the JTAC wanted the B-1B to destroy it. The B-1B crew found the abandoned vehicle with the ORS, mensurated its coordinates, and destroyed it with a well-placed GBU-38(V)1/B.

B-1B 85-0077 patrols the skies of Afghanistan on 10 December 2008. It wears the tail stripe and squadron badge of the 34th BS and is deployed with the 34th EBS. In this book, this aircraft can be seen in the markings of several squadrons. (*Staff Sergeant Aaron Allmon/US Air Force*)

A KC-10A refuels B-1B 85-0077. The H-configuration of the aerodynamic surfaces on the KC-10A refueling boom is in contrast to the V-configuration on the KC-135. (*Staff Sergeant Aaron Allmon/US Air Force*)

GBU-31(V)1/B JDAMs await loading on B-1B 86-0118 at al-Udeid AB. The olive bomb bodies and yellow nose bands mark these bombs as being filled with high explosives. With no radar proximity fuze on the nose, these bombs are fuzed for either instantaneous or delayed detonation upon contact. (*US Air Force*)

Three 34th EBS jets are lined up at al-Udeid AB in this 12 June 2010 photograph. B-1B 85-0087 in the foreground has just become the first B-1B to reach the milestone of 10,000 flight hours. Behind it, B-1B 86-0139 has the tail markings of the 28th BW commander. B-1B 86-0115 is in the background. (*Technical Sergeant Michelle Larche/ US Air Force*)

B-1B 86-0095 of the 34th EBS lands at al-Udeid AB in this 13 January 2012 photograph. The B-1B was originally intended to stand alert, with the occasional training flight. Years of frequent and long combat flights put wear and fatigue on the aircraft for which they were not designed. (*Staff Sergeant Nathanael Callon/US Air Force*)

On 4 April 2008, a B-1B was destroyed in a mishap at al-Udeid AB. The failure of two hydraulic systems on B-1B 86-0116 after landing ultimately led to the aircraft's destruction. Shortly after touchdown, the hydraulic systems in the B-1B's landing gear failed due to a hydraulic leak, causing a loss of braking ability and nosewheel steering as the aircraft moved down a taxiway. Unable to stop, the B-1B struck a barrier, ruptured its fuel tanks, and started a fire, which subsequently destroyed the BONE and damaged two C-130J Hercules aircraft. The B-1B aircrew escaped the aircraft without harm.

The BONE Gets an Eye

It had become common for fighters and attack aircraft such as the F-15E and F-16C to carry electro-optical (EO)/infrared (IR) targeting sensors. Such sensors provided full-motion high-resolution and high-magnification video to the crew during the day or night. They also had a recorder for the video and a laser designator for laser-guided PGMs. The benefits of having an EO/IR targeting sensor had been widely understood in the B-1B community for some time. Lieutenant Colonel Stephen W. 'Seve' Wilson advocated fitting the B-1B with a sensor of this type when he led the B-1B Division of the Weapons School in 1998 but he was unable to persuade ACC leadership. Partly it was a question of funding and prioritization, and there was also a dogmatic insistence that 'targeting pods are for fighters (only)' as if that was a law of physics (which it wasn't). The need for a B-1B EO/IR targeting sensor had been repeated in lessons learned reports from squadrons returning from OEF and OIF. In his after-action report on the 25 March 2003 close air support mission that saved 'Crazy Horse' Troop, 3rd Squadron, 7th Cavalry, now-Technical Sergeant Michael S. Shropshire wrote:

> The B-1 as a CAS platform is a flexible and effective platform. It was perfect for harsh weathers conditions such as my situation. The one drawback to this platform is its inability to see the enemy through a targeting pod. A B-1 with a Targeting Pod could only increase the capabilities of this platform. Especially with the situation as it is now. It would be completely insane not to give this aircraft the tools it needs to save the lives of guys like me and the soldiers who are dealing with dangers on a daily basis.

An aircraft can carry an EO/IR targeting sensor internally or in an external pod. An internal mounting on the B-1B would require an expensive and time-consuming structural modification. As early as 2004, two types of EO/IR targeting pods were fit-checked on the B-1B: the AN/AAQ-28 Litening and the AN/AAQ-33 Sniper. They were mounted on a custom pylon attached to a hardpoint on the left forward fuselage. The hardpoint had originally been for the ALCM and ACM and it had been disabled to comply with an arms control treaty, so it took some work to reactivate it. The 419th Flight Test Squadron conducted a ground vibration test of the AN/AAQ-33 Sniper pod in January 2006 to verify that the pod would not shake itself off the aircraft in flight.

In 2006, Lieutenant General Gary L. North became the American airpower commander in the Middle East and South-west Asia. He was a strong advocate of equipping the B-1B with an EO/IR targeting sensor. As the commander in the field during combat, North's July 2006 request to ACC was the impetus that previously had been missing. With North's executive

Above: The forward part of the Sniper targeting pod is the sensor head, which rotates in roll. The middle part of the pod contains the electronics. The aft module has the cooling system, required to handle the heat generated by the electronics. (*Author*)

Right: The rotating sensor head on the front of the Sniper targeting pod has windows which are used by the sensors and lasers. The pod is mounted on a pylon which connects to a fuselage hard point. (*Author*)

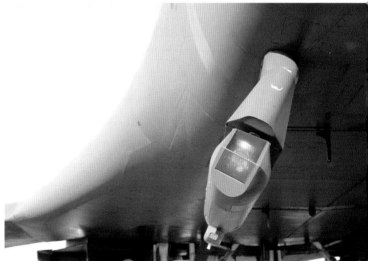

sponsorship, the program got moving. Major Marc N. 'Sporto' London was a B-1B WSO serving a tour on the Air Staff and arranged for funding.

The AN/AAQ-33 Sniper pod was chosen to equip the B-1B. The Sniper pod is loaded with equipment including high-definition EO and IR sensors, laser spot tracker, laser designator, two-way full-motion video datalink, digital data recorder, and precision geo-coordinate generation. With the Sniper pod, the B-1B has a vastly expanded range of capabilities. But the Sniper pod and its attachment to the hardpoint was only part of the solution. The WSOs must operate the pod and view its imagery. To fully integrate the Sniper pod into the OAS would be a major task, with hardware, software and wiring changes to numerous OAS components and probably a new control panel at the OSO crew station. Full integration was unaffordable and would take too much time. The same spirit of innovation that led to the 'Grumpy Jet' laptop computer again appeared for the Sniper pod. Building on the 'Grumpy Jet' solution, the WSOs used a laptop with specialized software for the Sniper pod and the pilots used another networked laptop computer.

Bringing the Sniper pod into service was a major coordinated effort. The aircraft needed to be modified with the pod and pylon. The 419th Flight Test Squadron conducted a test program with twelve flights that ran from June 2006 to January 2007, not only to test pod functionality but also to evaluate the structural integrity of the pod and pylon and their effects on B-1B performance and handling qualities. There was some concern that the wake coming off the pod and pylon would be ingested by the engine and cause problems, but this turned out not to be a problem. Drops of a GBU-31(V)1/B and a GBU-38(V)1/B also demonstrated that the wake coming off the pod and pylon did not affect the separation of weapons. The pod was relocated from the left forward fuselage to the right forward fuselage to improve maintenance access to the pod. A more comprehensive JDAM safe separation program during September–October 2007 involved eighteen drops and verified that no changes in the LAR were required when the pod and pylon were installed.

The Sniper pod is designed to be common to multiple aircraft but has a software module loaded that is specific to each type of aircraft. On 31 March–1 April 2008, the 419th Flight Test Squadron conducted a ground laser mask test to measure the limits of the pod field of view when mounted on the B-1B, so the laser beam would not impinge in the aircraft. These limits were programmed into the B-1B-specific software module. Further ground tests in April–May 2008 completed the integration of the Sniper pod with the aircraft systems and the laptop. The 419th Flight Test Squadron and the 337th TES conducted a combined DT&E/OT&E of the

B-1B 85-0075, the workhorse of the 419th Flight Test Squadron, carries a Sniper pod during the DT&E of the integration of that system on the BONE. (*Steve Zapka/US Air Force*)

Sniper pod on the B-1B during an eighteen-flight series of tests during April–May 2008. The pod worked well, although some deficiencies were noted which would be fixed in the future. The 337th TES moved on to train the 34th BS, the first operational squadron to be equipped with the Sniper pod.

Two years after Lieutenant General North articulated his urgent operational need for a B-1B EO/IR targeting sensor, it was used in combat. On 4 August 2008, a 34th EBS, 379th AEW B-1B used a Sniper pod to deliver a GBU-38(V)1/B on a target in Afghanistan. The Sniper pod dramatically increased the capability of the B-1B to delivery precision, discriminating close air support. B-1B aircrews could detect targets as small as individual persons, determine target coordinates themselves, transmit the video to personnel on the ground, and conduct immediate bomb damage assessment.

A 337th TES jet carries the Sniper targeting pod during operational testing at Edwards AFB. The development and testing of the pod on the B-1B happened in an admirably short time, a testament to the ability of wartime urgency to cut though the normally glacial pace of military acquisition. The 419th Flight Test Squadron and the 337th TES worked together closely on Sniper testing on the B-1B. The 337th TES aircraft became essential when the 419th Flight Test Squadron aircraft was grounded with a collapsed nose landing gear during the testing in 2008. (*Jet Fabara/US Air Force*)

The Sniper targeting pod transformed the B-1B from a bomb-dropper into a hunter/killer and an intelligence/surveillance/reconnaissance platform. (*Ken Middleton*)

The B-1B has undergone significant modernization since it was built, but the obvious external changes are few: a new paint scheme, the TDS, and the Sniper pod. (*Roelof-Jan Gort*)

The Sniper pod also added a new mission to the repertoire of the B-1B. The Sniper pod could transmit video to the ground and record the video, so the B-1B was now a full-fledged intelligence, surveillance and reconnaissance platform. A follow-on Sniper enhancement project added laser designation for the GBU-54(V)1/B Laser JDAM and the ability for the targeting pod to find stationary targets and automatically send the target coordinates to the OAS to be downloaded to the JDAMs. Automatically sending target coordinates from the pod removes the need for the WSO to enter the target coordinates manually, dramatically reducing both response time and the potential for error. The Sniper pod was as important to the evolution of the B-1B as was CMUP Blocks D and E. Modification of the B-1B fleet to carry the Sniper pod was completed in 2011.

Operation Odyssey Dawn

As the counterinsurgency ground on in Afghanistan and Iraq, changes were happening in other parts of the Islamic world. A rebellion against Muammar Gaddafi, the ruler of Libya, broke out in 2011 and escalated into a civil war with gross human rights abuses, and NATO intervened under the authority of a United Nations Security Council resolution. The American military activity in Libya was named Operation Odyssey Dawn.

On 24 October 2011, the 28th BW began to prepare for Operation Odyssey Dawn. It was a challenging situation. Not only had the 28th BW deployed much of its aircraft and personnel to al-Udeid, but the weather at Ellsworth AFB was miserable, with snow, ice, freezing fog, and cold temperatures. Under the command of Colonel Jeffrey Taliaferro, the 28th BW prepared the aircraft, built up and loaded munitions, and built mission plans. At dawn on 27 March 2011, four B-1B bombers launched on a mission to Libya, the first B-1B combat mission launched from the continental United States. After attacking their targets, the jets landed at a forward operating location. At the forward operating location, maintainers re-armed and refueled

Ellsworth AFB was hit by a major storm as it prepared bombers for Operation Odyssey Dawn. The GBU-31(V)1/B JDAM being loaded in this photograph was the weapon of choice for Operation Odyssey Dawn. (*Senior Airman Kasey Close/US Air Force*)

Ground crews de-ice a B-1B before take-off on the mission to Libya. (*Senior Airman Adam Grant/US Air Force*)

the aircraft while the crews rested. The B-1B bombers again attacked targets in Libya before returning to Ellsworth AFB. The attacks destroyed Libyan ammunition depots, missile and vehicle maintenance facilities, and command and control buildings with outstanding accuracy.

Tragedy in Afghanistan

On 26 February 2012, the BONE reached a milestone. The 9th EBS flew the 10,000th combat mission with the B-1B.

Close air support is a mission that is inherently dangerous. When friendly ground forces are in contact with the enemy, any number of mistakes can cause fratricide. Solid tactics, technology, and procedures, combined with excellent training and technology, had prevented the B-1B from being involved in friendly fire incidents until the terrible day of 9 June 2014.

B-1B 86-0111 of the 37th EBS launched from al–Udeid AB on 9 June 2014 to provide armed overwatch for three helicopter landing zones in the vicinity of Arghandab, Afghanistan which were being used to exfiltrate American special operations forces and Afghan National Army (ANA) soldiers. At 1915 local time, the B-1B aircrew checked in with the JTAC accompanying the special operations forces and established a right-hand orbit around the friendly forces. Because the Sniper pod was on the right side of the B-1B, a right-hand orbit enabled the aircrew to constantly point the sensors at the area of interest. Using the Sniper pod, the aircrew searched for enemy force which would threaten the exfiltration. At 1922 local time, the JTAC

A B-1B Lancer begins taxiing for takeoff at Al Udeid Air Base, Qatar, 8 Jul 2014. Day or night, the BONE was a guardian angel for troops on the ground in Afghanistan, Iraq and Syria, providing reconnaissance with the Sniper pod and precision close air support. (*Staff Sergeant Ciara Wymbs/US Air Force*)

passed the coordinates of the friendly forces to the OSO, who programmed them into the Sniper pod. The JTAC reported at 1949 local time that friendly forces were taking small arms fire. To maneuver on the enemy, five soldiers split from the main group and began to move up a hill. The leader of the five soldiers had an IR strobe light affixed to the back of his helmet so that friendly forces could identify them with night-vision sensors. Both the special operations forces and the B-1B were mistaken in believing that the Sniper pod could see the IR strobe light. In reality, the IR sensor in the Sniper pod was not sensitive to the wavelength of light emitted by the IR strobe light.

At 2001 local time, the JTAC transmitted a 9-line attack briefing to the B-1B aircrew which incorrectly reported the location of the five soldiers on the hill. The B-1B aircrew radioed the JTAC at 2007 to confirm the location of friendly forces. The JTAC responded: 'All friendlies are 300 meters west with IR strobes on taking effective fire; I need you guys in', which was incorrect. Communications and systems problems caused several bombing passes by the B-1B to be called off. At 2019, the issues were resolved and the B-1B called 'one minute' as it approached the target from the south. A minute later, the B-1B call of 'in, final' led to the JTAC responding with 'cleared hot, cleared hot, cleared hot'. The WSO was using the Sniper pod to observe the target. Expecting to see an IR strobe if friendly forces were there, the absence of the flashing IR strobe led him to believe that the friendly forces were not in the target area, although of course they were. Two JDAMs struck the target area, killing US Army Staff Sergeant Jason McDonald, Staff Sergeant Scott Studenmund, Specialist Justin Helton, Corporal Justin Clouse, Private Aaron Toppen, and ANA Sergeant Gulbuddin Ghulam Sakhi.

Killing ISIS

The Islamic State in Iraq and Syria (ISIS) was a jihadist organization in western Iraq and had a strong base of support among the disaffected Sunni minority in Iraq, as well as the Sunni majority in Syria. Unlike al-Qaeda, ISIS aimed to immediately establish a caliphate (state governed by Islamic law). The outbreak of the Syrian civil war gave ISIS the time and space to gain strength and flourish in Syria's ungoverned territories. ISIS had elements of both a state and a terrorist organization. It used exceptionally brutal tactics to conquer and control territory. By 2014, ISIS governed a large area in Iraq and Syria, including the major Iraqi cities of Mosul and Tikrit, and there was concern in the American government that the weak and ineffective Iraqi government might fall. In addition, ISIS was committing truly horrible crimes against humanity.

The American public was weary of the seemingly endless and inconclusive war against Islamic radicalism. President Barack H. Obama had been elected on a platform of disengaging the United States from the region. Reluctant as he was to increase American military operations, he also didn't want to see the emergence of an ISIS entity that could pose a direct threat to the United States. On 7 August 2014, President Obama authorized military operations to protect American personnel from ISIS and also to protect the Yazidis, a minority religious group in Iraq that was subject to genocidal violence and enslavement by ISIS.

On 8 August 2014, a B-1B from the 9th EBS preparing to depart on a mission over Afghanistan was redirected to northern Iraq to attack ISIS. The B-1B used its Sniper pod to locate an ISIS artillery position. Because the B-1B flew out of al-Udeid AB it could only employ weapons in strict accordance with the American agreement with the Qatari government over the use of that base, which did not yet include attacking ISIS. The B-1B crew passed the target information to two US Navy F/A-18 Hornets, which destroyed the target.

ISIS had captured the Mosul Dam in Iraq on 7 August 2014, thus threatening millions of people in the Tigris River valley downstream from the dam. On 14 August 2014, President Obama authorized limited airstrikes to assist Iraqi forces in recapturing the Mosul Dam. Starting on 16 August 2014, B-1B bombers as well as F/A-18 fighters and remotely piloted aircraft began an air offensive against ISIS forces near the Mosul Dam. The attacks continued for the two following days. Weakened by the airstrikes and isolated from reinforcement, ISIS was unable to prevent the Iraqi army from retaking the facility.

As well as in Iraq, airstrikes also started against ISIS in Syria. Operations in Syria were highly problematic. The Syrian regime still nominally controlled the state, although the actual scope of its rule only covered parts of the country. Iran and Russia supported the Syrian regime, and there was always the chance that the Russian aircraft based in Syria might intercept American aircraft. The American and Russian commands developed a communications channel to deconflict their operations and avoid a clash that neither wanted. The war against ISIS could be criticized as timid and lacking intensity, but President Obama's desire to avoid deeper entanglement in Iraq and Syria was understandable.

On 14 October 2014, the United States launched Operation Inherent Resolve (OIR) with allies to fight ISIS. The objective of OIR was this: 'In conjunction with partner forces Combined Joint Task Force - Operation Inherent Resolve (CJTF-OIR) defeats ISIS in designated areas of Iraq and Syria and sets conditions for follow-on operations to increase regional stability.'

From a strategic perspective, OIR had both similarities and differences to previous operations. Like OEF, the 'boots on the ground' would be mostly indigenous forces, with support from special operations forces and airpower. In the case of OIR, the indigenous forces included Iraqi army, Iraqi Shiite militias which were anti-American but also opposed to ISIS, and mostly importantly, Kurdish nationalists who hated and feared ISIS. Unlike the early days of OIF, OIR would not involve conventional American ground forces. But similarly to the initial phase of OIF, the enemy was a state (unrecognized but *de facto*) with territory, an army, and an economy, not merely an insurgency.

From October 2014 through January 2015, the focus of the war with ISIS was the town of Kobani in Syria. ISIS sought to capture the town, which was defended by a small force of Kurdish fighters. Not only was it important to protect Kobani from the depredations of ISIS, but the large concentration of ISIS fighters there offered a lucrative target. Given the intensity of the fighting around Kobani, and its remote location, the long range and heavy weapons load of the B-1B made it the combat aircraft of choice in this battle, and 9th EBS delivered 1,700 JDAMs in the Kobani area. The defense of Kobani was a great success and a serious blow to ISIS, displaying the power of the B-1B.

In March 2015, the offensive to reclaim territory in Iraq moved to the Iraqi city of Tikrit. By then, the 37th EBS had relieved the 9th EBS. The 37th EBS attacked ISIS military forces, vehicles, lines of communications, and facilities and resources. B-1B bombers also attacked oil production, processing, distribution, and storage facilities controlled by ISIS, greatly reducing its primary source of revenue. Concurrently with OIR, the fighting in Afghanistan continued, with the B-1B continuing to fly missions over it.

Above: A view of Kobani from a BONE during the war against ISIS. Notice that a bomb has just exploded. (*Lieutenant Colonel Chris Wachter*)

Right: This B-1B is taking on fuel prior to making an airstrike in Syria against ISIS. The area of the forward fuselage around the UARSSI shows evidence that not every air refueling hookup is perfect. (*Staff Sergeant Ciara Wymbs/US Air Force*)

Pilots fly the BONE during a 2015 OIR mission. The passage between the pilots going aft leads to the DSO and OSO crew stations. (*Lieutenant Colonel Chris Wachter*)

A GBU-54(V)1/B Laser JDAM destroys a truck carrying weapons for ISIS in Ramadi, Iraq. The combination of the Sniper targeting pod and the GBU-54(V)1/B gave the B-1B a capability against moving targets. (*Lieutenant Colonel Chris Wachter*)

Airmen perform pre-flight checks on a B-1B 86-0134 of the 34th EBS, 25 February 2015, at al-Udeid Air Base, Qatar in preparation of support for Operations Inherent Resolve and Freedom's Sentinel. Operation Freedom's Sentinel replaced OEF on 1 January 2015. During this deployment, Staff Sergeant Cody Patterson was the crew chief for 86-0134, with Staff Sergeant Jordan Roy as his assistant. Senior Airman Jake Davis and Senior Airman Will Jansma also worked on this jet. (*Senior Airman Kia Atkins/US Air Force*)

Right: In full afterburner, a BONE roars over al-Udeid AB. (*Senior Airman James Richardson/US Air Force*)

Below: A B-1B flies over the desert of western Iraq or eastern Syrian on its way to attack ISIS. (*Staff Sergeant Sandra Welch/ US Air Force*)

High-volume assembly of weapons is a critical wartime function. GBU-31(V)1/B bombs are in the foreground and GBU-31(V)3/B bombs are in the background. Munitions troops from the 379th AEW built thousands of bombs. (*Technical Sergeant James Hodgman/US Air Force*)

In 2016, it was time for the B-1B squadrons to focus on modernization. B-52H squadrons replaced them in the rotation. The B-52H squadrons also were assigned to the 379th AEW and based at al-Udeid AB. The B-1B returned to al-Udeid AB in April 2018, when the 34th EBS, commanded by Lieutenant Colonel Timothy Griffith, arrived. By this time, ISIS had been reduced to isolated pockets of resistance.

B-1B 85-066 of the 37th EBS is marked as the wing flagship for the 28th BW. When this photograph was taken in January 2016, the 37th EBS was imminently leaving al-Udeid AB. The next four bomber squadrons to rotate to the 379th AEW were equipped with the B-52H. (*Technical Sergeant James Hodgman/US Air Force*)

The BONE is back! The 34th EBS returned to al-Udeid AB in April 2018 after slightly more than two years of the 379th AEW bomber role being filled by the B-52H. (*Master Sergeant Phil Speck/US Air Force*)

This 34th EBS aircraft is departing from al-Udeid AB on the first combat mission since the return of the B-1B to the region. (*Staff Sergeant Joshua Horton/US Air Force*)

One of two 34th EBS B-1B aircraft conducting a JASSM attack on Syria on 14 April 2018 refuels from a KC-10A. (*Staff Sergeant Colton Elliott/US Air Force*)

In the civil war that racked Syria, the regime employed its extensive arsenal of chemical weapons. Not wanting to let the Syrian regime get away with this barbaric act, the United States, France, and the United Kingdom attacked Syrian chemical weapons facilities on 14 April 2018. Two 34th EBS jets (86-0129 in the lead accompanied by 86-0111) based at al-Udeid AB participated in this attack. Particularly noteworthy is that they launched nineteen AGM-158A JASSMs, the first use of that weapon in combat.

The roster of bombers squadrons that deployed to al-Udeid AB as part of the 379th AEW to fight ISIS was:

9th EBS	July 2014–January 2015
34th EBS	January 2015–July 2015
37th EBS	August 2015–January 2016
20th EBS	April–September 2016 (B-52H)
96th EBS	October 2016–February 2017 (B-52H)
23rd EBS	March –September 2017 (B-52H)
69th EBS	September 2017– April 2018 (B-52H)
34th EBS	April 2018–September 2018
9th EBS	October 2018–March 2019

The BONE at War

The 9th EBS, commanded by Lieutenant Colonel Erick Lord, departed al-Udeid AB in March 2019 to return home to Dyess AFB. It was not replaced by another bomber squadron. With the exception of a few relatively short periods, there had been a B-1B squadron deployed at Thumrait AB, Diego Garcia, or al-Udeid AB continuously since January 2003. It was an amazing run, attesting to the importance of the B-1B. Designed for a different mission and a different enemy, the B-1B had now spent half of its operational life in combat.

A 9th EBS B-1B flies in formation with two F-15E Strike Eagles. (*Staff Sergeant Clayton Cupit/US Air Force*)

Working with regional partners is an important aspect of American national security. A Qatar Air Force Mirage 2000-5EDA flies off the left wing of a B-1B. (*Staff Sergeant Clayton Cupit/US Air Force*)

The regular rotation of B-1B squadrons to al-Udeid AB ended in March 2019. The absence from the region was short-lived. B-1B 85-0079 is departing Ellsworth AFB on 24 October 2019 to fly to Saudi Arabia in response to Iranian provocations. (*Airman 1st Class John C.B. Ennis/US Air Force*)

Two B-1B Lancers fly in formation with an F-22A Raptor and two US Navy EA-18G Growlers over the Persian Gulf. (*Master Sergeant Joshua L. DeMotts/US Air Force*)

Chapter 13

Maintaining and Modernizing the BONE

'We are focusing on innovative ways to maintain and supply our aging fleets.'
USAF Posture Statement, Fiscal Year 2020

Sustainment

The B-1B is a maintenance-intensive aircraft. Each of the three levels of the B-1B maintenance concept is essential to supporting the aircraft. The first two levels occur on the flight lines and the shops of the operational wings. Each of the operational B-1B wings has a maintenance group with four squadrons:

- The Aircraft Maintenance Squadron provides flight-line maintenance and generates sorties.
- The Component Maintenance Squadron operates the shops for second-level maintenance.
- The Equipment Maintenance Squadron maintains AGE, does fabrication, and conducts phase inspections.
- The Munitions Squadron maintains the weapon release systems and stores and builds munitions.

The maintenance units have the same number as their parent wing. For example, the 7th Maintenance Group within the 7th BW has the 7th Aircraft Maintenance Squadron, 7th Component Maintenance Squadron, 7th Equipment Maintenance Squadron, and 7th Munitions Squadron.

OC-ALC at Tinker AFB, Oklahoma accomplishes the third level of maintenance, which is called Programmed Depot Maintenance (PDM). During PDM, the operational wing delivers the aircraft to OC-ALC for an intensive period of inspection, repair, and modernization, followed by painting. As the BONE ages, PDM provides an opportunity to systematically check the status of the fleet and create a database used to anticipate future problems. Each B-1B undergoes PDM at five-year intervals.

PDM is tailored to the needs of each individual aircraft, but a typical PDM involves approximately 17,000 staff-hours of labor and six months. Upon reception at OC-ALC, the aircraft is made hangar-safe by removing fuel and pyrotechnics. It is thoroughly inspected, including removing components and opening up areas. The necessary serving and overhauls are made. This includes both standard items and repairs made as a result of inspection findings. The aircraft is then reassembled including painting, and all systems are functionally checked on the ground. The 10th Flight Test Squadron conducts a thorough checkout of the overhauled aircraft at the end of PDM, after which it returns to operational service.

B-1B 86-0109 arrives at OC-ALC, Tinker AFB. This aircraft had a serious inflight emergency during a 1 May 2018 training flight. It is at OC-ALC for repairs and PDM. OC-ALC is a massive complex with responsibility for multiple aircraft including the KC-135R in the background, which has had its paint stripped as part of its PDM. (*Greg L. Davis/US Air Force*)

James Goers, OC-ALC aircraft ordnance mechanic, works on a B-1B ejection system. The primarily civilian workforce at OC-ALC is responsible for the heavy inspections, maintenance, and modernization that keeps the B-1B in the air. (*Kelly White/US Air Force*)

When it was impractical to bring an aircraft to OC-ALC, OC-ALC deployed its employees to the field to support the jets. For example, in July 2008 B-1B 86-0134 had a left precooler leak that could not be resolved by the maintainers of the 379th AEW. OC-ALC specialists Craig Bauman and Joel Canaga traveled to al-Udeid AB to fix the issue. Bauman returned to al-Udeid in October 2010 with Scott Meirs to repair an ORS wiring harness problem on B-1B 85-0090.

Modernization

While OC-ALC overhauls aircraft, the B-1B SPO manages the modernization of the aircraft, often contracting with Boeing or other companies. CMUP was a B-1B SPO program, as was installing the Sniper targeting pod on the B-1B. Not all B-1B modernization programs are as large and prominent as CMUP and Sniper. Replacing swivels on the brakes with flexible hoses reduced maintenance time. The new flexible hoses also reduced leaks, diminishing a source of brake fires and improving safety. Even a small change like this required considerable program management. The new flexibles hoses needed to be specified, procured, tested, and installed. Engineering drawings and TOs required changes.

Inertial navigation system upgrade was another program managed by the B-1B SPO. The original SKN-2440 inertial navigation system in the OAS was accurate and reliable by the standards of the time. But like any device based on moving parts (in this case spinning mass gyroscopes), the SKN-2440 required maintenance. The B-1B SPO contracted with Boeing to replace the SKN-2440 with an inertial navigation system that uses ring laser gyroscopes. The new inertial navigation was more reliable, more accurate, and essentially maintenance-free.

The ORS Reliability and Maintainability Improvement Program (RMIP) replaced two high-failure rate line-replaceable units in the ORS. The RMIP kit comprised a new radar transmitter/receiver, a radar processor computer and a re-implemented software package. The focus of the software portion of RMIP was to re-code the legacy ORS software into a modern and more maintainable programming language.

The 419th Flight Test Squadron at Edwards AFB executes the DT&E of the B-1B modernization programs. It plans, conducts, analyzes, and reports the tests. While the scope of B-1B flight testing has greatly decreased since the heyday of the B-1B CTF, the same disciplined and systematic flight test approach remains in effect. Before a new B-1B capability is released to the operational force, the 419th Flight Test Squadron makes sure that it meets requirements, works as desired, and is safe.

Integrated Battle Station

The most extensive B-1B modernization was the Integrated Battle Station (IBS). CMUP had revolutionized the operational capabilities of the B-1B, but the aircrew still was looking at what had become antiquated CRT monochromatic displays. The 'Grumpy Jet' laptops provided a work-around for these limitations, but the B-1B really needed fully modernized crew stations. The dependence on voice communications and the subsequent manual entry of data into the OAS was slow and error-prone, resulting in the three-pass close air support technique used in

The legacy B-1B crew stations with their legacy CRT-based displays are inadequate to handle the torrent of information that comes across the FIDL and is needed to rapidly target and deliver PGMs. (*Author*)

Afghanistan. With a data link on the B-1B, a JTAC could transmit target coordinates in digital form to the B-1B. The WSO could accept the transmitted target coordinates for entry into the OAS and then download to the PGM in seconds, also verifying the target by slewing the Sniper pod sensors to those same coordinates. To the ground unit in contact with the enemy and with an urgent need for close air support, the data link meant close air support on the first pass of the B-1B, not the third pass.

Also known as Sustainment Block 16 (SB-16), IBS consisted of Fully Integrated Data Link (FIDL) and upgraded CITS at the WSO crew stations and the Vertical Situation Display Upgrade (VSDU) for the pilots. FIDL is a Link 16 data link combined with new full-color displays with intuitive symbols and moving maps. The CITS upgrade added a new color display and replaced the ACU with a modern computer. The VSDU replaced two unsupportable monochrome pilot and co-pilot displays with four multifunctional color displays, giving the pilots greater situational awareness. For example, the LAR computed by the OAS is now depicted on the pilots' multifunction color displays as a yellow region with its size and shape corresponding to the actual LAR dimensions. To deliver a weapon, the pilots simply steer the B-1B so it enters the yellow region. The operational implication of IBS is an order-of-

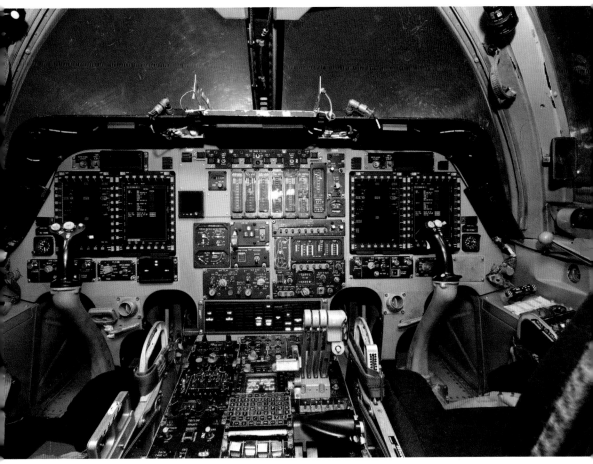

The IBS for the pilots has the VSDU with two color flat-panel displays for each pilot. On each side of the instrument panel, one display is used as the primary flight display and the other as a navigation display. Important information such as the weapons LAR is graphically depicted on the displays. (*Author*)

magnitude decrease in the time measured from when B–1B receives the target information to when weapons are released.

[Authors note: Link 16 is a military tactical data link network. With Link 16, military air, land, and sea forces exchange their tactical picture in near-real time. Link 16 also supports the exchange of text messages, imagery data and digital voice communications.]

FIDL was first tested in 2010. Flight testing of the full IBS by the 419th Flight Test Squadron began in 2013. The 337th TES received a B–1B modified with IBS later in that year to conduct DT&E. In 2015, the 9th BS was the first operational squadron to be equipped with IBS-modified jets, and it took them to Red Flag at Nellis AFB in January 2016. The 9th EBS conducted the first overseas deployment with IBS in February 2017 to Andersen AFB, Guam, followed by the 37th EBS in August 2017. The 34th EBS deployment to al-Udeid AB in April 2018 was the first combat deployment of IBS. OC-ALC completed the fleet modernization in September 2020, using kits provided by Boeing.

The OAS and DAS controls and displays were state-of-the art when the B-1B was developed. Thirty years later, they were antiquated, with inadequate functionality and unmaintainable because of parts obsolescence. IBS features a nearly complete renovation of the DSO and OSO crew stations, with the Radar Display Unit in front of the OSO being the only legacy display remaining. (*Chad Bellay/US Air Force*)

IBS gives the DSO a new set of color flat-panel displays. The color display on the right side of this photograph is for CITS. Note the laptop computer on a shelf under the CITS display. In theory, the Sniper targeting pod could be integrated with IBS, but until IBS/ Sniper integration is implemented, the laptop is still needed for the Sniper pod. (*Roelof-Jan Gort*)

When the B-1B was designed, the SAC concept of operations for the B-1B was to execute the SIOP mission with no outside inputs after the execution order was received. With FIDL, the B-1B is a node on a vast tactical information network. (*Roelof-Jan Gort*)

Members of the 10th Flight Test Squadron pose for a group picture in front of two BONEs after the completion of the IBS modification program. B-1B 86-0122 was the first production IBS modification and 86-0133 was the last BONE to get IBS at OC-ALC. (*Paul Shirk/US Air Force*)

External Captive Carry Demonstration

In addition to the DT&E of upgrades, the 419th Flight Test Squadron demonstrates proof-of-concept for new ideas that might become future upgrades to the B-1B if operational requirements emerge and funding is available. On 20 November 2020, B-1B 85-0075, the BONE currently assigned to the 419th Flight Test Squadron as its test aircraft carried an inert JASSM on an external pylon for the first time. The hardpoint for the pylon was originally used for ALCM and most recently for the Sniper targeting pod. The idea that led to the test was not so much the desire to increase the load of JASSMs, but rather to use the JASSM as a surrogate for hypersonic strike missiles which might arm the B-1B in the future and are too large to fit on the MPRL in a weapons bay.

Above: B-1B 85-0075 is the B-1B testbed used by the 419th Flight Test Squadron. In this photograph it has an inert JASSM shaped loaded on a pylon attached to an external hardpoint originally intended for ALCM. (*Second Lieutenant Christine Saunders/US Air Force*)

Opposite above: The 419th Flight Test Squadron B-1B Lancer flies with an external JASSM in the skies above Edwards Air Force Base, California on 20 November 2020. The flight was a demonstration of the B-1B's external weapons carriage capabilities (*Ethan Wagner/US Air Force*)

Opposite below: With modern weapon systems heavily dependent on software, the updates and testing of those updates never ends until the system is retired. In July 2016, the B-1B returned to the BAF at Edwards AFB to test recent improvements to DAS. (*Christopher Okula/US Air Force*)

The newest tanker in the USAF is the KC-46A Pegasus. The 419th Flight Test Squadron tested the B-1B with the KC-46A. *(Don Allen/US Air Force)*

Objectives of KC-46A/B-1B testing included handling qualities of the B-1B behind the KC-46A, fuel transfer evaluation, and the effectiveness of the KC-46A remote viewing system with the B-1B. *(Don Allen/US Air Force)*

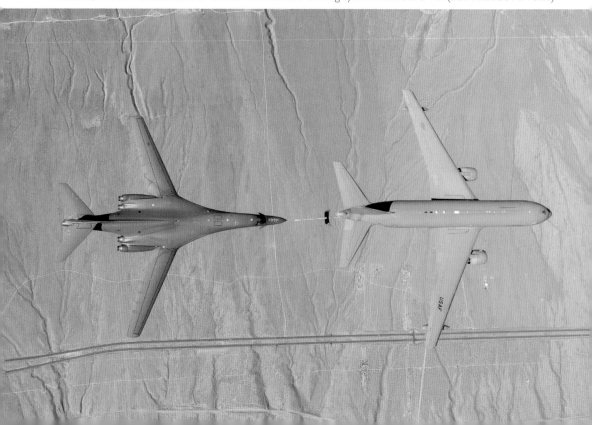

Chapter 14

The B-1B and Air Force Global Strike Command

'Airmen providing long-range precision strike . . . anytime, anywhere!'
Air Force Global Strike Command mission statement

Transferring to Air Force Global Strike Command

After the Cold War, the nuclear mission lost its priority within the USAF. The lengthy involvement in the Global War on Terror and the folding of SAC's bombers and ICBMs into the fighter-oriented ACC accentuated the trend. Yet even in the post-Cold War environment, the USAF retained thousands of nuclear weapons deliverable by the B-52H, B-2A, F-15E, F-16C, and Minuteman III. The nuclear threat to the United States and allies was considerably reduced compared to that of the Cold War, but it was not eliminated. China and Russia were nuclear weapons states with authoritarian governments. Pakistan had nuclear weapons, a

On 1 October 2015, the 7ᵗʰ BW and 28ᵗʰ BW transferred from ACC to AFGSC. AFGSC now controlled all USAF bombers (from left to right): B-1B, B-2A, and B-52H. (*Sagar Pathak/US Air Force*)

small nuclear arsenal, and an unstable government. North Korea was nuclear-armed with a mercurial, isolated, and extraordinarily inhumane regime.

SAC had been intensely focused on the security of its nuclear weapons. That focus was dissipated in ACC, which led to several incidents. To restore focus on the nuclear mission and its attendant disciplines, the USAF activated the Air Force Global Strike Command (AFGSC) on 7 August 2009. On 1 December 2009, AFGSC assumed control of the Minuteman III ICBM force. The B-52H and B-2A were reassigned from ACC to AFGSC on 1 February 2010.

The 7th BW and 28th BW were conspicuously absent from AFGSC, because by the time that AFGSC was activated, the B-1B's nuclear role had long since vanished. As AFGSC assumed a role providing long-range strike assets not limited to those with nuclear weapons, the 7th BW and 28th BW transferred from ACC to AFGSC on 1 October 2015.

Aside from a new chain of command and new emblems on the vertical stabilizers of the jets, the move to AFGSC had few effects on the B-1B force. The B-1B mission set and deployments continued unchanged. The major changes from the ACC years, including participation in Red Flag, Weapons School, and close integration with other kinds of airpower were deeply embedded in the institutional fabric and culture of the B-1B community.

B-1B 85-0088 is parked on the ramp at Dyess AFB as several maintainers attend to it. The slats are extended, revealing the white finish on the fixed part of the wing under the slats. (*Author*)

Nine BONES are visible in this photograph taken in the Dyess AFB flight line, with B-1B 85-0080 in the foreground. (*Author*)

B-1B 86-0123 has carried "Let's Roll" markings since shortly after the 11 September 2001 attacks on the United States. The tail stripe is for the 9th BS 'Bats'. The 9th BS is the operational squadron of the 7th BW at Dyess AFB. Note that in this 2019 photograph, the AFGSC shield above 'DY' has replaced the ACC shield seen in earlier years. (*Author*).

As USAF personnel like to say, it's not 'airplane noise', it's the sound of freedom. (*Ken Middleton*)

The blue and white checkerboard is the tail stripe for the 28th BS 'Mohawks', the B-1B Formal Training Unit. B-1B 85-0090 has 'Hellcat' nose art and the 28th BS emblem just aft of the nose art. The 28th BS is an element of the 7th BW. (*Author*)

Emergency over Texas

A noteworthy event during the AFGSC era was the in-flight emergency experienced by B-1B 86-0109 and its aircrew of Major Christopher N. Duhon (instructor pilot), Captain Matthew Sutton (instructor WSO), 1st Lieutenant Joseph Welch (student pilot) and 1st Lieutenant Thomas C. Ahearn (student WSO). During a routine 28th BS training flight on 1 May 2018, the B-1B indicated fire warnings in three areas of the aircraft. With fire visually confirmed by the aircrew, they took appropriate measures to extinguish the flames. One fire indicator light remained, however, which prompted the aircraft commander to order a controlled manual ejection.

Sitting in the OSO position, 1st Lieutenant Ahearn attempted to eject. The ejection hatch over Ahearn jettisoned, but his ejection seat did not activate. Alerted by another crew member, Major Sutton halted the ejection sequence and decided to attempt a two-engine emergency landing. The alternative would have been to leave 1st Lieutenant Ahearn behind to face a certain death. Despite auditory warning systems, depressurization and wind noise, the aircrew safely landed at the Midland International Air and Space Port in Midland, Texas, making it the first-ever successful landing of a B-1B experiencing these malfunctions.

Duhon, Sutton, Welch and Ahearn were decorated with the Distinguished Flying Cross for their actions in this flight. After an investigation discovered issues with the ejection system (although not the ejection seat itself), the entire B-1B flight was grounded on 7 June 2018. The grounding was lifted for each aircraft after it was inspected and found to have no ejection system problems. A crew from the 10th Flight Test Squadron flew the B-1B to OC-ALC on 26 October 2018 after maintenance that got the aircraft into an airworthy condition. During the flight, the aircraft had only three running engines.

Technical Sergeant Darnell A. Strawder, an engine dock chief and aerospace propulsion craftsman assigned to the 7th Component Maintenance Squadron, 7th Bomb Wing, inspects an F101-GE-102 engine. (*Author*)

B-1B 85-0084 'Hard Rain' carries the tail stripe of the 34th BS 'Thunderbirds', one of two operational squadrons in the 28th BW at Ellsworth AFB. (*Author*)

B-1B 85-0084 'Hard Rain' of the 34th BS 'Thunderbirds', 28th BW is illuminated by a South Dakota sunset. (*Roelof-Jan Gort*)

B-1B 86-0129 of the 34th BS, 28th BW is parked on the ramp of Ellsworth AFB. The 'Raiders' painted on the hangar refers to the famous Doolittle Raiders who conducted the first American bombing attack on Japan after the Pearl Harbor raid. The 34th BS and 37th BS had aircrews who flew on that mission. (*Technical Sergeant Jette Carr/US Air Force*)

B-1B 86-0108 of the 37th BS 'Tigers', 28th BW undergoes maintenance. (*Airman Jonah Fronk/US Air Force*)

B-1B 85-0064 carries the markings of the 337th TES, 53rd Wing. (*Author*)

On 7 February 2021, an example of each of the AFGSC bombers did a formation flyover of Superbowl LV, the most watched sports event in the United States. The B-1B that participated in this event was 86-0121. This aircraft had been a record setter in 1992 at Grand Forks AFB and the first B-1B to fly over Baghdad. (*Airman 1st Class Jacob B. Wrightsman/US Air Force*)

B-1B 86-0109 had a serious inflight emergency and landed at the airport in Midland, Texas. (*Greg L. Davis/US Air Force*)

The BONE in the Air Force Reserve

USAF reservists joined the BONE operational community in 2015. The 489th Bombardment Group was reactivated on 17 October 2015 and redesignated as the 489th Bomb Group in accordance with current contemporary USAF parlance. The 345th Bomb Squadron, 489th Maintenance Squadron and several smaller units were subordinate to the 489th Bomb Group. These units had a distinguished combat record in the Second World War II. The 489th Bomb Group was based at Dyess AFB with the 7th BW. [Author's note: The 10th Flight Test Squadron at OC-ALC is a reserve unit, albeit a test unit and not an operational unit.]

Although some jets are marked as 489th Bomb Group aircraft, in reality all B-1B aircraft at Dyess AFB remain assigned to the 7th BW. The 489th Bomb Group is an Associate unit in the Air Force Reserve, which means that by associating with an active duty unit it shares its aircraft and augments the active duty unit with additional personnel. Often the personnel in the 489th Bomb Group are experienced B-1B aircrew and maintainers who have left active military duty to pursue a civilian career but continue their military affiliation in a reserve capacity.

B-1B 85-0089 is marked as the flagship of the 489th Bomb Group of the Air Force Reserve. In reality, the 489th Bomb Group has no aircraft assigned to it and is the Associate of the active-duty 7th BW. (*Author*)

The 489th BG flagship is taxiing at Nellis AFB, Nevada. (*Ken Middleton*)

Chapter 15

Global Presence

'Our presence from the Arctic to Africa strengthens relationships with our allies and partners while sending a message to any adversary that we are committed to collective defense and ready to respond in a complex security environment.'

General Jeffrey L. Harrigian, Commander,
United States Air Forces in Europe and Air Forces Africa, 2020

'Despite the many cultural differences across the region, our principled values, our collective interests, and our mutual security concerns will drive us forward.'

Admiral Philip S. Davidson, Commander,
United States Indo-Pacific Command, 2020

In 1821, Secretary of State John Quincy Adams eloquently expressed the case for America's policy of non-interventionism:

But she goes not abroad, in search of monsters to destroy. She is the well-wisher to the freedom and independence of all. She is the champion and vindicator only of her own.

In the aftermath of two devastating world wars and the domination by Josef Stalin's Soviet Union over a major portion of the Eurasian landmass, the American statesmen who constructed the post-Second World War security architecture for an American-led international order rejected Adams's advice. The 'monsters' were more monstrous than Adams could have imagined. The oceans which separated America from Europe and Asia no longer protected it from those that threatened its interests and values. America had watched predatory regimes in Germany, Italy, and Japan pick off weaker nations one by one, each victory further whetting the appetite for greater conquest. In the post-war world order, one of the foundations of American foreign policy would be collective security – a web of alliances. In numbers there was strength. An attack on an American ally would be treated as an attack on the United States itself and invite an appropriate response, thus deterring aggression.

During the Cold War, this strategy was implemented by several means. Large forward-deployed American forces on the territory of allies not only helped defend those countries but acted as tripwires which ensured that aggression would immediately result in the direct involvement of the United States. In places like Korea and Vietnam, the United States became directly involved in combat. The rationale was not that the fate of Korea and Vietnam were vital American interests, but rather that failure to defend those countries would lower the credibility of American commitments to collective security. Finally, the American strategic nuclear forces backed up the other elements with the threat of truly massive destruction.

With the end of the Cold War, there was no single threat on the scale of the Soviet Union around which to organize American national security. Although the United States maintained its alliances and even expanded them to include some countries freed from Soviet control, its forward-deployed forces greatly decreased in size. After the 11 September 2001 attacks, the focus of American military operations shifted to the Middle East and South-west Asia. Unfortunately, new threats then arose. In Europe, Russia under the dictator Vladimir Putin threatened and occasionally invaded its neighbors, some of whom were in alliance with the United States. In the Asia, Pacific and Indian Ocean region, China became wealthy, confident, and powerful and began bullying other countries. The psychopathic Kim regime in North Korea had always been dangerous, but it became far more so when it built nuclear weapons and missiles.

To maintain its alliances, the United States needs credible military capabilities in these regions, all of which are distant from the United States. Long-range bombers are an excellent way to demonstrate American power. The bombers can fly missions directly from their bases in the continental United States to any place on earth. They can also be temporarily deployed to forward bases. Called Continuous Bomber Presence (CBP) and later Bomber Task Forces (BTF), these deployments have several purposes. They deter potential adversaries and provide tangible evidence of American commitment to its allies and alliances. During the deployments, the bomber squadron personnel become familiar with the airfields, airspace, and geography that they would use in wartime. Joint exercises with allied military forces increase interoperability and integration, which are critical to effectiveness if the United States comes to the defense of an ally. The exercises also build useful personal relationships between service members of the different countries.

In Europe, RAF Fairford in the United Kingdom has been the most common bomber deployment location. Andersen AFB on the American territory of Guam in the Pacific Ocean has been the focus of bomber deployments in that region. Both bases have large establishments which support the rotating BTF squadrons. More recently, the BTF deployments have gone to a wider variety of bases in countries such as Australia, Portugal, and Norway, as part of doctrine called Dynamic Force Employment. Dynamic Force Employment increases flexibility, creates uncertainty in the mind of an adversary, and reduces dependence on a small number of installations. The CBP and BTF deployments of the B-1B have not had the visibility of the extended combat operations, but they have been equally important to protecting American interests and they also form part of the B-1 story.

A Polish F-16C escorts B-1B 86-0129. Poland has a long history of conflict with Russia. The presence of the BONE flying over Poland sends a strong message that Poland would not be alone if it was attacked. (*Polish Air Force*)

B-1B 85-0073 takes off from Bodø AB, Norway. When a B-1B deploys to a base such as this one, the USAF verifies that the facilities are suitable for use by the big bomber. This information is valuable in a crisis. (*Torbjørn Kjosvold*)

B-1B 86-0127 of the 9th EBS takes off from Andersen AFB, Guam. Since the end of the Cold War, Andersen AFB does not have permanently assigned bombers, but its resident 36th Wing hosts bomber squadrons that rotate in and out. (*Airman 1st Class Jacob Skovo/US Air Force*)

B-1B 86-0120 is marked with the tiger-striped tail stripe of the 37th BS. When aircraft are selected for a EBS deployment, they do not necessarily all come from the squadron around which the EBS is formed. This photograph was taken at Andersen AFB. (*Airman 1st Class Christopher Quail/US Air Force*)

Three of four B-1B jets of a BTF at Andersen AFB can be seen in this photograph. (*Senior Airman Tristan Day/US Air Force*)

The 36th Wing has a large stockpile of munitions at Andersen AFB. The yellow band around the nose of this AGM-158A JASSM signifies that it has a high explosive warhead installed in it. (*Senior Airman River Bruce/US Air Force*)

Three generations of American bombers share the ramp at Anderson AFB. The forward-deployed CBP in the Indo-Pacific region deters aggression. (*Technical Sergeant Richard Ebensberger/US Air Force*)

A B-1B of the 37th EBS flies over the East China Sea. The vast distances in the Indo-Pacific region put a premium on the long range of bombers, which is one of their most important attributes. (*Staff Sergeant Peter Reft*)

Two F/A-18 Hornets, two F-35 Lightning IIs, and four F-15C Eagles fly in formation with three BONEs over the Pacific Ocean. *(Staff Sergeant Peter Reft/US Air Force)*

Two Japanese Air Self Defense Force F-15J Eagles escort B-1B 86-0118 (foreground) and 85-0081. Japanese-American security cooperation is demonstrated not only by the joint exercise but by the fact that the F-15J is a license-built version of an American design. *(Japanese Air Self Defense Force)*

Two B-1B bombers flying in formation with four Japanese Air Self Defense Force F-2A fighters and four US Marine Corps F-35B Lightning II fighters are sending a message to the North Korean regime after it conducted a round of missile tests. (*Japanese Air Self Defense Force*)

South Korea is another important American regional partner. In this picture, a B-1B deployed to Anderson AFB is exercising with two South Korean F-15K fighters. (*Republic of Korean Air Force*)

Chapter 16

Twilight of the BONE

'Our bomber force allows the commander in chief to hold targets at risk anywhere on the globe with unparalleled range and our most diverse payloads.'

General David L. Goldfein, USAF Chief of Staff, 2018

In 2016, the USAF revealed the first information about the Long Range Strike Bomber program, to be called the B-21 Raider. The B-21 is being designed and manufactured by Northrop Grumman. It is a stealthy flying wing with a strong family resemblance to its predecessor, the B-2A Spirit. The AFGSC Bomber Vector of 2018 described the roadmap for the future USAF bomber force. In perhaps the most ironic decision in USAF history, the B-21 is planned to replace the B-1B (based on the B-1A, which was intended to replace the B-52) and the B-2A (which might have replaced the B-52 if more than twenty-one B-2As had been built). The one bomber it will not replace is the B-52H, which will be modernized with new engines. As bizarre as this plan might seem, there is a rationale for it. The B-21 should be able to penetrate defended airspace better than the B-1B and the B-2A. What it cannot

The B-1B is in the last phase of its service life. The B-21 Raider is planned to be its replacement. *(Airman 1st Class Colin Hollowell/US Air Force)*

The Northrop Grumman B-21 Raider will be a stealthy flying wing with a strong family resemblance to the B-2A Spirit. As of the date that this book was written, the B-21 had neither been rolled out nor flown. The US Air Force released this artist's concept of the airplane in July 2021. (*US Air Force*)

do is externally carry very large weapons such as hypersonic missiles, as the B-52H can do with stores suspended from wing pylons. The B-52H is well-suited to carry and launch such weapons. It will probably be the first combat aircraft to attain a century of service.

In 2020, the average age of a B-1B was thirty-three years. At that time, the majority of B-1B aircrew, maintainers and support personnel were younger than the aircraft. The number of years since an aircraft was built is intrinsically meaningless, but other factors do act to limit its life. Metal fatigue is the result of the number of operating cycles and the stresses incurred in those cycles. Decades of high-speed, low-altitude TF flight have created a tremendous amount of metal fatigue in the B-1B airframes. Paradoxically, so have long hours spent loitering over battlefields with the wings swept forward, the B-1B structure not being designed for that mission profile. To preserve airframe life, low-altitude flight training of operational crews in the B-1B ceased in 2019, although the TF systems remained functional, and the 337th TES continued to do some low-level flight to maintain the capability within the B-1B force. Operational crews underwent some academic and simulator training of low-altitude and TF flight through 2021. To further conserve airframe life, peacetime maneuvers are limited to 1.5 G when the wing sweep angle is 15° through 55° and 2.5 G when the wings are swept fully aft. These limits are 0.5 G less than the design limits of the airframe. The wear and tear of frequent deployments and combat missions has consumed airframe life. Engine components also wear out because of repeated thermal and mechanical cycles.

The support of aging aircraft also faces other challenges. Many of the systems and components on the B-1B are unique to that aircraft. Stocks of spare parts are diminishing. It is often impractical or extremely costly to build more spare parts. The specialized tooling and test equipment may no longer be available. Electronic parts used in 1980s avionics often are

B-52H 60-0050 of the 419th Flight Test Squadron takes off from Edwards AFB with an AGM-183A Air-launched Rapid Response Weapon hypersonic test vehicle and an inert AGM-183A shape carried on its left wing pylon. The capability of the B-52H to carry large external loads will keep it in service after the B-21 has replaced the B-1B and B-2A. (*Matt Williams/US Air Force*)

B-1B 85-0080 took its last flight from Dyess AFB to Barksdale AFB, where it will join the collection of the museum on that installation. (*Senior Airman Jacob B. Wrightsman/US Air Force*)

B-1B 86-0109 'Spectre' is towed to a parking area at Tinker AFB after its last flight. It will be a maintenance trainer, allowing technicians and engineers to practice aircraft battle damage repair. (*Paul Shirk/US Air Force*)

unavailable, which means that avionics cannot be repaired nor replacements manufactured. In 2020, the USAF decided to retire seventeen B-1B aircraft, reducing the fleet size to forty-five. Although decried by some BONE supporters, in some ways the retirements ensured that the remaining aircraft will be viable until they are replaced by the B-21 in the 2030s. The specific aircraft to be retired were not chosen at random. Each had sustained such severe fatigue damage that it was estimated that it would take tens of millions of dollars to repair it. The retired aircraft will be cannibalized for usable parts to maintain the operational fleet. It is unfortunate that the retired aircraft had all been expensively modified with IBS and then achieved only a few years further use.

While the end of BONE operations approaches, it will remain an important element of American military power until its retirement. The remaining fleet of forty-five aircraft will undergo a Service Life Extension Program to keep them airworthy and effective. It is unlikely that there will be any further major modernization programs on the scale of CMUP or IBS.

One day around 2035, the last flying B-1B will land, and for the final time the roar of four F101 engines will fade out. Born after decades of controversy and false starts, the B-1B had a troubled childhood. Modernized to meet the challenges of a world situation very different than the one for which it was intended, the people and organizations associated with the B-1B adapted it to become one of the pillars of American airpower, with a highly successful combat record. Sleek, powerful, and beloved by those who designed, built and tested it, and who now fly, maintain and support it, the BONE is a legend.

B-1B 85-0092 was retired to the 'boneyard' at Davis Monthan AFB, Arizona. It was partially disassembled and trucked to the National Institute for Aviation Research (NIAR) at Wichita State University. NIAR will scan every part of the aircraft to create a digital twin that can be used for research. (*US Air Force*)

The drawdown of the B-1B fleet did not mean that improvements and testing of the aircraft came to a halt. B-1B 86-135 entered the BAF at Edwards AFB in May 2021 to evaluate the latest DAS enhancements. Elsewhere on Edwards AFB, the 419th Flight Test Squadron took delivery of retired B-1B 86-0099 on 23 February 2021. Called the Edwards Aircraft Ground Integration Lab (EAGIL), the squadron will use it as a non-flying integration laboratory for future upgrades to the BONE. (*1st Lieutenant Christine Saunders/US Air Force*)

Although aged, the B-1B remains highly capable and will be an important element of American airpower for the remainder of its service life. (*Roelof-Jan Gort*)

In one of the great examples of serendipity, what began as the quest for a supersonic bomber to deliver nuclear weapons targets in the Soviet Union ended up becoming an outstanding close air support platform against primitive fanatics. (*Staff Sergeant Manuel J. Martinez/US Air Force*)

The complex B-1B required extensive maintenance throughout its operational service. The dedicated and skilled US Air Force aircraft maintainers were essential to its success as a weapon system. (*Roelof-Jan Gort*)

An airplane can't itself have a soul; it is just an assemblage of metal, fasteners, and electronics. The soul of the B-1B is the collective souls of the men and women who have been associated with it. (*Senior Airman Dwane R. Young/ US Air Force*)

Bibliography

Books

Abzug, Malcolm J. and E. Eugene Larrabee. *Aircraft Stability and Control: A History of the Technologies That Made Aviation Possible*. Cambridge University Press: Cambridge, 1997.

Adams, Chris. *Inside the Cold War: A Cold Warrior's Reflections*. Air University Press: Maxwell Air Force Base, Alabama, September 1999.

Brown, Harold and Joyce Winslow. *Star Spangled Security: Applying Lessons Learned over Six Decades Safeguarding America*. Brookings Institution Press: Washington, DC, 2012.

Call, Steve. *Danger Close: Tactical Air Controllers in Afghanistan and Iraq*. Texas A & M University Press: College Station, Texas, 2007.

Carpenter, David M. *NX-2: Convair Nuclear Propulsion Jet*. Jet Pioneers of America, 2003.

Carter, Jimmy. *White House Diary*. Farrar, Straus and Giroux: New York, 2010.

Converse, Elliott V, III. *History of Acquisition in the Department of Defense: Volume I Rearming for the Cold War 1945–1960*, Historical Office, Office of the Secretary of Defense: Washington, DC, 2012.

Davies, Peter E. *North American XB-70 Valkyrie* (X-Planes 7). Osprey Publishing Ltd.: Oxford, 2018.

Deale, Melvin G. *Always at War: Organizational Culture in the Strategic Air Command, 1946-62*. Naval Institute Press: Annapolis, Maryland, 2018.

Doyle, David. *B-58 Hustler in Action* (Aircraft in Action No. 239). Squadron Signal Publications: Carrollton, Texas, 2015.

Drendel, Lou. *Bone in Action* (Aircraft in Action No. 179). Squadron Signal Publications: Carrollton, Texas, 2015.

Fontenot, Gregory, E. J. Degan and David Tohn. *On Point: The United States Army in Operation IRAQI FREEDOM*. Combat Studies Institute Press: Fort Leavenworth, Kansas, 2004.

Freedman, Lawrence. *The Evolution of Nuclear Strategy*. New York: St. Martin's Press, 1983.

Hallion, Richard P. 'Sweep and Swing: Reshaping the Wing for the Jet and Rocket Age'. *NASA's Contributions to Aeronautics, Volume 1: Aerodynamics, Structures, Propulsion, Controls* (SP-2010-570-Vol 1). National Aeronautics and Space Administration: Washington, DC, 2010.

Hallion, Richard P. and Michael H. Gorn. *On the Frontier: Experimental Flight at NASA Dryden* (2nd edition). Smithsonian Books: Washington, DC, 2002.

Hanson, Chuck. *U.S. Nuclear Weapons: The Secret History*. Aerofax, Inc.: Arlington, Texas, 1988.

Holder, William G. *The B-1 Bomber* (Aero Series 35, 2nd edition). Tab Books, Inc.: Blue Ridge Summit, Pennsylvania, 1988.

Jenkins, Dennis R. and Tony R. Landis. *North American XB-70A Valkyrie* (Warbird Tech Series Volume 34). Specialty Press: North Branch, Minneapolis, 2002.

Jenkins, Dennis R. and Tony R. Landis. *Valkyrie: North American's Mach 3 Superbomber*. Specialty Press: North Branch, Minneapolis, 2004.

Katz, Kenneth P. *B-52G/H Stratofortress in Action* (Aircraft in Action No. 207). Squadron Signal Publications: Carrollton, Texas: 2012.

Kennedy, Rick. *100 Years of Reimagining Flight: GE Aviation*. Orange Frazier Press: Wilmington, Ohio, 2019.

Kinney, Jeremy R. *The Power for Flight: NASA's Contributions to Aircraft Propulsion* (SP-2017-631). National Aeronautics and Space Administration: Washington, DC, 2017.

Klotz, Nick. *Wild Blue Yonder: Money, Politics, and the B-1 Bomber*. Pantheon Books: New York, 1988.

Knaack, Marcelle Size. *Encyclopedia of U.S. Air Force Aircraft and Missile Systems Volume II: Post-World War II Bombers 1945-1973*. Office of Air Force History: Washington, DC, 1988.

Logan, Don. *ACC Bomber Triad: The B-52s, B-1s, and B-2s of Air Combat Command*. Schiffer Publishing Ltd.: Atglen, Pennsylvania, 1999.

Logan, Don. *General Dynamics F-111 Aardvark*. Schiffer Publishing Ltd.: Atglen, Pennsylvania, 1998.

Logan, Don. *Rockwell B-1: SAC's Last Bomber*. Schiffer Publishing Ltd.: Atglen, Pennsylvania, 1995.

Logan, Don and Jay Miller. *Rockwell International B-1A/B* (Aerofax Minigraph 24). Aerofax, Inc.: Arlington, Texas, 1986.

MacIsaac, Bernie and Roy Langston. *Gas Turbine Propulsion Systems*. American Institute of Aeronautics and Astronautics: Washington, DC and John Wiley & Sons Ltd.: Chichester, West Sussex, 2011.

Mallick, Donald L. and Peter W. Merlin. *The Smell of Kerosene: A Test Pilot's Odyssey* (NASA SP-4108). National Aeronautics and Space Administration: Washington, DC, 2003.

Meilinger, Phillip S. *Bomber: The Formation and Early Years of Strategic Air Command*. Air University Press: Maxwell Air Force Base, Alabama, November 2012.

Merlin, Peter W. Gregg A. Bendrick and Dwight A. Holland. *Breaking the Mishap Chain: Human Factors Lessons Learned from Aerospace Accidents and Incidents in Research, Flight Test, and Development* (SP-2011-594).National Aeronautics and Space Administration: Washington, DC, 2012.

Miller, Jay. *Convair B-58* (Aerograph 4). Aerofax, Incorporated: Arlington, Texas, 1985.

Miller, Jay. *The X-Planes: X-1 to X-31* (revised edition). Aerofax, Incorporated: Arlington, Texas, 1988.

Moody, Walton S. *Building a Strategic Air Force*. Air Force History and Museums Program: Washington, DC, 1995.

Neufeld, Jacob. *The Development of Ballistic Missiles in the United States Air Force 1945–1960*. Office of Air Force History: Washington, DC, 1990.

Nicklas, Brian D. *The Complete Smithsonian Field Guide: American Missiles 1962 to the Present Day*. Frontline Books: Barnsley, South Yorkshire, 2012.

Pace, Steve. *North American Valkyrie XB-70A* (Aero Series 30). Aero Publishers, Inc.: Fallbrook, California, 1984.

Peebles, Curtis and Richard P. Hallion. *Probing the Sky: Selected NACA Research Airplanes and Their Contributions to Flight* (SP-2011-596). National Aeronautics and Space Administration: Washington, DC, 2014.

Perry, William J. *My Journey at the Nuclear Brink*. Stanford University Press: Palo Alto, California, 2015

Polmar, Norman and Timothy Laur. *Strategic Air Command: People, Aircraft and Missiles* (2nd edition). The Nautical and Aviation Publishing Company of America: Baltimore, 1990.

Polmar, Norman and Robert S. Norris. *The U.S. Nuclear Arsenal: A History of Weapons and Delivery Systems since 1945*. Naval Institute Press: Annapolis, Maryland, 2009.

Power, Thomas S. with Albert A. Arnhym. *Design for Survival* (revised edition). Coward-McCann, Inc.: New York, 1965.

Raymond, E. T. with C. C. Chenoweth. *Aircraft Flight Control Actuation System Design*. Society of Automotive Engineers: Warrendale, Pennsylvania, 1993.

Ross, Jerry L. with John Norberg. *Spacewalker: My Journey in Space and Faith as a NASA's Record-Setting Frequent Flyer*. Purdue University Press: West Lafayette, Indiana, 2013.

Simone, William J. *North American F-107A* (Air Force Legends Number 206). Ginter Books: Simi Valley, California, 2002.

Simonsen, Erik. *Project Terminated: Famous Military Aircraft Cancellations of the Cold War and What Might Have Been*. Crécy Publishing Ltd.: Manchester, 2013.

Wallace, Lane E. 'The Whitcomb Area Rule: NACA Aerodynamics Research and Innovation'. *From Engineering Science to Big Science: The NACA and NASA Collier Trophy Research Project Winners* (Pamela E. Mack, ed., NASA SP-4219). National Aeronautics and Space Administration: Washington, DC, 1998.

Werrell, Kenneth P. *Death from the Heavens: A History of Strategic Bombing*. Naval Institute Press: Annapolis, Maryland, 2009.

Werrell, Kenneth P. *The Evolution of the Cruise Missile*. Air University Press: Maxwell Air Force Base, Alabama, September 1985.

White, Alvis S. *The Times of My Life: A Pilot's Story* (2nd Edition). Self-published, 2003.

Withington, Thomas. *B-1B Lancer Units in Combat* (Combat Aircraft 60). Osprey Publishing Limited: Oxford, United Kingdom, 2006.

Yenne, Bill. *Rockwell: The Heritage of North American*. Crescent Books: New York, 1989.

Yenne, Bill. *The Complete History of U.S. Cruise Missiles: From Kettering's Bug & 1950's Snark to Today's Tomahawk*. Specialty Press: North Branch, Minneapolis, 2018.

Periodicals

_____. 'AEDC Tests B-1/SRAM Separation'. *Aviation Week & Space Technology* 96:2, 10 January 1972.

_____. 'Aero Engines 1970'. *FLIGHT International*. 1 January 1970.

_____. 'AFL-CIO, UAW Pass Pro-B-1 Resolutions'. *Rockwell International News* 5:5, 14 March 1977.

_____. 'Air Force Halts B-1B Testing'. *Aviation Week & Space Technology* 118:26, 27 June 1983.

_____. 'Air Force Seeks to Avoid Break in B-1'. *Aviation Week & Space Technology* 101:2, 15 July 1974.

_____. 'Air Force Starting Flight Tests Of B-1B Defense Avionics System'. *Aviation Week & Space Technology* 133:16, 15 October 1990.

_____. 'Air Force Uses Computer Lessons to Train Instructors, Flight Crews'. *Aviation Week & Space Technology* 124:22, 2 June 1986.

_____. 'AMSA Airframe'. *Aviation Week & Space Technology* 83:1, 5 July 1965.

_____. 'AMSA Bid Evaluation'. *Aviation Week & Space Technology* 84:24, 13 June 1966.

_____. 'ASD to Keep Major SCAD Responsibility'. *Aviation Week & Space Technology* 96:26, 26 June 1972.

_____. 'Aspin Threatens to Block Funding for B-1B Bomber'. *Aviation Week & Space Technology* 129:7, 15 August 1988.

_____. 'Automatic Machining Center Aids B-1B Productivity Effort'. *Aviation Week & Space Technology* 117:5, 2 August 1982.

_____. 'B-1 Bomber Crux of SAC Plans'. *Aviation Week & Space Technology* 104:19, 10 May 1976.

_____. 'B-1B Display Tests Flight Performance'. *Aviation Week & Space Technology* 117:11, 13 September 1982.

_____. 'B-1 First Flight to Evaluate Systems'. *Aviation Week & Space Technology* 100:22, 3 June 1974.

_____. 'B-1 Halt Generates Wide Impact'. *Aviation Week & Space Technology* 107:2, 11 July 1977.

_____. 'B-1 Makes Final Test Flight'. Aviation Week & Space Technology 114:19, 11 May 1981.

_____. 'B-1 Mockup Is Revealed'. *Aviation Week & Space Technology* 95:19, 8 November 1971.

_____. 'B-1 Spurs Air Force Offensive Strategic Effort for Next Decade'. *Aviation Week & Space Technology* 96:26, 26 June 1972.

_____. 'B-1 Tests Yield "Penetrativity" Data'. *Aviation Week & Space Technology* 112:24, 1 June 1980.

_____. 'B-1: A Year of Progress, Innovation'. North American Rockwell News 31:12, 11 June 1971.

_____. 'B-1A Avionics Study Proposals to Aid Airframe Competitors'. *Aviation Week & Space Technology* 91:19, 10 November 1969.

_____. 'B-1A Was Testing Stability, Control at Time of Accident'. *Aviation Week & Space Technology* 121:11, 10 September 1984.

_____. 'B-1B Bomber Production'. *Aviation Week & Space Technology* 124:13, 31 March 1986.

_____. 'B-1B Bombers Delivered to Operational Squadron'. *Aviation Week & Space Technology* 125:17, 27 October 1986.

_____. 'B-1B Checkout, Test Facilities Near Completion'. *Aviation Week & Space Technology* 122:18, 6 May 1985.

_____. 'B-1B Cockpit to be Fitted with Nuclear Flash Shield'. *Aviation Week & Space Technology* 120:9, 27 February 1984.

_____. 'B-1 Components'. *Aviation Week & Space Technology* 115:15, 12 October 1981.

_____. 'B-1B Delivery'. *Aviation Week & Space Technology* 122:19, 13 May 1985.

_____. 'B-1B Displays New Potential in Nonnuclear Tactical Roles'. *Aviation Week & Space Technology* 137:4, 27 July 1992.

_____. 'B-1B Flight Test Program Begins at Edwards AFB'. *Aviation Week & Space Technology* 118:14, 4 April 1983.

____. 'B-1B Flight Tests Begin at Edwards'. *Aviation Week & Space Technology* 118:13, 28 March 1983.

____. 'B-1B Production Work Involves 5,000 Firms'. *Aviation Week & Space Technology* 119:5, 1 August 1983.

____. 'B-1B Program Office'. *Aviation Week & Space Technology* 115:16, 19 October 1981.

____. 'B-1B Radar Profile'. *Aviation Week & Space Technology* 122:16, 22 April 1985.

____. 'B-1B Rotary Weapons Launcher Tested'. *Aviation Week & Space Technology* 118:22, 30 May 1983.

____. 'B-1B Sustains Engine Damage on First Flight'. *Aviation Week & Space Technology* 121:18, 29 October 1984.

____. 'B-1B Test Pace Quickens; Second B-1A Joins Effort', *Aviation Week & Space Technology* 121:8, 20 August 1984.

____. 'B-1Bs Developing Leaks in Fuselage, Wing Tanks'. *Aviation Week & Space Technology* 125:13, 29 September 1986.

____. 'Boeing, AIL Div. Supply B-1B Avionics Systems'. *Aviation Week & Space Technology* 119:5, 1 August 1983.

____. 'Brown Explains B-1 Bomber Decision'. *Aviation Week & Space Technology* 107:2, 11 July 1977.

____. 'C-5A Engines Feature Basic Differences'. *Aviation Week & Space Technology* 82:18, 3 May 1965.

____. 'Central Integrated Test System Monitors B-1B Data Points'. *Aviation Week & Space Technology* 124:10, 10 March 1986.

____. 'Cleveland Pneumatic Completes B-1B Main Landing Gear'. *Aviation Week & Space Technology* 119:20, 14 November 1983.

____. 'Columbus Div. Intermediate Fuselage Subassembly Checked by Technicians'. *Aviation Week & Space Technology* 119:5, 1 August 1983.

____. 'Combined Test Force Pilots Intensify B-1B Flight Activity'. *Aviation Week & Space Technology* 124:22, 2 June 1986.

____. 'Continued B-1 Development Urged'. *Aviation Week & Space Technology* 104:19, 10 May 1976.

____. 'Cost Determined B-1B Avionics Choice'. *Aviation Week & Space Technology* 115:23, 7 December 1981.

____. 'Decoy Tested for B-1B'. *Aviation Week & Space Technology* 146:27, 30 June 1997.

____. 'Defensive Systems to Undergo Full Flight Test in 1988'. *Aviation Week & Space Technology* 127:11, 14 September 1987.

____. 'Delivery of B-1B Changes Maintenance Procedures'. *Aviation Week & Space Technology* 124:22, 2 June 1986.

____. 'Design Review of B-1 "Favorable"'. *Aviation Week & Space Technology* 95:19, 8 November 1971.

____. 'DOD Halts SCAD Development as Costs Rise, Need is Debated'. *Aviation Week & Space Technology* 99:3 16 July 1973.

____. 'Eaton to Propose $600 Million Modification to ALQ-161 System'. *Aviation Week & Space Technology* 130:26, 26 June 1989.

____. 'Experience, Computers Aid Transition'. *Aviation Week & Space Technology* 124:22, 2 June 1986.

____. 'F-16, B-1 Launch Missiles in Tests'. *Aviation Week & Space Technology* 107:21, 21 November 1977.

____. 'First Major Subcontract Awarded on B-1 Program'. *North American Rockwell News* 31:7, 2 April 1971.

____. 'First Production B-1B Joins Flight Test Program'. *Aviation Week & Space Technology* 121:20, 12 November 1984.

____. 'Fourth B-1 Crewmember is Well Qualified for Flight'. *Rockwell International News* 4:7, 9 April 1976.

____. 'GE Reveals Building-Block Gas Generator'. *Aviation Week & Space Technology* 82:24, 14 June 1965.

____. 'GE Tests New Technology Engine for B-1'. *Aviation Week & Space Technology* 96:26, 26 June 1972.

____. 'General Electric Delivers First Engine for B-1B'. *Aviation Week & Space Technology* 119:16, 17 October 1983.

____. 'General Electric Undertakes Powerplant Qualification Tests'. *Aviation Week & Space Technology* 119:5, 1 August 1983.

____. 'High-Altitude Temperature Anomaly Causes Thrust Cutback during B-1 Climb Record Attempts'. *Aviation Week & Space Technology* 137:4, 27 July 1992.

____. 'Improvements Planned for B-1's SRAMs'. *Aviation Week & Space Technology* 104:19, 10 May 1976.

____. 'Industry Observer'. *Aviation Week* 58:1, 5 January 1953.

____. 'Industry Observer'. *Aviation Week & Space Technology* 124:19, 12 May 1986.

____. 'Initial B-1B in Automated Test Facility'. *Aviation Week & Space Technology* 121:1, 2 July 1984.

____. 'Jimmy's Weapons Choice'. *Aviation Week & Space Technology* 107:2, 11 July 1977.

____. 'Options Study Preceded B-1 Decision'. *Aviation Week & Space Technology* 107:2, 11 July 1977.

____. 'Palmdale and the Bomber Connection'. *Air International*, August 1986.

____. 'Potential AMSA Design Illustrated'. *Aviation Week & Space Technology* 89:12, 16 September 1968.

____. 'Pratt & Whitney Testing Basic Version of CX-HLS Powerplant'. *Aviation Week & Space Technology* 81:3, 20 July 1964.

____. 'Production B-1B Makes First Flight'. *Aviation Week & Space Technology* 121:17, 22 October 1984.

____. 'Red Flag Exercises Highlight Versatility of B-1B Bomber'. *Aviation Week & Space Technology* 137:4, 27 July 1992.

____. 'Rockwell Advances B-1B Rollout to September'. *Aviation Week & Space Technology* 120:19, 7 May 1984.

____. 'Rockwell B-1B Design to Be Studied in New Cab'. *Aviation Week & Space Technology* 118:3, 17 January 1983.

____. 'Rockwell Completes First B-1B Fuselage'. *Aviation Week & Space Technology* 120:4, 23 January 1984.

____. 'Rockwell International Mating Sections of First Production B-1B Bomber'. *Aviation Week & Space Technology* 120:3, 16 January 1984.

____. 'Rockwell Working With AIL to Develop B-1B Avionics Fix'. *Aviation Week & Space Technology* 130:1, 2 January 1989.

____. 'SAC Urges F-111 Stretch as Alternative to B-1'. *Aviation Week & Space Technology* 112:24, 16 June 1980.

____. 'Short Circuit Downed B-1B'. *Aviation Week & Space Technology* 148:26, 29 July 1998.

____. 'Some B-1 Avionics May Be Salvaged'. *Aviation Week & Space Technology* 107:2, 11 July 1977.

____. 'Special Markings Facilitate In-Flight Refueling of B-1B'. *Aviation Week & Space Technology* 122:20, 20 May 1985.

____. 'SRAM Launched From B-1'. *Aviation Week & Space Technology* 107:6, 8 August 1977.

____. 'SRAM Starts Successful Production'. *Aviation Week & Space Technology* 96:26, 26 June 1972.

____. 'SRAM-2 Rocket Propulsion'. *Aviation Week & Space Technology* 123:10, 9 September 1985.

____. 'Stuck Wing Forces No. 2 B-1B to Land At High Speed'. *Aviation Week & Space Technology* 124:11, 17 March 1986.

____. 'Swanson Adjusts Well to Project Manager Role'. *Rockwell International News* 5:5, 14 March 1977.

____. 'Systems Simulator to Cut Flight Testing'. *Aviation Week & Space Technology* 119:9, 29 August 1983.

____. 'Tests of B-1B ECM Systems Uncover Basic Design Flaws'. *Aviation Week & Space Technology* 129:3, 18 July 1988.

____. 'The Democratic Platform'. *Aviation Week & Space Technology* 113:17, 27 October 1980.

____. 'The Election Platforms'. *Aviation Week & Space Technology* 113:8, 25 August 1980.

____. 'USAF Expected Fully Operational B-1B By 1988 within Spending Limits'. *Aviation Week & Space Technology* 126:4, 26 January 1987.

____. 'USAF, Rockwell Test Systems Needed to Expand B-1B's Flight Envelope'. *Aviation Week & Space Technology* 129:22, 28 November 1988.

____. 'USAF to Test B-1B Operational Readiness'. *Aviation Week & Space Technology* 140:21, 23 May 1994.

____. 'World News Roundup'. *Aviation Week & Space Technology* 154:5, 29 January 2001.

____. 'World News Roundup'. *Aviation Week & Space Technology* 157:7, 12 August 2002.

____. 'World News Roundup'. *Aviation Week & Space Technology* 159:1, 7 July 2003.

Bond, David F. 'Bush's Cuts Are Little Threat to U. S. Military Capabilities'. *Aviation Week & Space Technology* 135:14, 7 October 1991.

Brownlow, Cecil. '15-Year AMSA Operational Life Forecast'. *Aviation Week & Space Technology* 90:16, 21 April 1969.

Brownlow, Cecil. 'B-1 Production Plan Approved'. *Aviation Week & Space Technology* 105:23, 6 December 1976.

Bullban, Erwin J. 'Vought Installs Automated System for Fuselage Work'. *Aviation Week & Space Technology* 119:5, 1 August 1983.

Butler, Amy. 'Jassm-ER Cruising Again'. *Aviation Week & Space Technology* 169:15, 20 October 2008.

Bulter, Amy. 'Jassm Redemption'. *Aviation Week & Space Technology* 171:15, 19 October 2009.

Canan, James W. 'How Electronic Countermeasures Went Wrong'. *Air Force Magazine* 72:8, August 1989.

Charleton, Linda. 'The People behind the Campaign to Shoot down the B-1 Bomber'. *The New York Times*. 25 July 1977.

Coleman, Herbert J. 'Rockwell Applies B-1A Experience to B-1B Development'. *Aviation Week & Space Technology* 119:5, 1 August 1983.

Dornheim, Michael A. 'Raytheon Decoy to Protect B-1'. *Aviation Week & Space Technology* 149:17, 26 October 1998.

Elson, Benjamin M. 'Boeing Delivers B-1B Avionics Shipsets'. *Aviation Week & Space Technology* 120:4, 23 January 1984.

Evans, David. 'The B1: A Flying Edsel for America's Defense?', *The Washington Post, 4 January 1987.*

Everstine, Brian W. 'The Bone is Back'. *Air Force Magazine* 103:1, January/February 2020.

Fink, Donald E. 'B-1 Aims for 3-Hr. Second Flight'. *Aviation Week & Space Technology* 102:1 6 January 1975.

Fink, Donald E. 'B-1 Avionics Test Vehicle Flight Nears'. *Aviation Week & Space Technology* 104:6, 9 February 1976.

Fink, Donald E. 'Paris Air Show 1987'. *Aviation Week & Space Technology* 126:25, 22 June 1987.

Fink, Donald E. 'Rockwell Designers Define New Derivatives of B-1'. *Aviation Week & Space Technology* 107:15, 10 October 1977.

Fink, Donald E. 'Rockwell Gears for B-1 Production'. *Aviation Week & Space Technology* 105:23, 6 December 1976.

Fink, Donald E. 'Rockwell Seeks Funding To Complete Two B-1s'. *Aviation Week & Space Technology* 107:13, 26 September 1977.

Fulghum, David A. 'B-1 Strike on Saddam'. *Aviation Week & Space Technology* 158:15, 14 April 2003.

Fulghum, David A. 'Finally, B-1s to Carry Advanced Weapons'. *Aviation Week & Space Technology* 145:2, 8 July 1996.

Fulghum, David A. and Robert Wall. 'Heavy Bomber Attacks Dominate Afghan War'. *Aviation Week & Space Technology* 155:23, 3 December 2001.

Fulton, Ken. 'GE Power for the B-1'. *FLIGHT International.* 26 December 1974.

Grant, Rebecca, 'Bomber Diplomacy'. *Air Force Magazine* 94:12, December 2011.

Greeley, Brendan M., Jr. 'Crash of Third Operational B-1B Could Raise Mission, Funding Issues'. *Aviation Week & Space Technology* 129:22, 28 November 1988.

Greeley, Brendan M., Jr. 'Inquiry Finds Crash Was Inevitable after Bird Strike Caused Fire in B-1B'. *Aviation Week & Space Technology* 128:4, 25 January 1988.

Grier, Peter. 'The Jet Age in Review'. *Air Force Magazine* 80:2 (February 1997).

Hieronymus, William S. 'B-1 Designed to New Standards'. *Aviation Week & Space Technology* 95:4, 26 July 1971.

Hoeber, Francis P. and Alton H. Quanbeck. 'Debating the B-1 Bomber'. *International Security* 1:4, 1977.

Hotz, Robert. 'Jimmy's Weapons Choice'. *Aviation Week & Space Technology* 107:2, 11 July 1977.

Hunter, Jamie. 'B-1 under Fire'. *Combat Aircraft* 21:5, May 2020.

Hunter, Jamie. 'Projecting Power in the Pacific'. *Combat Aircraft* 18:8, August 2017.

Johnsen, Katherine. 'Support for B-1 Decision Seen Mixed in Congress'. *Aviation Week & Space Technology* 107:2, 11 July 1977.

Keaveney, Michael. 'Lancers in the Depot'. *Combat Aircraft* 19:5, May 2018.

Klass, Philip J. 'Air Force Examines Deficiencies in B-1B Electronic Warfare System'. *Aviation Week & Space Technology* 125:25, 22 December 1986.

Klass, Philip J. 'ALQ-161 Flight Tests Set This Summer'. *Aviation Week & Space Technology* 120:13, 26 March 1984.

Klass, Philip J. 'B-1 Pioneers Airborne Phased Array'. *Aviation Week & Space Technology* 120:15, 9 April 1984.

Klass, Philip J. 'B-1B's EW Upgrade Open to Six Bidders'. *Aviation Week & Space Technology* 139:1, 5 July 1993.

Klass, Philip J. 'IBM Advances Systems Integrator Role'. *Aviation Week & Space Technology* 119:5, 1 August 1983.

Klass, Philip J. 'USAF to Upgrade B-1B Avionics'. *Aviation Week & Space Technology* 144:14, 1 April 1996.

Lenorovitz, Jeffrey M. 'B-1 Proposed as Core Aircraft'. *Aviation Week & Space Technology* 111:12, 17 September 1979.

Lowndes, Jay C. 'Avco Modifies Prototype Processes for Production'. *Aviation Week & Space Technology* 119:5, 1 August 1983.

Kozicharow, Eugene. 'B-1 for Cruise Missiles Urged'. *Aviation Week & Space Technology* 107:12, 19 September 1977.

Kozicharow, Eugene. 'FB-111H Proposal Cites Survivability, Low Cost'. *Aviation Week & Space Technology* 107:15, 10 October 1977.

Kozicharow, Eugene. 'Stretched FB-111 Version Urged'. *Aviation Week & Space Technology* 107:13, 26 September 1977.

Machat, Mike. 'Swinging on a Spar: The birth and development of variable-geometry aircraft'. *Airpower* 34:9, September 2004.

Machat, Mike. 'Valkyrie Flight'. *Airpower* 22:6, November 1992.

McCarthy, John F., Jr. 'The Case for the B-1 Bomber'. *International Security* 1:2, 1976.

McNamara, Robert S. *Testimony Before the House Armed Services Committee*, excerpted in *Aviation Week & Space Technology* 82:9, 1 March 1965.

Melampy, Jake. 'Sharpening the B-One'. *Combat Aircraft* 19:6, June 2018.

Merrifield, John T. 'Rockwell Upgrades Its Facilities Prior To Undertaking B-1B Simulation Role'. *Aviation Week & Space Technology* 124:13, 31 March 1986.

Miller, Barry. 'Rockwell to Submit R&D Options for B-1'. *Aviation Week & Space Technology* 107:2, 11 July 1977.

Mordoff, Keith F. 'General Electric F101 Production Nears'. *Aviation Week & Space Technology* 119:5, 1 August 1983.

Morrocco, John D. 'B-1B Defensive Avionics Meet Only Half of Intended Goals'. *Aviation Week & Space Technology* 129:5, 1 August 1988.

Morrocco, John D. 'Boeing Wins USAF Competition to Build Advanced Missile'. *Aviation Week & Space Technology* 125:24, 15 December 1986.

Morrocco, John D. 'Problems with Rocket Motor Delay Initial Flight of SRAM 2'. *Aviation Week & Space Technology* 132:5, 29 January 1990.

Morrocco, John D. 'Redesigned Boeing SRAM-2 Passes Critical Test, but Contract Issues Unresolved'. *Aviation Week & Space Technology* 134:21, 27 May 1991.

Newdick, Thomas. 'B-1B Lancer'. *Air Forces Monthly* 320, November 2014.

Noland, David. 'The Bone is Back'. *Air & Space Magazine* 23:1, April/May 2008.

Nordwall, Bruce D. 'Air Force Completes Flight Tests of B-1B's Defensive EW Systems'. *Aviation Week & Space Technology* 134:9, 4 March 1991.

Nordwall, Bruce D. 'Reliability of B-1B Improves As Line Crews Gain Experience'. *Aviation Week & Space Technology* 127:11, 14 September 1987.

North, David M. 'B-1B Combines Brisk Low-Altitude Handling, More Capable Avionics'. *Aviation Week & Space Technology* 127:11, 14 September 1987.

North, David M. 'Development Problems Delay Full B-1B Operational Capability'. *Aviation Week & Space Technology* 125:18, 3 November 1986.

Pace, Steve. 'Triplesonic Twosome'. *Wings* 16:1, February 1986.

Phillips, Edward H. 'JASSM Tested for B-1B Deployment'. *Aviation Week & Space Technology* 153:7, 14 August 2000.

Plattner, C. M. 'Variable-Geometry AMSA Studied'. *Aviation Week & Space Technology* 86:3, 16 January 1967.

Proctor, Paul and William B. Scott. 'Boeing To Buy Key Rockwell Aerospace and Defense Units'. *Aviation Week & Space Technology* 145:6, 5 August 1996.

Regis, Ed. 'Torture Chamber'. *Air & Space Smithsonian* 21:1, April-May 2006.

Robinson, Clarence A., Jr., 'B-1/Stealth Competition Emerges'. *Aviation Week & Space Technology* 120:9, 27 February 1984.

Robinson, Clarence A., Jr. 'Congress Presses Strategic Changes'. *Aviation Week & Space Technology* 107:15, 10 October 1977.

Robinson, Clarence A., Jr. 'USAF Recommends New Combat Aircraft'. *Aviation Week & Space Technology* 114:19, 11 May 1981.

Robinson, Clarence A., Jr. 'USAF, Rockwell Conduct Critical Design Review on B-1B'. *Aviation Week & Space Technology* 118:4, 24 January 1983.

Ropelewski, Robert R. 'B-1 Studied as Cruise Missile Carrier'. *Aviation Week & Space Technology* 111:24, 10 December 1979.

Ropelewski, Robert R. 'North American Gears to Produce B-1'. *Aviation Week & Space Technology* 96:26, 26 June 1972.

Ropelewski, Robert R. 'Rockwell Begins B-1B Production Plans'. *Aviation Week & Space Technology* 115:15, 12 October 1981.

Scharenborg, Martin and Ramon Wenink. 'Old Dog, New Bone'. *Air Forces Monthly* 288, March 2012.

Scott, William B. 'B-1B Combined Test Force Evaluating Next-Generation Short-Range Missile'. *Aviation Week & Space Technology* 134:26, 1 July 1991.

Scott, William B. 'B-1B Crews Adapt Readily to New, Conventional Role'. *Aviation Week & Space Technology* 137:4, 27 July 1992.

Scott, William B. 'B-1B Demonstrates Global Reach'. *Aviation Week & Space Technology* 141:20, 14 November 1994.

Scott, William B. 'B-1B Flight Tests Study Mission Needs'. *Aviation Week & Space Technology* 118:18, 2 May 1983.

Scott, William B. 'B-1B Stability Enhancement Tests Verify Low-Level Mission Capability'. *Aviation Week & Space Technology* 130:26, 26 June 1989.

Scott, William B. 'B-1B Unit Proves Capability in Operational Readiness Test'. *Aviation Week & Space Technology* 141:22, 28 November 1994.

Scott, William B. 'Better "Bomb Truck"'. *Aviation Week & Space Technology* 163:9, 5 September 2005.

Scott, William B. 'Flight Program Emphasizes Weapons Delivery, Stall Tests'. *Aviation Week & Space Technology* 127:11, 14 September 1987.

Scott, William B. 'Rockwell Management Plan Saving Costs, Time'. *Aviation Week & Space Technology* 119:5, 1 August 1983.

Scott, William B. 'USAF Building New Anechoic Chamber Capable of Accommodating B-1, B-2'. *Aviation Week & Space Technology* 130:9, 27 February 1989.

Scott, William B. 'Weapons, Avionics Upgrades Expand B-1B Options'. *Aviation Week & Space Technology* 142:7, 13 February 1995.

Smith, Bruce A. 'B-1A Testbed Crashes at Edwards AFB'. *Aviation Week & Space Technology* 121:10, 3 September 1984.

Smith, Bruce A. 'B-1B Assembly Operations Advancing'. *Aviation Week & Space Technology* 118:12, 21 March 1983.

Smith, Bruce A. 'B-1B Program on Time Despite Component Shortage, Engine Problems'. *Aviation Week & Space Technology* 121:24, 10 December 1984.

Smith, Bruce A. 'Production B-1B Tested in New Facility'. *Aviation Week & Space Technology* 120:22, 28 May 1984.

Smith, Bruce A. 'Rockwell Completes First B-1B Fuselage'. *Aviation Week & Space Technology* 120:4, 23 January 1984.

Smith, Bruce A. 'USAF Cites Fuel Transfer Error in B-1 Aircraft Crash'. *Aviation Week & Space Technology* 121:15, 8 October 1984.

Smith, Bruce A. 'Rockwell to Build CBU Kits for B-1B'. *Aviation Week & Space Technology* 142:21, 22 May 1995.

Smith, Kyle. 'Speed: Why The Fastest Bomber Faded at the Finish'. *Air & Space Smithsonian* 20:5, December 2005-January 2006.

Trimble, Steve. 'As Retirement Nears, USAF B-1Bs Gain New Roles'. *Aviation Week & Space Technology* 181:10, 20 May-2 June 2019.

Trimble, Steve. 'Maritime Threat'. *Aviation Week & Space Technology* 181:9, 6-19 May 2019.

Wall, Robert, 'B-1B Backers, USAF Clash Over Bomber Ax'. *Aviation Week & Space Technology* 155:3, 16 July 2001.

Wall, Robert. 'B-1B Fights Demotion in Combat Role'. *Aviation Week & Space Technology* 156:25, 24 June 2002.

Wall, Robert. 'New Weapons Debut in Attacks on Iraq'. *Aviation Week & Space Technology* 149:25, 21-28 December 1998.

Wall, Robert. 'Pentagon's EW Efforts Seen in Shambles'. *Aviation Week & Space Technology* 152:17, 24 April 2000.

Wallace, Ashley. 'Bone School House'. *Combat Aircraft* 18:8, August 2017.

Wallace, Ashley. 'Desert Bones: Bats at "The Deid"'. *Air Forces Monthly* 371, February 2019.

Warwick, Graham. 'B-1 back in the air'. *FLIGHT International*, 28 August 1982.

Wilson, George C. 'Congress, DOD Renewing Bomber Clash'; *Aviation Week & Space Technology* 82:9, 1 March 1965.

Wood Archie L. 'Modernizing the Strategic Bomber Force Without Really Trying – A Case Against the B-1.'*International Security* 1:2, Autumn 1976.

Yaffee, Michael L. 'GE Ships Final Engine for Flight-Test B-1'. *Aviation Week & Space Technology* 100:21, 27 May 1974.

Zumwalt, Elmo R. 'An Assessment of the Bomber-Cruise Missile Controversy'. *International Security* 2:1, 1977.

Handbooks, Manuals and Training Materials

____. *B-1 Aircrew Ground Training: Student Handout*. Rockwell International, B-1 Division: Los Angeles, March 1974.

____. *B-1 Flight Manual (AF74-0158A and AF74-0159A)* (NA-73-296). Rockwell International, B-1 Division: Los Angeles, 1 June 1976.

____. *B-1 Flight Manual (AF74-0158A and AF74-0159A)* (NA-73-296). Rockwell International, North American Aircraft Operations: Los Angeles, 29 October 1982.

____. *B-1 Flight Manual (AF74-0160A)* (NA-75-300). Rockwell International, B-1 Division: Los Angeles, 30 January 1976 (Change 4, 15 May 1977).

____. *B-1 Flight Manual (AF76-0174)* (NA-77-400). Rockwell International, Los Angeles Division: Los Angeles, 15 January 1979.

____. *B-1 Flight Manual (AF76-0174)* (NA-77-400). Rockwell International, North American Aircraft Operations: Los Angeles, 29 June 1984.

____. *B-1B Command Aircraft Systems Training (Programs 5551-5555)*. 436th Strategic Training Squadron: Carswell Air Force Base, Texas, 1 June 1990.

____. *B-1B Systems Familiarization Course No. 002A: Student Handout*. Rockwell International, North American Aircraft Operations, December 1982.

____. *B-52G Flight Manual: USAF Series Aircraft*. United States Air Force, 1 January 1975 (Change 25, 20 November 1981).

____. *Pilot's Flight Manual: USAF Series B-1B Aircraft*. Rockwell International, North American Aircraft Operations: Los Angeles, 1 January 1986 (Change 2, 1 December 1986).

____. *Preliminary Pilot's Flight Manual: USAF Series B-1B Aircraft* (PTO 1B-1B-1-1). Rockwell International, North American Aircraft Operations: Los Angeles, 27 May 1986.

Dissertations and Theses

Beatovich, Gary. *A Case Study of Manned Strategic Bomber Acquisition: The B-70 Valkyrie*. MS thesis, Air Force Institute of Technology, Systems Management: Wright-Patterson Air Force Base, Ohio, September 1990.

Creer, Jonathan. *Picking the Bone: The B-1 Bomber as a Platform for Innovation*. Student thesis, School of Advanced Air and Space Systems: Maxwell Air Force Base, Alabama, June 2010.

Frichtl, Paul J. *Limitations of the Conventional Role of the B-1B in the European Theater*. Research report, Air War College: Maxwell AFB, Alabama, May 1989.

Kugler, Richard L. *The Politics of Restraint: Robert McNamara and the Strategic Nuclear Forces, 1963-1968*. PhD dissertation. Massachusetts Institute of Technology, Political Science: Cambridge, Massachusetts, August 1975.

Orr, Verne. *Developing Strategic Weaponry and the Political Process – The B1-B Bomber: From Drawing Board To Flight*. PhD thesis, Claremont Graduate School, Political Science: Claremont, California, 2005.

Magiawala, Kiran R. *The B-1B Bomber: A Program Study*. MS thesis, Massachusetts Institute of Technology, Technology and Policy: Cambridge, Massachusetts, February 1988.

Papers and Research Reports

_____. *Adding Conventional Capabilities Will Be Complex, Time-Consuming, and Costly* (GAO/NSIAD-93-45), United States General Accounting Office, February 1993.

_____. *Air Force ADP: CAMS and REMIS* (GAO/IMTEC-92-43R). United States General Accounting Office: Washington, DC, 31 March 1992.

_____. *B-1B Cost and Performance Remain Uncertain* (GAO/NSIAD-89-55). United States General Accounting Office: Washington, DC, February 1989.

_____. *B-1B Maintenance Problems Impede Its Operations* (GAO/NSIAD-89-15). United States General Accounting Office: Washington, DC, October 1988.

_____. *B-1B Parts Problems Continue to Impede Operations* (GAO/NSIAD-88-190). United States General Accounting Office: Washington, DC, July 1988.

_____. *Evaluation of the Air Force Report on B-1B Operational Readiness Assessment* (GAO/NSIAD-95-151). United States General Accounting Office: Washington, DC, July 1995.

_____. *Flight Test Progress Report for B-1B Aircraft, Report No. 01* (NA-83-301-01). Rockwell International, North American Aircraft Operations, Los Angeles, California, 29 April 1983.

_____. *Flight Test Progress Report for B-1B Aircraft, Report No. 18* (NA-83-301-18). Rockwell International, North American Aircraft Operations, Los Angeles, California, unknown date.

_____. *Flight Test Progress Report for B-1B Aircraft, Report No. 45* (NA-83-301-45). Rockwell International, North American Aircraft Operations, Los Angeles, California, unknown date.

_____. *Flight Test Progress Report for B-1B Aircraft, Report No. 76* (NA-83-301-76). Rockwell International, North American Aircraft Operations, Los Angeles, California, unknown date.

_____. *Flight Test Progress Report for B-1B Aircraft, Report No. 77* (NA-83-301-77). Rockwell International, North American Aircraft Operations, Los Angeles, California, 30 November 1989.

_____. *Flight Test Progress Report: B-1B/SRAM II Program, Report No. 102* (NA-83-301-102). Rockwell International, North American Aircraft Operations, Los Angeles, California, 31 January 1991.

_____. *Issues Related to the B-1B's Availability and Ability to Perform Conventional Missions* (GAO/NSIAD-94-81). United States General Accounting Office: Washington, DC, January 1994.

_____. *Need to Redefine Requirements for B-1B Defensive Avionics System* (GAO/NSIAD-92-272). United States General Accounting Office: Washington, DC, July 1992.

_____. *Supportability, Maintainability, and Readiness of the B-1B Bomber* (GAO/NSIAD-87-177BR). United States General Accounting Office: Washington, DC, June 1987.

_____. *The B-1B Bomber and Options for Enhancements: A Special Study*. Congress of the United States, Congressional Budget Office: Washington, DC, August 1988.

_____. *U.S. Air Force White Paper on Long Range Bombers*. United States Air Force, 1 March 1999.

Benefield, Doug and LeRoy B. Schroeder. *B-1B Progress Report*. Proceedings of the 27th Annual SETP Symposium. Society of Experimental Test Pilots, 1983.

Bilien, J. and R. Matta. *The CFM56 Venture* (AIAA-89-2038). AIAA/AHS/ASEE Aircraft Design, Systems and Operations Conference, 31 July–2August 1989.

Bock, Charles C., Jr. *B-1 Flight Test Project Report*. Proceedings of the 19th Annual SETP Symposium. Society of Experimental Test Pilots, 1975.

Bock, Charles C., Jr. *B-1 Flight Test Progress Report* (AIAA 76-886). AIAA 1976 Aircraft Systems and Technology Meeting, 27–29 September 1976.

Bodilly, Susan J. *Case Study of Risk Management in the USAF B-1B Bomber Program* (N-3616). RAND: Santa Monica, California, 1993.

Broughton, R. N. *B-1 Flight Test Progress Report* (AIAA 78-1448). AIAA Aircraft Systems and Technology Conference, 21–23 August 1978.

Camm, Frank. *The Development of the F100-PW-220 and F110-GE-100 Engines: A Case Study of Risk Assessment and Risk Management* (N-3618-AF). Rand: Santa Monica, California, 1993.

Christensen, L. L. *Propulsion System Configuration Development for the B-1 Strategic Bomber* (AIAA 75-1040). AIAA 1975 Aircraft Systems and Technology Meeting, 4–7 August 1975.

DeJoannis, Jeffrey. *Development and Test of Towed Decoys: Applications from the B-1B Bomber*. Proceedings of the 34th Annual International Symposium. Society of Flight Test Engineers, 15–19 September 2003.

Derbyshire, Kenneth and Donald E. Pieratt. *B-1 Central Integrated Test System (CITS)* (AIAA 77-1502). AIAA Computers in Aerospace Conference, 31 October–2 November 1977.

Deptula, David A. and Douglas A. Birkey. *Building the Future Bomber Force America Needs: The Bomber Re-Vector*. The Mitchell Institute of Aerospace Studies, Air Force Association: Arlington, Virginia, September 2018.

Edkins, Craig R. and Richard M. Stuckey. *B-1B Flight Test Update*. Proceedings of the 39th Annual SETP Symposium. Society of Experimental Test Pilots, 1995.

Eichhorn, David J. and Harold R. Gaston. *B-1B Development Testing*. Proceedings of the 32nd Annual SETP Symposium. Society of Experimental Test Pilots, 1988.

Frederickson, Brian M. *The Laird-Packard Way: Unpacking Defense Acquisition Policy* (Wright Flyer Paper No. 74). Air University Press: Maxwell Air Force Base, Alabama, March 2020.

Fulton, Fitzhugh L., Jr. *Lessons From the XB-70 as Applied to the Supersonic Transport* (NASA TM X-56014, presented at the 21st Annual International Air Safety Seminar, Anaheim, California, 7–11 October 1968). National Aeronautics and Space Administration: Washington, DC, 1968.

Grant, Rebecca et al.*Operation Anaconda: An Air Power Perspective*. Headquarters, United States Air Force, 7 February 2005.

Grigaliunas, John M. *Integration Testing of the Sniper Targeting Pod on the B-1B from Concept through First Deployment*. Proceedings of the 42nd Annual International Symposium. Society of Flight Test Engineers, 8-12 August 2011.

Haagenson, W. Robert and L. M. Randall. *Inlet Development of the B-1 Strategic Bomber* (AIAA 74-1064). AIAA/SAE 10th Propulsion Conference, 21–23 October 1974.

Hampton, T. and W. E. Schoenborn. *Design for Durability–The F101-GE-101 Engine* (AIAA 78-1084). AIAA/SAE 14th Joint Propulsion Conference, 25–27 July 1978.

Harrigan, Jeffrey L. et al. *Investigation Report of the Fixed Wing Close Air Support Airstrike In the Vicinity of Arghandab, Afghanistan on 9 June 2014* (declassified and redacted).United States Central Command: MacDill Air Force Base, Florida, 5 August 2014

Hawkins, R. C. and T. L. Hampton. *The F101-GE-100 Engine Structural Design* (AIAA 75-1308). AIAA/SAE 11th Propulsion Conference, 29 September–1 October 1975.

Hendrix, Jerry and James Price. *Higher, Heavier, Farther, and Now Undetectable? Bombers: Long-Range Force Projection in the 21st Century*. Center for a New American Security: Washington, DC, June 2017.

Hodgson, Quentin E., *Deciding to Buy: Civil-Military Relations and Major Weapons Programs*. U. S. Army War College, Strategic Studies Institute: Carlisle, Pennsylvania, November 2010.

Humphey, Brian A. et al. *United States Air Force Aircraft Accident Investigation Report: B-1B, Tail Number 85-0051*. 19 December 2013 (approval date).

Humphries, John A. and David E. Miller. *B-1B/MJU-23 Flare Strike Test Program*. Proceedings of the 40th Annual SETP Symposium. Society of Experimental Test Pilots, 1996.

Lambeth, Benjamin S. *Airpower against Terror: America's Conduct of Operation Enduring Freedom* (MG-166). RAND: Santa Monica, California, 2005.

Lambeth, Benjamin S. *NATO's Air War for Kosovo: A Strategic and Operational Assessment* (MR-1365-AF). RAND: Santa Monica, California, 2001.

McMullen, Thomas H. *Evolution of the B-1 Crew Escape System* (AIAA 73-440). AIAA 4th Aerodynamic Deceleration Systems Conference, 21-23 May 1973.

Moeller, Michael R. *US Bomber Force: Sized to Sustain an Asymmetric Advantage for America*. The Mitchell Institute of Aerospace Studies, Air Force Association: Arlington, Virginia, 2015.

Morley, Richard A. *Ground Testing Approach for the B-1B Bomber* (SAE 851796). SAE Aerospace Technology Conference & Exposition, 14–17 October 1985.

Nalty, Bernard C. *The Quest for an Advanced Manned Strategic Bomber: USAF Plans and Policies*. USAF Historical Division Liaison Office: Washington, DC, August 1966.

Payne, William R. *B-1 Initial Operational Test and Evaluation*. Proceedings of the 17th Annual SETP Symposium. Society of Experimental Test Pilots, 1973.

Pixley, Greg and Ken Lockwood. *B-1B Weapons Conventionalization – A Seek Eagle Perspective*. Proceedings of the 41st Annual SETP Symposium. Society of Experimental Test Pilots, 1997.

Polhemus, Edward C. and Thomas A. Toll. *Research Related to Variable-Sweep Aircraft Development* (NASA Technical Memorandum 83121). NASA Langley Research Center: Hampton, Virginia, May 1981.

Quanbeck, Alton H., and Archie L. Wood with the assistance of Louisa Thoron. *Modernizing the Strategic Bomber Force: Why and How*. Washington, DC: Brookings Institution, 1976.

Robarge, David. *Archangel: CIA's Supersonic A-12 Reconnaissance Aircraft*. Center for the Study of Intelligence, Central Intelligence Agency: Washington, DC, 2007.

Silva, Jaime R. and Joginder S. Dhillon. *B-1B Terrain Following System Description*. Air Force Flight Test Center: Edwards Air Force Base, 1 April 1985.

Smith, John S., III and Frederick A. Fieldler. *Review of Five Years of Flight Testing the B-1*. Proceedings of the 23rd Annual SETP Symposium. Society of Experimental Test Pilots, 1979.

Staley, C. Wayne and Addison S. Thompson. *B-1B Flight Test Update*. Society of Experimental Test Pilots, 1988.

Sturmthal, Emil and T. D. Benefield. *B-1 Flight Test Project Report No. 2*. Proceedings of the 20th Annual SETP Symposium. Society of Experimental Test Pilots, 1976.

Sturmthal, Emil. *B-1 Operational Test and Evaluation 'An Early Look'*. Proceedings of the 17th Annual SETP Symposium. Society of Experimental Test Pilots, 1973.

Thompson, Addison S. *B-1B High AOA Testing*. Proceedings of the 32nd Annual SETP Symposium. Society of Experimental Test Pilots, 1988.

Tipton, Stephan and Thomas J. Blachowski. *History and Operational Performance for the B-1B Aircraft* (AIAA 96-2871). 32nd AIAA/ASME/SAE/ASEE Joint Propulsion Conference, 1–3 July 1986.

Ward, George H., Lewis L. Christensen and Rodney J. Sayles. *Application of New Development Concepts to F101 Engine for B-1 Aircraft* (AIAA 75-1290). AIAA/SAE 11th Propulsion Conference, 29 September–1 October 1975.

Wasser, Becca et al. *The Air War Against the Islamic State: The Role of Airpower in Operation Inherent Resolve* (RR-A381-1). RAND: Santa Monica, California, 2021.

Wolowicz, Chester H. *Analysis of an Emergency Deceleration and Descent of the XB-70-1 Airplane Due to Engine Damage Resulting From Structural Failure* (NASA TM X-1195). National Aeronautics and Space Administration: Washington, DC, March 1966.

Websites/Online

____. '1980 Democratic Platform'. 11 August 1980. https://www.presidency.ucsb.edu/documents/1980-democratic-party-platform, accessed 22 November 2020.

____. 'Republican Party Platform of 1980'. 15 July 1980. https://www.presidency.ucsb.edu/documents/republican-party-platform-1980, accessed 22 November 2020.

Adams, Charlotte. 'Building Blocks to Upgrade to B-1B'. 1 August 2002. https://aviationtoday.com/2002/08/01/building-blocks-to-upgrade-to-b-1b/, accessed 10 March 2020.

Birkey, Douglas A. and David A. Deptula. 'A Change in Vector'. 26 February 2019. https://www.airforcemag.com/article/a-change-in-vector/, accessed 24 August 2020.

Carter, Jimmy. 'The President's News Conference', 30 June 1977. https://www.presidency.ucsb.edu/documents/the-presidents-news-conference-111, accessed 22 November 2020.

Devereux, Kimberly E. 'B-1B Drops first GPS-guided JDAM'. March 1998. https://fas.org/man/dod-101/sys/smart/980300-jdam.htm, accessed 1 March 2021.

Grier, Peter. 'Aerospace World'. 1 February 1999. https://www.airforcemag.com/article/0299world/, accessed 1 March 2021.

Grier, Peter. 'The JDAM Revolution'. 1 September 2006. https://www.airforcemag.com/article/0906JDAM/, accessed 1 March 2021.

Hada, Zach. 'Operation Desert Fox: Recalling the 15th anniversary of the first B-1 combat operation'. 18 December 2013. https://www.ellsworth.af.mil/News/Article-Display/

Article/807685/operation-desert-fox-recalling-the-15th-anniversary-of-the-first-b-1-combat-ope/, accessed 23 March 2019.

Palyan, Hrair H. 'Coming of age: B-1 proves itself during Operational Allied Force'. 27 March 2012. https://www.ellsworth.af.mil/News/Features/Display/Article/217597/coming-of-age-b-1-proves-itself-during-operation-allied-force/, accessed 22 March 2021.

Palyan, Hrair H. 'Lessons learned, Operation Odyssey Dawn'. 21 March 2012. https://www.ellsworth.af.mil/News/Features/Display/Article/217598/lessons-learned-operation-odyssey-dawn/, accessed 5 February 2019.

Pate, Kristen, 'Sniper ATP-equipped B-1B has combat first', 11 August 2008. https://www.af.mil/News/Article-Display/Article/122748/sniper-atp-equipped-b-1b-has-combat-first/, accessed 29 May 2018.

Peninsula Senior Productions. 'B-1 Bailout: Hazards of Flight Test, Otto Waniczek'. https://www.youtube.com/watch?v=TN-mXzAFCqM&t=7s, posted 1 July 2018, accessed 16 January 2021.

Reagan, Ronald W. 'Remarks and a Question-and-Answer Session with Reporters on the Announcement of the United States Strategic Weapons Program'. 2 October 1981. https://www.presidency.ucsb.edu/documents/remarks-and-question-and-answer-session-with-reporters-the-announcement-the-united-states, accessed 22 November 2020.

Reagan, Ronald W. 'Remarks to Employees at a Rockwell International Facility in Palmdale, California'. 22 October 1984. https://www.presidency.ucsb.edu/documents/remarks-employees-rockwell-international-facility-palmdale-california, accessed 25 January 2021.

Secretary of the Air Force Public Affairs. 'Air Force outlines future of bomber force'. 12 February 2018. https://www.af.mil/News/Article-Display/Article/1438634/air-force-outlines-future-of-bomber-force/, accessed 15 March 2021.

Thum, Ashley J. 'B-1 bomber makes historic combat debut during Operational Desert Fox'. 7 March 2013. https://www.ellsworth.af.mil/News/Features/Display/Article/217539/b-1-bomber-makes-historic-combat-debut-during-operation-desert-fox/, accessed 29 May 2018.

Tirpak, John A. 'Repairing Broken Bones'. 25 January 2021. https://www.airforcemag.com/article/repairing-broken-bones/, accessed 12 February 2021.

Tirpak, John A. 'First of 17 B-1Bs Heads to the Boneyard'. 17 February 2021. https://www.airforcemag.com/first-of-17-b-1bs-heads-to-the-boneyard/, accessed 18 February 2021.

Miscellaneous

_____. *B-1 Aircrew Training*. Air Force Instruction 11-2B-1, Volume 1, 23 December 2011.

_____. *B-1 Operations Procedures*. Air Force Instruction 11-2B-1, Volume 3, 20 March 2015.

_____. *B-1 Rollout Media Information*. Rockwell International, B-1 Division: Los Angeles, October 1974.

_____. *Citation to Accompany the Award of the Distinguished Flying Cross to George F. Swan*, date unknown.

_____. *Global Power for America: Around the World Mission* (Coronet Bat pre-mission briefing to Commander, Air Combat Command), 7th Wing, 1995 (exact date unknown).

_____. *REVAMP 67* (after action report), 2003 (exact date unknown).

_____. *SWEDE 72* (after action report), 2003 (exact date unknown).

____. *VANDY 62* (after action report), 2003 (exact date unknown).

Greany, Gordon. Unpublished notes on Operation Desert Fox, 2021.

Henderson, Charles R. *Letter of Appreciation* (memorandum for 7 OG/CC), 7th Wing, 9 June 1995.

Hobbs, Daemon E. Unpublished combat mission journal, 2002.

Martin, Kenneth I. *My B-1A History.* 14 November 2020. Unpublished paper.

Moran, William J., Jr. *February 1992 it is warm outside: B-1B Time to Climb World Records, Grand Forks AFB, ND.* Unpublished paper.

Shropshire, Michael S. *B-1 CAS Situattions* [sic] (memorandum for record), 20th Air Support Operations Squadron, 1 June 2006.

Stewart, Chris. *After Action Report, Coronet Bat, B-1B Round the World Flight*, 9th Bomb Squadron, 5 June 1995.

Thompson, Addison S. *B-1B Three-Engine Ferry Operation, Aircraft S/N 86-0128* (TFD-90-2044), Rockwell International, 1990.

Interviews

Craig Baumann, 17 December 2020

Major 'Butch', USAF, 1 April 2019

Lieutenant Colonel Ricky W. Carver, USAF (retired), 12 March 2021

Lieutenant Colonel 'Chunks', USAF (retired), 11 January 2021

Senior Master Sergeant Wesley T. 'Skip' Clark, USAF (retired), 6 January 2021

Technical Sergeant 'Craig', USAF, 1 April 2019

Colonel Jonathan M. 'Claw' Creer, USAF, 22 December 2020

Colonel Charles R. 'Russ' Davis, USAF (retired), 29 October 2020

Captain Scott M. Dayton, USAF (honorably discharged), 7 December 2020

Kenneth Decker, 2 December 2020

Chief Master Sergeant Jerry Densmore, USAF (retired), 2 November 2020, 17 February 2021

Major Norman K. 'Keith' Dodderer, USAF (retired), 3 February 2021

Technical Sergeant Kyle C. Fagin, USAF (retired), 3 December 2020, 18 February 2021

Lieutenant Colonel Gary H. 'Smokey' Flynt, USAF (retired), 23 February 2021

Chief Master Sergeant George A. Gilbert, USAF (retired), 28 December 2020, 15 February 2021

Lieutenant Colonel Timothy Griffith, USAF, 2 April 2021

Technical Sergeant DaShon L. Hall, USAF, 1 April 2019

Lieutenant Colonel Lawrence H. 'Larry' Haskell, USAF (retired), 3 March 2021

Colonel Stephen A. Henry, USAF (retired), 23 November 2020

Colonel David L. 'Lowell' Hickey, USAF (retired), 24 March 2021

Lieutenant Colonel Daemon E. 'PBAR' Hobbs, USAF (retired), 4 January 2021

Lieutenant Colonel Kevin R. 'Hooter' Houdek, USAF (retired), 30 March 2021

Lieutenant Colonel John R. 'Ray' Houle, USAF (retired), 1 March 2021

Technical Sergeant Gamal A. James, USAF, 1 April 2019

Major General Perry L. Lamy, USAF (retired), 15 December 2020

James A. Leasure, 1 February 2021

Major Robert C. 'Von' Liebman, USAF (retired), 21 December 2020

Lieutenant Colonel Marc N. 'Sporto' London, USAF (retired), 23 March 2021
Colonel William J. Moran, Jr, USAF (retired), 21 December 2020, 15 February 2021
Lieutenant Colonel Steven R. 'Worm' Myers, USAF (retired), 6 January 2021
Lieutenant Colonel Kent L. Payne, USAF (retired), 5 December 2020
Major Theodore 'Brad' Purvis, USAF (retired), 26 October 2020, 15 February 2021
Lieutenant General Richard V. Reynolds, USAF (retired), 28 December 2020
Colonel Jerry L. Ross, USAF (retired), 16 December 2020
Major 'SCAM', USAF, 1 April 2019
Lieutenant Colonel Jaime R. Silva, USAF (retired), 8 December 2020
Erik Simonsen, 8 February 2021
Lieutenant Colonel C. Wayne Staley, USAF (retired), 24 February 2021
Lieutenant Colonel George F. 'Duck' Swan, USAF (retired), 22 February 2021
Lieutenant Colonel Ernest S. 'Turk' Taveras, USAF (retired), 22 December 2020
Lieutenant Colonel Addison S. Thompson, USAF (retired), 27 January 2021
Lieutenant Colonel Otto J. Waniczek, Jr, USAF Reserve (retired), 29 January 2021
Technical Sergeant 'Warren', 1 April 2019